Constituted by

The Grand Lodge of Pennsylvania, February 3, 1783

The Grand Lodge of Virginia, April 28, 1788

"The virtues which ennoble human character, are taught and cultivated in the lodge-room; and the mystic labors of the Master and his Craftsmen, when convened, are such as fit men for the domestic relations of life and the highest duties of citizenship. "

George Washington and His Masonic Neighbors such as Jonathan Swift, played an essential part of the foundation of society in Alexandria and the Virginia Colony. May their contributions remain in our perpetual memory and may the written record of those exploits long abound.

Hayden, Sidney. *Washington and his Masonic Compeers.* New York: Masonic Publishing and Manufacturing Co., 1867.

THE STRANGE CASE OF JONATHAN SWIFT AND THE REAL LONG JOHN SILVER

The Strange Case of
Jonathan Swift
and the Real
Long John Silver

Robert A. Prather

Introduction by Ron D. Bryant

ACCLAIM PRESS
MORLEY, MISSOURI

Acclaim Press

ACCLAIM PRESS, INC.
Your Next Great Book
P.O. Box 238
Morley, MO 63767
(573) 472-9800
www.acclaimpress.com

Book Design by:

Designer: Ellen Sikes
Cover Design: Emily K. Sikes

Publishing Rights: Acclaim Press

Library of Congress Catalog No. 2007934438
ISBN-13: 978-0-9798802-1-6
ISBN-10: 0-9798802-1-1

Printed in the United States of America
First Printing September 2007
10 9 8 7 6 5 4 3 2 1

Additional copies may be purchased from
Acclaim Press.

This publication was produced using available information. The Publisher regrets it cannot assume responsibility for errors or omissions.

CONTENTS

Dedicated to my wife, Karen, whose assistance
in the preparation of this work has been invaluable…

Acknowledgements

First and foremost, to Nadine Roberts for your intuitive editing skills, I am most appreciative. To Robert Ashley Prather, for your participation during the round-table process of "The Third Narrative" and to Melanie Prather Crady for your support and assistance your Dad will be forever grateful to you both. My gratitude goes to Jeffrey A. Crady for your notable contributions. To Keith Stivers, your early involvement into this subject will always be treasured. And, to my wife, Karen, your many talents, front-line editing and countless contributions was a constant support and inspiration.

Many thanks are due to Ron D. Bryant for his advice in matters of history, and for his insightful request to see more about Robert Louis Stevenson in this book. Also and especially, for your counsel, friendship, and being an early advocate for *The Strange Case of Jonathan Swift and the Real Long John Silver*.

A very special thank you to Robert G. Watkins, and the brethren of Alexandria-Washington Masonic Lodge #22, of Alexandria Virginia, for the great honor they have conferred on the author by hosting the premiere event of *The Strange Case of Jonathan Swift and the Real Long John Silver*. Also, to George Seghers, executive secretary of The George Washington Masonic National Memorial, for providing one of the world's great tourist attractions, and historic building, for the premiere event of this book. Also, I would like to thank Frank Dunaway for providing the images of Dr. James Craik and The Marquis de LaFayette.

I am also grateful to Rita Holtz of The Alexandria Library, for providing a glimpse into the past by furnishing pictures of the Colross excavation, for your excellent and notable research contributions, and especially for your gift of an original brick from Grasshopper Hall.

For loaning William H. Patten's book, The *Genealogy of the Roberdeau Family*, for providing additional information pertaining to William H. Patten, and for your dedication to this project, I am very grateful to Mrs. Loretta M. Patten. To a descendant of Jonathan Swift, Jean Roberdeau Patten Liotti, I am most appreciative for the information you provided regarding your grandfather, William H. Patten, the Swift portraits, and the dress Ann Roberdeau Swift wore at George Washington's Inaugural Ball.

Thanks to the following for their contributions in the development, and research of this book: Ann Bader of the Falls of the Ohio Archaeological Society, The Library of the Kentucky Historical Society in Frankfort, Kentucky, The Library of Virginia in Richmond, Virginia, The Filson Historical Society Library in Louisville, Kentucky, Robin Wallace of the Filson Historical Society for providing the image of John Filson, The Beinecke Rare Book and Manuscript Library of Yale University, Kandie Atkinson of the Kentucky Secretary of State Land Office for helping with the Kentucky Land Patent process, The Kentucky Archives in Frankfort, Kentucky, The Sons of the American Revolution Library in Louisville, Kentucky, Margery Miller of Princeton Day School in Princeton, New Jersey for furnishing photographs of Colross, Dennis Watson for providing pictures and information of Sand Knob, Miranda Caswell of the Hardin County Clerk Office, Twylane Van-Lahr of The Historic Brown-Pusey House in Elizabethtown, Kentucky, The Libraries of the University of Kentucky, The Nelson County Public Library in Bardstown, Kentucky, The Washington County Public Library in Springfield, Kentucky, The Meade County Public Library in Brandenburg, Kentucky, The Allen County Public Library in Fort Wayne, Indiana, Ruth Roberts, and The Indianapolis Museum of Art, Michael J. Brodhead, and James T. Garber of The U. S. Army Corps of Engineers for providing information and a picture of General Joseph Gardner Swift, George Parlier and Warren Perry of The Smithsonian National Portrait Gallery and to Kimberly Orcutt and Matthew Murphy of the New York Historical Society for providing the image of Ann Roberdeau Swift's portrait.

Appreciation and thanks to the following county clerk offices for the use of their historic archives, and for their preservation of these important documents: Hardin, Nelson, Franklin, Washington, and Breckinridge Counties in Kentucky and Alexandria County Clerk in Alexandria, Virginia.

And finally, to Doug Sikes and Acclaim Press, thank you for believing in this project and for contributing to the development of this book.

PREFACE

One of the oldest unsolved mysteries of the United States of America pertains to an alluring story about an eighteenth century merchant from Alexandria, Virginia. This centuries-old legend is known as "The Lost Silver Mines of Jonathan Swift." According to the findings of this investigation, it is probable that the mystery began during the desperate years of the American Revolution.

The legend of the Swift Silver Mine is a mystery; however, *The Strange Case of Jonathan Swift and the Real Long John Silver* will be best appreciated if read as a case-book to a complex investigation, rather than a mystery novel. While the discoveries revealed in this work provide historical evidence of the existence of Swift's mines, it is also a book of theory. In Part One many historical facts are presented, which pertain to the life of Jonathan Swift. Although many of these facts may appear trivial, it is these intricate details that form the necessary building blocks for the theories presented. The details of how an investigation is concluded are the most exciting parts of any mystery.

During the course of the investigation into the subject of Jonathan Swift and Robert Louis Stevenson, many remarkable people and places were discovered. One does not satisfactorily complete such a work without assistance. It has been the great privilege of this author to receive support from many willing and qualified people. At least fifteen libraries or genealogical research centers ranging from the county level to Yale University, the historic archives of six county clerk offices, The U.S. Army Corps of Engineers, The National Portrait Gallery, The Indianapolis Museum of Art, and descendants of Jonathan Swift were a few of the very memorable encounters along the way.

Another notable source of valuable information came from the Alexandria-Washington Lodge #22 in Alexandria, Virginia. It is a rare occurrence for a Masonic Lodge to share information from their historic lodge minutes and for information to be contributed from George Washington's Masonic Lodge is a great honor, and an exceedingly fortuitous occurrence.

It was in 1985 that I was pointed to an area of Kentucky which seemed a likely location for Swift's lost silver mines. At that time several long and enjoyable days were spent oscillating a metal detector; however, the only treasure that was inevitably to be found was fond memories of good times. A vital element of the lost Kentucky silver mine legend has always been the famed Swift Journal, which purportedly gives directions to the mine's whereabouts. This journal is thoroughly discussed in this book, but it is not considered a primary source of information.

It should be stated very clearly— this book is not a proclamation of a definite location of the Swift silver mine—it is one person's hypothesis based on the evidence to be presented.

The Swift legend has always been a popular Kentucky folk story, but in the early years of its inception it was known on a far greater scale. The widely believed existence of these silver mines was known throughout the United States in the late eighteenth century and early to middle nineteenth century. It is probable that the legend was also known throughout Great Britain, France, and Spain. In fact, the mines were marked on an early map of that time period. Gilbert Imlay's "Map of Kentucky" was published in London on February 1, 1793, and it illustrates the mine's location to be in the eastern part of Kentucky.

It should be noted, these mines would have originally been referred to as Swift's *Virginia* silver mines. Kentucky did not become a state until 1792 when it separated from Virginia; however, since the area where the mines were proposed to have been located is now within Kentucky, they shall from this point forward be referred to as Swift's Kentucky Mines.

After two centuries of searching for Swift's elusive silver mines without success, the once immensely popular legend has mostly settled into Kentucky folklore...or has it? It is proposed that the legend of Jonathan Swift attained worldwide fame in 1883, disguised in Robert Louis Stevenson's immortal classic, *Treasure Island*. In this spirited tale of tall ships, pirates, hidden treasure, and deception, Stevenson both conceals and reveals the real-life adventures of Swift through his most famous literary character...Long John Silver.

INTRODUCTION

For over two hundred years the legend of a treasure in silver has fascinated generations of adventurers and fortune hunters. In Kentucky, the mention of "Jonathan Swift's Silver Mine" immediately attracted attention. Dozens of stories regarding the location of the mine have surfaced through the years. None have ever been proven.

The lack of evidence to support the existence of a fabulously rich silver mine in the mountains of eastern Kentucky has not deterred treasure seekers from combing the hills and valleys of the commonwealth in a desperate search for untold riches. Often it seemed that the quest to discover the validity of Swift's mine became as important as finding treasure itself. The lure of the unknown, the sense of high adventure, and the hope of discovering vast wealth, has kept the Swift silver mine legend alive for more than two centuries.

No one has found Swift's or anyone else's silver mine in Kentucky. Much, however, has been written about the mine as well as the legend. A journal or journals attributed to Swift tell of a rich vein of silver ore found in a Kentucky cave. Different stories come down to us through different versions of Swift's Journal.

One account tells how Swift came into Kentucky about 1760 and began a mining operation that produced silver ingots and coins. The story varies, but in the end, Swift's mine is lost. In the retelling of the legend, Swift is forced to leave his treasure due to Indian attack. He walls up the mine and does not come back for fifteen years. By this time he is blind and is unable to again find the site of his fortune.

The Swift silver mine legend receives some acknowledgement from Kentucky's first historian, John Filson (1753-1788). In 1788, Filson laid claim to a tract of land that supposedly included a silver mine. Later historians would pick up the Filson story and the legend would continue to grow.

As efforts to discover the location of Swift's mine continued to fail, some of the adherents of the legend began to doubt the eastern Kentucky location of the site. The lack of geological evidence of silver ore in Kentucky did not seem to deter those who believed in the mine's existence. Some individuals decided to follow other clues to the whereabouts of the mine. The location varied from eastern, to southern Kentucky. Some claimed that the mine had to be located in the central or western part of the state. On a few occasions, searchers appealed to government agencies or individuals for assistance in uncovering Swift's treasure. These entreaties fell on deaf ears.

Notwithstanding the lack of interest in financing an expedition to find the mine, those dedicated to finding it persisted in their search. The fascination with the Swift legend prompted a few people to write about Swift and his mine. In 1975, the publication of Michael Paul Henson's book, *John Swift's Lost Silver Mines* rekindled interest in the story. The *Filson Club Quarterly*, a scholarly journal on Kentucky and Ohio River valley history published Joe Nickell's 1980 article "Uncovered—the Fabulous Silver Mines of Swift and Filson." Newspapers and popular magazines ran stories on the legendary treasure. Interest in the Swift legend did not disappear.

Throughout my career as a Kentucky historian, I have spoken with at least a dozen or more people who have firmly believed in the Swift story. Each person has brought his or her own interpretation to the legend. I must admit that I had my fill of the seemingly tall tale of Swift and his lost riches. When I thought I had heard every possible variation of the story, along comes Robert A. Prather with another one.

I had met Prather during my years with the Kentucky Historical Society. I found him to be a serious researcher of Kentucky history with a fascination for the Swift legend. His penchant for research made him stand out as one who had a healthy respect for history. It was for this reason that I listened to his account of Swift and his silver.

During our conversations regarding the Swift legend, Prather noted a number of intriguing comparisons to the Swift story and the Robert Louis Stevenson (1850-1894) classic, *Treasure Island*. He also began to look at the historical Jonathan Swift, as opposed to the pre-Daniel Boone character who discovered silver in the wilds of eastern Kentucky. The more he talked about similarities in the Swift story and the Stevenson story, the more I felt that he should pursue the historical and literary angle of Jonathan Swift and his treasure. Prather doggedly researched and compared notes on the Swift legend and the saga of Long John Silver and his treasure island. The results of his research are presented in the pages of *The Strange Case of Jonathan Swift and the Real Long John Silver*. In his work, Prather explores the fascinating comparisons between the Swift legend and the equally legendary author, Stevenson. He also purports in his work the possibility of a series of codes that link the Stevenson adventure story with the Kentucky legend of Swift's treasure.

Prather studied characters in *Treasure Island* in relation to their possible connection to the Swift story. His conclusions are remarkable and controversial. The readers of *The Strange Case of Jonathan Swift and the Real Long John Silver* will find themselves challenged to look at two enduring legends in a totally different light.

Those devoted to the Swift legend will not be disappointed by Prather's endeavors. The possible site of the treasure is discussed at length. Altogether, *The Strange Case of Jonathan Swift and the Real Long John Silver* is a refreshing attempt to redefine the Swift legend as well as to explore the literary connections between the Swift story and Stevenson's pirate classic. The reader will find much to consider when looking objectively at this work.

Where does legend and history successfully intermingle? Robert Prather has made a Herculean effort to separate fact from fiction. What he gives us is an interesting thesis that no doubt will find its detractors as well as its believers. After all, there has been much smoke regarding the Swift legend. Now it is up to the reader to decide whether or not there is any fire.

The controversy over the validity of the Swift legend, and the comparison with Stevenson's *Treasure Island* will continue. However, the author of *The Strange Case of Jonathan Swift and the Real Long John Silver* has given us another important chapter in the continuing saga of Kentucky's Jonathan Swift and his lost silver mine.

ɔɕ ɔɕ ɔɕ ɔɕ ɔɕ ɔɕ ɔɕ ɔɕ ɔɕ

Ron D. Bryant is Historian for the Kentucky State Parks System and adjunct professor of history at Lexington Community College. He is a well-known author and raconteur on Kentucky history. For nearly 20 years he was with the Kentucky Historical Society where he served as Curator of Rare Books, and Kentucky History and Genealogy Specialist. Bryant has written extensively on the subject of Kentucky history. He wrote over 80 articles in the *Kentucky Encyclopedia*, wrote *A Bibliography of Kentucky History*, writes a bi-weekly political history column for the *Kentucky Gazette* in Frankfort, and has completed a history of Kentucky State Parks. Presently he is finishing a book on the history of coal in Kentucky. He is a historical consultant for a number of authors and also has served as a historical consultant for a number of educational TV and radio programs. Bryant dedicates much of his spare time to making speeches on a wide variety of historical and genealogical subjects. In June of 2005 he won the National Genealogical Society's prestigious Filby Award for his contributions to genealogy. A ninth generation Kentuckian, he and his wife Jane live in Georgetown, Kentucky with their West Highland Terriers, Wesley and Kaspar.

THE SEA COOK OF ALEXANDRIA

PART ONE

THE LEGEND

CHAPTER ONE

Many rich, poor, famous and historical people have entertained a desire to find Swift's silver mine, ranging from a passing interest to a crazed and dangerous obsession. Early into this investigation, it was considered that most of the Swift journals and related tales were fictitious. In fact, many stories seemed as if they had been taken, at least in part, from Robert Louis Stevenson's *Treasure Island*. However, after investigating both Swift and Stevenson the opposite appears to be true, that Stevenson's *Treasure Island* is based upon the Swift silver mine legend. Articles exist which refer to the Swift legend as Kentucky's own treasure island story, but it is unknown whether anyone has made the case in which the two stories are the same.

Rumors of a silver mine located somewhere in the Kentucky wilderness may have existed as early as 1760, but based upon the discoveries of this investigation it appears that the Swift name was first associated with the silver mine stories in the 1780s. Most of the stories of the legend do not give significant information on the life of Swift. Generally, his name is given as John or Jonathan, and he is usually considered to be from Alexandria, Virginia. Legend also has it that he owned several tall ships, and many historical accounts refer to him as a pirate. In those early American times, one country's patriot may very well have been another country's pirate.

According to various accounts, Swift had mined silver in the Kentucky wilderness in the 1760s and 1770s and then he abandoned the mines for a period of fifteen years. When he returned in 1791, he had in his possession a journal describing his former mining activities. This journal gave directions to the silver mines, and he left it with Mrs. Renfro of Bean Station. There are many versions of the Swift silver mine journal. In *Lost Silver Mines and Buried Tresures of Kentucky*, the late Michael Paul Henson wrote that he possessed seven versions of Swift's journal, all different in wording but similar in facts and all written since 1900. In 1975 Henson provided another version in his book, *John Swifts Lost Silver Mines*. Michael S. Steely states in his book, *Swift's Silver Mines and Related Appalachian Treasures*, that he has acquired *forty* versions of Swift's journal.

An early publication of a Swift silver mine story is in *Collins History of Kentucky*, Volume II, and copyright 1882. In it Judge John Haywood writes in 1823—"One Swift came to east Tennessee in 1790 and 1791 and was at Bean Station. He had with him a journal of his former silver mining transactions." Haywood also declares the years that the mining took place, and mentions that Swift left the journal in the possession of a woman named Mrs. Renfro. These Swift stories are in the Josh Bell county section, page 414, and expanded by Collins on page 415.

All of Collins' reports on Swift are found in another history series: *History of Kentucky*, Judge Charles Kerr, editor, copyright 1922, Volume I, pages 110-133. Kerr's chapter on the Swift silver mines gives a great deal of early information on Swift and related tales as well as a version of Swift's journal.

In most accounts of the legend, Swift is associated with a man named Munday. The following information is taken from Kerr's *History of Kentucky*. In this excerpt, an account is given about Robert Alley, who was the owner of a Swift journal as well as the journal's contents

John Swift's Journal

"There are many forms of the Swift Journal and no doubt, many copies of each of these forms. They agree substantially. They are evidently all copies of some part or parts of Swift's Original Manuscript Journal left with Mrs. Renfro. Through repeated copying from copies by persons little capable of doing accurate work, the journal degenerated finally into a few pages of incoherent jargon, as will appear from an examination of the most common form of the journal, many copies of which are extant in Eastern Kentucky.

"The usual form of Swift's Journal is a document covering about four pages of legal cap paper and was very common in Eastern Kentucky half a century ago, and is a condensation of the whole of Swift's Journal.

"A better form of Swift's Journal was preserved by Judge Richard Apperson, of Mount Sterling, Kentucky. Immediately after the Civil war he was judge of the Circuit Court of some district, which included Magoffin County. While holding court at Salyersville, Judge Apperson stopped at the tavern conducted by William Adams, Esq., the founder of the town and a pioneer settler in that region.

"In the year 1878, a North Carolinian named James McLeMoore, came to Kentucky to search for Swift's Silver Mines and the hidden treasure left by Swift and his companions. He had some knowledge of geology and mineralogy and had spent some considerable time in mining in the gold-fields of North Carolina, South Carolina and Georgia. He was a man of easy and careless disposition and fond of roaming about the world. He was a minister of the Gospel, and belonged to the Baptist Church.

"McLeMoore had in his possession a number of copies of John Swift's *Manuscript Journal* of different forms. Some were very short and others quite long. He had also some maps and was certain that these indicated that much of Swift's treasure was hidden in Johnson County, Kentucky. A number of the residents of Johnson and Magoffin counties joined with him in a search for the mines and Swift's hidden silver. He said he had secured the maps in North Carolina, on the Upper Yadkin, where Swift had lived; [he also said] that Swift had died there, and was buried in that country.

"Robert Alley was a resident of Johnson County from 1859 to his death—about 1890. He came there from East Tennessee to search for Swift's mines, which he and some associates had sought unsuccessfully in the region of the Cumberland Gap. Among these associates was one William Turlington, sometimes known as William Spurlock. He was a very eccentric character. He tramped the roads of East Tennessee and Eastern Kentucky for half a century, and undoubtedly discovered some hidden treasure. He had in his possession a document, which, he asserted, was the original journal of John Swift. In the fall of 1873 he was at the house of Mr. Alley. At that time copies of portions of this journal were made. According to this document, Hazlitt, Ireland, Blackburn, McClintock, Staley and Swift made a preliminary journey into what is now Eastern Kentucky in the spring of 1760. This trip was for the purpose of making arrangements to work the silver mines supposed to be in that region. They built a furnace and burned a pit of charcoal somewhere about the breaks of the Big Sandy River. From that point they went southwesterly along the base of the mountains a considerable distance, where they found other mines. There, also, a furnace was erected and charcoal burned for use the next year. They then departed from these mountains and arrived at Alexandria, Virginia, December 10, 1760. They there set about preparations for taking up the work in the wilderness the next year. In this connection the following, taken from the journal, is of interest:

"'Montgomery bought two additional vessels to sail to the Spanish Seas and return with cargoes suited to our enterprise, and he began the work of engraving and cutting the dies with which the silver and gold was to be coined, he being in that matter very expert, having labored long in the Royal Mint in the Tower of London.'

"A reorganization of the company was effected during the winter. This company seems to have been a partnership, although the common fund was divided into shares of which there were fifteen. They took out a large number of packhorses, when they set out for the mines, leaving Alexandria on the 25th day of June 1761. At the forks of the Big Sandy the company was divided into two parties, one party going to work at each of the locations selected the previous year. Much progress seems to have been made in the development of their mines, during the summer. A large force was left to work during the winter, but the managers arrived at Alexandria, December 2, 1761. They found their vessels returned from the Spanish seas after profitable cruises, which gave them so much encouragement from this branch of their business, that they bought five more vessels for this service the next year.

"Swift and his company left Alexandria in the last week of March, 1762, and, as in the previous trips, they went by the way of Fort Pitt. A large pack-train was taken out. Two horses were drowned in the Kanawha. At the forks of the Big Sandy they cast lots to see who should go to the different points and work these mines. They found that the men who had been left all winter were dissatisfied and homesick, although much work had been done. Swift and others set out on their return to Virginia on the 1st day of September 1762, and arrived in Alexandria on the 12th day of October. They found that their shipping interests had prospered much. In the preparations for the work for the coming year, they more than doubled their number of pack-horses.

"In 1763, Swift and his train left Alexandria on the 21st day of April. They arrived at the mines on the head waters of the Big Sandy on the 17th day of May. Much progress had been made in their mining operations. Swift set out for Alexandria on the 16th day of September and arrived there the last day of October, and records that they had a successful year.

"In 1764 the operations of the company were hindered by wars in the wilderness, and it was deemed unsafe to go out by the way of Fort Pitt. They had now become somewhat more familiar with the geography of the country. They left Alexandria on the 7th day of June 1764, and went by the way of New River and the Cumberland Gap, reaching what they called their lower mines on the 11th day of July. This year was not a successful one. It seems that they abandoned the route by Fort Pitt for the time being. They left the mine on the 8th day of November, going out by the way of New River, and arrived at Munday's house the 1st day of December 1764.

"In 1765 the train set out from Munday's house on the 14th day of April 1765. They went by the way of Ingles' Ferry on the New River, arriving at their lower mines on the 2nd day of May. They had a profitable year, and gathered into a great cave, 'our immense store of precious metal, both of the coined and the uncoined, and hid it therein until we could in the providence of God convey it thence to the trade of the seas.' At another point of the journal says, 'that store of treasure lieth in that cave to this day.' Their geographical knowledge was increased, and in going out from their mines this year they went by a gap at the head of the Big Sandy, in all probability, the Pound Gap. They arrived at Munday's house on the 20th day of November, 1765.

"On the 6th day of June, 1766, they set out on their journey to the mines. Their delay this year was caused by wounds inflicted upon each other by two of their company, Fletcher and Flint. They were drinking heavily on Christmas Day and came to blows with swords. They made their wills and concealed their money in the vicinity of Munday's house, which was probably on the Yadkin. Flint buried 240,000 crown pieces, and Fletcher hid 360,200 crowns. Fletcher died on the 2nd day of July, and Flint recovered. This year the company was troubled with a mutiny of their workmen, who left and returned to the settlements. After taking every precaution to conceal their operations they left the mines on the 6th of November and set out for North Carolina, arriving at Munday's house on the 6th of December.

"In 1767 the company left Munday's house of the 1st day of October and arrived at the mines on the 4th day of November, bringing in their largest train, to that time. After a successful year they went out by the way of Fort Pitt and arrived at Alexandria on the 7th day of May, 1768.

"For the next year, a great train was made up, and on the 4th of June, 1768, they went by the way of Fort Pitt. The date of arrival at the mines is not given. This proved a prosperous year. Swift and some of his companions left the mines on the 29th of October. On the Big Sandy they were ambushed by Indians, and Campbell was killed. Hazlitt and Staley were badly wounded. The company arrived at Munday's house on the 14th day of December, 1768, and on the 24th Hazlitt died of his wounds. Mention is made of a settlement with the 'Scotch Company.' It is said that the settlement was not easily effected, as the company,

" 'Seeing that we prospered in all our enterprises, both at sea and on the land, took advantage of the nature of our business to extort from us a great sum, not their due, and this we paid, though very unwillingly, but fearing that worse might come of refusal to come to this agreement wrongfully exacted of us. In making that settlement we closed our business in North Carolina deeming it imprudent to longer move with our affairs there.'

"In 1769 the company left Munday's house on the 16th day of May and went by the New River and Cumberland Gap. The pack-train was large and unwieldy, and their progress was slow. The arrival at the lower mines was on the 24th day of June. This year it was determined to close up the affairs of the company and quit business. All their workmen were pledged to secrecy and paid seven-fold their agreed wages. The paragraph describing the close of their business is as follows:

" 'And it came up to us to settle what was to be done, and seeing that we had prospered beyond all our expectations, and had gathered gold and silver until we had heaped up great riches, and seeing also that the stormy life we had led in this wild land for more than a third of a century was wearing away our strength; and being minded that the works of men are always unfinished and unsatisfactory, leaving the heart at unrest and in tumult; and, too, being fully persuaded that the life of man should be at some period turned about for reflection on God and his mind drawn in from the wanderings of this world, we decided to quit and abandon this hard life for the present and mayhap for all time, returning here to carry out that store now hidden in the great cavern of the Shawnees, which fact is known to no living soul beyond our company.'

"They left the mines on the 9th of October going by the way of Big Sandy and Fort Pitt, and arrived at Alexandria the 11th day of December 1769. They closed out their 'sea-faring operations,' as it was written in the journal. 'So, we end the labor of ten years on seas and land, praising God that it was successful.' The journal ends with specific directions for finding the treasure left in all parts of the wilderness and for the discovery of the mines. If there is any reliance to be placed on the journal, there is concealed treasure in Eastern Kentucky in untold amounts.

"Whatever may be the facts concerning the Swift's mines, it is certain there were many expeditions made to Eastern Kentucky by men in pursuit of hidden minerals long before the central portion of the state was settled."

In this *History of Kentucky* excerpt, the town of Alexandria, Virginia is prominently mentioned. It describes the Swift silver mining operation having eight or more ships. In most accounts of Swift the silver miner, he is mentioned as living in Alexandria, Virginia.

The following is the full list of names gathered from Kerr's entire article about Swift: Shadrack Jefferson, Henry Hazlitt, James Ireland, Isaac Campbell, Samuel Blackburn, Joshua McClintock, Harmon Staley, Seth Montgomery, Jonathan Munday, William Wilton, John Motts, Alexander Bartol, Jeremiah Bates, Moses Fletcher and Abram Flint.

In M. Steely's *Swift's Silver Mine and Related Appalachian Treasures*, he states that, in various journals, Swift's first name is given as John, Johnathan, Jonathan, George, William, George William, Tom, William, and even called Smith, in place of Swift. Munday was also called Monday, Monde, Mundeau, Money, Mondeaux and Monie. Munday's first name variations where George, John Martin, Jonathan and Alfred. Steely also states that in some journal versions the silver mines are not referred to as Swift's but as Munday's. Also from Steely's book, James Ireland was also given as England and also given in southwest Virginia lore as Island. Other participants of the expeditions also had name variations and will be mentioned later.

The journal also gives directions to the mines and a description of the country with varying landmarks. The following landmarks mentioned in

Swift's journal are from Michael Paul Henson's book, *John Swift's Lost Silver Mines:* salt licks, lick creeks, rock houses [rock ledges] half moon cliff, Indian campground, Mecca Indians, hanging rock, balanced rock, bear den, great cave, haystack rock, lighthouse, sky rock, sinking creek, rock bridge, horseshoe bend, water falls, a large and very rocky creek, and a remarkable rock at a place where three creeks come together.

The journal describes places where they buried large amounts of silver bars and silver crowns they had made. It also mentions what they described as a "Great Cave" where an immense store of precious metal both coined and uncoined was hidden until they could retrieve it at a later time.

The following are two well-known anecdotes about Swift from Kerr's *History of Kentucky.*

Tale #1

"By Judge Haywood, we are told that Swift was at Bean's Station, in East Tennessee, in the years 1790 and 1791, and that he was deterred from going on to his mines by the troublesome presence of Indians in that region. A part of this conclusion is supported by tradition; and tradition has carried down, too, some things not set out by Judge Haywood. These additional matters are given here as traditions—traditions well defined and of common recital by the old people of Eastern Kentucky and East Tennessee and other portions of Appalachian America as late as fifty years ago.

"It is said in these traditions that Swift had become almost blind from some affection [infection?] of the eyes; and, also, that the Frenchmen who were with him at this time were not those French companions of his former journeys, but others having a knowledge of the mines worked and the treasure hidden by Swift and their countrymen. Any weakness in a man of cupidity invariably begets suspicion and distrust of those with whom he is associated in any business enterprise. Swift evidently realized that, in this affliction, he was at a disadvantage with these Frenchmen should they choose to exercise their opportunities. He feared that they might obtain possession of the written information which he alone had concerning the mines and treasure, and render him incapable of ever again finding them— while the Frenchmen would be enabled to easily discover them, and profit from the discovery, with the aid of his journal.

"It is said, in this connection, that Swift was desirous of procuring the hand of Mrs. Renfro in marriage. This lady was the widow of Joseph Renfro, who had been killed by the Indians in the defense of the country while it was a part of the State of North Carolina, the Legislature of which state granted his widow a large tract of land as a compensation for his loss and for claims he had then pending against the state for settlement; this grant was made in 1784. Renfro was a man of standing and consequence and a large property added to his prestige. He left his widow with a large estate. She is reputed to have been a woman of beauty and rare accomplishments, and to have lived on a large plantation near Bean's Station. Swift committed his journals to her for safe-keeping when he returned to North Carolina in 1790 and the Frenchmen descended the Cumberland River in a canoe and forever disappeared.

"Swift returned to Bean's Station in 1791, and attempted to re-discover his mines and treasure, but in the meantime the disease of his eyes had made such progress that his sight was almost wholly destroyed. He was unable even with the assistance of his journal to find any trace of his mines. He made a number of unsuccessful attempts to locate them, the last of which, it is said, he made with a dark bandage bound closely about his face and over his eyes. In this condition, he was mounted upon his horse, which was led by an attendant, while other attendants, or persons employed by him, endeavored vainly to trace the course to the silver mines, as set down in his journal, and as directed by him. He might have succeeded had not the condition of his eyes compelled him to cease his efforts. Leaving a large sum of money and his journals with Mrs. Renfro, Swift returned to North Carolina to consult a half-blood Cherokee Indian physician and surgeon. This physician had been educated at Paris, and for many years he was the leading surgeon in Western North Carolina. His name was Hicks, and he was in the army of the patriots who defeated the British at King's Mountain.

"Swift never afterward returned to Tennessee. He probably died in a comparatively short time. But precisely what became of him or what fate befell him is not positively known."

Tale #2

"Swift and his company had left concealed in the wilderness treasure amounting in the aggregate to a vast some. It was a rigid rule among them that no one member of their association should ever visit the place of concealment of any part of the hidden treasure. By a rule or law of their company, Swift (who was the leading man and principal) and any three others of the company might visit the mines or concealed riches and carry out money. An account was kept and an absent member was not wronged. It seems that there is no record of any visit made either by Swift or any of the company after the trip made in 1769 until 1790, and this tradition asserts that none was made. Why no one went out in all this time is not explained.

"In 1790 all the survivors of the company were gathered together to go into the wilderness and bring out the treasure left there in former days when the full company worked so persistently in the mines. This party was composed of Swift, Munday, McClintock, the two Frenchmen, and the two Shawnee Indians. These were the only survivors of the original company.

"The party arrived at the mines and examined the treasure hidden at the different points in the vicinity of their various furnaces. Nothing had been disturbed. The last place of concealment to be examined was the great cave. When Swift saw the immense sums lying on the floor of this ancient retreat of the Shawnees, the evil spirit of his nature was aroused, and he resolved to possess the whole of the great riches before him. He finally reached the conclusion to murder his companions if possible. His resolution deepened. At nightfall he set about the execution of his diabolical plot.

"At length, when his companions slept, unconscious of the bloody treachery in the heart of their leader, Swift stealthily arose from the group of prostrate forms about the fire. He was consumed with his passion for murder and bloodstained riches. His countenance was changed. The keen blade of his scalping-knife glittered coldly in the baleful light that fitfully fluttered up from the dying camp-fire. Noiselessly did he glide from one victim to another. The panther of the forest, a ghost, a phantom, a spectre, could not have moved or acted with greater stealth. Quickly was the dastardly deed done. With stroke sudden, silent, deadly, did the reeking blade enter the heart of each of his associates, companions, and friends.

"But not yet was his crime fully consummated. The Shawnees were sleeping in the great cave. Thither came Swift bent on further murder. His every faculty was quickened, his every act deliberate. There was no haste —there was manifested no premeditated order of events. With torches held aloft, at his solicitation, they together looked upon the treasure. At sight of it his inflamed passions broke into an insane fury. With the yell of a demoniac, he leaped upon the aged and unsuspecting Shawnees. In a moment they were lying lifeless, and

25

Swift was alone in the darkness. And from that hour did Providence smite him with almost total-blindness. He groped his way from the wilderness to civilization. The riches, bought with his soul, were left in the trackless forest wastes. They are guarded by the manes of the innocent slain. And no man hath looked upon them to this day."

It is reasonable to state that some, possibly many, of the old stories associated with the Swift legend *are* only fanciful folklore. One obvious question should be asked pertaining to Tale #2: If Swift killed all who were witnesses to the whereabouts of the treasure, who told the story? *History of Kentucky* also gives two separate accounts of Colonel James Harrod's disappearance while trying to locate Swift's silver mines. In his time, Harrod, a Kentucky pioneer, was as famous as Daniel Boone. He founded the first settlement in Kentucky, Harrodsburg.

"Dr. Christopher Graham gives the first account. Mrs. Harrod had told Graham that her husband went looking for Swift's silver mine near the three forks of the Kentucky River with a man claiming to know the location of the mine.
"Mrs. Harrod said that her husband had a lawsuit over property with that man and she believed that he lured Harrod into the wilderness to murder him, sometime in 1793."

The second account of Harrod's disappearance is given by Dr. R. G. Thwaites.

"In February of 1792, having made his will, Harrod set out from Washington in Mason County with two men in search of a silver mine reported to be at the three forks of the Kentucky River. No more was heard of him or his companions"

In Michael Cook's *Kentucky Record Series, Mercer County Kentucky Records Volume 1,* it was found that "on October 22, 1793, a summons to issue against five men from Mason County to appear in December court as witnesses to the last will of James Harrod, deceased." Also, in the same record series, "on December 24, 1793, Ann Harrod exhibits an instrument of writing purporting to be the last will of James Harrod, deceased." Both versions of Harrod's disappearance have him last seen looking for a silver mine. The Mercer county records confirm the approximate time of his disappearance.

Another Kentucky pioneer who went in search of Swift's silver mine, never to be seen again, was John Filson. Filson was Kentucky's first historian and one of the commonwealth's earliest cartographers. Filson, by way of a Kentucky land entry and the description of the property, appears to be the first to connect in print the name of Swift to a silver mine.

While there are numerous possible explanations for Filson's disappearance, the circumstances are suspect.

By using Jillson's *Old Kentucky Entries and Deeds* book, one finds that Filson made three land entries: 1) 5,600 acres entered on December 19, 1783, 2) 4,922 acres entered on December 19, 1783, and 3) 2,446 1/2 acres entered on December 20, 1783. These properties were in old Fayette County, Kentucky.

It was not until May 18, 1788, that Filson, along with Robert Breckinridge, made the entry of the land which was to include a silver mine: 1,000 acres in old Lincoln County. A copy of the original land entry is available at the Library of the Kentucky Historical Society in Frankfort, Kentucky.

The entry reads as follows:

"Robert Breckinridge and John Filson as tenants in common, enters 1,000 acres of land upon the balance of a Treasury Warrant #10117 about sixty or seventy miles North Eastwardly from Martin's Cabin in Powell's Valley to include a silver mine which was improved about 17 years ago by a certain man named Swift at said mine the said Swift reports he has extracted from the ore a considerable quantity of silver some of which he made into dollars and left at or near the mine. Together with the apparatus for making the same, the land to be in a square and the lines to run at the cardinal points of the compass including the mine in the center as near as may be."

A land entry was one of the early steps of having land granted from the state or commonwealth to an individual or group of individuals. The completed process resulted in a land patent. A four-step process had to be followed in order to complete a patent.

The following information on land patenting was primarily obtained from an article written by Kandie Adkinson titled, *The Kentucky Land Grant System.* Highlights regarding Virginia's land patenting process were found on *The Library of Virginia* web site under *Land Office Grants 1779-1993.*

Step #1: The Warrant

This document authorizes a survey to be made and the amount of land the person is entitled. It does not specify the exact location of the land. Warrants could be traded, sold, or reassigned to another person in whole or in part, any time during the patenting process. It was similar to a gift certificate where all could be used at once on one large tract of land or spread out and used several times on multiple tracts of land.

Step #2: The Entry

This record is often considered a patent in itself; when in all actuality, it is merely an intention to file for a patent. Once the warrant has been obtained, the person deposits it with the surveyor of the county in which the property was located. The surveyor records in his entry book the name of the person, a description of the property to be surveyed, warrant number and the date the intention is declared. Entries could be altered or withdrawn.

Step #3: The Survey

The next stage in land patenting is the preparation of the survey depicting the tract and describing metes and bounds, the name of the warrantee, warrant number or numbers, assignments made, the county the property is in, landmarks such as watercourses etc. are mentioned, properties and property owners bordering the land being surveyed are sometimes mentioned. The name of the surveyor and his deputy is also given.

Step #4: The Grant

Once the survey had been completed, the person then would deliver it to the land office for examination and if correctly executed, was filed for a period of no less than six months. If within that time, no caveat was entered on the survey the grant would be made, signed by the governor and delivered to the grantee. Virginia had a six-month waiting period and it is assumed that Kentucky did also.

The patent process would usually take a couple of years to complete and sometimes much longer. After the entry was made, it could take a year or two before it was surveyed. From the survey to the grant it could take that long as well. If a caveat was entered on the survey, the property could be tied up for many years.

During the course of this investigation, it was determined that a very short period of time existed between Filson and Breckinridge's initial awareness of the silver mine property to the time when the entry was made. It was likely a matter of days, weeks, or months—not years. It seems probable to state that Filson and Breckinridge ran all the way to the surveyor to make their entry and stake their claim on the property before someone beat them to it.

Neither Filson nor Breckinridge received a grant on this property. In fact, the year the entry was made, 1788, was also the year of Filson's disappearance. Filson and Breckinridge's 1788 entry is important in that it establishes the approximate time period when the Swift name became associated with the silver mine. It is also possible that the meeting of Swift and Filson, and the land entry that resulted, may have been somewhat responsible for a chain of events shortly thereafter that helps establish the complete identity of "a certain man named Swift."

Double Legend

Stevenson's classic *Treasure Island* is by no means only a better-written telling of the Swift stories. It is purely a Stevenson creation; however, the skeletal structure of the book appears to be based on the Swift stories and characters. How, one might ask, could the Swift legend be an inspiration for the Scottish novelist, Robert Louis Stevenson? To begin with, it is feasible that Stevenson was introduced to the Swift stories while living in Scotland. According to legend, Swift was involved with the "Scotch Company," and later in this book there is further evidence of Swift's Scottish connections. If Stevenson had heard the stories of Jonathan Swift when he was young, and found them amusing, he was in for both a writer's thrill and his luckiest day when he happened to meet Sam and Fanny Vandegrift Osbourne.

It was in July of 1876, that Stevenson met Fanny Osbourne at the artist colonies around Fontainebleau in Grez, France. Fanny was still married to Sam during that time. Stevenson was there for his health and Fanny was having marital problems. It was during their relationship in Grez that Stevenson met Fanny's husband, Sam Osbourne.

The following is from *Louis –A Life of Robert Louis Stevenson* by Philip Callow:

"Fanny Osbourne had arrived in Paris from California earlier that year after separating, not for the first time, from her husband. Sam Osbourne, sitting beside her at the hotel table as she chatted with Louis, had come over in a hurry to be at his youngest child's sickbed."

In August of 1879, Stevenson was alarmed at news of Fanny's illness and hurried to San Francisco, arriving in December. In May of 1880, they were married and spent their honeymoon in the desolate mining camp he describes in his book, *The Silverado Squatters.* As early as July 1881, Stevenson had written and published (in serial form) his most famous and successful book, *The Sea Cook,* later renamed *Treasure Island* when it was published in book form in 1883.

Stevenson scholars accept that Fanny was influential in some of Stevenson's writings. It is possible that, through Fanny and Sam Osbourne, a written form of the Swift legend was introduced to Stevenson, though no documentation to support this belief has been discovered. One must realize how unlikely it would be for Stevenson to acknowledge that his new bride's ex-husband was instrumental in the creation of his most successful book. How were the Osbournes responsible for this? How likely is this scenario that they delivered this old Kentucky legend into Stevenson's hands?

> The following is from *The Violent Friend* by Margaret Mackay:
> "Sam Osbourne was from Louisville, Kentucky. On December 4th 1857 Sam married Fanny Vandegrift of Indiana. Descendants of the families of Daniel Boone (on Sam's side) and Captain Cook (on Fanny's side) were in attendance at their wedding. In 1861 Sam went to war in an Indiana regiment. After his military service, Sam and Fanny moved to Nevada and tried their luck at prospecting in a silver mining camp. They spent several years prospecting in different mining camps, and, in Virginia City, Sam bought a silver mine."

Anyone interested in treasure and silver mines that came across a copy of the Swift journal would copy it for their own use from person to person. Sam Osbourne was clearly the type of person who would be interested in the location of a silver mine. With these interests and his Kentucky heritage, Mr. Osbourne would have had the opportunity to possess a copy and it is believed that Sam Osbourne did own a Swift journal and possibly maps of the mine.

To compare, following is a list of some of the similarities between *Treasure Island* and the Swift legend.

Treasure Island	Swift Legend
• Long John Silver (not Goldman or Copperpott)	• Jonathan/John Swift, (associated with silver)
• Pirate, Captain Flint	• Abram Flint
• Captain Flint, murdered his six crew members so he would not share the treasure.	• John Swift, murdered six crew members so he would not share the treasure.
• Blind Pew, looking for treasure map at Benbow Inn	• Blind John Swift, looking for treasure, left map with Mrs. Renfro
• Benbow Inn	• Swift lodges at Renfro's
• Billy Bones leaves map and book at Benbow Inn	• Swift leaves journal with Mrs. Renfro
• The Barsilver, left undiscovered on the island	• Lost silver mine
• Treasure hidden in cave	• Treasure hidden in cave
• Tall ships	• Tall ships
• Pirates	• Pirates
• Widow Hawkins at the Benbow Inn	• Widow Renfro

As mentioned, it is possible that Stevenson created his book, *Treasure Island*, based upon elements of the Swift legend, and the story was passed to him through the Osbournes. Another reason for believing this is the Flint factor. As noted in *History of Kentucky*, John Swift's journal section, Robert Alley's journal mentions Flint as one of Swift's mining associates; this journal was at least eight years older (probably much older) than Stevenson's *Treasure Island*. Where did Stevenson get the name of the pirate Captain Flint?

Captain Flint has always been considered Stevenson's fictitious creation because there was no known pirate named Flint. It is probable that Flint was the one name from Sam Osbourne's Swift journal that Stevenson could not resist using in his book. Because Abram Flint is one of the secondary characters of the Swift journal, it is likely Flint's name would not have been mentioned if Stevenson had only heard an oral version of the story. This is further evidence to support the belief that Osbourne owned a Swift journal and Stevenson had access to it.

As previously mentioned, in the John Swift's journal excerpt from Kerr's *History of Kentucky*, there were many forms of the Swift journal and many copies made of each of those forms. From James McLemoore's account it is known that seekers of Swift's silver collected as many forms of the journal as they could get their hands on. It was probably common in those days that, when one person would have one version of Swift's journal and another person would have a different version, and hearing of this through family or friends they would seek each other out so a swap for information could be made. Both parties would make copies of one another's journal to add to their collection. In the early days of silver mine hunting, if anyone was interested in finding Swift's silver, there were always family members or friends who knew someone who could acquire a Swift journal. Sam Osbourne definitely fits the profile of someone interested in Swift journals in as many forms of it as he could find.

The evidence of looking no further than one's own family to find one of Swift's journals is found through Robert Alley who provided John Swift's journal for Kerr's *History of Kentucky*. A history of how the Osborne and the Alley family trees relate is available in the book, *Early Osbornes and Alleys* compiled by Rita (Kennedy) Sutton, about their lives on the Clinch and New Rivers. This book documents the lives of Sam and Fanny Osbourne, Robert Louis Stevenson and Robert Alley, and has the same excerpt from Kerr's *History of Kentucky* about Robert Alley's "John Swift's Journal." Sam was the first in his line to include the letter "U" in the spelling of Osborne. Sam Osbourne's grandfather was Solomon Osborne. He married Mary (Polly) Stewart who was the second child of John and Hannah (Boone) Stewart, Daniel Boone's sister. From *Hannah Boone and Her Descendants*, compiled by Bess L. Hawthorne, one finds that Solomon Osborne was born in Scott or Lee County Virginia. Stephen and Comfort (Langrum) Osborne are believed (unresolved) to be Solomon's parents and were from Osborne's Ford in Scott County Virginia. Mary (Polly) Osborne was the eldest daughter of Stephen and Comfort Osborne, and in 1786 she married Samuel Alley. Robert Alley and David, his father, were also from Scott County Virginia. David Alley was born in 1791 and Robert in 1817 in Scott County Virginia.

Robert Alley possessed a Swift journal and, as previously noted, came to Johnson County Kentucky seeking Swift's silver mine. Sam Osbourne also had an interest in silver mines, but unlike Alley, found the search for a lost silver mine less exciting than digging for silver in a known Nevada silver mine. Both men's families intersect in Scott County Virginia; an area where Swift's silver mine was on everyone's tongue. Considering the profile of Sam Osbourne, the fact that it was possible to obtain a Swift journal in those days, and the obvious similarities between the Swift legend and *Treasure Island,* it seems nearly impossible to believe that Sam Osbourne did not possess a Swift journal. In fact, he probably owned several versions of it.

32

The following is from *Robert Louis Stevenson* by James Pope Hennessy: "Stevenson wrote the first fifteen chapters of *Treasure Island* in fifteen days and when he resumed writing he finished the remainder of the book in another fifteen days. Stevenson regarded it as his 'quickest piece of work,' and the rapidity with which the tale flowed from his pen is indeed astounding."

The following excerpts are acknowledged to be the genesis and inspirations of Stevenson's *Treasure Island*. The first is from *The Violent Friend* by Margaret Mackay.

"One day [Stevenson] found Lloyd painting a map he had drawn of an imaginary island. Louis loved charts and joined in, adding a number of swashbuckling place names such a Spyglasse Hill and Skeleton Island. In the top right-hand corner he wrote 'Treasure Island.' Something lit up his mind like a smuggler's lantern. In five minutes he had jotted down a list of chapter headings. 'Then,' remembered Lloyd, '...he put the map in his pocket, and I can recall the little feeling of disappointment I had at losing it.'"

So, in a way, Stevenson does credit the genesis for *Treasure Island* to Sam Osbourne, Samuel Lloyd Osbourne that is, the son of Sam and Fanny, and it is S.L.O. to whom the book is dedicated. There is some speculation as to who drew the map first, Lloyd or Louis. These next excerpts are from *Louis--A Life of Robert Louis Stevenson*, by Philip Callow:

"...Then one day, dabbling with watercolor and ink, he (Stevenson) made the map of an island. Lloyd later claimed wrongly that it had been his work." Callow goes on to say, "*Treasure Island* began with the map. Writing later of 'My First Book,' Stevenson realized that it was most of the plot. Beyond doubt this was the engendering catalyst. It was like 'a fat dragon standing up'; it contained harbors 'that pleased me like sonnets.' Before he knew it, poring over his imaginary map, the future characters of the book began swarming out. He snatched up some paper and was writing out a list of chapters which seemed to write themselves. 'On a chill September morning, by the cheek of a brisk fire, and the rain drumming on the window, I began *The Sea Cook,* for that was the original title.' Owing up the work of others he didn't forget his father, who contributed, as well as the apple barrel idea, the inventory of Billy Bones's chest. He acknowledged a debt to Washington Irving's *Tales of a Traveller,* to *Robinson Crusoe,* and someone, playing the game of influences, told him that the stockade came from *Masterman Ready.* Not that he cared. An artist in full flow plunders as if by right, and the book flowed effortlessly, and he with it. He picked up whatever he fancied like a magpie. Whatever he made use of, he knew the story would still be his. Maybe he found the skeleton in Poe, but what of it? No one, he remarked happily, 'can hope to have a monopoly of skeletons or make a corner of talking birds.' Something out of Fenimore Cooper's *The Sea Lions* may have found its way in there. It all worked. He admitted to Colvin in 1884 that the book 'came out' of Charles Kingsley's *At Last,* from which he had lifted the Dead Man's Chest, and that he owed something to a *History of Notorious Pirates,* borrowed from Henley in August. Johnson's *Buccaneers* was dipped into, and his own recollections of canoeing and a cruise through the Western Isles in a fifteen-ton Schooner yacht made up the rest of his material. He should have made the *Hispaniola* a brig but was unable to describe handling one. Then had an idea for John Silver, 'from which I promised myself funds of entertainment.' He was recalling Henley with his one foot, his 'maimed strength and masterfullness.' He would take his admired friend, deprive him 'of all his finer qualities and higher graces of temperament,' and leave him with 'only his strength and courage and his geniality, and try to express these in terms of raw tarpaulin.' "

The books acknowledged by Stevenson to be influential in the creation of *Treasure Island* were primarily used to create the writing style and the vivid descriptions to help create the sea-faring pirate story he had envisioned it to become. Stevenson's admired friend, Henley, who was used to bring a descriptive personality into Long John Silver, is a good example.

The following is from *Robert Louis Stevenson* by James Pope Hennessy: At twelve years of age W. E. Henley, whom Stevenson had collaborated writing plans with, developed a tubercular disease, which made him a cripple, and one foot had been amputated... "...He was a big, broad-shouldered man with a bushy head of yellow hair that stood straight upward, and a copious reddish beard..." " ...He was of a jealous nature, very noisy and drank too much whiskey.

"Henleys' talk was 'boisterous and piratic.' 'He will roar you down, he will bury his face in his hands, he will undergo passions of revolt and agony.'"

Henley, of course, was never a sea-faring man, pirate, or treasure hunting silver miner.

If Stevenson did have access to a Swift journal and the Swift stories are, as proposed, the skeletal structure of Treasure Island, or in this case the Billy Bones of it, then is it possible that an unacknowledged Osbourne Swift journal could have contained clues and information of Swift's silver mine that the typical extant Swift journals found in Kentucky today do not? To be sure, Treasure Island is an unlikely source of clues for Swift's lost silver mine, but it is proposed that it does contain valuable supporting evidence, and Part Three of this book is devoted to proving this point.

THE DARK AND BLOODY SOJOURN

CHAPTER TWO

"The history of Kentucky has features not shared with other States west of the Allegheny Mountains. Because of the incessant wars between the Iroquois and the Cherokees for its possession, the Indians knew it as the 'Dark and Bloody ground.'" ~ *The Encyclopaedia Britannica*

The objective of this investigation was to find anything that might tie the Swift legend or Jonathan Swift to the general area of the 1985 and 1986 searches. By employing the old investigative technique of beginning with the information that was readily available, imagining various possible scenarios, and then basing the research on those suppositions, the connections that were found exceeded all expectations. The first evidence presented for consideration is an area of land in Kentucky located in Breckinridge County, the northern part of Grayson County and the western part of Hardin County.

The following eleven landmarks demonstrate why this area is of particular interest. Each is located on Map #1 with corresponding numbers.

1. A Remarkable Rock, at an area where three streams of water come together.

In Swift legend, the Remarkable Rock at an area where three streams of water come together, is considered one of the most important landmark clues left by Swift to designate the approximate location of the silver mine.

A unique rock formation is located in the southwestern part of Breckinridge County, Kentucky. This geologic formation is called Sand Knob, and it is located in the area of Rough River Lake. Around the base of Sand Knob, the ground is as sandy as an ocean beach. Its highest point is approximately 150 feet tall. Its walls are nearly vertical, and it is 450 to 500 feet in length.

From the owner of the property, it was discovered that on top of the main formation one can see over twenty miles in any direction on a clear day. Being on top of this natural wonder is very similar to being atop a large natural rock bridge. There is also a natural rock house, which is another landmark relevant to Swift legend, on the side of the main formation.

Another singular rock formation is on the backside of Sand Knob. This rock protrudes skyward approximately 30 feet. It is as big around as a silo, and is called Buttercup or Butter Stack. The Buttercup is very interesting for those investigating the Swift silver mine legend because of its cylindrical shape. It seems probable that if these geological formations where mentioned in the Swift journals, the Buttercup/Butter Stack may have been referred to as the landmark called the lighthouse, haystack rock, or sky-rock.

The three streams of water near these remarkable rocks are Long Lick Creek, the North Fork of Rough River, and Rough River.

One feels like a delighted tourist at a national park, while visiting this magnificent geological wonder, rather than being in its owner's back yard.

Sand Knob is not a tourist attraction. It is located on private property and is not open to the public.

2. Long Lick Creek—This creek empties into the North Fork of Rough River. The mouth is approximately one mile from Axtel.

3. Sinking Creek

4. Big Clifty Creek—Named for the big cliffs nearby, from Historical Sketches and Family Histories Grayson County, Kentucky. The mine/mines were described to be in a place that was rough and "clifty."

5. Rough River—The mine/mines were described to be in a place that was "rough" and clifty.

6. Hanging Rock—"The locals say, 'this community was named for a commodious cliff that was large enough for a team and wagonload of people, a load of hay or corn, too…to pull under and get out of bad weather. It became a place to stop while traveling to Leitchfield to get out of the rain.'" from Historical Sketches and Family Histories Grayson County, Kentucky.

7. Falls of Rough—"The town is named for the water falls of the Rough River. Rough River or Rough Creek is named in boundary descriptions dating to the late 1700s," from Historical Sketches and Family Histories Grayson County, Kentucky.

8. Indian Valley—"This Rough River Reservoir lake subdivision was named for the numerous Indian artifacts found along the river in this area," from Historical Sketches and Family Histories Grayson County, Kentucky.

37

9. Horseshoe Bend
10. Rocky Branch
11. Great Cave—Breckinridge County has some of the greatest cave systems in the world.

Each of these landmarks is like or very similar to the descriptions of landmarks given in Swift's journal that are used to describe the locations of silver mines. Landmarks such as these can be found in various areas in Kentucky, but the close proximity of these and the number of matches, especially the remarkable rock and its location, make this a most interesting place.

There is one other major reason for interest. Somewhere in this area Jonathan Swift owned property.

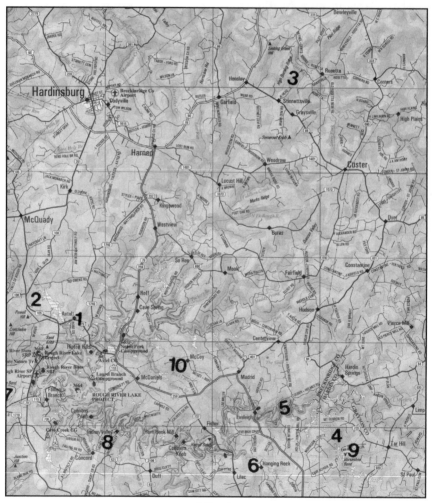

Map 1

"X Marks the Spot"

Before proceeding into the dissection of Swift's Kentucky properties, a question should be asked. What was and is the one vital element of the Swift silver mine legend? The answer is land or property, there can be no silver mine without it, and this chapter specifically addresses Swift's properties.

It would merely be considered land before it was patented; however, once it was legally obtained through the Virginia and Kentucky land patenting systems, it became someone's property. It is proposed that each tract of property to be presented is a piece of the Swift silver mine puzzle, and each has numerous points of pertinent details. Only by meticulously accumulating the many points of information which may be gathered from his land purchases, can a remarkable discovery be revealed.

By means of a systematic method of locating property, an "X MARKS THE SPOT" treasure pointer on one of Jonathan Swift's properties will be presented in Part Two of this book.

From the Hardin County clerk's office in Elizabethtown, Kentucky, one finds in *Deed Book A*, The Quarter Sessions Book (red binder) on page 19, an indenture (contract) between James Kerr and Julia, his wife, from the town of Alexandria, Fairfax County, Virginia and Robert Walsh of Baltimore, Maryland, merchant of the other part, on the 23rd day of March 1795. Kerr sells to Walsh a certain tract or parcel of land containing 20,718 ¾ acres for $10,000 dollars. Reading further into the indenture, the original land patent belonged to Mordecai Barbour and that patent was conveyed by the said Mordecai Barbour to a certain Jonathan Swift. The patent date was August 5, 1788. Barbour conveyed the land to Swift on September 15, 1791. Swift conveyed the land to James Kerr May 8, 1792. This property was entered three times. Mordecai Barbour made the final and correct entry May 7, 1784, and the survey date is March 1, 1787.

From the Virginia County Court Records, *Deed Abstracts of Fairfax County, Virginia 1791-1792*, one finds that Swift sold this same property to Kerr for five shillings CMV (current money of Virginia) and the first name of Swift's wife was Ann. The profit on this transaction should be noted and is surely due to Jonathan Swift being a previous owner.

The indenture from Hardin County *Deed Book A* was vague in describing where the property was located; it listed no watercourse, etc. The information it did give was the county where the property was located, "old" Nelson County (the indenture was filed in Hardin County—Hardin County came off of Nelson County in 1793). It also gave the name of the original patent owner as Mordecai Barbour, and the names and acreage of two bordering properties, Barbour & Banks 60,000 acre survey and Bell's 70,000 acre survey mentioned as now belonging to Blair Elliot & Co.

The procedure to determine the approximate location of this property was to use the original Virginia and Kentucky land surveys and the measurements given in poles (one pole equals 16½ feet) plus the angles given and converting those measurements to correspond with the topographical maps used. The original surveys were then put together like a jigsaw puzzle to be overlaid on the topographical maps.

On the original survey for Mordecai Barbour, one finds that the property was located on the waters of Rough Creek (now called Rough River). It also mentions Bell's 75,000 acre (not 70,000 as on the Kerr/Walsh indenture) survey mentioned as now belonging to Blair Elliot and Company. Blair Elliott and Company assigned the 75,000 acres to William Bell. It also mentions Barbour & Banks 60,000 acre survey adjoining the 20,718 ¾ acre property. The survey determined that the property was located somewhere on the waters of Rough Creek. In order to get a more precise location of the property, the two adjoining properties were used to see what further landmarks or watercourses were revealed to describe their location.

The Bell survey was very helpful in its description of the watercourses that the property was situated on. Using the Old Virginia Surveys and Grant Book, one finds that William Bell had a 75,000 acre land patent mentioned as being located on the waters of Rough Creek. The original survey describes this property as being located on Rough Creek and adjoining Barbour & Banks' two 50,000 acre surveys that extend to Otter and Mill Creeks, located in present day Meade and Hardin Counties. Also, the surveyor's drawing, shows at the top left the waters of the North Fork of Rough Creek; in the middle it shows Rough Creek, and at the bottom left it shows Big Clifty Creek. This 75,000 acre tract adjoins the former Swift property on its top right portion. The surveyors listed were William May and George Wilson.

The survey of the second property adjoining Swift's former property, which is the Barbour & Banks 60,000 acre tract, mentions being on the waters of Wolf and Rough Creeks; bordering their (Barbour & Banks) 121,782 acre entry. From the *Deed Books A-G* by Michael L. Cook C.G. and Bettie Cook C.G. volume #1 on page 17, one finds that Robert Townsend Hooe of Alexandria District of Columbia had purchased the 60,000 acres from Philip Barbour on August 5, 1792 for 3,000 pounds. From Breckinridge County Kentucky Records Volume #4, also by Cook and Cook, page 252, on May 19, 1817 the title to the property had been to a great part defective and was sold to four other individuals. On page 295 of the same book is an indenture that describes the property being on the waters of Sinking Creek (instead of Wolf Creek) and Rough Creek.

From the Breckinridge County Clerk's Office in Hardinsburg, Kentucky, in *Deed Book D* pages 355 and 356 is an indenture dated October 23, 1818, which describes the property as being on Sinking Creek and Rough Creek and lying mostly in the County of Breckinridge. The northeast tip may have been in Hardin County.

The 121,782 acre entry mentioned adjoining the 60,000 acre survey actually surveyed to be 113,482 acres and this property borders the 60,000 acre tract on the north and extends all the way to the Ohio River. From the river to the adjoining property line on the north side of the 60,000 acres, is 14 miles as mentioned on the 113,482 acre survey. The 60,000 and 113,482 acre tracts were surveyed for Philip Barbour and Henry Banks, and the surveyor was Mordecai Barbour.

For all six of these surveys that were used to determine the approximate location of the 20,718 ¾ acre Swift property, the property line angles matched up, and where corners met and trees were used as markers, such as "beginning at three white oaks", they satisfactorily matched as well.

This property just described, will be referred to as Rough Creek/Remarkable Rock Jonathan Swift Property #1. Swift Property #1 is arguably the most interesting of all the land that he owned in Kentucky. After some research, it was discovered that Swift owned 62,056 ¾ acres in eleven tracts of property in Kentucky. All eleven tracts of properties are listed in order by the time of purchase.

Early in the quest for information on Swift and the legend, it was decided to find all available information on Jonathan Swift of Alexandria, Virginia even though, according to various books and articles, it seemed that he could not be the same Swift of the Swift journal. The writings of the journal state that Swift's mining operation took place approximately from 1760-1769. This particular Jonathan Swift of Alexandria was born in 1764, which would obviously make him too young to be the Swift of the Swift *journal*. But could he be the Swift of the Kentucky silver mine *legend*?

The original surveys of Swift Property #1 (Mordecai Barbour's 20,718 ¾ acres), Barbour and Banks 60,000 acre tract, their 113,482 acre tract, their two 50,000 acre tracts and William Bell's 75,000 acre tract may be viewed in Appendix A of this book in transcribed and original form.

The transcribed Kerr/Walsh indenture and the first and second pages of the original document may be found in Appendix B of this book identified as B-1. Further information on this property will be presented later.

Gold Vault / Mill and Cedar Creeks
Swift Property # 2

The early surveyors of Kentucky, in describing the general whereabouts of the property, would often use the best known landmarks in the area closest to the property such as: "five miles south of Hardin's Fort" or "the property lies on the Ohio River 60 miles west from the falls."

An immediately recognizable description of this property's location is – the northern-most property line is in a near level line approximately five miles east of the U.S. Bullion Depository (the Gold Vault) on the Fort Knox Military Reservation. How bizarre that out of all the people in the world Jonathan Swift, a man who is at the very heart of a two hundred and twenty year-old Kentucky silver mine mystery, owned 5,000 acres of land near the U.S. Gold Depository. The same jigsaw puzzle method mentioned in property #1 was employed to approximate the location of this property. Once again, this indenture between Jonathan Swift and a Stephen Cook can be found in the archives room of the Hardin County Clerk's office in Elizabethtown, Kentucky. The original indenture can be found on page 83 in the *Deed Book* marked only 1795.

The transcribed indenture and the first page of the original document may be found in Appendix B of this book identified as B-2.

The points of interest pertaining to this indenture are:

1. Swift sells the property to Cook on March 1, 1792.
2. Jonathan Swift and his wife, Ann, of Alexandria, Virginia
3. At the time the indenture was made, the property was located in old Nelson County. This property would be located in present day Hardin County; Hardin County came off of old Nelson County in 1793.
4. Robert Brook Voss was the original patent holder of the property. The property was surveyed May 20, 1789 and granted March 3, 1791.
5. The property adjoins another property that includes a salt lick, Hynes Lick.
6. The property lies on Cedar Creek.
7. William May's 1,600 acre survey borders the property.
8. Swift buys the property from Robert Brook Voss in November of 1791.
9. It states that Jonathan Swift personally appeared before Gabriel Cox and Andrew Hynes, justices of the peace of Nelson County on February 22, 1794.
10. It seems, that this is the only property Swift profited from; Cook paid Swift 386 pounds and 15 shillings, and three rights of land in Massachusetts plus five shillings.

Below is a list of other points of interest from the original survey:
1. The property is situated between Mill Creek and Rolling Fork River.
2. The surveyors were William May and William Roberts.
3. The property was originally surveyed for Edward Voss, and he assigned it to Robert Brook Voss.

From the book *Old Kentucky Entries and Deeds*, one finds that Edward Voss made the entry on June 4, 1784.

The following properties adjoin the 5,000 acre Swift tract:
1. Jacob Myers- 400 acres

This property borders the top left of the 5,000 acres and was the most useful in helping to approximate the positioning of the property to a map location. That survey mentions that Myers' 400 acres is on Mill Creek, which empties into the Salt River, about 2 miles from the mouth of the south side.

From *The Kentucky Encyclopedia*, John E. Kleber, editor in chief, on page 451: "Jacob Myers constructed the bourbon iron furnace thought to be Kentucky's first, in 1791 on Slate Creek in Owingsville in Bath County where he had claimed 8,000-10,000 acres. The charcoal-burning furnace with water-powered bellows produced one ton of iron per day."

The same year that Jacob Myers constructed the bourbon iron furnace was the same year of this indenture. Two important points pertain to this: Myers constructed the furnace in 1791, and this indenture mentions that Swift's 5,000 acre property shares a property line with Myers' preemption that includes Hynes Lick (a salt lick).

The following is an excerpt from *Salt- A World History* by Mark Kurlansky:

"Obsessed with the extraction of precious metals, the Spanish invented the 'patio process' for silver mining in mid sixteenth-century Mexico. In this process, silver was separated from ore by using salt because the sodium in the salt extracted impurities. Silver mining by the 'patio process' required huge quantities of salt, and the Spanish built large-scale salt works adjacent to silver mines."

This makes the lick creek mentioned in the journal an even more believable and important landmark. Is it just a coincidence that Jacob Myers (metal expert) happens to own property with a salt lick that borders Jonathan Swift's 5,000 acres?
2. Andrew Hynes – 280 acres, first tract and 352 acres, second tract, both on Mill Creek.

3. Reuben Camp – 400 acres on Hynes Lick
4. Travis (or Francis) Nash – 586 acres on Mill Creek
5. William May – 1,600 acres on Mill Creek and a drain of Cedar Creek.

Note: William May did receive a grant on this property and sold it to a Dr. John Staton. Out of the 1,600 acre tract, Staton sold 283 acres on September 2, 1803 to Thomas Lincoln (father of the president). This indenture can be found at the Hardin County Clerk's office Archives Room in Elizabethtown, Kentucky.

The following is an excerpt from The *Kentucky Lincolns on Mill Creek* by R. Gerald McMurtry.

"The urge of a pioneer farmer caused Thomas Lincoln to purchase land, and his first homestead was located on the waters of Mill Creek. This tract is located between the Shepherdsville Road and the Dixie Highway, some seven miles from Elizabethtown. Why he selected this portion of Hardin County for the homestead of the Lincolns will likely always remain a matter of speculation. Before making this purchase, his home was in Washington County, although he had been living in Elizabethtown for spasmodic periods, since the year of 1796. Sometime between September 6, 1802, and April 3, 1803, the Lincoln family migrated to Hardin County. After the massacre of Captain Abraham Lincoln, the grandfather of the president, in Jefferson County in the year 1786, the family settled in Washington County. Hardin County was to be the third and last Kentucky County in which the Lincolns were to find a home.

"The Lincoln migration, from Washington County to the Mill Creek farm, included the widow Bathsheba Lincoln, the wife of the pioneer Abraham Lincoln, her youngest son, Thomas and their youngest daughter, Nancy Ann."

There is some speculation as to the actual date of the pioneer Abraham Lincoln's death. Later in this book, another arguably more accurate date of his death is given.

In summary, this 5,000 acre Jonathan Swift property has one landmark that relates to the Swift journal, which is Hynes Lick, a salt lick. There is no Hynes Lick referenced on the topographical maps of that area. It is believed that Hynes Lick was renamed Flat Lick.

Other points of interest pertaining to Swift Property #2 will be presented later.

Bear Creek
"Mines, Metals, Ores or Minerals"
Swift Property #3

When Jonathan Swift bought property on Bear Creek on February 26, 1794 from Jadia (Jedia) Ashcraft, there was no mention of mines, metals, ores or minerals (the transcribed indenture and the first page of the original document may be found in Appendix B of this book identified as B-3). However, when Swift sold the property to Dr. James Craik of Alexandria Virginia on August 1, 1795, the section of the indenture that describes all that comes with the property reads—"and all houses, buildings, gardens, orchards, meadows, woods, under woods, huntings, fisheries, coals, licks, mines, metals, ores or minerals of any kind above or under the ground and all the waters and watercourses etc..."

There are no clues in the indenture that would indicate the type of metals, mines or ores that Craik or Swift were concerned about (iron, silver etc). However, when the seller of the property is Jonathan Swift of Alexandria in that time period, one would have to take notice.

On page 81, from the *Deed Book* marked 1795, the points of interest from the indenture in which Swift buys this property are as follows:

1. Jadia Ashcraft of Hardin County sells to Jonathan Swift of Alexandria, Virginia 568 acres of land for 5 shillings on February 26, 1794.
2. The property lies on the second large west branch of Bear Creek, waters of Green River.
3. This property is part of a 1,276 acre patent owned by Jadia Ashcraft and was granted on May 20, 1786.
4. The property adjoins James Craik's land. (probably 708 acres)
5. Mines, metals, ores and minerals are not mentioned.
6. Witnesses to the indenture were Philip Philips, John Taylor and Isaac Morrison.

A copy of the Swift to Craik indenture and can be found at The Library of the Kentucky Historical Society in Frankfort, Kentucky on microfilm under *Kentucky Court of Appeals Book N (or A2)* page 307. The transcribed indenture and the first and last pages of the original document may be found in Appendix B of this book identified as B-4. Note Jonathan Swift's signature on the last page of the original document.

The points of interest pertaining to this indenture are as follows:

1. Swift sells property to Craik for 5 shillings on August 1, 1795. Note: Dr. James Craik of Alexandria, Virginia was the noted physician and close personal friend of George Washington.

2. This indenture does mention mines, metals, ores etc.

3. The name of Swift's wife, Ann, is also on the indenture.

This property is almost certainly located near Claylick Branch and Hargus Creek on Bear Creek in the south part of Grayson County Kentucky.

Two landmarks pertaining to this property could tie in with the Swift journal/legend:

1. Horseshoe Bend

The horseshoe bend in Bear Creek just north of this property belonged to Thomas Helm. The survey and grant mentions that the 300 acres includes the horseshoe bend bottom about ten miles below the sulfur lick.

2. Bear Creek

Some have suggested that the Swift journal was written in code or shrouded in symbolism and could only be interpreted by those having actual knowledge of the silver mine. If so, could this Bear Creek be the same bear, according to another Swift legend from Henson's *John Swift's Lost Silver Mines*, that Munday tracked to a cave and found a silver mine? One who tracks this bear (Creek) south they will find that it and its branches come close to the Mammoth Cave National Park. In the journal it is said that Swift and Co. stored up enormous riches in a "great cave" (not big or large)—a *great* cave. Mammoth Cave is *definitely* that.

From the *Encyclopaedia Britannica*: "The cave is said to have been discovered in 1809 when a hunter named Hutchins is reported as having pursued a bear into the entrance. It must have been discovered earlier than 1809, because its entrance was designated in the county records in 1797."

20,720 Acres
Swift Properties #4 thru #8

This next indenture included five properties that totaled 20,720 acres and appears to be a joint effort between Jonathan Swift, Philip Philips and William May to procure the lands for Dr. James Craik.

This indenture was made on February 19, 1794, and Philip Philips of Hardin County is selling (conveying) the properties to Jonathan Swift of the town of Alexandria and County of Fairfax Virginia for five shillings, current money of Kentucky. The transcribed indenture and the first page of the original document can be found in Appendix B of this book identified as B-5.

Swift Property #4

The first tract or parcel of land mentioned on this indenture is described as being on the waters of Green River in the county of Hardin (Old Hardin)

formerly of Nelson County. The watercourses that the property laid on were described as follows:
  –the second large branch of Bear Creek;
  –waters of Big Reedy Creek;
  –near the head of Raymers Fork;
  –the property line crosses several branches of Caney Creek;
  –the first west branch of Bear Creek, below the claylick.

This tract of land contained 8,912 acres and was a part of an original patent granted to Philip Philips of 11,870 acres on May 25, 1790.

Swift Property #5

The next tract of land on this indenture is described as being on the waters of Green River in the county of Hardin. The watercourses the property lay on were described as the second large west branch of Bear Creek and on the head of one of the main branches on Big Reedy Creek. The tract contained 3,000 acres being one half of an original land patent obtained by William May and adjoined the first tract of 8,912 acres (Swift Property #4). William May conveyed this property to Philip Philips on the same day of this indenture, February 19, 1794, for five shillings. The transcribed indenture and the first page of the original document may be found in Appendix B identified as B-6.

Swift Property #6

The next tract of land on the indenture is the remainder of the 1,276 acre patent of Jadia Ashcraft mentioned in the Bear Creek Swift property #3 of 568 acres. This tract has 708 acres, and Ashcraft conveyed the property to Philips on the same day of this indenture, February 19, 1794, for 5 shillings. Swift along with John Taylor and Joseph Barnet, were witnesses to the Ashcraft to Philips indenture. The transcribed indenture and the first page of the original document may be found in Appendix B identified as B-7.

Swift Property #7

The next tract of land on the indenture is described as being located on the waters of Green River in Hardin County. The watercourses it laid on is described as– one pole south of a large run branch of the middle fork on Indian Camp Creek. There were 4,700 acres that made up this tract which was originally patented by Philip Philips.

Apparently, Philips had patent problems on the tract. In the *Kentucky Court of Appeals Book N* (or A-Z) on microfilm at the Kentucky History Museum and Library, one finds an indenture dated September 5, 1809 between Michael Campbell of the county of Davidson and state of Tennessee executor of the last will and testament of Philip Philips deceased of the first part and Jonathan Swift of Alexandria and District of Columbia of the other part.

The indenture goes on to say that due to patent problems the indenture of February 19, 1794 for the 4,700 acres was not valid and Philips deeded this property to Swift in his will. Also, in the *Kentucky Court of Appeals Book N,* another indenture dated April 4, 1809, Jonathan Swift of Alexandria sells for $1.00 the 4,700 acre tract to John McIver also from Alexandria. It mentions that the property is now located in Ohio County (formerly Hardin) and it states that this is the same property conveyed by Philips to Swift on February 19, 1794 in which Swift then conveyed to Craik in February of 1794.

Swift also mentions in the indenture—"and I do covenant with the said John McIver his heirs and assigns, that I am lawfully seized in fee simple of the said premises, that they are free and clear of all claims (except any taxes that may have [arisen] since the said conveyance to the said James Craik) or encumbrances whatever etc..."

This indenture ends with a very impressive Jonathan Swift signature (seal).

Swift Property # 8

The final tract of land of this indenture contains 3,400 acres and adjoins the just mentioned 4,700 acres on its northeast corner. The watercourses it lay on are described as one of the main branches of Indian Camp Creek and by the head of one of the main branches of Indian Camp Creek. The indenture from William May to Philip Philips gives additional description of the watercourses this tract lay on as "dividing ridge between the southern branches of Big Caney Creek and the waters of Welches Creek and Indian Camp Creek."

This tract is one half of an original patent obtained by William May of 6,800 acres. May conveyed the 3,400 acres to Philips on the same day of this indenture, February 19, 1794, on the same indenture that he conveyed the 3,000 acre tract.

The points of interest pertaining to this indenture of these five tracts are as follows:

1. Properties 4, 5, and 6 share adjoining property lines.
2. The primary creek mentioned in Properties 4, 5, and 6 is Bear Creek
3. Properties 7 and 8 border each other and the primary creek mentioned is Indian Camp Creek.
4. The portion of the indenture that describes all that the property in-

cludes does mention mines, metals, ores and minerals of any kind above or below the ground.

5. When May conveyed both the 3,000 and 3,400 acre tracts to Philips, mines, metals etc. were not mentioned.

6. These properties are probably located in the southern parts of Grayson and Ohio Counties and the northern part of Butler and Edmonson Counties.

7. Jonathan Swift of the town of Alexandria in Virginia, merchant of the first part, buys the land package from Philip Philips on February 18, 1794.

8. Witnesses were William May, Benjamin Frye, Robert Foster and Gabriel Cox. Note: Several of these men lived in Nelson County near Bardstown.

9. The indenture was filed at Hardin County. However, the transaction may have actually taken place at Bardstown in Nelson County.

10. The property was formerly in Nelson County.

Another Interesting piece of evidence pertaining to this five-property land package was found at the Nelson County Clerk's Office in *Deed Book* #4, located in the Sutherland Building in Bardstown, Kentucky in the Archives Room, pages 843 (see A-1) and 844 (see A-2). On page 843 Craik is interested in two properties, one with 20,720 acres situated on the waters of Green River; this is the five parcels in the aforementioned indenture. The second property is the 20,718 ¾ acres which was mentioned earlier in the Rough Creek/Remarkable Rock Swift property #1. Apparently, Dr. Craik also had an interest in this land, but as mentioned before, it was already sold by Swift to James Kerr on May 8, 1792. Nothing questionable was happening there, but apparently it had been some time since Swift and Craik had seen each other. This could be an indication of Swift being in Kentucky on prolonged business affairs. The transcribed communiqué can be found in Appendix A of this book identified as A-1.

Both pages 843 and 844 appear to have been written by the same hand, probably by the county clerk of Bardstown, Kentucky. Page 844 is a letter document in which Swift is acknowledging that he received Dr. Craik's letter and concludes by saying "witness my hand at Bardstown Kentucky this fourth day of March 1794," Jonathan Swift. This Swift letter may be found in transcribed form in Appendix A of this book identified as A-2.

Another communiqué from James Craik authorizing John Taylor, his attorney, to purchase land (the 20,718 ¾ acres) through Jonathan Swift was found at the Hardin County Clerk's Office in the *Deed Book* marked 1795,

(343)

By virtue of a power of attorney from Doctor James Craig Senr. of Alexandria dated the third day of September 1793 I have received of Jonatha Swift for said Craik his heirs Executors Admi nistrators or assigns peaceable and quiet possession of twenty thousand seven hundred and twenty acres of land situated on the waters of Green River in the County of Hardin and State of Kentucky with his general warranty Deed of them to the said Craik and all the papers of the same and will deliver them to the said Craik or his aforesaid. by the Records both of Hardin & Nelson County they appear to be perfectly free and clear from all incumbrances and are su perior in quality and situation to the twenty thousand seven hundred and eighteen acres & three quarters of an acre of land on Rough Creek which I could not receive in consequence of their being incumbered. Witness my hand at Bairds Town Kentucky this fourth day of March 1794

John Taylor
attorney in fact for
James Craik Senr.

A-1

50

A-2

pages 92 and 93. It reads as follows:

"To all persons to whom these presents shall come James Craik of the town of Alexandria, County of Fairfax of the Commonwealth of Virginia send Greetings, know ye that for courses and considerations and there unto moving, I have made, ordained, constituted and appointed and by these presents make, ordain, constitute and appoint John Taylor of the Town of Alexandria and State of Virginia my true and lawful attorney for me and in my name behalf and Stead to receive of and from Jonathan Swift of the said Town twenty thousand seven hundred and eighteen acres and three quarters of an acre of land in the State of Kentucky and to do all the things relative thereto contained in my letter of Instruction to him of this date hereby relying and confirming whatsoever my said attorney Shall lawfully do in the promises I witness whereof I have hereunto Set my hand and Seal this third day of September in the year of our Lord one thousand seven hundred and ninety three."

Jas Craik

Signed Sealed and Delivered
In presence of
Josiah Watson, Clion Moore

The original document of Dr. James Craik's letter may be viewed in Appendix B of this book, within the indenture section, identified as B-13.

The day after Swift purchased the five-parcel land package, he and Ann, his wife, conveyed the properties to Dr. James Craik, commonwealth physician from the town of Alexandria Virginia, for the same price he purchased it for: five shillings. The transcribed indenture and the first page of the original document may be viewed in Appendix B of this book identified as B-8.

Near the end of the Swift and Craik indenture is the following: "Personally appeared before us two Justices of the Peace in and for the County of Nelson, Jonathan Swift acknowledged this indenture by him Subscribed to be his free act and did given under our hands this 20th day of February 1794."

Signed Gabriel Cox and Andrew Hynes

Both Cox and Hynes lived in or near Bardstown, Kentucky.

All of these indentures may be found at the Hardin County Clerk's Office in Elizabethtown, Kentucky in *Deed Book marked "1795"* (only) pages 81-105.

This indenture and the Swift letter document proves that Swift was in Kentucky and, as previously mentioned, Swift was listed as a witness on the 708 acre tract #6, where Ashcraft sells to Philips and also on Swift Property #2 the indentures states that Swift personally appeared before Gabriel Cox and Andrew Hynes of Nelson County on February 22, 1794.

From the *Kentucky Court of Appeals Deed Books A-G Volume 1* by Michael L. Cook C.G. and Bettie A. Cook C.G., one finds that Dr. Craik had sold the 568 acre, the 8,912 acre, the 708 acre, the 3,400 acre and the 3,000 acre properties to the same John McIver to whom Swift had sold the 4,700 acre tract (the one Philips had patent problems with) on two indentures each for $1.00.

In summary, in the five parcel package (Swift Properties #4 thru #8) that Swift bought from Philips and then sold to Craik, two landmarks could tie to the Swift legend/journal:

1. Indian Camp Creek
2. Bear Creek

Although Swift owned these properties for one day, he is officially one of the previous owners. These are properties whose indenture mentions mines, metals, ores and minerals. It is certain that this Jonathan Swift was in Bardstown, Kentucky in 1794, and may have been in Kentucky for some time at this point.

Indian Camp Creek
Swift Property #9

The following is an abstract description of this indenture:

This indenture was made on March 10, 1794 and was between William May from Nelson County, Kentucky of the first part and Jonathan Swift of Alexandria, Virginia of the other part. William May sells for five shillings, current money of Kentucky, to him in hand paid by the said Jonathan Swift at and before the sealing and delivery of the 1,950 acres.

The watercourses mentioned to describe this property are Indian Camp Creek and Welches Creek, which are both waters of Green River. May was the original patent holder, and the property was granted to him on July 10, 1786. There is no mention of mines or metals in the indenture. The way the payment is described "to him (May) in hand paid by the said Jonathan Swift at and before the sealing and delivery etc…" it appears that Swift was there in person at Bardstown at this time. This was about nineteen days after the five-parcel indenture (Swift Properties #4 thru #8).

There was one other indenture on the pages following this one between William May and Swift where May is selling Swift the same 3,400 acres (Swift Property #8 of the Properties #4 thru #8) for five shillings. Apparently, there was a lack of communication between Swift, Philips and May. Both of these indentures can be found at the Nelson County Clerk's Office located in the Sutherland Building in Bardstown, Kentucky in *Deed Book #4*, pages 845 thru 854.

The 1,950 acre property was sold in 1799 by the late sheriff of Hardin County, George Helm, for back taxes. This information can be found at the Nelson County Clerk's Office in Bardstown, Kentucky *Deed Book #7* pages 480 and 481.

No further Jonathan Swift properties will be presented at this time. There are two more indentures presented later in this book.

These nine properties have many of the landmarks mentioned in the

Swift journals. The following is a list of those landmarks pertaining to the properties that Jonathan Swift owned thus far:

1. Remarkable Rock being at a place where three creeks come together
2. Lick Creek
3. Sinking Creek
4. Hanging Rock
5. Great Cave
6. Indian Camp Creek
7. Horseshoe Bend
8. Three creeks that come together
9. Indian Valley (Property #1)
10. Clifty and Rough
11. Bear Creek (subject to opinion)
12. Rocky Branch

Of these five Jonathan Swift indentures, two of them mention mines, metals, ores or minerals (six of the nine tracts).

Could this man named Jonathan Swift, a merchant from Alexandria, Virginia, who had purchased these properties with the relevant landmarks during the years 1791-1794, be the person John Filson had referred to as "a man named Swift," only three years earlier, in 1788? Could he be the Swift who was at Bean Station in 1790-1791, and be the same Swift of the "Swift silver mine" which Col. James Harrod was last known searching for in 1793?

JONATHAN SWIFT

CHAPTER THREE

The historic importance of Jonathan Swift, of Alexandria, Virginia, has for the most part been unrecognized, and therefore, it has been overlooked. His life journey was adorned with a host of historic personages. Among his daily associations were city officials, high-ranking military leaders, representatives of foreign nations, Presidents of the United States, and the city's poor. His accomplishments in life were great, and great also were his losses, in both family and monetary terms.

The following information in this chapter has primarily been assembled from the writings of researchers/authors of Alexandria's history, and the books—*The Memoirs of Gen. Joseph Gardner Swift LL. D., U.S.A., First Graduate of the United States Military Academy, West Point* — and also from *Genealogy of the Roberdeau Family* by Roberdeau Buchanan.

In addition to obtaining as much relevant information pertinent to Jonathan Swift for the purpose of determining his life accomplishments, another desired objective was to define his life in chronological sequence, and therefore, a particular time period of his activities may be established.

From this information, one may determine how Jonathan Swift, of Alexandria, Virginia, compares with the Alexandrian, John/Jonathan Swift of the silver mine legend.

In the beginning, information on the personal life of the man responsible for this legend was only considered somewhat important, as opposed to finding concrete evidence in support of his mining operation. It is now realized that the relevance of a lost silver mine is insignificant in comparison to the re-discovery of the lost stories of Jonathan Swift's life. While the silver mine aspect of this work is the common thread, from which many of the theories are woven, the life stories of Swift and his family are a gold mine of historic importance. Before the investigative results of Jonathan Swift of Alexandria, Virginia is told, one would be remiss in reportorial obligation if the tragic, yet heroic account of Samuel and Ann Foster Swift of Milton, Massachusetts were not first explored.

Jonathan Swift was born March, the 27th (or 22nd) 1764 to Samuel, and Ann Foster Swift of Milton, Massachusetts, the seventh of nine children. Samuel Swift (1715-1775) was one of the participants masquerading as "Mohawk Indians" during the Boston Tea Party, and according to one source was a partner with John Adams. The following excerpt is from *The Memoirs of Gen. Joseph Gardner Swift, LL. D., U. S. A.* "*First Graduate of the United States Military Academy, West Point*" and refers to Jonathan's father, Samuel.

"Mr. Swift was graduated at Harvard College in 1735, studied law with Counsellor Gridley and became a barrister and fellow practitioner with John Adams, afterwards President of the United States.

"Mr. Swift was a highly esteemed citizen of Boston, and was frequently invited by the selectmen to visit the schools with many other distinguished citizens.

"He was one of those fearless and determined men who set the revolutionary ball in motion, and early gave up his life to the cause of freedom.

"As a proof of his prominence and the esteem in which he was held, the town records of Boston attest. At a town meeting of the freeholders and other inhabitants of the town of Boston, legally warned, at Faneuil Hall, Monday, April 3, 1775, -- an adjournment of the March meeting – Mr. Samuel Adams, moderator of the meeting, being at the Congress then sitting at Concord, Samuel Swift, Esq., was chosen moderator *pro tempore*. It was, indeed, no small honor to preside at one of the famous town meetings in those stirring times, and to take the place of such a patriot as Sam Adams.

"Mr. Swift was a member of the Ancient and Honorable Artillery in 1746, and he is said by his friend, Colonel May, to have been one of those active in promoting the destruction of the tea in Boston Harbor.

"However that may be, he is known to have been an active and influential patriot. President John Adams told his [Samuel Swift's] distinguished grandson, General Swift, while on a visit to his seat in Quincy in 1817 with President Monroe, that Samuel Swift was a good man and a generous lawyer, and was called the widows' friend; that he was a firm Whig whose memory the State ought to perpetuate. The same sentiments Mr. Adams expressed in a letter to William Wirt, of Virginia. Mr. Adams also said it was owing to the zeal and resolution of Samuel Swift that caused many Bostonians to secrete their arms when Gov. Gage offered the town freedom if arms were brought in to the arsenal; and that Mr. Swift presided at a freemason's meeting where it was covertly agreed to use the arms concealed, and, in addition, pitchforks and axes, if need be, to assail the soldiery on the common; which scheme was betrayed to Gage, causing the imprisonment of Swift and others. This imprisonment brought on disease from which he never recovered, and he died August 30, 1775, aged 60 years, as President Adams said, 'a martyr to freedom's cause.' His remains were interred in the tomb in the stone chapel ground that had belonged to Samuel Tylly, Esq., the father of his first wife.

"He had acquired a competency by his profession, which, excepting a house in Boston and a few acres of land in Dorchester, was lost, including bonds, through the unfaithfulness of his agent, while Boston was garrisoned."

Another account of Samuel Swift is given at the end of this chapter, and it further describes his imprisonment by saying –"that he was permitted to occupy his own house under surveillance. From disease induced by confinement, he died a prisoner in his own house…"

Samuel Swift's second wife was Ann Foster (1729-1788), of Dorchester, by whom he had two sons, Foster and Jonathan, and four daughters. In *The Memoirs of Gen. Joseph Gardner Swift*, Samuel's first wife is listed as being Eliphal Tilley, and in *The History of Milton, Mass. 1640 to 1887 by A. K. Teele*, his first wife is listed as Sarah Tyler. The following excerpt describing the hardships of Ann of Dorchester, as well as her children, due to the imprisonment of Samuel, is also from *The Memoirs of Gen. Joseph Gardner Swift*.

"Mrs. Swift appears from her diary to have been a woman of more than ordinary intelligence, and of great piety.

"She commenced to write before her marriage, and continued it, at intervals, for many years after. Her compositions, which are of a deeply religious character, are mostly in verse, commemorating the death of relatives and friends. She writes, May 6, 1758, that she was taken into Mr. Byles' church, and of her religious duties, etc. She was in the habit of writing out her thoughts on the sermons she heard preached, and she often wrote on passing events, as – on the frequenting the tavern Saturday nights; on Lisbon being shaken by an earthquake, Nov. 1, 1775; on the taking of Quebec, 1759, on the vanity of the world; on the safe delivery of a child; on the repeal of the cruel stamp act, May 20, 1766. She also wrote verses on the death of 'the universally beloved Capt. Larrabee,' and says 'this worthy gentleman departed this life in the 75th year of his age, lamented by all who knew him.'

In June, 1775, she is at Springfield, and writes: 'Here I am in the woods, Boston being so surrounded by armies that we could not enjoy our home: no school for the children, and the town forsaken by the ministers – the pillars of the land.' About this time she wrote the following letter:

"Capt. HANDFIELD Sr.
"Your kindness in undertaking to get a pass for me emboldens me to ask the like favor for my dear husband whom I hear is in a very weak state of health. The anxiety of my mind is great about him. A word from you would have more weight than all the arguments that he could make use of.
"Could I come to him, this favor I would not ask. O, Sir I trust in your goodness that you will do what you can to forward Mr. Swift to me and in doing so you will greatly oblige
"Should be glad if he would bring out two trunks which there is clothing in that I want very much for myself and children.

Your distressed friend
ANN SWIFT."

"The appeal seems to have failed, for she writes under date Aug. 30, 1775: 'Departed this life, in the 61st year of his age, my dear husband, Samuel Swift. He died in Boston, or in other words, murdered there. He was not allowed to come to see me and live with his wife and children in the country. There he gave up the ghost – his heart was broken; the cruel treatment he met with in being a friend to his country was more than he could bear, with six fatherless children (in the woods) and all my substance in Boston.' Mrs. Swift was a woman of delicate health, but of much energy. She was living, Nov. 16, 1787, in her own house in Orange Street, Boston, when she deeded a small portion of her land to Ebenezer Pope, whose estate in joined."

In Samuel Swift's will Jonathan was bequeathed "five shillings." It is unknown what he may have inherited upon his mother death, though it is probable that it was very little.

In the following excerpt from *The Memoirs of Gen. Joseph Gardner Swift*, General Swift further describes Samuel Swift's participation in The Boston Tea Party.

"...In Boston I met my friend Mr. Gardner and Colonel Samuel Bradford. To the latter I had a letter of introduction from his brother-in-law, Colonel Williams. I also met Colonel Joseph May of Boston, who gave me many particulars of the 'Mohawk Indians,' who had destroyed the tea in Boston Harbor—the precursor of the Revolution. Colonel May had been a friend of my grandfather, Samuel Swift, who he said had been active in promoting that event of destroying the tea."

In this next excerpt from *The Memoirs of Gen. Joseph Gardner Swift*, General Swift's father Dr. Foster Swift (Jonathan's brother) recalls the events of his father Samuel's death, and also the beginning of Jonathan's merchant career.

"...Among his details he said that the death of his father had occurred under the tyranny of General Gage when he was in his sixteenth year, and had been prepared at Mother Lovel's school to enter Cambridge College, but being the oldest child it was necessary for him to remain with his mother, sisters and brother. His father had been an active Whig, and his moderate property in Boston had suffered injury while the town was a garrison; that in returning to Boston with the family after the evacuation by the British troops they found their residence sadly dilapidated, as was also the similar case of many a neighbor; that the residence in town and a small country place on Dorchester Point formed nearly all the means of support to the family, aided by the needles of his mother and sisters; that his brother Jonathan was apprenticed to Mr. May, a merchant, and that himself commenced in 1779 the study of medicine with Doctor Joseph Gardner..."

The Mr. May mentioned in this excerpt, in which Jonathan was apprenticed to, is Colonel Joseph May, who was mentioned in the previous excerpt as being a friend of Samuel Swift. Joseph May and Thomas Patten were partners in the merchant trade, May conducted the Boston business and Patten the trade in Alexandria. Jonathan also had a close connection to the Patten's, which is mentioned later in this chapter. It is also probable that Jonathan came to Alexandria, Virginia due to this May-Patten business partnership. No record was found to determine the exact year the town of Alexandria got their first look at the young swashbuckler; however, it is known that he arrived in the year of 1784, or sometime prior, which is also the same approximate time his father-in-law, Daniel Roberdeau came to Alexandria.

Also from *The Memoirs of Gen. Joseph Gardner Swift*, a physical description is given of the General's Uncle Jonathan.

"...A gentleman of dignified and elegant manners, tall, of commanding aspect; his eyes were blue, and his complexion dark.

"He was an intelligent traveler, visiting England and Ireland in 1786-7, when he improved the opportunity of a visit to Rotherham, in Yorkshire, the home of his ancestors. Here and elsewhere in the county he found the name respectably represented; some having the tradition that a branch of the family had migrated to Boston in the previous century. On visiting Dublin some members of St. Patrick's Society thought they traced a resemblance between him and the Dean, and with the characteristic poetry of Irish feeling, they gave him a dinner and presented him with a portrait of the Dean, with the arms of the Yorkshire family. His valuable papers, among which were many letters from Gen. Washington, were all lost at sea soon after the death of his son [William Roberdeau Swift], while being sent to New York. His portrait, which was painted abroad, was so injured on the voyage home that he destroyed it."

The "Dean" mentioned in this excerpt is of course, Dean Jonathan Swift, author of *Gulliver's Travels*. The following excerpt from *Genealogy of the Roberdeau Family*, further clarifies the family relation of the two Jonathan Swifts.

"The arms of Jonathan Swift [of Alexandria, Virginia], as shown by an engraved book-mark, appear to be *Sable, three bucks trip-pant or; Crest, a demi-lion rampant or, holding between the paws a helmet of the first*. A watch-seal, 'Swift' impaling 'Roberdeau,' now in the possession of Mrs. Dr. Wheat, shows for Swift, *or a chevron vair, between three bucks at speed (proper?);* Crest as in the previous coat. The latter arms, save the crest, are the arms of the celebrated Dean Swift's family, who was a near relative of Mr. Jonathan Swift, the subject of this sketch."

Since none of the forebears of Jonathan Swift of Alexandria was named Jonathan, it seems highly probable that he was named for Dean Swift.

Through an unpublished article written by Jean Elliot, titled, *Kindly but Alien Hands,* a peculiar characteristic of Jonathan was found from an article in a November, 1863 edition of the *Alexandria Gazette.*

"He [Swift] was a gentleman of very fine exterior, but what was most notable about him was the great rapidity of his pronunciation. Let me see if I can convey to your mind any idea of this peculiarity. Repeat as fast as you are able: 'if Peter Piper picked a peck of pickled peppers, where is the peck of pickled peppers Peter Piper picked?' "You can't?" "Then, sir, I can give you no idea of the rapidity of Mr. Swift's utterance."

Also from General Swift's Memoirs it is found that "Mr. Swift [Jonathan] was for forty years a prominent citizen of Alexandria, Virginia. He was bred to mercantile life by Mr. May of Boston, and early (before 1785), established himself in commerce at Alexandria, where he met with success, accumulating a fortune."

As mentioned, it is unclear when Jonathan Swift first came to Alexandria. It seems the first record of him is from the *Virginia Gazette* and *The Alexandria Advertiser* when he placed two ads on October 20, 1784, and at twenty years of age he seemed to be already well established in the merchant trade.

The following are from *The Virginia Gazette* and *Alexandria Advertiser* by Wesley E. Pipenger and James D. Munson PHD:

Jonathan Swift, HAS just arrived from London,
In the Ship Henry, James Dennison, Commander, and brought with him
a general Assortment of Fall and Winter Goods, which will be sold by
Wholesale, at the lowest Advance, for Cash or Crop Tobacco, at the Store
lately improved by Messrs. Williams, Cary, and Company, on Capt.
Harper's wharf. ALX, October 20, 1784. Also, a few Hampers of excellent Porter and Baskets of Cheese.

For LONDON, THE Henry, James Dennison, Master, -- She is a fine vessel, about 200 tons burthen, a fast Sailer, well sound, has good Ac-

commodations for Passengers, and will sail for London by the 20th of November, having part of her Cargo engaged, --For Freight or Passage apply to J. SWIFT and COMPANY, or the Master on board. ALX. October 20, 1784.

On the nineteenth day of January, 1785 Swift along with a Mr. Watson – late of the House of Watson and Cossoul of Nantes—paid a visit to George Washington at Mount Vernon spending the night there and leaving after having breakfast.[26] (For sources of information in this chapter, refer to the endnote numbers which correspond to the matching numbers within the bibliography section.)

In February of 1785, Swift was passed as a Mason in Washington's own Lodge, No. 22.[15]

In 1785 Swift had taken out eight ads. The following are five of those ads and the dates they were placed:

Jonathan Swift, and CO. Have for Sale, at their Store on Capt. Harper's Wharf, a general Assortment of European Goods, suitable to the Season, which they will sell by the Package or Piece at a very moderate Advance, viz. Broadcloths of all colours and prices, corduroys, royal ribs, velvets, velverets, sarrandines, crapes, camblets, cambleteens, linens, dowlas, osnaburgs, carpeting, gauzes, millenary, ladies' calamanco and lasting shoes, misses Morocco ditto of different colours, gentlemens' shoes and boots, beaver, castor and felt hats, canvas, cordage, porter in hampers, and assortment of hardware, fowling-pieces, 10d. and 20d. Nails, elegant looking glasses, cut glass, and a few crates of queen's ware for sterling cost and charges. Their terms are for ready money, for which they allow two and an half per cent. —They will give the market price, in cash or goods, for good Tobacco. ALX-- Jan. 10, 1785. (43)

Jonathan Swift and CO. TAKE the earliest opportunity in town and country, that they have received, per the ship Ceres, Captain St. Barb, from London (via Boston) an additional assortment of European GOODS, which they will dispose of at a moderate advance for cash, bills of exchange or tobacco. —They have received, per the ship Triton from Boston, West-India and New-England rum, molasses, Port wine, tea, coffee, chocolate, allspice, cheese, butter, soap, candles, beef, mackerel, mens' and womens' leather shoes, womens' coarse calamanco and lasting shoes; a few tons of iron hollow ware, and many other articles, --They discount 2 ½ percent. For ready-money, and give the market price as usual, in cash or goods, for good tobacco. ALX, March 5, 1785 (43)

To be LET, and immediate possession given, THREE UPPER STORIES of a large commodious BRICK STORE, situated on Capt. Harper's wharf, which is well calculated for a wholesale store and very convenient for the reception of produce of every kind. —For terms, apply to Capt. Harper, or Jonathan SWIFT and Co., ALX, August 25, 1785. (43)

Jonathan Swift and Company, Take the earliest opportunity to inform their friends and customers in town and country, that they have removed from Captain Harper's Wharf, to a store on the south side of Fairfax-street, where they have now open and ready for sale, A GENERAL assortment of WINTER GOODS, which they will dispose of by wholesale and retail, on the most reasonable terms, for cash, produce, or good bills of exchange on any part of Europe.—They return their grateful thanks to those gentlemen in the town and country who have favored them with their custom, and flatter themselves that the moderate prices of their goods, and their endeavors to give satisfaction, will induce them to continue their favors.—They have now on hand, excellent hyson, souchong and bohea tea, London porter, soap in boxes, chocolate, pimento, New England rum, molasses, Liverpool ware, well assorted, and a few casks of nails of different sizes, which they will dispose of very low. Wanted, a Negro Woman, who has served in a decent family, who can cook in a plain way, and wash and iron.—None need apply but those who can be well recommended for their honesty, industry and sobriety. ALX, Sept. 22, 1785. (43)

MARRIED.] Mr. JONATHAN SWIFT, Merchant, to the amiable Miss NANCY ROBERDEAU, elder Daughter to General ROBERDEAU, of this TOWN. ALX, Sept. 29, 1785. (43)

The following excerpt is from *Genealogy of the Roberdeau Family*, by Roberdeau Buchanan, which was loaned to the writer by descendants of Jonathan and Ann Roberdeau Swift.

"Ann (Roberdeau) Swift. Born in Philadelphia, December 3, 1767; baptized March 27, 1768. Removed to Alexandria, Virginia, with her father, where, on the 24th of September 1785, she married Jonathan Swift, an importing merchant and man of means, who became a resident in that town before 1785, and for forty years was a prominent citizen. He was the uncle of the veteran General Joseph G. Swift, mentioned in these pages. Mr. Swift's fine place bore the unique name of Grasshopper Hall, but being afterwards purchased by one of the Mason family, is now known as Colross."

Brigadier-General Daniel Roberdeau

Brigadier-General Daniel Roberdeau (1727-1795), father of Ann Roberdeau Swift, was an important participant of the American Revolution, and the following nine excerpts from *Genealogy of the Roberdeau Family*, are the points of his life, considered relevant pertaining to the theories presented in this work.

Two of the following topics are of particular importance regarding Jonathan Swift, and the silver mine legend. The first pertinent point of information which comes under point number five titled "Privateers" establishes the truth of a previous statement which was "In those early American times, one country's patriot may very well have been another country's pirate." It is unknown if Jonathan Swift had ever operated as a privateer, or if he served under someone else's command as such. Also, it is unknown if any of Swift's merchant ships were obtained as a result of "privateering." The second pertinent point of information which comes under point number seven is titled "Lead Mining and Stockade Fort," and from information gained through this excerpt, the veil of the Swift silver mine mystery is slightly lifted.

The following excerpts from the rare book *Genealogy of the Roberdeau Family* describe the life of a true American hero, General Daniel Roberdeau, the father-in-law of Jonathan Swift.

1) "The family of Roberdeau, in this country is of French origin, the first of whom we know of, being Isaac Roberdeau, a Hugnenot, who fled from Rochelle, France, on the revocation of the Edict of Nantes, and took refuge on the island of St. Christopher's, one of the British West Indies, in 1685. Here he married Mary Cunyngham, of that place, the descendant of an ancient and noble Scotch family. She, after her husband's death, came to Philadelphia with her children, and is the progenitor of all of these two families in this country."

2) "...He [Daniel Roberdeau] was born, as already stated, on the island of St. Christopher, one of the British West Indies, in the year 1727. Of his early years we have no account. His after-life, however, shows that he received a good education, and it is believed that he studied, for a time at least, in England. During his minority, as we have already seen, his widowed mother removed with her family to Philadelphia, in North America, 'where, after having finished his education,' his son Isaac writes, 'he qualified himself for mercantile business, and became a merchant of respectability in that city.'"

John Filson- Kentucky's first historian and cartographer

1788 Land entry of John Filson

Long John Silver "The Sea Cook"
From a 1920 Charles Scribner's Sons publication of *Treasure Island*.)
([Not Original Caption]

Sand Knob – Main Formation

View from top of Sand Knob

Crescent moon-shaped rock house on the side of Sand Knob

Buttercup/Butter Stack Rock

Dr. James Craik
Purchased Kentucky properties through Jonathan Swift.
Picture provided by The Alexanderia-Washington Lodge #22. Portrait photographed
by Authur W. Pierson

Ann Roberdeau Swift- Wife of Jonathan Swift

3) "A few years after this, we find Daniel Roberdeau a member of the 'Mystic tie,' the evidence being a paper now framed and hanging in a conspicuous place in the Masonic Hall in Philadelphia. The import is as follows, and constitutes the earliest documentary record of our ancestor in this country:

PHILADELPHIA, March 13, 1754.

'Whereas, at a meeting of the Grand and First Lodges, on Thursday the 12th day of March, 1752, a committee was then appointed and fully authorized to look out for a suitable lot, whereon to erect a building for the accommodation of said Lodges, Philadelphia Assembly, and other uses. The undersigned subscribe the several sums:'…etc.

"Following which, are the names of thirty or forty subscribers, and among them we read:

'For Mr. John Mather, Jr., Daniel Roberdeau, 15 pounds; Benjamin Franklin, 20 pounds.'"

4) "The writer [Roberdeau Buchanan] has often heard his mother and aunt speak of the large stature and great physical strength of Daniel Roberdeau, which account they had from their father. The Tories of the Revolution, who would naturally caricature the most prominent characteristics, spoke of him as a 'specter of portentous show.'"

5) "PRIVATEERS"

"While engaged in the army, now that England had destroyed the commerce of the Colonies, their vessels were converted into privateers. Daniel Roberdeau's receipt-book shows that, April 2, 1776, he paid 100 pounds for one-eighth share in the sloops *Congress* and *Chance,* privateers, and a month or two afterwards is a receipt for 400 pounds from him as treasurer of this company.

"It appears that these vessels were successful in making some valuable captures, and John Adams, in a letter to his wife, May, 1776, refers to the 'valuable prize' taken by the privateer fitted out by Daniel Roberdeau and John Bayard.—(P. Force's Am. Archives, 4, V L., 489.) In the receipt-book of Colonel Roberdeau is the following: 'Received, July 25, 1776, of Daniel Roberdeau, treasurer to the privateers *Congress* and *Chance,* the sum of 6,097 pounds, 1s., 3d., which, with five bags of silver coin and plate, is in full of the trust reposed in him. Received by order and in behalf of owners of privateers *Congress* and *Chance,'* and co."

6) "IN CONGRESS"

"Before General Roberdeau had sufficiently recovered his health to resume command in the army, he was destined to serve his country in a high sphere. The General Assembly of Pennsylvania conferred upon him the highest honor within their power to bestow; and elected him a member of the Continental Congress. To this august and dignified body, he was chosen on the fifth of February, 1777; the delegation consisting of the following gentlemen: Benjamin Franklin, Robert Morris, Daniel Roberdeau,…"

General Roberdeau would be elected to serve a second term in Congress.

7) "LEAD MINE AND STOCKADE FORT."

"Leave of absence was granted to General Roberdeau April, 11, 1778, to allow him to superintend the working of a lead mine, from which to procure lead for the army. How it was that *he* became connected with it does not appear, unless it was his ceaseless and untiring exertions in the cause of liberty led him to those scenes where he could be of most service. So, leaving his duties in Congress and the comforts of his own fireside, he braved the hardships and dangers of the backwoods, where he had to erect a fort for protection against the Indians.

"But little regarding this fort is now known. The traditions in the family relate simply the fact, so we must look elsewhere for an account of it, and the only record we find is in *Hazard's Pennsylvania Archives,* in twelve volumes of 800 pages each, published by the State, a work which contains, together with his *Colonial Records,* in sixteen volumes, all documents that could be collected relating to the revolutionary history of that State. In the former work are fifty or sixty letters of General Roberdeau's, some of which have been here quoted on the previous pages. From these letters, also, Hazard has given a history of this fort, on page 454 of the Appendix.

"FORT ROBERDEAU" [Altoona, Pennsylvania]

"From a letter from General Roberdeau, dated Carlisle, April 17, 1778, it appears that he was then on his way to work some lead mines to supply the great scarcity of lead to the public. He was at that time a member of Congress, of whom he asks and afterwards obtains leave of absence for the purpose. He says:

'The confidence the honorable the representatives of our States have placed in me by a late resolve, together with the pressing and indispensable necessity of a speedy supply of lead for the public service, induced me to ask leave of absence of Congress to proceed with workmen to put their business in a proper train; and have reached this place on that errand and have collected men and materials and sent them forward this day, proposing to follow to-morrow. My views have been greatly enlarged since I left York, on the importance of the undertaking and hazard in procuring it, for the public works here are not furnished with an ounce of lead but what is in fixed ammunition. On the other hand, the prevailing opinion of people as I advance into the country, of Indian depredations shortly to commence, might not only deter the workmen I stand in need of, but affright the back settlers from their habitations, and leave the country exposed and naked. To give confidence to one and the other, I have drawn out of the public stores here twenty-five stand of arms and a quantity of gunpowder, and intend to proceed this morning, but was applied to by John Caruthers, Esq., lieutenant of the county, and William Brown, commissary of provisions for the militia, who advised with me on the subject of their respective departments; and by the account they give of the orders from your honorable Board to them as to calling out and supplying the militia, I find the State is guarding against the incursions of the savages. This confirmed me in a preconceived intention of erecting a stockade fort in the immediate neighborhood of the mine I am about to work, if I could stir up the inhabitants to give their labor in furnishing an asylum for their families in case of eminent danger, and prevent the evacuation of the country. Mr. Caruthers convinced me of the necessity of the work for the above purpose, condescendingly offered one company of the militia, which he expected would consist of about forty men, under my command to cooperate in so salutary a business, as it consists with the order of the Council respecting the station, being only a deviation of a very few miles; and that one other company of about the same number should also join me, for the greater expedition, until the pleasure of the Council was known.....Mr. Brown expressed much concern for the scarcity of provisions. I was advised very lately by Judge McKean of a quantity of salted beef in the neighborhood of Harris' Ferry, and before I left York I applied to him by letter to advise me of the quantity and quality, with a design to purchase, as I intended to employ a much greater number of men than are already employed at the lead mines, to carry on the business with vigor....'I intend to build such a fort, as with sufficient provisions, under the smile of Providence would enable me to defend it against any number of Indians that might presume to invest it. If I am not prevented by an opportunity of serving the state eminently, by a longer stay in the wilderness, I propose to return to my duties in Congress in about three weeks. Will the Council favor me with the exemption of a number of men, not exceeding twenty if I cannot be supplied by the adjutant-general, who has orders co-extensive with my want of smelters and miners from deserters from the British army, to suffer such to come to this part of the country, contrary to a preceding order?...

"Besides the supplying of provisions to the militia in Bedford, it is very important that the intended stockade should be seasonably furnished with that article.

"'My landing is at Water street in Juniata, but I could, on notice, receive any supplies from Standing Stone.

'I am most respectfully, Sir, your most ob. And very hum. Servt., 'Daniel Roberdeau.'

"On the 23rd of April, he writes from Standing Stone to John Caruthers.... An attack is threatened by thirty Indians who expect reinforcements of 300 more; other reports not so reliable say 1000 whites and savages. Desires him, therefore, to call out the militia if he has authority to do so. General Roberdeau has only ten Continental soldiers with him.

"On the 27th of April, General Roberdeau writes from Sinking Spring Valley to President Wharton, 'I am happy to inform you that a very late discovery from a new vein promises the most ample supply, but I am very deficient in workmen. Mr. Glenn is with me to direct the making and burning of bricks, and is come up to build a furnace; by which time I expect to be in such forwardness as to afford an ample supply to the army. Of 40 militia-men, I have at most 7 with me, which retards building a stockade to give confidence to the inhabitants who were all on the wing before I reached this.'

"But little is known to us about this fort or where it was erected.

In a letter from General Potter, dated Penn's Valley, May 19, 1779, three forts are spoken of in this valley, as having together but one lieutenant and fifteen men as a guard. He says: 'I cannot help being surprised that there has been no militia sent to this part of Bedford county that joins us, neither to Frankston nor Standing Stone, except a small company of Buchanan's battalion that would not go to Fort Roberdeau.'

"August 6, 1779, Capt. Cluggage dates a letter from Fort Roberdeau, and says: 'This morning I arrived at this point, bringing with me what men I could collect on the way. I think from the accounts of my brother, that the number of the enemy in these parts must be very large,' and adds another postscript: 'This moment there is twelve men arrived, and with what can be spared from this garrison, I will march immediately to Morrison's Cave.'

"In another letter, dated at this fort, October 10, 1779, Capt. Cluggage says: 'My company has been received, and passed muster, three officers, and forty-three rank and file, one of the latter killed or taken.'

"We presume, therefore, that this was Fort Roberdeau built on account of the lead mines, and named after him, in Sinking Spring Valley. In an article in the *Columbian Magazine* for 1788, allusion is made to the attempt to procure lead from the mine in this valley during the Revolution, and says 'a large fort of logs was erected and some miners employed, also a considerable quantity of ore procured and some lead made,'

[R. Buchanan continues]

"Thus does Mr. Hazard record this interesting subject. The tradition in our family states that the expense of erecting this fort was met wholly by General Roberdeau, which is abundantly verified by his letters as published by Hazard, and other evidence.

"June 6, 1788, he writes from York, where Congress was in session, to Vice-President Bryan:

…'My account exhibited to the Assembly, when last in Lancaster, refers to a debit, of which I was not then possessed, paid Capt. Piper, who guarded Wm. Todd to Lancaster, for his expenses, which is now before me in a proper entry of 6.11.3 pounds,' and hopes the Council will include it in the above account and remit the whole, adding, 'my late engagement in the lead works has proved a moth to my circulating cash, and obliged me to make free with a friend in borrowing.

"On the 30th of March, 1778, General Roberdeau, with others, petitioned the General Assembly, and reciting that upon the recommendation of Congress, having opened a lead mine, they desire the lands whereon the mine lies, be vested in the petitioners; and the next day the Assembly resolved as follows:

" 'On considering the petition of the Honorable Daniel Roberdeau and company, for vesting the lands therein mentioned, whereon there is a lead mine, in Frankstoun township, in Bedford county, in the said Daniel Roberdeau and company, to which they lay claim; Resolved, That this house will not determine in whom the title of said lands is; but being of opinion that the utmost encouragement should be given to opening said mine and smelting the ore therein for public benefit, will indemnify the said Daniel Roberdeau and company from any loss they have already sustained or may sustain in opening the said mine and smelting the ore, if they shall immediately proceed upon said work, and diligently and faithfully prosecute the same.'

"The following appears upon the journals of Congress after General Roberdeau's return from the mine, but I can find no report of the Board of War on the subject, or any further mention in Congress:

"June 23, 1788. Ordered: That the Board of War estimate the expense of the fort lately built by Mr. Roberdeau, in Bedford county, in Pennsylvania, and report the same to Congress, with their opinion by whom the same ought to be defrayed.'

"It does not appear that any remuneration was made to General Roberdeau for his expenses in working this mine and erecting the fort, although it is seen to have been done by the orders of, or at least with the consent of, Congress and the Assembly, both of whom it seems felt themselves in a measure responsible. On the 1st of April, 1779, the Assembly reiterated its resolve of March 31, that General Roberdeau be indemnified; and the matter remained before the house as late as 1781, without settlement, although the journals show that it was repeatedly brought up for consideration."

8) "REMOVAL TO ALEXANDRIA, VA."
"After General Roberdeau's return to Philadelphia, he removed his family to Alexandria, Virginia, sometime between March, 1784, and April, 1785, probably early in this latter year. For this step, he

doubtless had good reasons; which being unknown to us, it seems a great mistake of his, in leaving a community where he had so long resided, and with whom he had been so closely identified. He gave up all his associates for a comparatively small town. His removal could not have been for commercial reasons, for it is believed that he did not again engage in business after the Revolution.

"Here General Roberdeau had purchased a house in 1776, which he now made his permanent residence. It is still standing, situated on the east side of Water, now Lee street, between Wolfe and Wilkes streets. It is of brick, twenty-eight by forty-two feet, three stories and an attic in height...."

9) "In a letter to his daughter, Ann Swift, of March 4, 1794, he writes upon religion, then a few words of English politics, and concludes: 'I have experienced great debility for a long time past, but blessed be the Source of all my mercies, it had a check yesterday, and this day His providence will do for me all that His goodness shall graciously dictate, and that will suffice. I think to pay Isaac a visit, who solicits it; besides, it may be of use to restore my strength. I expect you here this spring, and possibly shall not be disappointed. I am, my dear Selina's affect. Father, Daniel Roberdeau.

"....At this time he sold his house in Alexandria; disposed of part of his furniture, and advertised the remainder at auction; saying, he proposed moving to New York. His sons-in-law, Thomas Patten and Jonathan Swift, offered a higher price for the house, to keep it in the family, but the deeds had already been signed."

From *The History of Old Alexandria, Virginia* by Mary G. Powell is another interesting story of the marriage of Jonathan Swift and Ann Roberdeau –

"General Daniel Roberdeau was a distinguished officer in the Revolution, and was afterwards a member of Congress. He was born at Philadelphia of Huguenot descent. At the close of the war he came to Alexandria and built upon Water Street (now Lee Street) one of the most stately homes in Alexandria. It still remains in perfect condition. He had a large family of children. Of these Ann Foster married Jonathan Swift, a native of New England, who came to Alexandria about 1780, and was a prominent merchant here for forty years. As consul of several foreign nations he was able in the time of the British occupation [War of 1812] to protect much valuable property here. "For some reason General Roberdeau opposed this union with his daughter, and after waiting vainly for his consent, the couple resorted to stratagem. As they were forbidden to meet, Miss Nancy became very intimate with a young married friend around the corner from her home; confiding in her, they managed to elude the vigilance of her parents. She threw her clothes out of the window one night where they were received by Mrs. Rosa Harper, and in the morning she stepped around to see her friend, and from there the lovers eloped. Of course, they were forgiven, and some years later she appears as mistress of "Belle Aire" or Colross, as it is now called, and her son William Roberdeau Swift married the beautiful and charming Mary Harper, daughter of his mother's friend."

By this elopement, one may conclude that Jonathan Swift was no coward, considering the high social rank and enormous physical size of his future father-in-law, Daniel Roberdeau.

Swift's wife is sometimes referred to as Nancy and other times as Ann, however, it is incorrect when she is referred to as "Ann Foster" in this story. The Foster name came from Jonathan's mother's maiden name. Jonathan and Nancy/Ann had a daughter named Ann Foster who was named for her Grandmother Swift.

It is believed that Nancy was her nickname. Her name in *Implied Marriages of Fairfax County Virginia* by Morty Hiatt and Craig Roberts Scott is "Nancy." In all the indentures she is always referred to as "Ann," and in church records she is referred to as either Nancy or Ann. In the book, *Genealogy of the Roberdeau Family*, she is listed as Ann.

On Wednesday the twenty-third of November, Jonathan's brother, Dr. Foster Swift, was introduced to George Washington by General Benjamin Lincoln who was a friend of Foster Swift. Swift, Lincoln, Miss Kitty Washington, Colonels Hooe and Lyles, Mr. Porter, Captain Goodwin, Mr. Potts, and others were dinner guests at Mount Vernon.[26]

The following are three of the six ads that ran in 1786 along with the dates when they were placed:

To be SOLD, FREIGHTED OR CHARTERED, The _Schooner Suky,_ *Baxter Downs, Master; she is a strong well built vessel and only nine months old---for further information inquire of JONATHAN SWIFT, ALX, June 8, 1786. (43)*

PHILADELPHIA PACKET,

THE sloop CHARMING POLLY, JOHN Ellwood, Master, will ply constantly as a Packet between Philadelphia and ALX,--She has good accommodations for passengers, and will sail the 30th inst.—For freight or passage, apply to the master on board JONATHAN SWIFT and CO. , ALX, July 27, 1786. (43)

LUMBER

Now landing from the Brig Endeavor, John Riley, Master, from Portsmouth, New-England, PLANK of all sizes. Also, NEW-ENGLAND Rum, PICKLED and Dry CODFISH, &c. All which will be sold cheap by JONATHAN SWIFT and Co. ALX, November 9, 1786.(43)

In July 23, 1786, in an indenture—Swift buys for 457£ and 12 shillings cmv from Richard Chichester and Sarah, his wife a certain piece of ground in Alexandria being a part of lot #51 or #52 and being on Fairfax Street on the south side of a 12' alley, which extends from Fairfax to Water Streets. Witness—George Gilpin and Robert T. Hooe from the *Fairfax County Deed Book Q series* by Ruth and Sam Sparacio.

In July 25, 1786, in an indenture—Jonathan Swift and Ann, his wife, sell to Richard Chichester for 457£ and 13 shillings cmv a piece of ground in Alexandria on the east side of Fairfax Street and to the southward of King Street. George Gilpin and Robert T. Hooe witnesses from the *Fairfax County Deed Book Q series* by Ruth and Sam Sparacio.

No actual money changed hands on these indentures—it was just a land swap.

Sometime between 1786 and 1800, Swift served as Senior Warden of the Alexandria Washington Lodge #22.[2]

September 1786, "SWIFT, JONATHAN & CO. ...removed to the opposite side of Fairfax Street between Col. Fitzgerald's and Dr. Craik where he will sell: gilt looking glasses, tankards, tea-pots, copper tea kettles, razors, penknives, nails, hoister, and pocket pistols, fowling pieces, queens ware, port wine, cognac brandy, molasses, and salt".[39]

Sunday the 26th of November 1786, Swift along with Dr. Craik, Colonels Hooe and Henley and others dined with George Washington at Mount Vernon.[26] This is the same Dr. Craik of the Bear Creek and Properties #4 thru #8 indentures.

The following are three of six ads Swift placed in 1787:

Jonathan Swift and Company, Have Imported per the Charlotte, and Olive Branch, from London. A GOOD assortment of linens from 6d1/2. to 2/6 cost, Yorkshire sheetings, low priced printed linens, cottons and chintzes, fustians, sham jeans, jeanets, drabbets, satinets, needle worked aprons and handkerchiefs, sewing silks, oil-skin umbrellas, silver watches, &c.&c. They have just received by the brig Commerce, and other vessels from Boston, fresh bohea tea in ½, ¼ and 1/8 of chests. 10d. nails, inch plank, sprits of turpentine, mens' leather shoes, womens' leather, calamanco, everlasting and neat russel ditto, also a pair of elegant looking-glasses. ALX, June 7, 1787. (43)

Stop Saddle Thief!

STOLEN from Mr. Smith's livery stable on Tuesday night the 14th inst., an English SADDLE and BRIDLE: The saddle is full welted, very neatly made, has a scarlet striped cloth, two girths, double skirts, plated stirrups, and two silver staples in the front bosses which are plated; the bridle has a plan snaffle, double plated bit, and black reins.—Any person who will secure the thief and deliver the saddle and bridle to the Subscriber, shall receive a generous reward. JONATHAN SWIFT. ALX, August 16, 1787. (43) Jonathan Swift and Company, Have just imported from London, per the brig Ceres, Capt. Traverse, via Baltimore, and the ship Potomack Planter, Capt. Johns, an assortment of EUROPEAN GOODS, Suitable to the season; among them are the following, viz, DUFFILS of all colours and prices, double milled drabs, wide and narrow coatings, low priced broadcloths, cardinals of all prices, a large assortment of brown Irish linens, white ditto ditto from 7d. to 3/6 cost, British shirtings, ditto dowlas, Yorkshire sheetins, checks, thicksets, corduroys, velverets, plushes, king's cord, queen's ditto, ditto twilled, Rodney's ditto ditto, drabbets, beaver satinets, jeans, fustians, white cotton linings, coloured ditto ditto, calamancoes, tammies, draw boys, chintzes, ell-wide fancy calicoes, printed cottons, ditto linens, glazed ditto, elegant copperplate furniture, very common ditto, muslins, red sprigged India ditto, muslinets, gloves of all kinds, ladies' dress hats trimmed, Royal lustres, Denmark ditto, silk cords, glossinets, silk crapes, missionets, shawls of all kinds, pullicat handkerchiefs, worsted vest patterns, ditto hose, silver watches, fowling pieces, holster pistols, gentlemen's elastic boots, smith's London-made shoes in trunks from 21s to 84s. cost per dozen, viz. gentlemen's dress dogskin shoes, neat ditto ditto, men's and women's common ditto ditto ditto pumps, youths' and boys' ditto, ladies' Spanish leather ditto, best calamanco ditto , common ditto ditto, misses' ditto ditto, ditto Morocco ditto, ditto leather ditto, childrens' Morocco ditto, ditto leather ditto, patent blacking cakes, &c. &c.&c. Which they will dispose of by wholesale or retail on the most reasonable terms, for cash, bank notes, bills on any part of Europe, tobacco, hemp, flour, wheat, corn, or flax seed. They have a few crates of queen's ware, among which are complete blue and green edged table services.—also 4d. 6d. 10d and 20d nails, New-England made shoes. West-India rum, port wine, spirits of turpentine, Leiper's snuff, allspice, &c. ALX, Oct 25, 1787. (43)

"Rev. Bryan Fairfax (Lord Fairfax) preached a charity sermon before the Lodge, December 27, 1787, and the contribution raised for the benefit of the poor was handed to Rev. Mr. Fairfax for distribution. At night the festivities of the day were terminated with a ball, which was numerously attended. Among those present were: Dr. Dick, George Richards, John Allison, Capt. John Hawkins, William Bird, Col. West, Thomas West, Col. Ramsay, Robert McCrea, Jonathan Swift..." [2]

From Presbyterians In Alexandria, 1770-1830 by Marylou Gjernes – "Authorizations in 1789 and 1790 to raise lotteries to pave the streets of Alexandria were given to William Hunter, Jun., Josiah Watson, William Hunter, Sen., John Dundas and Jonathan Swift among others."

"The act for incorporating the Academy of Alexandria named Presbyterians Isaac S. Keith, and Josiah Watson, in the group of trustees to conduct the business of the Academy until the first scheduled election of trustees. Other Presbyterians, who signed the petition requesting incorporation, were William Lowry, Jonathan Swift..." [17]

Swift ran four ads from October to December of 1789. The following are three of the four ads:

For CHARTER,
To any Part of Europe or the West-Indies,
The BRIGANTINE
WILLIAM,
Capt. STODDART,
Burthen 150 Tons, an American
Bottom, a fast Sailer, and has good
Accommodations for Passengers. – For
Further information, apply to the

Captain on board at George-Town, or
Jonathan Swift.
ALX, October 26, 1789 (43)

Jonathan Swift, HAS JUST IMPORTED, per the Ships Commerce
and Menter, from Liverpool, and Ship Changeable, Capt. Bowrey,
from London, A general Assortment of EUROPEAN GOODS, Suit-
able to the Season—Among them are Cassimers; 7-4,6-4,5-4,7-8
and 3-4 brown, drab, mixed, olive and fashionable coloured Cloths;
Hunters' Plains; German Serges; green, red and crimson Drapery;
Baizes; Welch Flannels; white, blue and green Negro Cottons; plain
Plaidings; Duffil Blanketing; 7-4, 8-4, 9-4 Rose ditto; Rugs; mat-
tresses of all Sizes; Beds with Bolster and Pillows; Filed-Bedsteads;
a large Assortment of Cardinals; ditto of Worsted, and Silk and
Worsted Hosiery; Shoes and Boots; Velvet and Velverets; Queen Royal
Cords; Thick-setts; Drabbets; Satinets; Royal Ribs; Jeans; Denims;
Fustians; 3-4, 7-8 and 4-4 Irish Lines; British, Scotch and Irish
brown and bleached Sheetings; ditto Dowlas; stout shirting Linens;
3-4 and 7-8 brown Hollands; Cotton and Linen Checks; Furniture
ditto; Crankies; British and Scotch Flax and Tow Osnaburgs; Dia-
pers; Quiltings; a large Assortment of printed Linens, Calicoes and
Chintzes of the latest Fashion; ditto of Soucee; Britannia, Romal,
Malabar, Barcelona and Bandano Handkerchiefs; ditto Shawls;
coloured Threads assorted; Osnaburg ditto; Mohair and Twist;
low-priced Hats in Boxes assorted; and—irons, Shovels and Tongs;
Shovel-Pans; Scale-Beams; small ditto with Scales; Desk and Side-
board Mounting; Planes; double and single Plane-Irons; Sash-Line;
Hammers; Augers; Gouges; Firmer's Chisels; Mason and Plaisterer's
Trowels; Closet, Till and Door Locks; Cupboard ditto and Handles;
H, HL, Chest and T Hinges; Table Buts and Catches; Nails; Brads;
Screws, lackered and plain; House and Hearth Brushes; Cloth, Bot-
tle and Shoe ditto; Cloak-Pins; Steel, Iron and japanned Tobacco
and Snuff Boxes; Graters; Rat-Traps; Bed-Screws; Pistols; Webbing;
Table, Carving and Dessert Knives and Forks of all Kinds and
Prices; ditto Penknives; Cutteaux; large and small Pewter Spoons;
Whitechapel, Osnaburg and Darning Needles; plated and common
Buckles; gilt, plated and Metal Buttons; Matthewmen ditto; Horn
ditto of all Kinds; Entick's Dictionaries; Psalm-Books; Spelling ditto;
Primers; Children's Books; Histories; Voyages; Novels, &c. Queen's,

Stone and black Ware; best London Porter in Hampers and Casks; a few Sets of Beach, japanned and Mahogany Chairs; Tea-Caddies; Pembroke and Dining Table, &c.&c.&c.
ALX, Nov. 16, 1789. (43)

For LONDON,
The Ship
CHANGEABLE,
Robert Bowrey, Master,
Will sail with all convenient Speed. She is a British Bottom, with a Pass—stands A No. 1; burthen 420 Hhds. Well found, a fast Sailer, and has good Accommodations for Passengers.—For Freight, with Liberty of Consignment, apply to the Master on board, or to
Jonathan Swift.
ALX, November 16, 1789 (43)

In 1790 Swift ran six ads. The Following is two of the six ads:

Jonathan Swift, Has just imported, Per the Mary, Capt. Bayshore, from Liverpool, A Further Assortment of BIRMINGHAM, MANCHESTER and YORKSHIRE GOODS.---Also, Orange-striped, blue and white and yellow QUEEN'S WARE, in Crates, well assorted, and very low; STONE, BLACK and SPOTTED WARE: SALT; 4d. d.d.10d. and 20d. NAILS: BRADS; LONDON PORTER: IRISH LINENS: and SCOTTISH OSNABURGS.
ALX, January 6, 1790 (43)

For CHARTER,
THE SNOW MARY,
William Bayshore, Master:
A British Bottom, with a Pass; a strong, well-built Vessel; burthen 200 Hogsheads.
If not chartered in a few Days, she will take 100 Hogsheads of Tobacco on Freight for Liverpool with Liberty of Consignment.--- For Freight or Passage, apply to
Jonathan Swift.
ALX, January 6, 1790 (43)

From the book *Lodge of Washington* by F. L. Brockett one finds, in 1791, Swift was listed as being present at a Masonic ceremony of lying [erecting] the first cornerstone of the District of Columbia. This was laid at Jones' Point, at the mouth of Great Hunting Creek, on the west bank of the Potomac, and marked the southeast corner of the District of Columbia. The ceremony and those who attended are described in the following excerpt:

"Dr. Elisha Cullen Dick, Worshipful Master, accompanied by the Lodge, performed the ceremonies on the 15th of April 1791, in the presence of the commissioners appointed by President Washington, the Mayor and Common Council of Alexandria, citizens and strangers, after which Rev. James Muir, D.D., Chaplain of the Lodge, delivered an address. After partaking of refreshments, the company returned to John Wise's Tavern, which a number of toasts were drank.

"Among those present were: John Allison, Joseph Greenway, Benjamin A. Hamp, Michael Madden, Col. Dennis Ramsey, Col. Charles Simms, Thomas West, Jesse Taylor, Jr., John Harper, Peter Waggoner, James Taylor, Capt. John Hawkins, Jonathan Swift, Robert McCrea, William Hodgson, John Dunlap, William Herbert, Robert Sanford, William Hunter, Sr., Edward Harper, William Hunter, Jr., Charles Turner, and Michael Gretter."

On the 18th day of September 1793, Swift was present at one of this country's most historic events and one of the most important Masonic ceremonies in history that of laying the corner-stone of the United States capitol in the city of Washington.[2]

On January 12, 1796, Swift purchases a parcel in Alexandria located south of King Street and west of Union Street, for 5#, current money of Virginia, from Thomas and Mary Patten of Alexandria, and Joseph and Dorthy May.[41]

On October 4, 1796, Swift buys a parcel in Alexandria located east of Union Street and south of King Street for 4,000# from Alexander and Rachel Smith.[41]

The following is from *Artisans and Merchants of Alexandria Virginia* by T. Michael Miller: "DARBY, JOHN - Merchant - Fairfax St. Lately occupied by Jonathan Swift; 1796, Spring & Summer goods, Irish linens, India nankeens, expects from Philadelphia & New York a variety of articles in the fancy line, salt, rum, old port..."

In April 24, 1797, an indenture – Swift buys a certain piece of ground in Alexandria upon the east side of Union Street and to the northward of Prince Street to the front of the wharf, for 90# cmv.[50]

On the 28th day of March or May 1797, Ann Selina daughter of Jonathan Swift and Ann, his wife, was baptized.[68 & 64]

On the 19th day of July 1797, Isaac Roberdeau Swift was buried. He was three years old. The cause of his death was listed as "Cho: morb:".[64] There is no listing of the parents but it is very likely that he is Jonathan and Ann Swift's child. He was undoubtedly named for Ann Swift's grandfather, Isaac Roberdeau.

April 1797, Swift, "will lease a warehouse at the corner of King and Union St. which was lately occupied by Thomas Patten..."[39]

In February of 1798, Swift was listed as one of the officers of the Mutual Assurance Society, fire insurance company.[39]

Also on February the 16th in 1798 on an indenture — Swift bought a parcel of land on Four Mile Run in the county of Fairfax containing 356 acres for 1424# cmv.[50]

June, 1798 Swift leased the house and store on Fairfax Street adjoining Messrs. Joseph Riddle.[39]

On the 19th of July 1798, Ann Selina Swift was buried; she was one year and five months old, and her cause of death was listed as "flux." [68 & 64]

On August the third 1798, Swift and John Fitzgerald purchased for 1,200# a parcel of land east of Water Street and north of Prince Street in Alexandria.[40]

In February of 1799, Swift was listed among managers of a ball at Gadsby's Tavern: "on Monday the 11th of February in commemoration of the birth of our illustrious and greatly esteemed, Lieutenant-General Washington." Jonathan Swift also signed on November 9th a paragraph advising, "members of the Golf Club will please to take notice that the club will meet at their room, Gadsby's Hotel, this evening." [16]

In November 1799, a ball was given at Gadsby's Tavern; the managers were Jonathan Swift, Charles Alexander, Georgia Deneale, Robert Young, James H. Hooe, and William Newton. An invitation was sent to General and Mrs. Washington, and the following oft-quoted reply was received; the following letter was sent to Jonathan Swift:

November 13, 1799

Gentlemen,

Mrs. Washington and myself have been honored with your polite invitation to the assemblies of Alexandria this winter, and thank you for this mark of your attention. But, alas! Our dancing days are no more. We wish, however, to all those who have a relish for so agreeable and in-

nocent an amusement all the pleasure the season will afford them; and I am, gentlemen, your most obedient and obliged humble servant.

George Washington [15,2 & 44]

The following is an excerpt from the *Story of Old Town and "Gentry Row" in Alexandria Virginia* by Robert H. Wilson:

Death of George Washington

"Not long after daylight on December 14, 1799, a messenger from Mount Vernon reached Dr. Craik's home with an urgent summons from Martha Washington. The General had been seriously ill all night from the effect of a cold horseback ride in the rain two days before, but had insisted his old friend, the doctor, not be summoned until morning. Hurrying as much as possible, Dr. Craik reached the bedside about 11 a.m. He recognized the situation to be terminal and called in two colleagues for consultation, Dr. Dick and Dr. Augustus Brown, who lived across from Mount Vernon on the Maryland side of the Potomac. They arrived at 3 o'clock in the afternoon. Washington died that night, his last words to Dr. Craik. 'Doctor, I die hard, but I am not afraid to go.'"

Dr. James Craik was a close personal friend of George Washington and was the first surgeon general of the United States Army.

Monday, December 16th 1799, Jonathan Swift was present at the funeral lodge to make arrangements for George Washington's interment, and on Wednesday the 18th he was one of the Masonic members of the Alexandria Lodge #22 in attendance at George Washington's funeral. All of George Washington's pall-bearers were masons except Col. Philip Marsteller.[2]

Mrs. Washington had left the funeral arrangements in the hands of the Masonic Lodge, making but one request, which was to allow Colonel Philip Marsteller, who as not a mason, to be included among the pall-bearers. [63]

According to the family records, Swift "sprinkled ashes on the bier." [15]

The following excerpt from *Genealogy of the Roberdeau Family*, by Roberdeau Buchanan, refers to the aforementioned letter, from Washington to Swift, and it also describes Swift's participation in the first President's funeral, which further defines the friendship of George Washington, and Jonathan Swift.

"The note of General Washington to Mr. Swift and others, here referred to, was presented by him to the Museum of Alexandria

Washington Lodge of Alexandria, which was burned a few years ago with all its contents; among which was this letter and some other valuables, placed there by Mr. Swift, including a saddle presented to the government by the Dey of Morocco, while Mr. Swift was his consul. A photograph of the letter was however taken a short time previously, a facsimile of which appeared in the *Chromotype* of July 1873, published in New York. It is probably one of the last that General Washington ever wrote, being dated November 12, 1799, within a month of his decease. Jonathan Swift was a member of the Masonic Fraternity, having received his degrees in this lodge:--initiated and passed February 25, 1785; and raised to a Master Mason February 24, 1786. As a brother mason, Mr. Swift attended General Washington's funeral; and was the one who sprinkled the earth over the body during the services."

This account of Jonathan Swift being mentioned as the one who "sprinkled the earth over George Washington's body" is also mentioned in *The Memoirs of Gen. Joseph Gardner Swift.*

Also from *Genealogy of the Roberdeau Family,* is another historical account of the interaction of the Swift and Washington families.

"Mrs. Ann Swift was present at the inauguration ball in honor of General Washington, and during the evening, was led out to dance by him. A lifelike miniature of her on ivory, at the age of twenty-two, is in possession of her daughter, Mrs. Patten; who has also an oil painting at the age of sixty."

"One month to the day of the first president's demise his admirers founded the Washington Society at Gadsby's; Swift became treasurer, holding the post several years. Both Swift and [John] Potts were among the Justice-of-the-Peace "midnight appointments" made by John Adams which Jefferson would not recognize thereby precipitating the notorious Madison-Marbury case." [16]

January 1800, "All Swedish and Danish vessels entering Alexandria reported to Mr. Swift -- the consul for those countries..." [39]

In 1800, Swift was elected a director in the Marine Insurance Company. Also, in 1800 Swift bought 202-204, three story buildings on King Street, from Bernard Chequiere. [39]

February 22, 1800 George Washington Swift, son of Jonathan Swift and Nancy, his wife, was baptized. He was born February 9, 1800. [68 & 64]

July 1800, Swift offers, "20 guineas reward for a runaway slave..." [39]
In November of 1800, Swift had the following indenture:

Fm Jonathan Swift, Twn ALX, Ffx Co. St VA
To William Hodgson-do -: lease for 10 years from 01Jan1801 @ 1000 silver $/an-num, quarterly payments, first due 31Mar1801:

1. Jonathan Swift's pier and the "Docks and Dockheads upon each side thereof Extending to the Lines of John Fitzgerald deceased and John & Thos. Vowell "known by the Name of Merchants Warf."

2. "Also all the vacant ground lying between the said Merchants Warf and the fence which Incloses the other Vacant Ground of...Swift Immediately joining upon his Warehouse."

3. "Also all the Part of the Inclosed Ground" within: Begin at NE corner of Swift's Warehouses on S side of the alley dividing him from Fitzgerald...E w/alley line the "full length of the fence and shed erected upon the said [enclosed] ground"...S w/fence ½ its length...W//alley to the warehouse wall... N w/wall to BEGIN—plus use of the Shed.

4. Other items: "Hodgson may at his own expense build within the fence, removing same at the lease end if he and Swift can't agree on a purchase."

   --Hodgson agrees not to stop up the "Passage now lying open between the Docks and the...fence but suffer [it] to remain as the means of Communication along the several Docks to the North and South";

   --"Hodgson will adhere to the Wharfage and Dockage Regulations dated 06Jun97 drawn up by Swift and other ALX wharf owners 'until...new modeled by a majority of the...owners'";

   --When Swift rents his warehouses on King Street and adjoining this area, he will stipulate renters must use Merchants Warf for their goods and vessels (except for goods assigned to persons other than the tenants of these warehouses).

WTT: John McIver, Chr. Robinson, Jas. Kennedy Jr.[40]

"June 24, 1801 — on this day the Lodges united in a procession, and attended service at the Episcopal Church. Rev. Thomas Davis officiated, for which he received the thanks of the Lodge, through Jonathan Swift." [2]

December 1801, Swift – "lease of several properties in Alexandria including: 1) warehouse at the corner of King and Union St. lately occupied by C. Wilson, 2) plantation in Fairfax County, 3) elegant brick building adjacent to George Gilpin..." Also in December 1801, "a black horse was stolen or strayed from the subscribers stable..." [39]

August 1802, Swift – "lease of the stores lately built by the subscriber--one fronting Merchants Wharf, the other fronting said wharf and the south alley leading thereto..." [39]

September 1802, Swift – "lease of a convenient store with cellars under it with a good sail loft--warning to numerous persons who cut his timber in Alexandria and Fairfax Counties..." [39]

General Joseph Gardner Swift

October 11, 1802, Ann Foster Swift was born of Jonathan Swift and his wife, Ann. [64]

On October 12, 1802, Jonathan Swift's nephew, Joseph Gardner Swift, was the first cadet to graduate from the West Point Military Academy. The following are highlights of the life of General Swift, from information, which was provided by the U. S. Army Corps of Engineers located in Alexandria, Virginia.

"Joseph Gardner Swift, was born December, 31 1783, and died July, 23 1865. He was a soldier and engineer. He was born on Nantucket Island, Massachusetts, the son of Foster Swift, a physician who served in both the army and the navy of the early American republic, and Deborah Delano, who was part of a large Quaker congregation on the island...

"Although Swift intended to enter Harvard College, he instead became a cadet with the U. S. Artillery at Fort Wolcott, Newport, Rhode Island, on 12 may 1800. He studied there under Lieutenant Colonel Louis Tousard, who headed the first apprentice program for artillery officers and engineers in the U. S. Army. On 14 October 1801 Swift arrived at West Point, New York, as a member of the first class of cadets to study at the newly formed U. S. Military Academy...

"The academy, founded formally on 16 March 1802, grew out of Thomas Jefferson's interest in establishing an institution that could provide American-trained engineers for an expanding country as well as officers drawn from a broad spectrum of society. Swift graduated from West Point on 12 October 1802 and is considered the first graduate of the Military Academy and thus the first American-trained engineer in the United States. Assigned at West Point to act as an instructor until 1804, Swift founded the Military Philosophical Society, the first professional development organization for military officers in the United States...

"In 1805 [General] Swift married Louisa Margaret Walker, they had twelve children…

"During the War of 1812, [General] Swift was in demand throughout the Northeast. He participated in the abortive American invasion of Canada in 1813 and was brevetted to brigadier general for his services, particularly in the battle of Chrysler's Field, Nov. 11 1813, where he was second in command and chief engineer for the American army. At the same time he was chief of engineers of the army and superintendent of the Military Academy…

"A man of great integrity, Swift was frequently called upon as a consultant to railroads and other engineering projects throughout his life. He is generally regarded as the first American-trained engineer…"

Roberdeau Buchanan, author of *Genealogy of the Roberdeau Family*, gave the following account of General Joseph Gardner Swift.

"…The writer remembers with pleasure once having seen General Swift when he called upon the writer's mother, and dined with the family. He also heard him relate the cause of his resignation, but was too young to pay much attention to it. During this visit an incident occurred not to be forgotten by those present. This old gentleman, at the age of 74, asked his daughter to accompany him while he sang My Orra Moor, 'I wish to sing that song here once again in memory of old times, and in front of that picture,' said he, pointing to a portrait of Colonel Roberdeau hanging over the piano. While singing, his eyes rested on the likeness of his old and valued friend, and the tears rolled down his cheeks. There was hardly a dry eye in the room."

June 12, 1803, Ann Foster Swift was baptized.[68 & 64] Ann Foster would later marry Jonathan T. Patten. [22]

Grasshopper Hall

December 1, 1803, Swift bought one of Alexandria's largest mansions, Belle Aire, from John Potts and wife Elizabeth of Alexandria for $9,000 and assumed annual ground rent of $133.33 to Charles Alexander. The Swifts did call it Belle Aire, but nephew, Joseph Gardner Swift, who was a frequent visitor, spoke of his Uncle Jonathan's "fine place" in Alexandria that bore the name of Grasshopper Hall, since known as Colross and (Jonathan and Ann) frequently entertained General Washington. [15]

Apparently until recent years, it was believed that Swift built Belle Aire/

Colross for his bride, Ann, in 1799. Alexandria's researchers have discovered that John Potts built Belle Aire in 1799 and sold it to Swift in 1803. Since Swift did not own the house until 1803, he could not have entertained General Washington, who died in 1799, at Belle Aire. Washington's visits would have been at Swift's previous home which was most likely on Fairfax Street, or possibly at the Long Glades.

The following is an excerpt from *Days In an Old Town* by Mrs. Bettie Carter Smoot, who lived in the Colross/Belle Aire mansion from 1885-1917:

"Colross dated from the year 1799. It was built by a wealthy, Scotch merchant of Alexandria, Jonathan Swift. He resided there with his young wife, formerly a Miss Roberdeau, with whom he had eloped in romantic fashion. He eventually failed in business, and the house was purchased by Charles Alexander, of Preston, who already owned the land. Charles Alexander bequeathed Colross to his son, Lee Massey Alexander; from him it passed into the hands of Judge Thompson F. Mason, of Alexandria. The Mason family owned the place until it was purchased by my husband, Mr. W. A. Smoot, in 1885, but it had been unoccupied by them for a number of years previous.

"The grounds of Colross included a whole square and were enclosed with an ancient brick wall ten feet in height. There were the remains of pretty old trees about the place, and it was these that were most valued.

"On the interior, the house was of the invariable style of the colonial period, with a hall through the center and large, airy rooms on either side. There was a broad stairway at the back, and an intersecting hall opening upon a small breakfast room. The rooms on the second floor corresponded, as did the four rooms in the attic.

"In addition to the main building, there were wings and various out-buildings. In one of the wings, there was the conservatory, and another the kitchens, and over these a cozy little suite, with a hall-way, built for servants, in the olden days. There were cupboards and closets without number at Colross, some of them dark closets under stairways, where a family skeleton, if there were one, might safely hide. In the attic, too, there were some dark cubby-holes. Below were some little back stairways and narrow halls, apparently leading to nowhere. To one who lived there it was all plain enough, but to a new-comer, these little by-ways were often mystifying. On one occasion a girl who had come on an errand was discovered on some back steps, sobbing bitterly. She said she had been everywhere and was sure that she could never find her way out.

"Much of the interior woodwork of Colross was of mahogany, such as the stair rails, newel posts, and door sills, and on the lower floor the large mantels were of black and gray Irish marble. Above these were deep cornices and centerpieces of stucco. At the entrance of the house, there was a handsome pillared porch, and semi-circular walks, paved with granite, leading to iron gates at the front. At the back there was a long portico, also with pillars, and a tessellated floor of marble and slate. Surrounding all, there were extensive brick walks. Jonathan Swift had certainly built his house on a noble plan."

"Unfortunately in 1929, Alexandria's largest mansion, Colross, located on the 1100 block of Oronoco Street, was carted off brick by brick to Princeton, New Jersey, after being ravaged by a tornado in 1927." [48]

"This most interesting interstate move resulted from the ambitious determination of Princetonian John Randall Munn '06 to relocate Colross, one of the most historical architectural landmarks of Alexandria, Virginia, to The Great Road in Princeton, where it now stands as part of the Princeton Day School Campus." [15]

This next description of Colross is by John Randall Munn. What a coincidence that a man named Munn would buy, raze and move Swift's old mansion to Princeton.

"Colross, as it was called, was built in 1799, as evidenced by that date on a leader head, and was the home of Jonathan Swift and his bride, Ann Foster Roberdeaux, a daughter of General Roberdeaux, of the American Army under Washington.

"The house, three stories high with five windows along the front and back with three gabled windows on the third floor, was all of brick and stone. There were two large irregular wings, one containing a passageway used as a greenhouse leading to a square two story brick building, the office of the estate on the ground floor and a bedroom above. The other wing was two stories and had a kitchen, smoke house, storage rooms, servant's rooms, etc., and was almost as large as the main part of the house." [15]

June 1804, (Swift) "elected to the city council from the first ward." [39]

On the twenty-third of January 1805, Swift ran this humorous ad in the Daily Advertiser and is presented in Jean Elliot's *Kindly But Alien Hands*:

"Those persons who have been in the habit of stealing my fence, for a considerable time past, are respectfully informed, if equally agreeable to them, it will be more convenient to me, if they will steal my wood, and leave the fence for the present—and as it may be attended with some little inconvenience getting over the palings, the gate is left unfastened for their accommodation." J. Swift

May 21, 1805, Mary Selina Swift, daughter of Jonathan Swift and Ann, his wife, is baptized.[68 & 64] Mary Selina would later marry Henry Allison.[22]

"1805, [Swift] owned a three story brick warehouse occupied by Wm. J. Hall on the east side of the 100 block of S. Union St.; 1805, owned four buildings occupied by Jon Potts on the south side of the 200 block of King St. -- 3 story brick dwelling, 2 story brick warehouse, 2 story brick kitchen and a necessary..."[39]

"1807 & 1810 Swift will lease the Merchants Wharf with the middle store and the warehouse on Union St...."[39]

"4/1808, subscriber [Swift] will rent the store at present in the occupancy of S. Moore fronting Merchants Wharf and the warehouses at the corner of King and Union St...." [39]

Swift, "8/1808, sale of several parcels of land including the White House tract..." [39]

September 20, 1808—William Taylor Swift, son of Jonathan Swift and Nancy, his wife, was baptized, born this morning. [68 & 64]

September 21, 1808—William Taylor Swift, son of Jonathan Swift and Ann, his wife, dies, one day old. [68 & 64]

Swift, "5/1809, advertised for a runaway slave..."[39]

September 1809, "...Swift's White House Tavern and buildings at the Long Glades were destroyed by fire. 'We are happy to hear that the incendiary, a Negro, has since been discovered, by dropping a button half a mile distant.'"[16]

January 1810, Swift, "will lease the Merchant's Wharf with the middle store in front and the warehouse on Union Street...also the sail loft formerly occupied by Mr. Sanford..."[39]

April 1810, Swift, "sale of the Long Glades where the White House Tavern and store stood containing 1,350 acres of land–three miles from the Great Falls of the Potomac, in Fairfax County..." [39]

May 1810, Swift, "will sell a warehouse on Union St. adjoining John M'Pherson and Co..." [39]

April 15, 1811, Foster Swift, son of Jonathan Swift and Ann, his wife, was baptized...born May 20, 1810.[68 & 64]

October 1813 ---Jonathan Swift and Ann, his wife, to Isaac Entwisle for $4,000, lots #5, 6 and 23 allotted to Ann Swift, daughter of Daniel Roberdeau. #23 on East side Potomac Strand sometimes called Strand and on South side Wolfe (Street). (#5 & #6) On East side Wolfe (Street) and East side of Water (Street). [45]

Swift's Role in the War of 1812

The following excerpt from *Fairfax County, Virginia A History*, by Netherton, Sweig, Artemel, Hickin, and Reed, describes Swift's role in Alexandria during the War of 1812 and the great losses of ships and merchandise that Swift and other merchants of that town suffered:

"On 25 August, the Reverend James Muir of Alexandria along with Dr. Dick, Johnathon Swift and William Swann came to Dr. James Ewell's house near the Capital in Washington where Admiral Cockburn and General Ross were making their headquarters. They came carrying a white flag and said that Alexandria was completely defenseless—what surrender terms could they expect? The following account describes the meeting as seen by Dr. Ewell.

"The terror struck into the good people of our city, by the capture and conflagration as aforesaid, rolled on in such conflomorating floods to Alexandria, that, by the time it reached that place, It had acquired a swell of mountainous horrors, that appear to have entirely prostrated the spirits of the Alexandrians. Men, women and children in that defenseless place saw nothing, in their frightened fancies, but the sudden and total destruction of their rising city, by the British army then at Washington, and the British squadron, under Captain Gordon, coming up the river.

"In this alarming situation, they very wisely determined to throw themselves on the generosity of the enemy, and supplicate security for their town, on the humble conditions of capitulation. As men in the time of their troubles seem naturally to look for a blessing through the ministration of the godly, the Alexandrians selected four of their citizens distinguished for piety and morals, as Dr. Muir and Dick, and Messrs. Johnathon Swift and Wm. Swann. They arrived during the dreadful tornado, which we experienced on that memorable day and as I happened to be sitting in my dining room with Admiral Cockburn, when these delegates presented themselves, I had a fair opportunity to hear every word that passed on this occasion. Soon as they communicated to the admiral the object of their mission, he replied, with the brevity that characterized him, 'Gentlemen, I have nothing to say, until you first tell me whether captain Gordon is in sight of Alexandria.'

"The reply was, that captain Gordon was not in sight of Alexandria.

"'Well, then, gentlemen', continued he, 'I am ready to negotiate with you. And now, all I have to say is, that we want provisions, and must have them. But let me tell you, that for every article we take, you shall be allowed a fair price.'

Upon this they very soon retired.

"The same situation was reported by William Chamberlayne in a letter to his wife. He further added, 'A deputation from Alexandria waited on the British Commander who recd for answer that persons not found in arms, shd. Be respected in their persons and property. [h]e sayd that he wanted flour & wed. have it, but he wd. pay a fair price for it....'

"This was, as stated, even before any sight of a British squadron on Potomac. However, Alexandrians were most anxious to avoid a conflict in their own city. They were not alone. The people of Georgetown were also attempting to surrender.

"In the meantime, there was a real danger to Alexandria. For, after leaving Fort Washington, which had deliberately destroyed its own ammunition, the way was opened to Alexandria, and a small boat came toward the frigate Seahorse, the flagship of the expedition of forces on the Potomac under Captain James Gordon. About 10 a.m. on the 24th, three of Alexandria's leading citizens came bearing a white flag and asked to see Captain Gordon. Gordon Swift, spokesman for the group, began by saying that they hoped Captain Gordon would show respect for the city of Alexandria. [The name, Gordon Swift, is apparently a misprint—obviously confusing 'Capt. Gordon' with 'Jonathan'.] Gordon replied that he planned to respect all shops and houses, but planned to seize all ships and cargo waiting for export. Swift thought this unfair.

"It seemed as if the major concern of the commerce-minded Alexandrians was that someone might try to rescue them from British control, and that shooting would ensue. Alexandrians felt unprepared for their town to be the site of a major battle, since they knew that Brig. General John P. Hungerford's 1,400 member Virginia militia, hurrying toward them, was just 24 miles away. The committee sent a resolution to General Hungerford asking him to stay away as Alexandria had no military force to protect itself and intended to surrender at its own discretion.

"By 7:00 p.m. Captain Gordon's squadron was anchored two miles away, but the vessel Aetna continued up to the city. Consequently, the city again renewed its apprehension and a Committee of Vigilance sent businessman William Wilson to Gordon asking to be left alone. Captain Gordon refused.

"By Monday, 29 August 1814, the British squadron came opposite the town and asked for:

1. all naval stores, public or private
2. all scuttled vessels
3. all goods intended for export
4. all goods sent out of town since 19 August 1814, to be retrieved and given up.

"Naturally the town leaders balked at such an extensive list of demands, but the only concession given by the British was that of not raising and delivering vessels at the bottom of the river because it would be too lengthy and difficult a task.

"Thus, for the next three days, until 31 August, the crew loaded the three vessels with goods from the Alexandria warehouses, principally tobacco, flour, cotton, wine and sugar. But the owners were not allowed 'a fair price.' In general there was no overt friction between the town fathers and the British seaman, but Mayor Simms might be cited for overstating the case when he wrote to his wife; 'it is impossible that men could behave better than the British behaved while the town was in their hands.' "

From the same chapter:
"By 2 September 1814, the British had finished their job in Alexandria and left empty warehouses; they took with them 21 vessels, 13,786 barrels of flour, 757 hogsheads of tobacco, and tons of cotton, tar, beef, and sugar, as well as other merchandise valued at $100,000. And not a shot was fired."

"Conditions were intense in Alexandria in 1814 after the British took it, although the town escaped small damage 'due to the intercession of Jonathan Swift,' who by this time was prominent in diplomatic circles."[15]

Apparently Swift's efforts and accomplishments in the seize of Alexandria, did not go unnoticed. In "March of 1815 he was appointed to the Consulate of Holland," and he advertised furnishing certificates to vessels bound to Holland, Sweden, Denmark and Russia.[15]

August 1, 1815, Jonathan and Ann's oldest son William R. Swift marries Mary D. Harper.[16]

"EXCHANGE COFFEE HOUSE - Cameron St. -- Market House...
...1817, Officers: George Deneale, Phineas Janney, Noblet Herbert, J.P. Thompson, Joseph Dean, Jonathan Swift, T. Mountford, Jr., Sec...."[39]

"March 1819, Jefferson by proclamation recognized Swift as consul to the United Kingdom of Portugal, Brazil and Argaves, and in November as 'Consul of his Majesty King of the Netherlands for the Port of Alexandria and places thereto belonging.' In those days, that Harbor [Alexandria] was second to few in a bustling international commerce." [15]

During Thomas Jefferson's term as President, a saddle of crimson velvet, heavily embroidered with gold, was sent to him as a gift from the Dey of Morocco. The President of the United States was inhibited from accepting a gift from the hands of a foreign prince. Jonathan Swift, Esq., The Consul of Morocco, through whom the saddle was sent, deposited it in a museum. [2]

August 9, 1819, George Washington Swift, Jonathan Swift's son, died.[39] (He would have been 19 years old.)

Jonathan, Ann and their children were members of the Presbyterian Church of Alexandria. During 1789-1820 Rev. Dr. James Muir was minister. [65]

Belle Aire was then considered way out in the country; there for the healthier climate, the venerable James Muir, D.D....repaired in the summer of 1820. Dr. Muir failing to recover slipped away under the Swifts' hospitable roof.[16]

March 1821, Swift was elected to the third ward on the common council.[38]

In 1821, Swift was president of the Trustees of the Poor.[38]

March 1822, Swift was elected president of the Common Council of Alexandria.[38]

August 1822, it was ordered that Jonathan Swift, Thomas Swann and Humphrey Peak be appointed a committee to meet commissioners from Washington and Georgetown and to confer with them on the permanent improvement of the navigation of the Potomac River.[38]

March 1823, Swift is re-elected president of City Council.[38]

"ALEXANDRIA MUSEUM - Market House... ...6/1823, Thomas Mountford, the manager of the museum, executed a deed of trust which included the museum to Christopher Neale, mayor and Jonathan Swift, president of the Common Council and their successors forever..." [38]

"Alexandria suffered a major loss when in 1871 the market building burned. The Masonic museum, dating from 1811, with most of its historic contents, was destroyed in the conflagration." The saddle, which Jefferson could not accept from Morocco, was destroyed in the fire. It was valued at $15,000.[16]

October 1823, "resolved, that Messrs. Thomas Swann, Jonathan Swift, Humphrey Peake, Phineas Janney, Robert J. Taylor, and Charles I. Catlett be appointed delegates to attend a general meeting of the friends of the Potomac Canal in the city hall in Washington on November 6, 1823."[38]

From the *Alexandria Gazette and Advertiser*:
Thursday morning, August 26, 1824 issue-- (under 'DIED' column)
On Monday evening about 8 o'clock, Jonathan Swift, Esq., long respectable inhabitant of this town. The poor will have much cause to lament his death, to whom he devoted much time and feeling attention in distributing public and private charities.
Alexandria Library, reel #39 of *Alexandria Gazette*

The only reference discovered as to where Jonathan Swift is buried is from a publication by T. Michael Miller and William Francis Smith, A Seaport Saga: Portrait of Old Alexandria, which states that Swift died at Colross (Belle Aire) and was buried there with Masonic honors.[48]

The following information was contributed by Alexandria-Washington Lodge of Alexandria, Virginia, and is the lodge minutes of August 24 1824 and was transcribed by Rita Holtz of the Alexandria Library.

Alexandria Washington Lodge No. 22
Augt. 24th 5824
Lodge of Emergency

The Master and Wardens being absent the Lodge was called to order by the Junior Deacon who directed them to make choice Master Pro tem. When Bro. Jno B. Hammatt was unanimously called to the chair, The Lodge being opened on the 1ST Degree the W.M. states the object of the meeting was to pay the last Masonic honors to our late Bro. Jonathan Swift –

Present
John B. Hammatt – Worshipful Master pro tem
Joseph Eaches – Senior Warden pro tem
R. T. Ramsay – Junior Warden pro tem
John Dunlap – Secretary pro tem

T. Mountford – Treasurer pro tem
Robert Conway – Senior Deacon pro tem
John H. Runnels – Junior Deacon pro tem
John Shakes – Steward
M. T. Stubling – Steward
B. C. Wood – Tyler
William A. Williams, Past Master

Members
Alfred P. Gilpin, Thomas J. Minor, Edw. Pittman, Robert Barry, George H. Smoot A.Moore, Philip H. Minor, Thomas S. Martin, and Washington C. Page

Visitors
Jas. Carson, W.M.
A. Alexander, S.W.   } Brooke Lodge
E.A. May, J.W.
Robt. Brockett, Sr.,
Robt. Brockett Jr.,   } No. 2
L. T. Shields

Wm. Hayman – W. M.
Levi Hurdle   Potomac Lodge No. 5   Geo. Town

W. Devaughn, J. W. Beedle, James H__y (?), Uriah Jenkins, W. Bailey, Robert Hall, William Gilham – former visitors

B. G. Thornton S. W.
John Symburn
(?) James Jack   } Evangelical
John F. Wheat
Samuel Isaacs
Phares Throop   } Lodge No. 8

Brother W. C. Page was appointed Marshal who made the following assignments:
Brother T. J. Minor bearer of the great lights –
Robert Brockett Jr.
T. L. Martin and   } Bearers of the lessor lights
Edw. A. May

Brothers Alexander, Gilham, Thornton, Gilpin, Carson, Williams, Brockett Jr. and Hall, Pallbearers –

At 4 o'clock the Lodge moved in procession accompanied by the military band to the dwelling of our deceased Brother and from thence to the burial ground where the last Masonic obsequies were paid to his remains – The Lodge then returned to their Hall and were called off from Labor to refreshment for a short time. Labor being resumed, the following resolution was moved and seconded.

Resolved that the thanks of the Lodge be returned to the gentleman composing the Band for their prompt and kind attention – which was unanimously carried –

Ordered that the Secretary transmit a copy of the above resolution to the leader of the Band – nothing further appearing the Lodge closed in harmony at 7 o'clock.

Jno. Dunlap Secretary pro tem

The Lafayette Factor

The same year Jonathan Swift died, "Ann Foster Swift sat for her portrait to Rembrandt Peale; considered one of his finest, it is much valued by her descendants. Her father, Jonathan, since 1822 President of Council, passed away at Belle Aire on 22 August in his sixty-first year." [15]

From the records of Alexandria Washington Lodge, Jonathan Swift was listed as having made a toast to General Lafayette at the banquet given in his honor during his visit in October of 1824. This would have been impossible since Swift died in August, two months earlier.

This visit from Lafayette to Alexandria was celebrated in grandiose style and undoubtedly was planned in great detail. It is likely the toasts were planned and it is probable, that the following is the toast Swift was to give to Lafayette— "Jonathan Swift Esq.— The man whom ten millions of freemen delight to honor." [2]

From the book *Lodge of Washington* by F. L. Brockett, is a description of the red carpet treatment Alexandria's citizens had planned for Lafayette.

"About 3 o'clock, General Lafayette, accompanied by the residue of the procession, passed through the Grand Arch, under a national salute of twenty-four guns. Of this Arch we can, indeed, say that for simplicity of style and yet for all of the beauties of design and ornament, it exceeded our most sanguine expectations. It extended from one side of Washington Street to the other, forming a front sixty-four feet, and in height forty feet. From the columns on which the Arch rested, rose two pyramids, surmounted with flag-staffs, upon one of which was hoisted the national flag of France, and on the other that of the United States. On the north front of the Arch, in large letters, was painted: 'Welcome Lafayette—a Nation's gratitude thy due.' And on the south front: 'For a Nation to be free, it is sufficient that she wills it.' On the top of the Arch, were a liberty cap, and a real mountain eagle, which was politely furnished by Mr. Timothy Mountford, of the Museum.

"As the General passed the Arch, on the first gun being fired, the eagle spread his wings, and showed too much advantage. A ship, fully rigged, emblematical of the Navy, was hung beneath the Arch, and added much to the appearance. The columns were splendidly ornamented with national designs. From the large Arch two smaller ones were thrown over the side pavement tastefully decorated. On the top of one was an elegant figure, representing peace; on the other, one representing plenty. On the north front of the side arches, the following inscriptions were placed: 'Washington, 1824, Lafayette; Lafayette, 1777, Washington.' On the south front: 'Honor, virtutis praemium, 1781,'—'Ubi libertas ibi patria, 1778.' The portraits of Washington and Lafayette were conspicuously hung on the sides of the columns. The whole was handsomely ornamented with flowers, the cedar, the laurel, the oak, and various other products of the forest. Nothing on paper can give a proper idea of the beauty of the whole. It was not only the admiration of our own citizens, but strangers from all quarters spoke of it in high terms. This Arch was erected by the patriotic citizens of the town, and as a free-will offering of the spirit of our town, we should hope it might be allowed to stand. It is ornamental, and it at least might abide as it is till the General returns."

The following is another account of that visit from Lafayette passed down to descendants of Jonathan Swift. "When Lafayette revisited America in 1824, a triumphal arch was erected in Alexandria, Virginia, to welcome him. This portrait was placed in the center of the arch. When his carriage reached the arch, Lafayette stopped it, rose, took off his hat and, turning to my Grandmother, Ann Foster Swift, who sat beside him, said 'That is the most life like portrait of my good friend that I have ever seen.'" [16]

Art of the Swift's

The portrait of George Washington mentioned in these excerpts was owned by Jonathan Swift, and was painted by Charles Willson Peale (1741-

1827). The name of the portrait is "George Washington at Princeton." On January 21st of 2006, another Washington portrait by Peale, which was also called "George Washington at Princeton", sold at Christie's auction house in New York for $21.3 million dollars. As mentioned, Rembrandt Peale, also a famous American artist, and son of Charles Willson Peale, painted Ann Foster Swift's portrait in 1824. John Wesley Jarvis, the artist who painted the portrait of General Joseph Gardner Swift for the Military Academy, West Point, also painted a portrait of Jonathan Swift's son, William Roberdeau Swift. Charles King painted Ann Roberdeau Swift's portrait in 1827. Charles Willson Peale was one of the most important American artists of his time, and knowing this certainly contributes in bringing the life of Jonathan Swift into clearer focus.

It is believed that there is no individual portrait of Jonathan Swift. The following excerpt is from *The Memoirs of Gen. Joseph Gardner Swift*. "His [Jonathan] valuable papers, among which were many letters from Gen. Washington, were all lost at sea soon after the death of his son, while being sent to New York. His portrait, which was painted abroad, was so injured on the voyage home that he destroyed it." The book, *Genealogy of the Roberdeau Family*, also supports this assertion.

The locations of the portraits of Ann Foster, William R., and Ann Roberdeau Swift are unknown at this time.

The Indianapolis Museum of Art (IMA) now owns this marvelous portrait of Washington, and its provenance is recorded as follows: Painted with the consent of George Washington for Jonathan Swift, of Alexandria, Virginia; William Patten, Rhinebeck, New York; Mrs. William (Grace Bigelow) Patten; Mr. John Bigelow Patten, Rhinebeck, New York; and, Mr. and Mrs. Nicholas H. Noyes, who presented the portrait to The John Herron Art Museum. Herron's art collection formed the nucleus of what would become one of the largest art museums in the United States, the IMA. The portraits accession number is 53.64.

The following is from "The Bulletin of the Art Association of Indianapolis, Indiana-John Herron Art Institute" Vol. XLI October 1954, page #26-29.

"THE SWIFT-PATTEN PORTRAIT OF WASHINGTON"
"The painting George Washington at Princeton, reproduced on our cover, has come to be known as the "Swift-Patten" portrait of Washington for the names of its previous owners. The picture has now been presented to the Museum by Mr. and Mrs. Nicholas H. Noyes,

of Indianapolis.

"The standard reference work on the painter Charles Willson Peale is that by Charles Coleman Sellers, published in 1947; our picture was not mentioned in that book, but Mr. Sellers has now studied the picture in the original, as well as the existing documents concerning it, and has made for us the following report of his findings. –EDITOR"

"'I [Charles Coleman Sellers] have examined with great care and great interest the Swift-Patten portrait of Washington, together with a statement of the family tradition concerning it, and the documentation by which this tradition is supported.

"'The tradition follows a pattern common to many Washington portraits. It is said to have been painted from life, by Charles Willson Peale, soon after the Battle of Princeton, the scene of which is represented in its background, and to have been the gift of Washington to his friend, Jonathan Swift (1764-1824), a merchant of Alexandria, Virginia. On June 11, 1858, General Joseph Gardner Swift (1783-1865) noted in his diary: 'June 11th, my cousins, the Pattens, visited us. I gave them my certificate of my knowledge of a portrait of Washington by the elder Peale, after the 'Battle of Princeton,' painted by the consent of Washington for my uncle Jonathan Swift of Alexandria, where in 1804, and onward, I saw it, and my uncle gave me its history as above.'...The "certificate" referred to here is published in full in the *Genealogy of the Roberdeau Family* by Roberdeau Buchanan...Its significant statements are: 'My Uncle Jonathan, whose property it was, used to say it was 'more natural' than Stuart's, and was painted by the elder Peale before the surrender of Yorktown... Cousin Nancy, Mrs. Jonathan T. Patten, daughter of Jonathan Swift, told me Rembrandt Peale recognized the portrait above mentioned as being from the pencil of his father.'

"From my experience in tracing many such statements to their foundations, I can accept the following as facts: (1) The portrait was in the Alexandria home of Jonathan Swift in 1804, and, since that had been Joseph G. Swift's first visit to his uncle there, may well have been, in the house for a period of years. (2) The portrait was painted 'by consent of Washington.' This is a different matter from the oft-repeated tradition of a gift. Washington actually gave very few portraits of himself to others. As a point of politeness, however, friends and acquaintances asked his permission to hang portraits of

105

him in their houses, and from this exchange of courtesies has grown the stories of gifts. The diary statement has the ring of truth, and I believe it should be accepted that this portrait was purchased by Jonathan Swift during Washington's lifetime and with Washington's permission. Washington first met Swift at Mount Vernon, January 19 1785, as his diary records: Elkanah Watson 'and a Mr. Swift, Merchant in Alexandria, came in, and stayed all Night.' There is sufficient evidence that Swift called at Mount Vernon on other occasions, that he and Washington had business relations relating to land, and social relations, in fact that Swift was one of the managers of the Alexandria Dancing Assembly, to which the Washington's were invited.

"The statement that the painting was by 'the elder Peale,' and the concurrence in this of his son, Rembrandt Peale, is worthy of consideration. But both factors have appeared so often in connection with paintings proven to have been the work of other members of the Peale family that they cannot be considered conclusive. Final evidence must come from the picture itself, and from a knowledge of the Peale family and of the Peale studio in Philadelphia where it was probably painted.

"The portrait is in its original condition, with no evidence of retouching or overpainting. The face repeats the likeness of the so-called 'Constitutional Convention' portrait, painted by Charles Willson Peale from life at Philadelphia in July, 1787 (Pennsylvania Academy of the Fine Arts, and repeated by him in a replica of December, 1788 (Yale University Art Gallery). The face in the Swift-Patten portrait is strikingly similar to that in this replica of 1788, and could certainly be attributed to Charles Willson Peale.

"The rest of the picture, however, a half-length pose with hat and sword hilt and Princeton background is known positively to have been repeated a number of times by Charles Willson Peale's student and ward, his nephew, Charles Peale Polk (1767-1822). The red tone in the sky is particularly characteristic of Polk. It is worthy of note that while Charles Willson Peale would have given us the background scene in darker color and clearer definition, this younger painter has either a sense for atmospheric perspective which his elder lacked, or realizes, as his uncle apparently did not, that these pale tones give greater prominence to his central figure. Polk, whose father had been killed in a Revolutionary naval battle and whose mother had died at about the same time, had been from the age of ten a member of a painting family. Charles Willson Peale did not take up the brush until about the age of twenty-two, but had had the advantage of European training. These different beginnings and their reflection in the styles of the two men present a most interesting contrast which can be seen in this and other Washington portraits from the Peale studio.

"Polk was married in 1785. Charles Willson Peale helped him in every way possible to establish himself as an artist, as he did with his brother, James, and, later, with his son, Rembrandt Peale. An essential to a good start in the profession was a portrait of the First Citizen. There would be a steady demand for repetitions of it. It would be a valuable attraction in the artist's exhibitions. And it would serve as a recommendation to new business, especially if the original had, in some way, Washington's sanction.

"Inconclusive as it may be, there is internal evidence that the Swift-Patten portrait is the first of Polk's series, that it was painted in Peale's Philadelphia studio in 1788 or 1789, and that Peale himself brushed in the likeness. Polk's earliest signed Washington of which I know bears the date 1790. His first exhibition to include a WASHINGTON of which I have a record was advertised in the Maryland Gazette, May 24, 1791. The fact that this canvas is unsigned is evidence, again, of a joint effort. It interested me that in certain lights it can be seen that the fence was painted complete across the right side of the canvas before the addition of the hat, which now covers much of it. This carries a suggestion that the hat was added over a simpler composition, then repeated thus in the other portraits –that this may be the first in Polk's series.

"It has some significance that the wife of Jonathan Swift was a daughter of General Daniel Roberdeau, who had known Charles Willson Peale well. They had served together in the Philadelphia campaigns and had been associated in politics afterward. The Swift's would have been friendly to Polk, but likely to insist that their portrait of Washington be by Charles Willson Peale. It may have been sold to them with the understanding that it was 'by the elder Peale.' All this is in the realm of supposition, as Polk still remains a shadowy figure, much on the road, whose future biographer must reconstruct his life mostly from the portraits scattered through Maryland and Virginia, and his character from his precise, his simply and boldly forthright style of painting.

Charles Coleman Sellers"

[Footnotes]

"Oil on canvas, 32 X 29 inches. This portrait was exhibited at the Opera House, New York, at the time of the Inaugural Centennial. In 1931 the picture was lent for exhibition at the Smithsonian Institution by its owner William Patten of Rhinebeck, New York. In 1932 the portrait was reproduced, in part, on a four-cent stamp in one of the George Washington Bicentennial series of postage stamps. The Princeton University campus is represented in the background of the painting."

In this letter written by Mr. Sellers, the "certificate/letter" he refers to, but omits, was written by General Joseph Gardner Swift. Several important historical issues pertinent to the family tradition of the portrait are listed in this letter. The following excerpt is Gen. Swift's letter in its entirety from *Genealogy of the Roberdeau Family*, by Roberdeau Buchanan.

"...Jonathan Swift was also consular or commercial agent for seven European nations. He was an intimate friend of General Washington, and had a portrait of him by Peale, which is the subject of the following letter:

"Geneva, 12 June, 1858

"Jonathan T. Patten, Esq.

"Dear Sir: The portrait of Washington in your house has always appeared to me more natural than most of the attitudes of his that I have seen. The background in the painting is Princeton College, as it was in 1776. My Uncle Jonathan, whose property it was, used to say it was "more natural" than Stuart's, and was painted by the elder Peale before the surrender of Yorktown. In 1824, at the reception of Lafayette in Alexandria, this portrait was in the procession, as I was told, by loan of Aunt Nancy, and was recognized by Lafayette as a good likeness. At the museum he recognized the handwriting of Washington, "his early friend," in a note found on the wall, written to my uncle, Jonathan Swift, regretting, &c., "Mrs. Washington and his own dancing days were over." Cousin Nancy told me Rembrandt Peale recognized the portrait above mentioned as being from the pencil of his father. Tell your children, the grandchildren of Jonathan Swift and Nancy Roberdeau, his wife, that I have heard Alexander Hamilton, and Chief Justice Marshall, General C. C. Pinkney,

say that the vulgar report of Washington swearing at Lee at the battle of Monmouth was an idle tale, not true. His uniform language and deportment was ever grand and correct, tho' violent when provoked.

"Your friend and hum. Servt., J. G. Swift."

Charles Coleman Sellers (1903-1980) was a noted historian of early American, he was best known for his numerous works on the life, and artistry of his own great-grandfather, Charles Willson Peale. Mr. Sellers was the noted authority on the works of Charles Willson Peale. By his action of determining the authenticity of this Charles Willson Peale painting, it also determined Swift's portrait of Washington to be a national treasure.

In this letter of authentication written by Mr. Sellers, one will notice that he had obviously observed many portraits, which were purported to have been a Charles Willson Peale, but were not. While his confirming that this Swift-Patten portrait of Washington is indeed an authentic Peale was the primary importance of Mr. Sellers positive evaluation, he understandably had to "make a call" when it came to the family tradition account of the portrait. It seems obvious that the information made available to Mr. Sellers, pertinent to Jonathan Swift of Alexandria, was minimal. Apparently, the primary bit of information he was given about Swift was, that he was a merchant, and that he had on occasion, met George Washington. Had he been provided with more relevant information pertinent to Jonathan Swift's personal integrity, and historic importance, perhaps he may have more readily accepted the long told family tradition, that the portrait was a gift to Swift, from George Washington. The historical family tradition aspect of this great portrait surely equals or exceeds its worth as a Peale.

The family tradition of this portrait passed down from Jonathan Swift to General Joseph Gardner Swift, who was "a man of great integrity," and also to daughter, Ann Foster Swift-Patten, and on to William H. Patten, is as follows: Jonathan Swift said that the portrait was painted by "the elder Peale," Charles Willson Peale, and was painted sometime, "soon after the Battle of Princeton, in 1777," and "before the surrender of Yorktown in 1781." This would mean that the portrait would have originally been in the possession of George Washington, and was as family tradition indicates, presented by him to "his intimate friend Jonathan Swift," as a gift. Another family account of this historic portrait was as mentioned, when it was displayed on the "Triumphal Arch" in Alexandria, Virginia, during General Lafayette's return visit in 1824, which is also supported in part by F. L. Brockett's account of this event, in his book, *Lodge of Washington, A History of the Alexandria Washington Lodge #22.*

According to family tradition the provenance of the portrait would be as follows: Painted by Charles Willson Peale, and presented to George Washington, who presented the portrait to his friend Jonathan Swift, and upon his death was in the possession of his widow, Ann Roberdeau Swift, then passed to her daughter, Ann Foster Swift-Patten, and her husband Jonathan T. Patten, then passed to son, William Swift Patten, then passed to son, William H. Patten, then passed to son, John Bigelow Patten, which it then went to Mr. and Mrs. Nicholas Noyes, who presented the portrait to The Herron Art Gallery, which is now the Indianapolis Art Museum.

Another proud moment in the history of this portrait occurred in 1932, when it was included in the issue of the "Washington Bicentennial Commemorative U. S. Postage Stamps." The following information is from the web site-- "United States Postage stamps. History." "The stamp is printed in warm brown and has a narrow rectangular border indented at the sides and end…" "Within the large oval is the likeness of Washington taken from a painting by Charles Willson Peale. The painting was donated to the National Portrait Gallery by its former owner, Mr. William Patten, Rhinebeck, N.Y."

In regards to the portrait being donated by Mr. Patten, it is believed that the portrait was only on loan to the National Portrait Gallery.

Of the early caretakers of the portrait, it seems apparent there were none more proud of that responsibility than, William Hardman Patten (1865-1936), of Rhinebeck, New York. Among Mr. Patten's accomplishments was being the art editor for Harper's Weekly, and in 1899 the portrait was featured on a title page. From Jean Elliot's unpublished article "Kindly But Alien Hands," there is a quote from Mr. Patten-- 'At the time of the Washington Memorial Exhibition at the Metropolitan Opera House, N.Y., in the spring of 1889, this portrait was accepted by the late Charles Henry Hart of Philadelphia, the recognized authority on Washington portraits at the time and author of a book on the subject. Standing in front of the portrait, which he had not seen before, he said to me 'Probably the most painstakingly drawn portrait of Washington in his prime. It is to Charles Wilson Peale that we must look if we would see how Washington looked at that time…'" It is because of W. H. Patten, that the U.S. Postal Service used the likeness of the portrait for the Four-Cent stamp of that commemorative issue of 1932. This portrait is in perfect condition, and the Patten families were the caretakers of this portrait for well over one hundred years.

Swift's portrait of Washington may be further evidence of many months of preplanning for Lafayette's return visit; Swift no doubt volunteered the use of the portrait before he died.

"Though Jonathan Swift's affairs were left in poor shape, his widow sent Foster, their youngest, to Quaker Benjamin Hallowell's famous school in January. Alas, Foster, just sixteen, expired early the next year." Ann Swift, finding it increasingly difficult to meet the annual $133.33 for ground rent, proffered Belle Aire for sale in March 1827.[16]

Ann (Nancy) Swift died, January 31, 1833.[66]

"Ann Roberdeau Swift, was buried in Madison Court House the...; her only surviving son, William Roberdeau, would only out live her 'til October, dying in Washington, North Carolina, at forty-six." [15]

From a document signed at Madison Court House in June 1834, it states in part:

"Whereas Jonathan Swift, late of the county of Alexandria...was at the time of his death seized and possessed of a certain house and lot situated in the said Town of Alexandria...and which house and lot was subject to a certain annual rent of $133.33 payable to Charles Alexander, his heirs and assigns and which rent having been long in arrears and unpaid and William R. Swift and others as heirs of the said Jonathon Swift declining to pay up said arrears and entering again into the possession of said property..etc."[15]

Commentary and Miscellany

As mentioned, in 1929 Belle Aire/Colross was moved from the 1100 block of Oronoco Street in Alexandria to Princeton, New Jersey where present day it stands, and is used as the main administration building for Princeton Day School. From the years 1929 to 2004 the 1100 block of Oronoco had been used for commercial purposes. A large Printers facility, a car wash, and an electric sub-station were built there.

In 2004/05 all these structures were razed, for the purpose of building a large retail and condominium complex. As required under the Alexandria Archaeological Protection Ordinance the project developer was required to hire an archaeological firm to excavate and document the Colross site before construction could begin.

Amazingly, if not miraculously, under the slabs of concrete from the former commercial structures the last remnants of Swift's Grasshopper Hall was waiting to be rediscovered, allowing one final glimpse into it's former glory. A brief description of the unearthed discoveries is as follows: 1) The basement floor, which was mostly intact, was laid in brick in a stylish herringbone pattern. 2) The basement walls, which were also laid with brick. 3) The foundation remnants of outbuildings such as the smokehouse, servants quarters, and stables. 4) A complete cistern, which is described as being complex in its design, and 5) What is surmised to be "remnants of a burial vault."

To quote archaeologist, Steven J. Shephard, from an "Alexandria-Arlington" article in "The Washington Post" dated September 8, 2005, "The house may be gone, but the site's excavation will have a lasting impact on the city."

The burial vault was built by, Thomson Mason some time around 1833. Mason lived in the mansion after the Swift's. One of the primary objectives of the archaeological excavation was to determine if there were undiscovered human remains, and none were found on the site.

It is unknown at this time where Jonathan Swift is buried.

The logical place of his interment is the historic First Presbyterian Church of Alexandria. There are many unmarked graves there, and it is there where at least three of their children are known to be buried. The only reference discovered during this investigation mentioning his burial indicates that he was buried at Colross, with Masonic Honors. According to conversations with local archaeologists, "it is believed that Swift may have owned the block property to the north of the Colross city block, and it is possible he may have been buried there." When researching cemeteries that have been typically used when a body is exhumed and relocated no mention of Swift was found. The records searched at this time have only been pertinent to city burials. It is hoped, due to recent events such as the Colross excavation, as well as this work, an arousal of public interest may lead to the discovery of the burial site of one of Alexandria's and the United States of America's most colorful citizens, Jonathan Swift.

It is probable that the British financially ruined Swift in 1814 when they plundered Alexandria. One can only guess the amount of merchandise and ships that were stolen, scuttled etc. that he lost due to the British invasion.

As far as finding anything to tie Swift to any sort of silver connections, one would not expect to find anything. However a few curiosities were found by way of possible family connections and one interesting story of a silver mine. Swift leased a sail loft to Thomas Sanford, a sail maker [39], sometime prior to January of 1810. One of the oldest known silversmiths of Alexandria, Edmond Sanford, operated from 1773-1813. Other silversmiths in Alexandria were John Mason from 1785-1798, John Mason II from 1808-1810, and Thomas Mason from 1795-1797.[23] It is unknown if Sanford, the sail maker, and Sanford, the silversmith, was related or that the Masons, the silversmiths, and the Mason who purchased Belle Aire were related. Although, it is probable they were related.

The following is an excerpt from *The Silver and The Silversmiths of Alexandria, Virginia.* by Barbara E. Taylor, April 1976:

"…Another source documents the presence of silversmiths in Alexandria in 1775. On March 16, of that year, Nicholas Cresswell, a young Englishman in Alexandria, confirmed the existence of manufacturing smiths in town when he wrote in his journal 'Got some silver trinkets made by a silversmith in town…' mention of 'trinkets' indicates another aspect of the silversmithing business—the Indian trade. Pieces of American-made silver were given to Indians as tokens of peace or in exchange for furs. The custom started at an early date and was not unique to Alexandria silversmiths. 'Gorgets, protective throat plates, and the last vestiges of full suits of armor were among the earliest desirable ornaments presented to the Indians.' "A few days later, Cresswell writes in his journal that he went to look at a silver mine. It seems he was unconvinced that the metal he saw was silver. This is a particularly interesting comment as it is an unresolved question where the Alexandria silversmiths got their silver. It has generally been assumed that old pieces of silver or silver coins were melted down and refashioned into newer styles. If a silver mine had existed in the area, it is probable that it would have been mentioned in the Alexandria papers."

Approximately forty-eight silversmiths and apprentices lived in Alexandria during Swift's forty years there.[23]

Robert Townsend Hooe, whose name appears on Swift's indenture in Alexandria as witness and was at noted Swift activities, bought the 60,000 acres that Banks & Barbour owned that adjoined the Swift Property #1 of 20,718 ¾ acres; Hooe bought it on August 5, 1792.

In 1787, Swift moved his business between Dr. Craik and Fitzgerald, which seems that Swift and Craik would have seen each other frequently. As noted in the 1793 and 1794, letters from Craik (Chapter Two of this book) to Swift and Swift to Craik at the Nelson County Clerk's Office in Bardstown, Kentucky, it seems they had not seen each other for some considerable time, because Craik was interested in the 20,718 ¾ acres (Swift Property #1) that Swift had already sold to Kerr on May 8, 1792, which could be some indication of the amount of time Swift spent in Kentucky.

As mentioned, on the 18th of September 1793, Swift was recorded as being present at the Masonic Lodge at the laying of the cornerstone of the United States Capitol Building. Dr. Craik's letter to Kentucky authorizing his attorney, John Taylor, to purchase property from Swift was dated September 3, 1793. If John Taylor or Dr. Craik had seen Swift before the letter was written, they would have known that the 20,718 ¾ acres of land had already been sold by Swift to Kerr in 1792. If Dr. Craik had given the letter to Taylor at Alexandria, then apparently Taylor and Swift (who were both present at Bardstown in February of 1794) did not travel to Kentucky together. All this makes one consider the possibility that Swift may not have been present at the cornerstone laying, but may have been in Kentucky on business as well as putting together another land package for Dr. Craik.

If Swift was an officer of the Masonic Lodge in 1793, it is possible that he was only listed as an officer of the attending lodge. Without seeing the way the secretary of the lodge actually worded the minutes, one can only assume he was there at the cornerstone function, which would mean that he did not see Dr. Craik or John Taylor some considerable time before and after the September 3, 1793 letter, (which seems very improbable) and he left for Kentucky sometime after September 18, 1793. To reiterate a previous point--he was listed as a lodge member making a toast to Lafayette two months after he had died.

There are other points of information in regards to constructing a Jonathan Swift timeline, which should not be considered as conclusive at this time. There were different years and time periods with little or no information on Jonathan Swift. There were primarily two of these time periods that provoke the most curiosity. From December 27, 1787 to February of 1789, no information of his activities was found. This would have been in the time period that John Filson had met "a certain man named Swift." Swift was present in December of 1787 when Lord Fairfax preached. From the *Virginia Journal and Alexandria Advertiser* by Pippenger and Munson, Swift ran ads in April, June, August and October 25, 1787. The ads stopped and reappeared again in October 26, 1789, where four ads were listed from October to November of 1789. From *The Memoirs of Gen. Joseph Gardner Swift*, it was found that Swift's wife, Ann Roberdeau Swift, gave birth to a son November 12, 1789. If the normal nine month pregnancy applies, this would have placed Jonathan in Alexandria as early as February of 1789. The unnamed boy child died the following day. Also, from 1790 to 1795, very little information on Swift was available. This was the time period he was purchasing properties in Kentucky. In 1790, from January to May, ads are listed, but nothing else after May 1790. The *Virginia Journal and Alexandria Advertiser* series, by Pippenger and Munson, used in this investigation was in five volumes with dates from February 5, 1784 to November 1790. There was no additional information on ads that Swift placed after November 1790.

In 1791, he was recorded as being present at the District of Columbia cornerstone laying.

No information on Jonathan Swift was found for 1792.

In September of 1793, he was present at the laying of the United States Capitol corner stone. (As previously noted, this may be questionable).

No information on Jonathan Swift was found for 1794 and 1795.

In 1796, Swift purchased property in Alexandria in January and October.

For other years, of course, little or no information is found, but from 1788 and early to middle of the 1790's, are the time periods that are most important to this investigation. Not all of the old gazettes and advertisers and court records of Alexandria and Fairfax County etc. have been scoured. The time gaps just mentioned should not be considered conclusive of his actions/transactions of those years.

Jonathan Swift of Alexandria, Virginia, does match the profile given of the "Swift" described in the Swift journals and the legend, nearly perfectly. He had definitely, heaped up great riches, owned or was in charge of several ships, was adventurous and he was in Kentucky and owned property there.

There is one major exception-- this Swift was by all indications, a good man, who was a devoted husband, father, civil servant, church member, mason, and president of the Trustees of the Poor. He proved himself courageous and self-sacrificing for his fellow Alexandrians during the War of 1812. The quality of people he was associated with was beyond comparison and he came from a long line of good people.

Jonathan Swift had come from Milton, Massachusetts.[67 & 59] The following excerpts are from *The History of Milton, Mass. 1640-1887* edited by A.K. Teele, which further verifies previous information on Swift already mentioned. It also provides his genealogy back to the first Swift, in Jonathan's line, who came to America. This book also provided some interesting information on the origins of Gulliver's Travels by Dean Jonathan Swift 1667-1745, and the lives of the Swifts and the Gullivers of the town of Milton.

Swift Estate

"In the old survey made by James Blake, 1747, from the Town House in Boston to the Governor's farm in Milton, the estates are given along the line, and probably all the principal houses then standing. On the south side of Neponset river appear two buildings, one on the site occupied by the present chocolate mill, another where the house occupied by the late Dr. Ware stands; then, ascending the hill on the east side, the "Stanley house," occupied by Wade; the next is the Miller house, far over the hill; and on the south-west side of the road, nearly opposite the Miller house, the Swift house; the Daniels, Kinsley, Babcock, Holman, and Gulliver houses follow.

115

"The old Swift house stood in the field on the south-west side of Adams Street. About forty rods from the street, below the barn of Mr. Dudley, a depression in the field plainly indicates the position of the cellar and house.

"Thomas Swift, [first generation American] son of Robert, of Rotherham, Yorkshire, England, first appears in the Town Records of Dorchester, November 22, 1634. He was a maltster by trade, but followed agriculture. He left a large estate, for the times. Among the household goods that he brought from England was a carved oak chair, very antique and beautiful, which is now in the possession of Miss Elizabeth R. Swift of Milton Hill. At one time he owned a large tract of land extending over many hundred acres, said to be about 1,400, in the north-east part of Unquity. On this were two houses, one of them built as early as 1649. In one of these Mr. Swift lived; the other was occupied by Henry Merifield. (See Suffolk Deeds, Lib. 13, Fol.408) He died May 4, 1675, and was buried in the old Dorchester burying ground, where are now to be seen the large slabs of stone then placed over his grave to protect it from wolves.

"Deacon Thomas Swift [second generation American], oldest son of Thomas, was born June 17, 1635. He married Elizabeth Vose, daughter of Robert Vose, of Milton, in 1657. She died January 15, 1675. He married again October 16, 1676, Sarah Clapp, of Milton. Deacon Swift received from his father-in-law Vose, in 1659, nineteen and three-fourths acres of upland in Milton, confirmed to him by deed February 23, 1663. (Suffolk Deeds Lib. 42, Fol.33) This was in the region of School street, opposite the house of the late Wm. Davis, Canton avenue, stretching towards Churchill's lane. Here he settled at the time of his first marriage, and became one of the most enterprising and useful citizens of Milton. He was selectman for thirty-five years, 1668-1704, inclusive, excepting the year 1677, and filled various other offices in the town and colony. May 5, 1676, he was made quarter-master of a troop of horse, as had been his father, with the rank of lieutenant. He was appointed by the General Court to the charge of the Neponset Indians, and was constantly active in the Indian wars. He was one of the founders of the Milton Church, signing the covenant August 24, 1678. August 20, 1682, he was ordained deacon. He died January 26, 1718. His wife died the day after his funeral.

"We have no data from which to decide when the Swift house was built on the south-west side of Adams street. It is known, however, to have been standing there in 1747, and may have been the house built prior to 1649. Subsequently a house was built on the opposite side of Adams street, where most of the family yet to be spoken were born.

"William Swift, son of Deacon Thomas, was killed in the disastrous expedition against Quebec, 1690. He was a member of Captain John Withington's Company, Dorchester.

"Col. Samuel Swift, [third generation American] the youngest son of Deacon Thomas, was born in Milton, December 10, 1683. He married Ann, daughter of Thomas Holman, of Milton, a prominent man of his day. Col. Samuel Swift was one of the wealthiest and most influential men of Milton. He, like his father, filled many offices of trust and importance in the town. He was Judge of the Court of Common Pleas, Colonel of the militia, and Representative to the General Court; moderator of the town-meetings for eleven years, between 1734 and 1747, and selectman for fifteen years, between 1735 and his death, 1747. His second son, Samuel Swift, [fourth generation American] was a distinguished barrister in Boston to whom reference is made in another place."

Anthony Gulliver

"Anthony Gulliver was born in 1619, and died in Milton November 28, 1706, aged 87 years. He removed from Braintree to Unquity in 1646. He bought land of Edward and Richard Hutchinson, sons and heirs of Richard Hutchinson, bounded north by Gulliver's creek, to which he gave the name. He married Elenor, daughter of Stephen Kinsley, and had five sons and four daughters. Lydia, b. 1651, m. Jas. Leonard; Samuel, b. 1653, d, 1676; Jonathan, b. October 27, 1659; Stephen, b. 1663; John b. December 3, 1669; Hannah, m. Tucker; Mary, m. Atherton; Elizabeth b. November 6, 1671; Nathaniel, b. November 10, 1675, m. Hanna Billings.

"His house, built on Squantum street, on the north side of the brook, was taken down about thirty-eight years ago. The imported brick used in the chimney bore date of 1680. This house was known later as the Rawson house, --David Rawson having married into the Gulliver family.

"At an early date Anthony Gulliver came into possession of a large tract of land in the central part of the town, most of which is now embraced in the estate of Col. H.S. Russell. This land was long owned and occupied by the Gulliver family, and here or on land adjacent thereto some of his descendants have lived ever since.

"His second son, Lieutenant Jonathan Gulliver, one of the leading men of his day, married Theodora, daughter of Rev. Peter Thacker, Milton's first pastor.

"Anthony Gulliver was the progenitor of a long line of solid and trustworthy men and women, who have been conspicuous in the history of the Church and Town of Milton, holding many of the important offices, and faithfully meeting the trusts imposed on them for nearly two centuries. The family is still represented amount our citizens. This name appears under various forms of spelling, as: Caliphar, Colliford, Cullifer, Gullwer, Gouliver, Gulliwer, Gullifer, Gulliver."

Foot-Path From Country Highway to Meeting-House

"In May 1672, a foot-path, four feet wide, was laid out by Anthony Gulliver, Thomas Swift, and John Fenno, from the 'County Heigh Waye' to the meeting house. It began at, or near, Algerine corner, and ran for a short distance nearly in the course of Centre street then it passed over upon the land of B.F. Dudley."

"Gulliver's Travels"

"It is said that Dean Swift received the suggestion of his 'Gulliver's Travels' from one of this family. Capt. Lemuel Gulliver, who, according to James M. Robbins, once lived at Algerine Corner, returned to Ireland in 1723, and described the country and its productions and resources to his neighbor, Jonathan Swift, in the most extravagant and high-wrought colors; in which line of description he was favored with especial gifts. The frogs, he declared, reached up to his knees, and had musical voices like the twang of a guitar, and the mosquitoes had bills as large as darning needles; from these and similar exaggerated stories, the fertile mind of the great writer conceived and wrought out the famous 'Gulliver's Travels,' which appeared in 1726, exhibiting a singular 'union of misanthropy, satire, irony, ingenuity, and humor.'"

Samuel Swift, Esq.

"In 1768 there were twenty-five barristers in the whole of Massachusetts. Ten of these were Boston; of this number was Samuel Swift [fourth generation American]. He was the second son of Col. Samuel Swift, born at the homestead of Milton Hill, July 19, 1715.

He graduated at Harvard in 1735, and studied law with the distinguished counselor Jeremiah Gridley; he was a member of the Ancient and Honorable Artillery. He married Sarah Tyler, by whom he had one daughter. His second wife was Ann Foster, of Dorchester, by whom he had two sons—Foster, born January 20, 1760 and *Jonathan*, born 1764 --and four daughters. Foster was a physician in Taunton, and was the father of General Joseph G. Swift. U.S. Army, who was one of the first cadets at West Point. Jonathan became a merchant and settled in Virginia. President Adams often speaks of Samuel Swift in his diary. He says, 1766, --'Spent the evening at Sam Adams very socially with brother Swift.'
"In a letter to William Wirt, who was writing the life of Patrick Henry, he says; --
'Among the illustrious men who were agents in the Revolution must be remembered the name of Samuel Swift.'

"When General Gage offered the freedom of the town of Bostonians who would deposit their arms in the British Arsenal, Mr. Swift opposed the movement. He presided at a meeting where it was covertly agreed to use their concealed arms, also pitchforks and axes, to assail the soldiers on Boston Common. This scheme was revealed to General Gage, and Mr. Swift was arrested. He was permitted to visit his family, then at Newton, upon his parole to return at a given time. At the appointed time he returned, against the remonstrance of his friends, and so high an opinion of his character was entertained by General Gage that he was permitted to occupy his own house under surveillance. From disease induced by confinement, he died a prisoner in his own house, a martyr to freedom's cause, August 31, 1775. He was interred in his tomb, which had formerly belonged to the father of his first wife, Samuel Tyler, Esq."

The following excerpt from *The Memoirs of Gen. Joseph Gardner Swift* is a complete list of the children of Jonathan and Ann Roberdeau Swift—
"CHILDREN"
--"A son, still born Oct. 10, 1786
--William Roberdeau, b. Aug. 29, 1787; d. Oct., 1833; m. Aug. 1, 1815, Mary Donaldson (s. Apr. 30, 1870, aged 83), dau. of Edward Harper, of Alexandria; early was in the counting-room of Wm.

Taylor, and made voyages for this house as supercargo with great success; was afterwards established as a merchant in Baltimore with Eli Adams; finally moved to Washington, N.C., where he died, s.p. Oct. 1833.

--A son, b. Nov. 12, 1789; d. Nov. 13, 1789.

--Daniel Roberdeau, b. Nov. 9, 1790; d. unm. Aug. 1825.

--Jonathan, b. Dec. 2, 1792; d. July 1, 1793.

--Isaac Bostwick, b. Feb. 2, 1795.

--Ann Selina, b. Feb. 18, 1797; d. July 18, 1798

--GEO. Washington, b. Feb. 11, 1800; d. unm. Sept. 19, 1819.

--Ann Foster, b. Oct. 11, 1802; m. Jan. 13, 1829, Jonathan T. Patten, a prosperous wholesale merchant of New York, where they still reside. For their children, see Roberdeau Genealogy.

--Mary Selina, b. Jan. 18, 1805; m. Aug. 8, 1826, Henry Allison, b. in Ba. Dec. 23, 1793; d. Dec. 26, 1871; settled in Missouri, where, at Brownsville, Mrs. A. lives For children, see Roberdeau Genealogy.

--Wm. Taylor, b. Sept. 20, 1808; d. next day.

--Foster, b. May 20, 1810; d. unm. Sept., 1825."

From *Genealogy of the Roberdeau Family* further information is obtained in regards to "Isaac Bostwick" Swift.

"Isaac Bostwick Swift.—Born February 2, 1795; died July 18, 1797. The church register, probably erroneously, gives the name Isaac Roberdeau; the family record is as above."

The following is believed to be the list of countries Swift served as consular or commercial agent—

1. Sweden
2. Denmark
3. Holland
4. Portugal
5. Brazil
6. The Netherlands
7. Morocco
8. Russia

Due to the incredible amount of information on Jonathan Swift of Alexandria, Virginia, he certainly is not the man described in some of the Swift silver mines stories and journals, but the information gathered makes a convincing case that he is the Swift of the silver mine legend. To be sure whatever silver mining activities he may or may not have had in Kentucky, it would have been by no means a definitive description of his life.

THE SILVER MINE TWIST

PART TWO

QUINCUNX

CHAPTER FOUR

From this point forward, the assembly of the Swift silver mine hypothesis begins and this point should be stressed: conjecture will be mingled with the facts, which have been and will be presented.

In these next pages reasonable proof will be provided to better establish that the Jonathan Swift of the prior biographical chapter is indeed the very Swift of the silver mine legend. Providing further remarkable information on Swift Property #1 (the 20,718 ¾ acres), would seem to establish it as a possible location of the Swift silver mine. By piecing the original surveys together to approximate the location of the property, according to this method, the heart of the 20,718 ¾ Swift property is near the Hudson Lookout Tower. This is near the little town of Hudson in south Breckinridge County, Kentucky.

By using only the survey of William Bell's 75,000 acre property that borders the Swift property on the northeast, it appeared that the Swift land was located more near the town of Madrid in south Breckinridge County. By using, in addition to the Bell property, the two 50,000 acre tracts that adjoined Bell's land on the northeast, the 60,000 acre Barbour and Banks property that adjoined Swift's land on the north and the 113,482 acre tract that adjoined that 60,000 acre tract on the north, it proved one half of the property to be located in Breckinridge County and the other half located in west Hardin County. As previously mentioned the landmark most easily recognizable which is nearest the center of the property is the Hudson Lookout Tower near Hudson, Kentucky.

Historically, when the Spanish were in this country mining silver and gold, they marked their mines and caches of silver or gold bars by using landmarks on high points or easily recognizable areas to the cardinal points of the compass, north, south, east and west, of the mine/cache. The intersecting

123

lines of the marked areas would reveal the area of the mine. This method of marking is what Swift described to John Filson, judging by the wording of Filson's 1,000 acre land entry he made in 1788, noted in Chapter One on this book. Swift said the mine was in the center of the four cardinal points of the compass where the lines intersect. Then other methods would be used to hone in on the exact location, such as engraved stones, commonly called Spanish markers, or a detailed map.

If this is true, the Swift Property #1 has become more than just interesting.

The following information is based on the process of piecing together the original surveys of Virginia and Kentucky land grants. The size of the properties, their relation to the watercourses, and their proximity to each other as mentioned on the surveys and indentures, was the method used to determine the general location of the properties. While the information to be presented is believed to indicate an approximate location of Swift Property #1, it should not be considered conclusive at this time.

Based on the method of piecing together the original land surveys to approximate the location of the property, about 6½ miles in a straight line from the eastern most property line of the 20,718¾ acre tract is the town of "Eastview" in Hardin County, five and one half miles west of the west property line of the 20,718¾ acres is the town of "Westview" in Breckinridge County, five and one half miles north east from the northern most point of the 20,718 ¾ acres is the town of "Grandview" in Hardin County, and one mile south of the south property line of the 20,718 ¾ acres is the town of "Centerview" in Breckinridge County.

If one draws a straight line from Grandview to Centerview and from Eastview to Westview, the lines intersect at the Hudson lookout tower in the very heart of the 20,718 ¾ acres of land that Jonathan Swift of Alexandria, Virginia purchased in 1791… **"X Marks The Spot!"**

Some will choose to believe that this is only coincidental. It must be pointed out, though, that Jonathan Swift, the very man known to be associated with the elusive silver mine, owned this 20,718 ¾ acre property with the many matching landmarks described in the Swift journal. With it being located within the intersecting lines of the four "View" towns, the odds are enormously against it being a coincidence. It would seem that Swift Property #1 is indeed a possible location of Swift's silver mine.

One should also consider this to be a very solid affirmation indicating that Jonathan Swift of Alexandria, Virginia and husband of Ann Roberdeau Swift was the *Swift* of the Swift silver mine legend. Theoretically speaking;

these four view towns, which are located to "the cardinal points of the compass" of the Swift property, conceivably, could have been checkpoints on the old traces/roads leading into the heart of the property. It certainly does appear that someone believed there was something of importance there.

It is also probable, as indicated by the naming of these towns, that from a hill or knob one would have a clear view of the portion of the property, of which the names of these towns imply. An elevated point near the town Eastview would have a clear view of the "east side" of the 20,718 ¾ acres. A clear view of the west side of the property may be had from an elevated point near Westview. The town of Centerview indicates that the central area of the property may be viewed from there. The word "grand," in Grandview, alludes to an exalted or elevated level, which clearly indicates that it is located in a position from which one may view the "north" side of the property.

Another elevated point, from which one may view Swift property #1, is a landmark, which is extremely relevant to the Swift silver mine legend. This viewpoint is none other than the "remarkable rock," which as mentioned in Chapter Two of this book is called Sand Knob. As mentioned in Chapter Two, when on top of Sand Knob one may see for twenty miles in any direction. It is approximately ten miles from Sand Knob to the southwest corner of the Swift property. Knowing that an unbroken line of sight exists, which extends from Sand Knob to Swift's property, is a very substantial affirmation. It indicates that Sand Knob is *the* "remarkable rock" mentioned in Swift legend. This reinforcing fact, which coincides with Swift legend, likewise appears to indicate that Swift Property #1 is the area of Swift's silver mine

Another interesting fact is that about three miles west of the town of Sonora in Hardin County, Kentucky is an old road called "Silver Mine Road," which most likely pertains to Swift Property #1. Looking at old maps of different time periods, it appears probable that this winding old road may have once been part of old Kentucky Highway 84, the road that connects Sonora to Hudson. According to the older maps, this road at one time also went to Madrid. The end of the Silver Mine Road is about 6 ½ miles (in a straight line) from Eastview and 13 miles from the eastern property line of Swift's 20,718 ¾ acre tract.

Many of the roads used today run near or actually are some of the very early roads and wilderness trails. No one locally in Hardin County could shed any light on how this road got its name. One thing is certain; someone, for some reason, named it Silver Mine Road, and, if it is part of Old Hwy 84, it would certainly be quite a coincidence that it ran through the very heart of Jonathan Swift's "X Marks the Spot" property in Hudson.

On Map #2 one sees approximately where Swift's 20,718 ¾ acre Property #1 is located and also how the adjoining properties are situated. Also shown is where Swift's Property #2 (the 5,000 acre Gold Vault Property) is located. Notice on Swift Property #1 how the adjoining properties are positioned. The two northern-most properties adjoining Swift's property extend to the Ohio River. The northeast properties extend in the direction toward Swift's gold vault Property #2. It is unclear just how close the tip of these two 50,000 acre tracts of Barbour and Banks came to the 1,600 acre tract of William May which adjoins Swift's 5,000 acre tract (Property #2) on the southwest, but it would have been fairly close. One must admit that if there was a secret silver mine somewhere on that 20,718 ¾ acres of land this would, strategically speaking, be a very large area for a safe and secret removal of silver.

Also refer to Maps #2a and #2b.

Also notice that, of these adjoining properties, Bell's 75,000 acres, Barbour & Bank's two 50,000 acres tracts, Barbour and Bank's 60,000 and 113,482 acre tracts, 342,482 acres was the total acreage and only three owners are involved: Bell, Barbour and Banks.

The following points of interest are shown on Map #2 with the corresponding numbers:

1. The location of Swift's 20,718 ¾ acres located at Hudson Lookout Tower

2. The intersecting point of the towns of Grandview and Centerview and of Eastview and Westview, which is very close to the Hudson Lookout Tower.

3. How the adjoining properties of Swift's Property #1 are positioned, and how they extend to the Ohio River and also in the direction of Swift's Property #2.

4. The location of Swift's Property #2 and how William May's and Jacob Myers' properties adjoin it.

5. The location of Silver Mine Road.

While on the subject of Highway 84, consider a location about nine to ten miles east of Sonora, the town of Hodgenville, Kentucky in Larue County. From *United States Treasure Atlas Volume #4* by Thomas P. Terry, there is

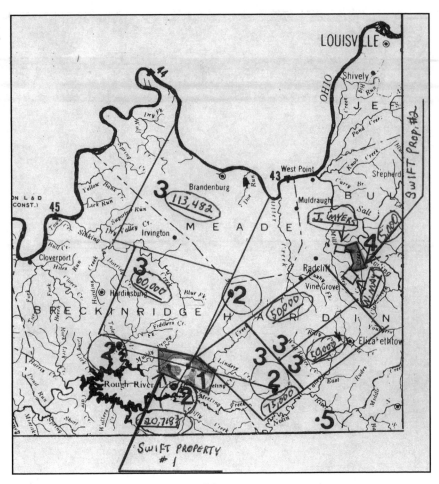

Map 2

127

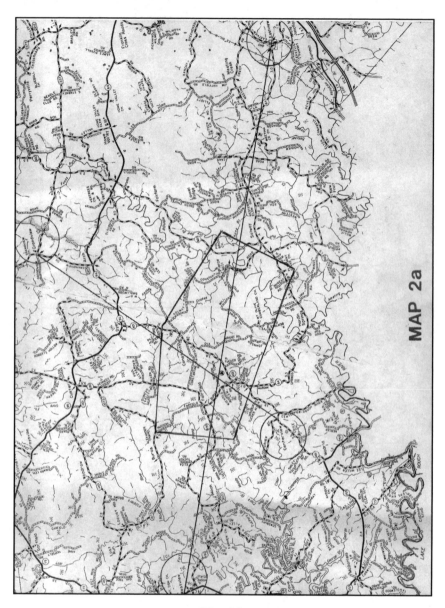

Map 2A

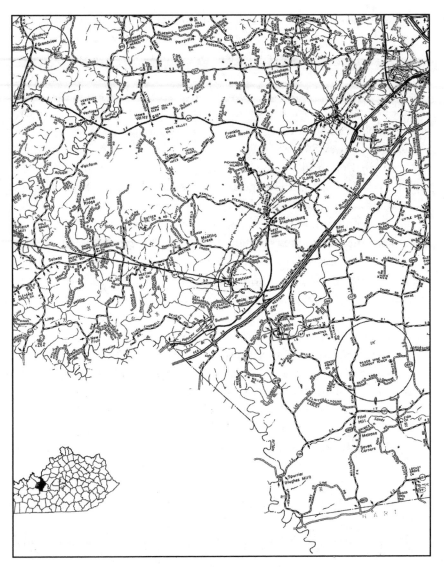

Map 2B

a short story that perhaps ties Hodgenville to the 20,718 ¾ acre Swift property, which Highway 84 runs through: In 1830, a silversmith had a cabin near the head of a creek [near President Abraham Lincoln's boyhood home]. Somewhere close to the silversmith's cabin he had a native source of almost pure silver nuggets. He was found dead one day, killed by a mountain lion, and the exact location was never learned. This area is a couple miles northeast of Hodgenville. Going from Hodgenville to Sonora (about 9-10 miles) one would use Highway 84.

One other point of interest at Hodgenville is that this is the area where Philips Fort was located, the original settlement of that area. It was built by Philip Philips, the man who sold Jonathan Swift the properties in which the indentures mention mines, metals, ores and minerals.

When considering the possibility that Swift Property #1 could be a relevant factor in regard to the Swift silver mine legend the following, which recapitulate the previously mentioned discoveries, should be the primary information used to provide one with a preliminary statistical evaluation.

1) Four view-towns, which have correctly corresponding names to describe their proximity in relation to Swift's property.
2) The intersecting point of said view-towns is near the town of Hudson, which is also proposed to be the central part of Swift's property.
3) A line of sight, which extends from the top of the Remarkable Rock to the entirety of Swift's property.
4) Jonathan Swift from Alexandria, Virginia owned this property.
5) Swift purchased this property in 1791, which was a time period that the Swift silver mine stories were in full bloom.
6) There are eleven landmarks identified in the area of this Swift property that are identical in description to landmarks, which are mentioned in Swift legend.
7) The close proximity of "Silver Mine Road" to this "Jonathan Swift" property.

Gullible's Travels by Jonathan Swift

There is a conundrum, which has perplexed Swift silver mine researchers for generations. If the Jonathan Swift who lived in Alexandria, Virginia for forty years and was born in Milton, Massachusetts in 1764 was the Swift of the silver mine legend, then what can be made of the Swift silver mine journals? Perhaps a more suitable name for the journals would be 'Gullible's Travels' by Jonathan Swift, written for all those who may try to find the Swift silver mine. Not only did he and all his men forget the location of not one but three or four silver mines by the late

1700's, but apparently so did all the many Spaniards and French who had supposedly worked the mine.

Because so many people were supposedly involved in the operation of the silver mines, it is not realistic to believe that it or they were lost. As mentioned in Chapter One of this book, the authenticity of the many varying Swift journals is doubtful, and it is likely that the journal has been added to and embellished upon for the many years it has been copied from person to person. If the journal's dates have been set back too far in the past, one might consider the whole journal a total work of fiction, however, there are simply too many landmarks mentioned in the journal that seem to match Jonathan Swift's Kentucky properties. The fact that, in the journal, Swift was mentioned as being from Alexandria, Virginia and he owned ships there helps one believe that whoever did write the journals had at least some facts correct.

It is believed that the Swift journal is not just a work of fiction, it is much worse than that for would-be Swift silver mine searchers; it is full of half-truths. A lie that is half true is a much more effective way of twisting the truth. Too much was known in those days about the silver mine for a supposed journal of Swift's to have been completely fabricated. It would have been too easily recognized as fiction; therefore, it would have been ineffective. It is proposed that the journal is authentic: an authentic lapwing or Kildee, created to do what a lapwing does; lead attention away from its nest, or in this case, the silver mine.

So with that said, the Swift journals may indeed have useful information pertaining to the location of the silver mine. Much of what is in them could be solid information, provided that one is able to weed out the false or misleading material. It is a glass half full. Until the mine is found and all conjecture is ended, it may still be one of the best sources of information available for would-be searchers who are not content to wait for a happenstance discovery.

The Swift journals were used as a means to distort facts that were known during that day about the silver mine to lead astray those who already knew a great deal of information pertaining to the real mine. A false journal with incorrect dates, would also effectively create anonymity in the personage of Swift. With the evidence that has already been provided, the mine was probably never lost, as the journal would have people believe. However, it was in danger of being discovered by the early Kentucky pioneer settlers and surveyors of that time period. Those who did have knowledge of the actual location of the real silver mine executed an extensive cover-up operation.

Once the possibility of such a cover-up is accepted, it clears up a number of perplexing questions. One such question was Filson's 1788 land entry mentioning a man named Swift who had worked a silver mine somewhere in old Lincoln County some seventeen years prior to the 1788 entry. The Jonathan Swift of this research would have been too young to be involved in a mining operation that would have taken place, according to Filson's entry, in 1771. It also would make sense to have bits and pieces of a so-called Swift journal (like Judge Haywood presented in 1823) placed in a strategic locations to help propagate the new false but similar information of the silver mine operation. The Swift journals were only one method used in achieving the successful cover-up. It is probable that John Filson may have been step one of "Operation Silver Mine Cover-Up." Was it not peculiar that John Filson, known writer of the Daniel Boone story and Kentucky's first historian, would happen to bump into Swift? Which leads to the question, did Filson seek out Swift or did Swift seek out Filson? From a cover-up viewpoint, it makes more sense to believe that a pretext meeting of the two was set in motion with the purpose of manipulating Filson to respond to the intentions of those who were putting the cover-up into action.

What other means would they have used to mislead, confuse, overwhelm and discourage those who already knew a great deal of information about the mine? It is simple: send the only person who could do the job, Jonathan Swift of Alexandria, Virginia.

Perhaps Swift was either the one who leaked the information or was caught with his hand in the cookie jar, disclosing secretive information pertaining to the location or operation of the actual silver mine. Therefore, only he could effectively fix the problem. No one would believe for a moment that Swift alone could pull off such an elaborate and complex cover-up operation. However, he was the one who had to be observed and witnessed by those who knew him as well as those who had only heard of him for the cover-up to be effective.

What part did Swift play in the cover up? Why did Jonathan Swift, a merchant from Alexandria, Virginia, leave his successful business and family to come to Kentucky to purchase properties that he had no intention to keep? Why did he go to the expense and great effort to acquire these properties and not make money from it? If he had no intention to keep the land or to make money, why would he risk personal harm from hostile Indians, mountain lions etc, to purchase the Kentucky Swift Properties?

Swift's major role in the operation was to go to Kentucky and to be seen scouting out properties, which would immediately cause a stir of gossip, to buy properties, forever leaving his name on the indenture as owner and as a former owner, and to leave false information along the way playing the role of a lapwing-diversion.

As previously noted, it seems that Swift's 20,718 ¾ acre property is indeed a possible location of Swift's silver mine, and that is exactly what Swift and his cover-up cohorts wished the early surveyors, settlers, etc. to believe. These properties were large tracts and enough of them to confuse, discourage and overwhelm any potential seeker of the silver mine.

The genuine facts and physical evidence of Jonathan Swift and his properties were presented in a way that would hopefully lead some to believe or give serious thought that Swift Property #1 was a very possible location of Swift's silver mine. This effort was to illustrate the effectiveness of Swift's Pied Piper Operation. If the reader believes that Swift Property #1 is a probable location of the silver mine, then a first hand experience of the **very same twist** that the surveyors and settlers experienced during the years 1788 to 1795 has been effectively reproduced.

The effort of presenting all the facts pertaining to this investigation and withholding key information until now was nothing compared to the expense, effort, expertise and complex planning that Jonathan Swift and Co. put into it. It was Swift's job, while secretively being helped by others, to purchase properties with similarly known landmarks and other qualities of the actual silver mine.

This is Jonathan Swift's Silver Mine Twist: To distort the facts of what was known about the location of the real silver mine, by entwining those known facts with the diversion Properties #1 through #11, which had similarities to the area where the real mine was located. Further, he intended to make people re-associate what they thought they knew about the silver mine with something new and real that seemed to make sense with what they already knew. This was probably a certain landmark, watercourse description or even people who may have been living near the real silver mine. Throw into the mix some new landmarks along with the old, and everything makes perfect sense to the seekers of the mine. The silver mine seekers have then disassociated most of their thoughts of the real silver mine. More examples and comparisons of the dis-association and re-association technique of the cover-up operation will be presented later.

THE SECOND SPRINGFIELD

CHAPTER FIVE

A s mentioned in Chapter Two, the final two Jonathan Swift Kentucky indentures will now be presented. In one of these indentures is the first point of evidence that suggests a cover-up. It is also the first point of evidence presented to indicate an approximate area that could be the *real* silver mine location.

The cover-up operation appears to have been effective and successful, by using what was known of the actual mine and entwining it with Swift's diversion properties, all of which had similarities of the actual silver mine. While Swift and Co. were duplicating characteristics of the real mine, they were also unwittingly painting an abstract picture of the mine they were attempting to hide.

The Jonathan Swift of this investigation does indeed appear to be the Swift of the silver mine legend. Very early in this investigation, though, the possibility that he could have been a diversion for some other Swift seemed possible. If that was possible, there would probably be important clues of the silver mine to be found in the paper trail that he had left. At that point in the investigation, it became irrelevant for him to be the *real Swift* as long as the evidence of his paper trail could sketch a picture of the *real silver mine*.

The following are abstracts of each deed, detailing the main points of interest of both indentures. These two indentures may be found at the Hardin County Clerk's Office in Elizabethtown, Kentucky in the *Deed Book* marked only 1795, and pages 9-26. Both transcribed indentures and the first page of each original document may be found in Appendix B of this book, identified as B-9 and B-10.

Swift Property #10
"Greenwich"

This indenture was made the fourth day of August 1794. Daniel Ferry of Nelson County Kentucky sells to Jonathan Swift of Alexandria, Virginia 3,900 acres of land called "Greenwich," for five shillings, current money of Virginia. The property is mentioned as being located on the north side of Green River in Hardin County, formerly part of Nelson County. This 3,900 acre tract is a part of a patent of 5,000 acres granted to William May, surveyor of Nelson County, on June 1, 1786. William May and wife, Mary, conveyed the property to Daniel Ferry on July 15, 1794. The transcribed indenture and both pages of the original document may be found in Appendix B of this book, identified as B-11. In the description of all that comes with the property, it does mention "mines, metals, ores or minerals of any kind above, upon and under the ground, as well as, all watercourses, licks, woods etc." Witnesses to the indenture were Thomas Lewis, Amos Allison and Charles Bennett. Present day, this property would be approximately located in southern Ohio County near Lewis Creek and somewhere near the town of Rockport.

Swift Property #11
"Springfield"

This indenture was also made on the fourth day of August 1794. Daniel Ferry of Nelson County Kentucky sells to Jonathan Swift of Alexandria, Virginia 9,200 acres of land called "Springfield" for five shillings, current money of Virginia. The property is mentioned as being located on the waters of Green River between little Reedy Creek and Welches Creek about two miles from Green River in Hardin County, formerly a part of Nelson County. This 9,200 acres of land was originally granted to William May, surveyor of the County of Nelson, on July 10, 1786. William May and wife, Mary, conveyed the property to Daniel Ferry on July 15, 1794. The transcribed indenture and the first page of the original document may be found in Appendix B of this book, identified as B-12. The description of what all is to be included with the property does mention "mines, metals, ores or minerals of any kind above, upon, or under the ground, as well as all watercourses, licks, woods etc." Witnesses to the indenture were Thomas Lewis, Amos Allison and Charles Bennett. The property is believed to be located in present day Butler County. Swift actually kept this important diversion property until October 19, 1802. At that time, he sold the property to William Mattocks Rogers of Boston, Massachusetts for $1.00. This 1802 indenture can be found in Deed Books A3 and B1 at the Franklin County Courthouse Annex Building Deed Room.

On Map #3 Swift Properties #3 thru #11, are identified in their approximate location.

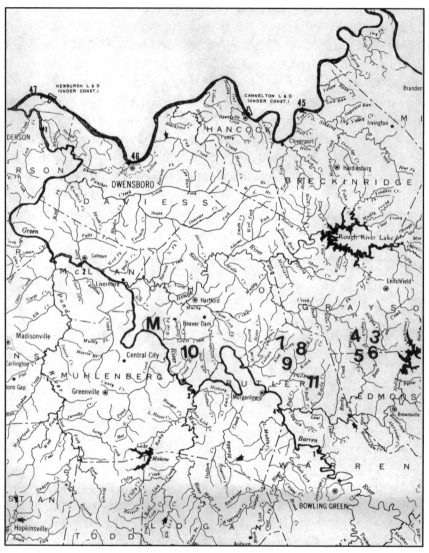

Map 3

Foster Swift, M.D.
Brother of Jonathan Swift

Mrs. Foster Swift

Swift Alley

202-204 King Street-Once
owned by Jonathan Swift

Gen. Joseph Gardner Swift
First cadet graduate of West Point Military Academy and nephew of Jonathan Swift.

Colross at Princeton

Belle Aire/Colross in Alexandria before 1927

The Marquis de Lafayette
Close friend of the Roberdeau and Swift families. Picture provided by The
Alexandria-Washington Lodge #22. Portrait photographed by Arthur W. Pierson

George Washington at Princeton by Charles Willson Peale. Family tradition states that Washington presented this portrait to his friend, Jonathan Swift.

Above and Below: Remaining floor and walls of Colross/Belle Aire

Cistern of Belle Aire

Possible burial vault at Belle Aire

It seems that Ferry had traveled to Alexandria to sell these properties to Swift. All the witnesses were from Alexandria, and in both the Greenwich and Springfield deeds on the final page under Virginia Fairfax it says, " 'Daniel Ferry personally appeared before us two justices of the peace', signed by Robert Townsend Hooe and William Herbert, both of Alexandria."

This property transaction and the two indentures apparently were not recorded in Hardin County until April 15, 1795, which is the date of the indentures between William May and Daniel Ferry, where May sells both properties to Ferry for five shillings, current money of Kentucky. On the Ferry to Swift indenture, it states that May had actually conveyed the properties to Ferry on July 15, 1794. The names of the properties, Greenwich and Springfield, are not mentioned on the indentures when May sells them to Ferry in Hardin County, but are only mentioned when Ferry sells them to Swift in Alexandria.

On Swift Property #9, Indian Camp Creek, (see Chapter Two) the indenture was dated March 10, 1794. May actually conveyed Ferry the Greenwich and Springfield properties on July 15, 1794, as mentioned in the Ferry to Swift indentures. Swift purchased Greenwich and Springfield from Ferry on August 4, 1794 in Alexandria. The Swift Property #9 indenture was made at Bardstown, Kentucky in Nelson County where Swift had also purchased Properties #4 thru #8 on February 19, 1794. It was sometime between March 10, 1794 and July 15, 1794 that Swift had left Kentucky and returned to Alexandria. It is probable that Swift and Ferry had left Kentucky together after July 15, 1794 and traveled to Alexandria. It is apparent that Swift stayed around long enough to make sure all the details of these final two properties were taken care of, such as naming them Greenwich and Springfield. It seems probable that this would be the last time that Kentucky would ever see Jonathan

Swift; however, according to the end of the indenture marked B-2, he may have been in Elizabethtown, Kentucky in 1821.

On the Greenwich and Springfield Indentures it would have appeared to the indenture witnesses at Alexandria and to those who would have seen the indentures recorded in Hardin County, that Swift purchased these properties, which were already named Greenwich and Springfield.

As previously mentioned, it is likely that Swift named these two properties. Being the "intelligent traveler" that he was, traveling to various foreign countries, he would have known that" any place in England where the name ends in 'wich' at one time produced salt, such as Northwich, Nantwich, and Middlewich" [and Greenwich], as mentioned in the book, *Salt: A World His-*

tory by Mark Kurlansky. This property, being on the north side of Green River, if there was a salt lick on it, it is probable that is how this property got the name of Greenwich. Of course, this is only one possibility of its naming, but as mentioned in Swift Property #2, if there is a silver mine on a property, a salt lick is needed for the refining process. Swift may have intended to identify the salt lick property, Greenwich, with the Springfield Property #11.

In the area where the real silver mine is proposed to be located, there was also a major salt lick and salt works in the 1700's about eight and one half miles north of the town of "Springfield" in Washington County Kentucky.

Before getting into the details of the Springfield of Washington County (the second Springfield) and a possible location of the silver mine, an explanation should be provided on how the evidence should be classified. The found evidence not only reveals the possible existence of a Swift silver mine cover-up, but also presents a very possible location of an actual Kentucky silver mine. The Swift indentures, found in Chapter Two, and the Swift biography, found in Chapter Three, are the physical evidence of this investigation. By presenting all the physical evidence which Jonathan Swift had left behind, the circumstantial evidence of the investigation will now be presented in a way where it can logically prove the possibility of a cover-up operation.

Circumstantial evidence is defined as a presentation of facts that are closely associated with an event from which a logical deduction may be concluded. The objective in presenting this case is to compare the physical evidence that has already been presented, as well as the physical evidence now to be presented and comparing all the similarities of Swift Properties #1 thru #11 to the Washington County area. At this time, new points of interest will be presented, showing that all of this *is* closely associated to this silver mine investigation.

By comparing the similarities of landmarks of the Washington County properties to the landmarks of Jonathan Swift's properties, it indicates a pattern of *landmark duplications* as well as *name duplications*. From these comparisons one may logically establish that there is a high degree of probability of the existence of a Swift cover-up operation, which was done for the purpose of concealing the location of a silver mine operation in Washington County, Kentucky at that time.

If there were a secret silver mine in Kentucky in the 1780's and information had been leaked, what sort of details of the location would have been known? There were no towns in Kentucky, to speak of, and only a handful of the old forts. Landmarks such as watercourses, salt licks, springs and old wilderness trails or traces, either left by man or buffalo, are the landmarks that would have been used to describe its location.

Many of these traces very early acquired names. One such example is Sandusky's Path, the trail connecting Sandusky's Station (located on Pleasant Run near the present county line of Washington and Marion Counties) and Walton's Lick, located present day in the town of Polin in north Washington County.

If the information of the location of the silver mine had been leaked in the 1780's, which is when the leak of information is believed to have occurred, then landowner names could also have been known. One example of this scenario would be--Jonathan Swift, after sharing one too many pints of rum with someone at Alexandria at his White House Tavern or Gatsby's Tavern, and in his notable "rapidity of speech" starts to divulge certain facts of a silver mine located in Kentucky. The details that he revealed were certain landmarks, watercourses, a salt lick and even a landowner. This hypothetical landowner is given a fictitious name for now: George Munday.

Of course, the following morning Swift starts remembering most of the fantastic story that he revealed the previous night, and realizing that his loose lips could sink the silver ship, the cover-up was set in motion.

This demonstration of how information was leaked of the silver mine is only used to express what would have to be done if Swift had divulged such information in the 1780's or early 1790's. It also makes sense that it was Swift who either leaked the whereabouts of the mine to someone, was caught in a situation at his wharf in Alexandria, or a ship of his had been seized with a load of silver. There are countless such possibilities. Logically, the man responsible for the leak would also be the man who could be most effective in the success of the damage control part of a cover-up operation. That man was Jonathan Swift.

It is suggested that Springfield of Washington County is one of the points of information of the silver mine about which Swift had divulged secretive information pertaining to its whereabouts. The Swift/Ferry Springfield indenture was used so the people that Swift & Co. wanted to be aware of the indenture would disassociate their thoughts of the Springfield in Washington County and re-associate what they knew of that Springfield with the Springfield of the Swift/Ferry indenture, located in present Butler County. Both of the properties were in old Nelson County from the years 1785-1792. If the leak occurred after 1785 and before 1792 and the divulged information included the county where the mine was located, both the Springfield of Washington County and Swift's Springfield property of present day Butler County would have been in Nelson County.

Matthew Walton

According to *Pioneer History of Washington County, Kentucky* by Michael Cook and Bettie Anne Cook, the town of Springfield in Washington County was laid off in 1793, from the lands of Gen. Matthew Walton. This was only one year before the Swift/Ferry Springfield indenture. In order for the theory that the leak occurred after 1785 to be valid, the area where the town of Springfield in Washington County is located would have been called Springfield years before it was officially named that in 1793. The originally leaked information was probably that the silver mine was north of a spring or a number of springs.

Also from *Pioneer History of Washington County, Kentucky*, it is discovered that Matthew Walton settled in the Springfield area as early as 1780, and it was Walton who named Springfield. In *Washington County, Kentucky Bicentennial History 1792-1992* by David Hurst, one finds that at one time Walton owned 260,000 acres and was the largest landowner of his time. Of these 260,000 acres, 45,500 were located in what later became Washington County.

The following is an excerpt from *Pioneer History of Washington County, Kentucky*:

"Matthew Walton Was Richest Man"

"According to an article appearing in print in the Washington County Leader in 1890, General Matthew Walton of Springfield was the richest man who ever lived in Kentucky, and in his days, the richest man west of the Allegheny Mountains.

"At the time of his death, Gen Walton owned one hundred thousand acres of land and many hundred slaves. It was said of him he was the first man in Kentucky who freed his slaves, which was done according to his will at the death of his wife.

"A distinguished lawyer of his day stated that Gen. Walton's success in life was due to the fact that he never said a smart thing and never did a foolish thing.

"Gen. Walton built the residence on old Bardstown Road in which John R. Barber lived for many years. It is said he carried the finishing nails used in the building from Lexington in his saddle pockets. It is known that he could ride from Springfield to Louisville and never get off his own lands.

"He was a large salt manufacturer and had salt works all over this section of the country."

From *Washington County, Kentucky Bicentennial History 1792-1992*, one finds that "John Richard Barber purchased the old Walton mansion from his father, Philetus Swift Barber in 1866." Why Philetus *Swift* Barber bore the middle name of *Swift*, is unknown.

According to *Kentucky Settlement and Statehood 1750-1800* by George Morgan Chinn, Walton was also a member of the elite Danville Political Club and was a political figure in Nelson and Washington Counties for many years.

The following is an excerpt from *Washington County Kentucky Bicentennial History 1792-1992*:

"Born in 1759 at Farmville Virginia, he was the first cousin of George Walton, signer of the Declaration; consequently, after attending William and Mary College of Williamsburg, he found all social and political doors open to him. He was in Kentucky Territory as early as 1776 on surveying assignments and before 1800 he held or shared titles to over 200,000 acres. After his years of service in the Kentucky Legislature, he served in the U.S. Congress from 1803-1807 and was presidential elector for James Madison in 1809. The present St. Catherine Motherhouse and College stands on General Walton's former orchard where his friend, Thomas Jefferson, helped with the selections including the 'Gilead Balm' trees prized as a source of body creams and lotions. Matthew and Frances Walton had no children. He died in 1819 leaving collateral heirs who contested his 1804 will."

Walton was a large salt manufacturer in his day, and his most famous salt lick was called Walton's Lick. It was noted on some of the very earliest and better-detailed maps of Kentucky, as early as 1792. From *Pioneer History of Washington County, Kentucky*, one finds that, "Walton's Lick, so-named because it was located on the lands of Matthew Walton, very early became a popular resort for the settlers in this section. For many miles some of them traveled to get salt. The place was located on Powell's Trace, a multi-traveled trail extending from the Falls of the Ohio to Harrodsburg." The location of the actual silver mine would need to be proximate to a salt works. Walton's Lick is very possibly that salt works. It was located just across the creek from one of the four areas considered, in Washington County, in this investigation.

Walton's Lick was located on Powell's Trace, the trail that connected Harrodsburg to The Falls of the Ohio, near the present-day city of Louisville.

Powell's Trace appears to be another piece of leaked information pertaining to the whereabouts of the real mine. John Filson's 1788 land entry states that sixty or seventy miles north eastwardly from Martin's cabin in Powell's Valley is a silver mine on the entered property improved by Swift some seventeen years ago; it was a Lincoln County entry. This was the only description of where the property was located. It is hard to believe that in that entire area there were no notable landmarks or watercourses given to better describe the location of the Filson/Breckinridge entry.

As previously mentioned, this false information was given to Filson so a land entry would be made to further cloud what was actually known of the real mine. In doing this, Swift & Co. were entwining what was known of the real mine, with the new false knowledge to compel those with the divulged information to re-associate what was known of the silver mine on "Powell's Trace," to the Filson land entry mentioning a silver mine and "Powell's Valley."

Each point of interest to be presented in this Washington County area is located with the corresponding number on Map #4. Because there is no longer a Powell's Trace or Walton's Lick, they will each be identified on the map as #1 located at the town of Polin.

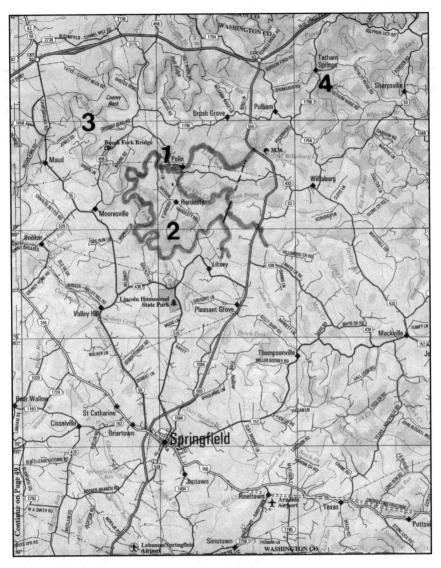

Map 4

TREASURE ISLAND ?

CHAPTER SIX

"Squire Trelawney, Dr. Livesey, and the rest of the gentlemen having asked me to write down the whole particulars about Treasure Island, from the beginning to the end, keeping nothing back but the bearings of the island, and that only because there is still treasure not yet lifted..." ~ *From the first paragraph of Treasure Island by Robert Louis Stevenson*

Four areas in Washington County, Kentucky will be considered in this book as potential areas for Swift's real silver mine. Each of these areas is equally likely to have a silver mine, though it seems most likely that the areas mentioned in northern Washington County are the most significant. The readers will no doubt choose for themselves an area they believe to be most suitable.

The first area is considered to be somewhere near the town of Springfield. This is due to the reference made in Swift's Springfield indenture. Matthew Walton owned the land that the town of Springfield is on, and he owned much of the land in that area. Walton lived only two miles from Springfield on Cartwright's Creek, and further information of Cartwright's Station will be mentioned later. Another reason for interest in this area is that Jonathan Swift signed an indenture, as witness, for Philip Marstellar. Philip Marstellar was mentioned in Chapter Three as a pall-bearer for George Washington, and Swift was in attendance. This Marstellar indenture that Swift signed, as a witness, will be described later in this chapter.

The second area to be considered in northern Washington County is Walton's Lick. Location of Walton's Lick can be found on present-day maps by the town of Polin. Matthew Walton and Anthony Hundley placed a 1783 land entry of 12,000 acres for this area. The entry states the property is located "in the fork of Chaplin's Fork and the Beech Fork, and to run up the Beech

Fork to the mouth of the first large creek, which is called the main north fork of the Beech Fork [this creek would shortly thereafter be called Long Lick Creek] the creek that the trace [Powell's]…" Of the 12,000 acres listed, 2,650 acres was withdrawn from the entry making it 9,350 acres total.

The following excerpt is from *Pioneer History of Washington County, Kentucky*:

"Matthew Walton and Anthony Hundley jointly owned 9,350 acres of land lying on the Beech and Chaplain's Fork. In 1797 commissioners were appointed by the Washington County court to divide the land. Walton's share began on the Beech Fork at Terrels and Hawkins upper corner and from thence until it intersected Penn's line. The salt lick was included in his portion. Descendants of William Hardesty still treasure an old iron kettle that was used at the salt works at Walton's Lick."

The third area of interest is also in the northern part of Washington County. It is the area near a *Spanish marker*, which will be described later in this chapter, and the approximate location is Brush Grove, Willisburg, Tatham Springs, and Sharpsville. There are also other landmarks in this area that could pertain to landmarks given in faked Swift journals and can be located on most topographical maps. The landmarks are Big Rock Run and Rock Bridge.

The fourth area of interest in Washington County is located just south of Walton's Lick. This property was originally granted to a man named Benjamin Moody. For the remainder of this chapter, a scenario will be presented using Benjamin Moody, Matthew Walton and Jonathan Swift as the primary characters. The evidence presented is factual; however, the theories presented should only be considered one of many possible scenarios. As previously mentioned, this fourth area may be no more likely to have a silver mine than the other three.

The Swift, Walton and Moody Scenario

As previously proposed, Jonathan Swift Properties #1 thru #11 were used as a diversion to lead people away from the real silver mine and by doing that, Swift and Co. were also unwittingly painting an abstract picture of the location of the actual silver mine. If this theory is correct, then the legendary Swift silver mine could be located somewhere on the northern Washington County property owned by Benjamin Moody from Alexandria, Virginia.

The property is highlighted and identified on Map #4 as #2. The portion of Moody's property, which is referred to as *the island*, is the largest section and is bounded by the Beech Fork on the property's south boundary line and Long Lick Creek on the property's north boundary line. This portion of Moody's property is surrounded by water, except for what is estimated to be about 700 feet on the property's east side.

If part of the divulged information of the silver mine had been the name of the landowner, then it would be an absolute must that the landowner's name be changed to a fictitious one. It is proposed that Benjamin Moody, or possibly one of his sons or both, was the one known in Swift legend as "Munday" and the other variations of that name as noted in Chapter One of this book. If the silver mine was on Moody's property, his name had to be altered, but the Swift name would need to remain the same because Swift was known to have been connected in some way to a silver mine. As noted in Chapter One of Michael Steely's book *Swift's Silver Mines and Related Appalachian Treasures,* in one version of the Swift journal, the silver mine was Munday's, not Swift's.

The most effective way to disguise this name-twist would be to change the name as little as possible, so it would not be recognized as an obvious fake and possibly ruin the cover-up operation. Who knows just how similar the pronunciation of Moody and Munday may have been in those days.

In *Pioneer History of Washington County, Kentucky,* William Moody, son of Benjamin Moody, purchased lot #86 in the new town of Springfield on March 4, 1799, and his name was spelled Mudey. This can be further verified from an early town map of Springfield that is in *Washington County Kentucky Bicentennial History 1792-1992.*

From *Old Kentucky Entries and Deeds,* one finds that Benjamin Moody made two entries for the entire Beech Fork/Long Lick Creek property on November 21, 1783. The west portion of the property (one of the two entries) was, by the date on the survey, surveyed on March 12, 1784, and the surveyor was George May. George May was a brother of William May. There were, according to the survey, 3,000 acres in this west section of Moody's land. Patrick Henry granted the land on May 1, 1786. The east portion of the property was surveyed on December 15, 1784. A name of interest on the survey was William May as surveyor. There were, according to this survey, 1,800 acres in this property that adjoined the previous survey of 3,000 acres. Isaac Shelby issued the grant on February 19, 1793.

Benjamin Moody, Sr. did not live to see this property granted. It would, however, be inherited by his children. From *Abstract of Wills and Inventories Fairfax County, Virginia 1742-1801,* two dates are given. The first date, February 13, 1784, is probably the date Moody's will was made, and the second date, April 6, 1784, is probably the date he died. It states his children as being William (to have land in Kentucky), James, Thomas, Frances, Ann, Sarah and Benjamin. The executor was his son, William.

The following document identified as A-3 was found at the Washington County Courthouse in the County Clerk's Office in *Court Order Book A*, pages 263-266. It is a copy of the original re-survey of Benjamin Moody's land, which was completed prior to September 5, 1797. It shows how the property was divided among his children. According to this document, there were actually 5,226 acres in this property. Also, note the location of Walton's Lick, which designates the property's north side. Several of Benjamin Moody's children are believed to have settled on this property and, as noted, William owned a town lot in Springfield.

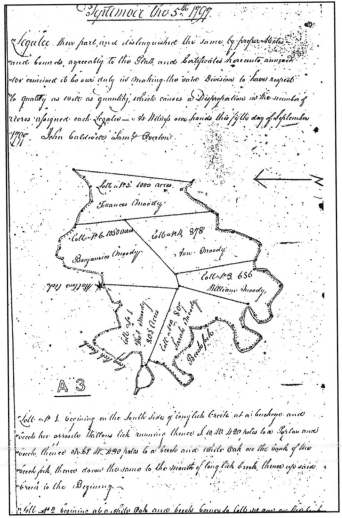

From *Washington County, Kentucky Bicentennial History 1792-1992*, one finds that Thomas Moody married Mary Berry. Mary Berry was a daughter of Richard Berry, who owned property just south of Moody's land in the Beech Fork neighborhood. This is also where Abraham Lincoln (grandfather of the President) lived and is located on Map #4, south of Moody's property. This is the site of the Lincoln Homestead State Park.

It is interesting how many times in this investigation that a Lincoln or their property was near an area of interest.

1. The William May 1,600 acre tract that adjoined Swift Property #2 on the southwest is the tract that Thomas Lincoln bought a portion of in the Mill Creek area.
2. Swift Properties #3 and #4 were just north of Lincoln Branch in Grayson County.
3. The story of the silversmith near Hodgenville was near Abraham Lincoln's Boyhood Home.
4. Lincoln Homestead State Park is just south of Moody's land.
5. Swift's brother, Foster, was a close friend of General Benjamin Lincoln, for whom Lincoln County Kentucky was named.

Going back once again to the John Filson 1788 land entry which mentioned Swift, a silver mine and Powell's Valley, the land entry was a Lincoln County entry. Could Filson's land entry have served a dual purpose? To be not only the diversion of Powell's Trace (the trail next to Moody's Island), but also of a settlers name mentioned in the leak of the mine's whereabouts, the pioneer Abraham Lincoln. Lincoln settled in the Washington County area in 1782.

The following is an excerpt from, *Pioneer History of Washington County Kentucky*:

"When Abraham Lincoln, Sr. reared his little cabin on Richard Berry's land in the Beech Fork neighborhood, he established his family in the midst of the hunting grounds of numerous Indian tribes. All of that territory had long been used by the redskins who came down each year from the north."

Could this be the Mecca Indians associated with the Swift legend and journals? Mecca: any place that many people visit or hope to visit. It seems a likely name that someone of Swift's experience would have referred to the Indians, since he was consul to many foreign countries such as Morocco.

Continuing:

"The Indians, seeing their hunting grounds rapidly becoming farms of numerous white settlers, carried on a campaign against the 'intruders' from the east with terrible results. From 1782, the year in which the Lincolns and Berrys came, until after the death of Abraham Lincoln, Sr., the family lived in constant fear of the dusky savages…Tradition says that Abraham Lincoln was busy planting the spring crop and that he was working about a half mile from the cabin when he was slain by an Indian lurking in the forest nearby…. it is highly probable that Lincoln was killed in April 1788."

There is speculation as to the actual burial site of Abraham Lincoln, Sr. This excerpt provides one possible location. It is also possible he was buried in Long Run Cemetery in eastern Jefferson County.

Also from *Pioneer History of Washington Country*, in an article dated May 2, 1935, titled "Indian Mounds in This County," three prehistoric Indian mounds and other sites in Washington County, Kentucky, are described in detail in "An Archaeological Survey of Kentucky," a one thousand-page volume, published by the University of Kentucky. Another article dated March 28, 1935, titled "Indian Peace Pipe is Found." This article goes on to say that the Indian peace pipe was found near Willisburg, just east of Moody's property. Washington County has many land shapes that resemble Indian mounds and almost 99% of these are just earth. There are shapes in the northern Washington county area that are symmetrically shaped like an Indian burial mound.

In most legends and myths, there is usually a kernel of truth. There is an interesting, old Nelson County legend. The following is an excerpt from, *Legends of Nelson County* by Sarah B. Smith:

"Lover's Leap"
"In the east part of Bardstown from the bluff above the valley, extends a flat rock known as 'Lover's Leap.' The story goes, an Indian princess leaped to her death from here, when abandoned by her lover.
"In the valley below, in an Indian burial ground lies a great warrior whose name was a terror to the pioneers.
"Somewhere near, so tradition says, is a vast quantity of treasure, if interred, – undiscovered to this day."

It is only about 10½ miles from the east part of Bardstown to the west side of Moody's Island. For this legend to apply to Moody's Island, its creation would have to be between 1785, the year Nelson became a county, and

1792, the year Washington County came off of Nelson County, which seems a likely time period.

The following are further examples as well as those already noted of what could be evidence of the duplication/diversion and re-associate/disassociate theory. The Washington County landmarks and people are mentioned first and then secondly, their diversionary counterpart:

1. Moody's property was nearly surrounded by water and was partly bounded by Long Lick Creek. *Diversion*: Swift Property #1 was nearly surrounded by water and was near another Long Lick Creek.

2. Matthew Walton owned the salt works on Long Lick Creek, which was Walton's Lick, near Moody's land. *Diversion*: Matthew Walton also owned the property at the mouth of the Long Lick Creek near Swift Property #1. This 500 acre property was surveyed for an Edward Herndon by William May on January 18, 1786. Herndon assigned this property to Matthew Walton and Walton received the grant on February 9, 1789.

3. Just to the northwest of Moody's property, where Chapline River and Beech Fork intersect, Samuel Bell was granted 1,180½ acres, and that property shared a property line of a 973 acre survey of a Joseph Bell. Samuel Bell's property and Joseph Bell's entry is identified on Map #4 as #3. *Diversion*: The 20,718 ¾ acre Swift Property #1 adjoined the 75,000 acre tract of William Bell, who had been assigned to the property by Blair Elliot and Co. In Michael Paul Henson's *John Swift's Lost Silver Mines* is a Robert Alley map, which Henson had attained in 1959 from Alva Rice (deceased). Robert Alley's Swift journal is listed in Chapter One of this book. In the northwest (top left) of this Robert Alley map, is a drawing of a bell. Henson reports that this map "is an exact copy of what is believed to be John Swift's original map of his mines, that he drew in 1769." This map shows what could be interpreted as an island area, bounded on its north side by a Lick Creek. This map property could be interpreted as a crude drawing of Moody's island property.

4. As noted, Matthew Walton owned property all the way to the Ohio River. *Diversion*: Barbour and Banks properties that adjoined Swift Property #1 also extended all the way to the Ohio River.

5. Bear Wallow in Washington County is located seven miles south of Moody's land. *Diversion*: the head of Bear Creek is located seven miles south of Swift Property #1.

6. May's Creek (probably named for William May) is located to the east

of Moody's land. *Diversion*: May's Run is located to the east of Swift Property #1.

7. A Joshua Renfro owned at least 2,000 acres just to the east of Moody's land on Long Lick Creek. On a map of early settlers in Washington County, in the book, *Washington County Kentucky Bicentennial History*, it shows Renfro's property being located above Taylor's Branch and south of Danbow Creek. *Diversion*: Mrs. Renfro at Bean Station.

8. The town of Springfield in Washington County *Diversion*: Swift's Springfield indenture.

9. Spring of Springfield, south of Moody's land *Diversion*: Hardin Springs, south of Swift Property #1.

10. Powell's Trace *Diversion*: Powell's Valley mentioned on Filson's 1788 entry.

11. Pioneer Settler, Abraham Lincoln *Diversion*: Lincoln County, the county in which John Filson filed the 1788 land entry.

12. The Indian campgrounds/hunting and burial grounds at Moody's land *Diversion*: The Indian Camp Creek indenture of Jonathan Swift.

13. Walton's salt lick *Diversion*: Swift's Greenwich indenture (implying a salt lick).

14. Moody *Diversion*: Munday

15. Matthew Walton *Diversion*: Wilton and Walden (of the journal) from Michael S. Steely's *Swift's Silver Mines and Related Appalachian Treasures*.

16. Benjamin Moody's 4,800 acres *Diversion*: Swift's 3,900 acre Greenwich property-- Swift's Springfield and Greenwich properties are the best example and evidence of the diversion/duplication, confuse and overwhelm cover-up theory. Swift's Greenwich named property is northwest of his Springfield named property and Greenwich had 3,900 acres. It was situated within a large nearly island area (Green River on the south and Rough, Muddy and Three *Lick* Fork on the north) near a large horseshoe bend in Green River. As mentioned, Swift may have named the property Greenwich to associate it with Moody's property across from Walton's Lick. Moody's property is north of Springfield in Washington County and had 4,800 acres according to the 1784 surveys. The 1784 surveys are the relevant surveys pertaining to this because Swift's properties were purchased before 1794. Therefore, the 1797 resurvey of Moody's property would not be relevant. Much of the Moody property is situated within a nearly island area with a horseshoe bend on the Beech Fork and it was just across Long Lick

159

Creek from Walton's well known salt lick. When William May was granted the Greenwich property (as it was later known), it originally had 5,000 acres and Daniel Ferry purchased the full 5,000 acres from May. When Ferry sold the property to Swift at Alexandria, Swift purchased only 3,900 acres of the 5,000 acre tract. The original 5,000 acre tract of the Greenwich property was nearly the same acreage as Moody's 4,800 acres, which when resurveyed was found to be 5,226 acres.

It is possible that some of this is merely coincidental, but the question to be asked is *Could there be something to this?*

It is suspected that Swift and Co. would have rather had the Greenwich property located more due north instead of northwest from Swift's Springfield property. But if they had done that, Swift's Springfield property would have been south of Green River, which would have placed it in old Lincoln County. It is proposed that the leaked information included that the silver mine was located north of Springfield and that Springfield was known to be in Nelson or Jefferson Counties. As previously mentioned, both the Greenwich and Springfield properties were once in Nelson County (1785-1793) and Jefferson County (1780-1785), Kentucky.

Benjamin Moody was also granted 1,000 acres on the northside of Beech Fork. This property's location was described as five miles above the mouth of Chapline Fork. This property was probably near his 4,800 acres, but did not adjoin it. He had 5,800 acres total in that area. Daniel Ferry's tract of land had 5,000 acres total and was used to duplicate the acreage leaked out about Moody's 4,800 acres.

If, due to an unknown reason, Swift divulged secret information and the information he leaked included 1) the location of a silver mine in Kentucky, 2) the property being north of Springfield in Nelson County, 3) the land being in a nearly island area, 4) near a major salt lick, 5) an approximate number of acres, 6) landmarks, and 7) the name of the property owner, Benjamin Moody, which would automatically associate Swift with Moody and a silver mine; what did Swift and Co. do to make diversion/duplication arrangements for the Swift, Moody and Kentucky silver mine divulged information?

Incredibly, but in all probability not coincidentally, both the Swift Property #1 and the Greenwich property were located near two other Benjamin Moody properties. Moody received a grant on 1,000 acres of land just west of Swift's Greenwich property near Williams Creek, which is just east of the great horseshoe bend on the north side of Green River. For the location of this 1,000 acre Moody property see Map #3, identified as "M." Moody's land is within the same nearly island area as Swift's Greenwich property. Moody also had a land entry on the North Fork of Rough Creek near Swift Property #1, the 20,718¾ acre tract, which was located in an area nearly surrounded by water (See Map #4). Perhaps Moody had diversion in mind himself in 1783 when he made the entries on these two properties, and luckily it worked to Swift and Co.'s advantage that Moody had made these entries when they began to purchase the Swift properties eight years later, in 1791.

Benjamin Moody had an interest in only two tracts of land, other than his Washington County Beech Fork/Long Lick Creek property, and they were located in different areas. One was near Williams Creek on Green River and the other on the North Fork of Rough Creek, and Swift's two principal diversionary properties were located near both.

When Swift purchased the properties near Benjamin Moody's entries, located far from his (Moody) Beech Fork/Long Lick Creek properties, therefore showing an interest in areas where Moody also had a documented interest, this and all the previously mentioned evidence completed the cover-up operations as well as all the information which had been divulged pertaining to the silver mine.

It is interesting that both Swift's Springfield and Greenwich properties are near two different Bull Creeks. Of course, when the creeks were named, they could have had bull bovine, bull elk, or bul-lion in mind.

From *Swift's Silver Mines and Related Appalachian Treasures*, there was a Mary Cartwright connected with the Swift Legend who cooked for Swift and his men while they were mining silver in Kentucky. She was never shown the location of the mine. Could this Cartwright connection be linked to the Cartwright Station of old Washington County? In *Pioneer History of Washington County, Kentucky*, one finds that Cartwright and Sandusky Stations where the first two settlements in that area. Sandusky's Station was built in 1776 and Cartwright's Station was built in 1779. Matthew Walton owned much land on Cartwright Creek and also lived near the creek. Jacob Myers, the iron furnace builder, also owned property on Cartwright's Creek and other properties in Washington County. In 1793, Jacob Myers served on the first grand jury of Washington County.

Moody's property does have some landmarks in that area that also closely resemble those mentioned in the journal:

1. Three creeks: Chapline River, Beech Fork and Long Lick Creek
2. A lick creek
3. Just to the east of Moody's property is an area called "Rock Bridge"

4.   The "horseshoe bend" in Beech Fork

5.   Big Rock Run and Little Rock Run

No information could be found on how the Rock Bridge area got its name, or if a natural rock bridge was located there.

As previously mentioned in this chapter, there is, or was, one landmark in the north Washington County area that is far more interesting than any of these landmarks and when it comes to investigating a silver mine, the discovery of this particular landmark is a very significant point of evidence: a Spanish marker. This shows that there is or was something in that area of significant interest to the Spanish explorers who were in this area long before Jonathan Swift, James Harrod, Daniel Boone and Dr. Thomas Walker.

The following is an excerpt from *Pioneer History of Washington County Kentucky*:

"A Mysterious Stone"

"In the northern part of Washington County, near Chaplin River, and about two miles from the Nelson County line, about twenty years ago, [this was from an article by O.W. Baylor written in 1935 which makes the year of discovery 1915] a Mystery Stone was found by D.P. Casteel. The stone is said to have been about four feet high and two feet wide and quite thick. One side was smoothly dressed and on it there was a lengthy inscription in Spanish.

"The discoverer of the Mystery Stone said that he had been sitting up all night with a sick neighbor and was returning home in the morning, following an old path along the river, when he noticed an unusual rock setting edgeways in the roots of an old tree. His attention was directed to the rock more than it otherwise might have been because he was building a stonewall in front of his home and needed a top step for the stone stairway that was made a part of the wall.

"Upon examining the rock, Mr. Casteel found that it bore a lengthy inscription in a language he knew nothing about. Others who examined the rock at later dates told him the inscription was in Spanish. The inscription covered nearly the entire surface of the smoothed side. The letters were one-half inch tall and the lines quite close. Near the middle of the stone the numerals 207711 appeared, and at the bottom was the date 1703.

"Within 30 or 40 feet from the spot where the rock was found, there was and is a small mound. Whether there was any connection between the stone and the mound has never been determined as no one has ever disturbed the mound. Mr. Casteel removed the rock to his home and it served as a step for many years. He placed the inscription side up and the continued use wore the lettering away. No effort was made to have the lettering translated or to determine the purpose of the stone. Some interested parties in the neighborhood plan to explore the ground in the vicinity of the spot where the stone was found and they will open the mound in an effort to solve the mystery."

It would certainly be a worthwhile search to determine exactly were D.P. Casteel lived, and try to locate that 2'x4' stone and see if the modern technologies available to archaeologists today could revive some of the inscriptions.

From the county clerk's office at the Springfield, Washington County courthouse, one finds that on October 6, 1898, D. P. Casteel had purchased three acres from John H. Spratt and Artemace Spratt, his wife. The property is described as bordering on Chaplin River and the Chaplin and Rockbridge turnpikes. If State Road #1796 from Rockbridge to Chaplin River is that turnpike, then Casteel's three acres would have been located near Tatham Springs. Casteel described the Spanish Marker as located about two miles from the Nelson county line, near Chaplin River. This is also near Tatham Springs and is marked as #4 on Map #4. Casteel also mentions that the stone marker was located near a small mound that seems to indicate further Indian presence.

This marker is definitely evidence that the Spaniards were in this area and that there was something of importance to them there. It is hard to believe that someone would forget the whereabouts of a silver mine. The Spanish system of markers would likely have allowed them to return 100 years later to find its location. Certainly there was no reference to the silver mine on the stone, but it did have an identification number for their records, which no doubt were very detailed with accurate mapping. Swift credits the Spaniards for locating the silver mine. This is further verification there were facts entwined in the Swift stories. In *The Virginia Gazette Index 1736-1780*, there were several listings under, "Silver seized from Spanish, French, British and Genoese ships." Perhaps a Spanish ship was seized with a load of silver and the location of the mine was discovered through its crewmates.

The Chaplin River mentioned in the "spanish marker" story was named for the Kentucky pioneer Captain Abraham Chapline. While researching John Filson, one finds an interesting story about Captain Chapline. From *John Filson, The First Historian. His Life and Writings*, one finds that Filson had investigated the stories that Prince Madoc of Wales had established a Welsh colony in America in the twelfth century. To bring further credit to his investigation, Filson brings forward another prominent Kentuckian in support of his theory.

The following is an excerpt from *John Filson, The First Historian. His Life and Writings*:

"Captain Abraham Chaplin [his last name was spelled various ways] of Kentucky, a gentleman whose veracity may be entirely depended upon, assured the author [Filson] that in the late war, being with his company in garrison at Kaskasky, some Indians came there and speaking in the Welsh dialect, were perfectly understood and conversed with by two Welshmen in his company, and that they informed them of the situation of their nation as mentioned above."

The town of Chaplin in Nelson County, just north of Chaplin River, was also named for Abraham Chapline, and is about five and one half miles due north of Polin (Walton's Lick).

The Swift-Alexandria, Moody-Washington County Connection

If there were a cover-up operation designed to conceal the whereabouts of a Benjamin Moody silver mine in Washington County Kentucky, would one expect to find anything? If Swift was the one known to be connected in some way to the mine, it would be absolutely necessary for him to have no documentation in the county wherein the mine was located. However, significant evidence was found to connect Jonathan Swift to Washington County, and most importantly, to the Moodys. From *Virginia County Court Records Deed Abstracts of Fairfax County, Virginia 1791-1792* by Ruth and Sam Sparacio, one finds that the first of two points of evidence loosely ties Swift to Washington County by an indenture between a Thomas Cunningham and a Phillip Marsteller from Alexandria, Virginia, where Swift, John Taylor and James Kerr all signed as witnesses. Swift, Taylor and Kerr could have been called as witnesses who were familiar with the area where this property was located. Of course, Taylor and Kerr were mentioned with the Swift properties in Chapter Two of this book. The properties were located in the southwest corner of Washington County and located on Beech Fork and Hardin's Creek. The indenture was made at Alexandria.

The second point of evidence establishes a definite connection between Jonathan Swift and the Moodys. Benjamin Moody and Jonathan Swift were both from Alexandria, Virginia. This point alone is a strong connection; however, finding that they attended the same church during the same years is a solid connection. From the *Register of Baptisms, Marriages and Funerals, During the Ministry of the Rev. Doc. James Muir in the Presbyterian Church of*

Alexandria D.C., under marriages: September 12, 1799, Benj. Moody and Elizabeth Blunt married. This was Benjamin Moody, Jr., son of the Benjamin Moody who was granted the property in Washington County Kentucky.

Under "Baptisms" it was noted that on November 2, 1800 Benj. Moody, son of Benj. Moody and Elizabeth, his wife, was baptized. Under funerals: October 22, 1803, Mrs. Elizabeth Moody died at 25 years of age.

What would be the odds that a property that was considered to be a possible location of Jonathan Swift's silver mine in 1985, would be owned by someone that Swift attended church with and that his name would closely resemble Munday?

Salt, Silver and 202-204 King Street

If the mysterious Swift silver mine was located in northern Washington County, and a covert silver mining operation was going on there in the late 1700's, then an ideal opportunity for a safe and secret removal of smelted silver or silver ore (most likely) existed there via Matthew Walton. As previously noted, Walton was one of the earliest and largest salt manufacturers in Kentucky in those days.

Salt was a precious and scarce commodity in those pre-refrigeration days. It was valuable not only in the preservation of meat, but in great monetary value as well. It would have been expected that an adequately armed escort would accompany any salt shipment that Walton sent out from Walton's Lick. This normal and logical protection of his merchandise would arouse no suspicion from anyone along the way. All that Walton and Moody would need was security around the island, safe transport from point A to point B and a logical and believable place for point B.

Which brings up the next important point: **Matthew Walton manufactured salt – Jonathan Swift sold salt.** This is verified by three advertisements Swift placed during a ten-year period. The first was in September 1786, the second was on January 6, 1790, and the third in 1796. These ads may be found in Chapter Three of this book by the dates just mentioned.

There would be absolutely nothing to arouse suspicion if a shipment of Walton's Salt was delivered to one of Swift's places of business. No one would be the wiser that only the top half of Walton's Salt barrels had salt in them. If the smelting of the silver ore was done in Alexandria, then this was a most ingenious operation to have the silver ore and the salt needed for the refining process all delivered at the same time in Walton's salt barrels. Swift's part of the operation, getting the silver from point B to point C, would have been the most precarious link in the chain of delivery. Point C was overseas.

What possible reason would there have been for these men to keep a silver operation a secret? There are many possible scenarios that one could come up with to explain why Swift and those involved would need a cover-up operation. Only two will be considered here. The first scenario would be the old Swift story from *History of Kentucky*, Judge Charles Kerr, editor. It is listed as Swift "Tale #2" in Chapter One of this book and it is basically the same old story of greed and murder. The second scenario is based upon the facts of this investigation. There have already been enough negative stories associated with the Swift legend. For the sake of new discussion and possibilities that are based upon the evidence of this investigation, an alternate scenario is offered, which considers the characters of this story to be innocent until proven otherwise.

Scenario #1 is the most obvious and simple to accept and, as noted, it is Kerr's Swift "Tale #2" in Chapter One of this book. It does seem that some of the evidence presented in this book could be interpreted to support the old stories. If the old stories were true, it would certainly explain why a cover-up was needed, due to the disappearance of people who went looking for the mine never to return. It was well known that both Filson and Harrod disappeared while looking for Swift's silver mine. As mentioned in Chapter Three of this book, no information was found on Swift during December 27, 1787 thru October 26, 1789, which is the documented time period (1788) that Filson had met "a man named Swift," and it is also the same year of John Filson's disappearance. It was also presented in Chapter Three that little information was found on Swift during the 1790 to 1795 time period. This, as cited in Chapter Two, is the documented period of time he was in Kentucky purchasing land, and as mentioned in Chapter One, it was during this time, 1793, that Colonel James Harrod disappeared. Also as discussed in Chapter Three, the first known record of Swift in Alexandria was by the October 20, 1784 ads he placed, and, previously mentioned in this chapter, Benjamin Moody, the man who is proposed to have possibly owned a Kentucky silver mine, died in 1784. To claim the mine, and attempt to set up a legitimate mining operation would most definitely have brought a serious investigation from the law. To own up to it would undoubtedly mean a sudden stop at the end of a rope for all involved.

Scenario #2 is the theory presented in this investigation of why a cover-up was needed, and is more difficult to believe and would be even harder to prove. This is the more plausible of the two scenarios, based on the evidence. This second scenario would also explain the need for a secret operation, because in the years to come, public opinion could and no doubt would have forced the secret agreement to be broken. One obvious reason that this scenario is possible is due to the evidence in support of the good reputations of the men involved in this investigation. Also considered was the possibility that the Swift journals and the old stories are designed to conceal the truth, then it is probable that Kerr's Swift "Tale #2" (Chapter One) is also just a convenient and easily believable diversion.

The second scenario is primarily based upon the following eight reasons:

1. The time period of the 1780s and 1790s where shortly after the American Revolution.
2. Jonathan Swift and the men involved in this Swift silver mine investigation were some of the finest and outstanding citizens and patriots of their day.
3. The mention of the French working a silver mine in the Swift journals.
4. Lafayette paying homage to the recently deceased Jonathan Swift. This is indicated by Swift's daughter, Ann Foster Swift, riding along with the General at his return celebration in Alexandria in October 1824 as mentioned in Chapter Three of this book. Lafayette's tribute to Swift by this public display of sentiment is further indicated when the General stops the procession, turns to Ann Foster Swift, and comments on her father Jonathan's portrait of Washington which was displayed on the "triumphal arch."
5. Jonathan Swift married Gen. Roberdeau's daughter, which indicates further French connections.
6. Jonathan Swift was in charge of ships and in the business of shipping overseas.
7. The possible involvement of Dr. James Craik.
8. The complexity of the cover-up operation. It is beyond the capabilities of just one man or even a small organization to pull off such a complex operation.

The second scenario: The silver mine was used as a bargaining chip before or during the Revolutionary War for military support from France. The mine operation would have been under military control supervised by those doing their duty to honor a verbal contract made with Lafayette. It is also likely that Spain and Holland (Swift would later be consul to Holland) were in on various bargaining chips. Swift's lawyer father, Samuel, from Boston was involved in the beginning stages of the American Revolution by his participation in The Boston Tea Party. Could it be that Jonathan was involved in an operation that put the finishing touch to it by making deliveries to honor this agreement? Considering how harshly his father was dealt with by the British, he would have jumped at the chance. If this scenario should be proven true, it is probable that Jonathan Swift would have temporarily been active military in merchant guise. It is possible that Swift ended up the scapegoat resulting from a momentary breach of the mine's whereabouts. One thing seems certain: The stories of slander against Jonathan Swift seem mostly untrue. If the Jonathan Swift of this investigation is the Swift of the silver mine legend, then it is possible that he has been vilified for matters that would have been out of his control. Of all the merchants, officials and citizens of Alexandria, Jonathan Swift was chosen by the people to take charge of protecting their valuables, during The War of 1812.

The Relevance of Lead Mining, and the Notation of William H. Patten

In Chapter Three of this book, highlights were given of Jonathan Swift's father-in-law, General Daniel Roberdeau, which was taken from *Genealogy of the Roberdeau Family*, written by Roberdeau Buchanan. Considerable detail was given to the fact that, during the Revolutionary War General Roberdeau was called upon to oversee the production of a lead mining operation, for the purpose of procuring lead for the army. Roberdeau's first duty was to erect a stockade fort in the immediate vicinity of the mine. His other duties included obtaining men for mining the ore, building a furnace for the smelting of ore, opening said mine, and smelting the ore. It was also stated "a considerable quantity of ore [was] procured and some lead made."

The fact that Daniel Roberdeau was solidly documented as having been in charge of a lead mining operation has a tremendous relevance to that of his son-in-law, Jonathan Swift of Alexandria, Virginia, who is suspected of being a participant in a secret silver mining operation. The correlative importance of the fact that Swift's father-in-law operated a mining operation, built a furnace for smelting, and smelted the ore he mined is great indeed; however, the most significant connection to the Swift Silver Mine Legend is the fact that the ore being mined by Daniel Roberdeau was "lead."

In nature, silver is generally found in the combined state, usually in copper or *lead*. The mineral galena, which is found in Kentucky, is the principal source of lead production. Silver occurs in the free or uncombined state only in small quantities, and then usually in conjunction with deposits of gold and copper. Only twenty-five percent of the world's annual production of silver comes directly from silver ores. The remaining *seventy-five percent* is obtained as a by-product of the refining of lead, zinc, copper, and gold ores.

Silver-bearing lead ores contain the most silver, and zinc concentrates the least. Lead ore is smelted to produce an impure lead-silver alloy. From this, impurities such as arsenic, tin, and silver must be removed. Silver is removed by adding zinc to the molten lead.

This information, coupled with the fact that Swift's father-in-law had mined lead ore in an obscure place in the wilderness in 1778, it certainly seems to identify more of the missing pieces of the Swift Silver Mine puzzle. The search for *Jonathan Swift's Lost Lead Mine*, may sound ridiculous but it may very well be true, and the following remarkable evidence, corroborates this supposition.

As it was with Swift's portrait of Washington, and the family tradition pertaining to it, one must be able to determine if the tradition has reason for merit. Does history lend support for the tradition? As mentioned, it is probable that the documented family traditions relating to Jonathan Swift, which had been passed down through the Patten family, are reasonably accurate. A two hundred year old family tradition will be harder to accept than one that is fifty years old. It is not difficult to believe that one could tell a story with accurate detail, which was told to them by their grandmother, and through this assertion the following information is presented.

When an investigation into a subject such as this is begun, one hopes for affirmations along the way. Realizing that Swift Property #1 was located in the center of the four *view towns*, recognizing that the man named Swift in the John Filson land entry was describing an "X marks the spot" as to where the mine was located, finding an undeniable Kentucky connection pertinent to Robert Louis Stevenson, and discovering that Jonathan Swift's father-in-law mined, and smelted lead ore, are only a few of the many affirmations, which have been presented in this work that are relevant to this investigation.

One such affirmation came like a voice out of the past from the pencil of a person who loved the many stories of Jonathan, and Ann Roberdeau Swift. This remarkable person from times past is none other than the Swift's great-grandson, William H. Patten.

As mentioned in Chapter Three, a family of Swift's descendants lent to the writer of this work a copy of *Genealogy of the Roberdeau Family*, by Roberdeau Buchanan. It is a rare, very hard-to-find book; however, the most fortunate singularity pertinent to this acquisition occurred upon the realization that William H. Patten once owned the book. While researching the "Lead Mine and Stockade Fort/Fort Roberdeau," section of the "Daniel Roberdeau" chapter of the book, an extraordinary discovery was made by means of a penciled in *notation*, being located at the top of page number 83 of said book. The transcription of that notation is as follows—

169

"Grandmother often told me that Jonathan Swift had large investments in a lead mine, the location of which was unknown. WP"

The initials "WP" stand for William Patten. It has been determined that it was William H. Patten, and not William Swift Patten who authored the notations. His grandmother, whom he mentioned, was Ann Foster Swift-Patten, the daughter of Jonathan Swift. See scanned copy of page number 83 of said book with Mr. Patten's notation.

The notation by William H. Patten, coupled with the discoveries previously mentioned throughout this book, affirms that Jonathan Swift (1764-

DANIEL ROBERDEAU.   83

can find no report of the Board of War on the subject,
or any further mention in Congress:
"June 23, 1778. Ordered: That the Board of War estimate
the expense of the fort lately built by Mr. Roberdeau, in Bedford county, in Pennsylvania, and report the same to Congress,
with their opinion by whom the same ought to be defrayed."
It does not appear that any remuneration was made to
General Roberdeau for his expenses in working this mine
and erecting the fort, although it is seen to have been
done by the orders of, or at least with the consent of,
Congress and the Assembly, both of whom it seems felt
themselves in a measure responsible. On the 1st of
April, 1779, the Assembly reiterated its resolve of March
31, that General Roberdeau be indemnified; and the
matter remained before the house as late as 1781, without settlement, although the journals show that it was
repeatedly brought up for consideration.

SECOND MARRIAGE.

But a very few days after General Roberdeau's last
election to Congress, he contracted a second marriage
with Miss Jane Milligan, of Philadelphia. A notice of
the event appearing in the *Pennsylvania Packet*, of December 3d, 1778, as follows:
"Last night, was married, General Roberdeau to Miss
Milligan, an agreeable young lady, who has every quali-
fication to felicitate the nuptial state."
From the similarity of the name which she gave her
son, born some years after, it is presumed that she was a
daughter, or at least a near relative, of James Milligan,
of Philadelphia.
This gentleman is frequently mentioned in public
affairs of this time, in connection with the finances. He
was, in March, 1776, one of the numerous Signers of
Bills of Credit; July, 1776, one of three Commissioners
to Settle the Accounts of the Northern Department; in
March, 1778, spoken of as Commissioner of Claims at
the Treasury; Nov., 1778, one of six Commissioners of
the Chamber of Accounts; Nov., 1779, Auditor-General
to the Treasury; Oct., 1781, Comptroller of the Treasury.

THE MEETING OF MAY 24-25, 1779.

No sooner had General Roberdeau retired to private
life, than he was again called before the public, to pre-

1824), of Alexandria, Virginia, was involved in a potential, if not probable, *silver-bearing lead mine.*

While Kentucky is not traditionally known as a lead mining state, it does have a well-documented history of lead mining. The following excerpts from Collins' *History of Kentucky*, Volumes One and Two, provide documentation of lead as well as silver- bearing ore.

The following nine excerpts are from, *History of Kentucky*, Volume One, "Annals of Kentucky"

1) "April 1 [1866] – Discoveries of lead ore in Owen, Scott, Fayette, Grayson, and other counties, …

2) "November, 25 [1865] – Mining for lead ore, in Fayette Co., 7 miles from Lexington, on the Lees-town Pike.

3) "December, 1 [1865] – Lead ore discovered in Owen, Henry, and several other counties.

4) "March, 10 [1868] – Lead mines discovered in Bath Co., near Sharpsburg.

5) "February, 25 [1868] – Lead ore taken from several places in Bourbon Co., the finest vein on Payne's farm, 3 miles west of Millersburg – a vertical vein, commencing at the top of a cliff 60 feet high, on the bank of Hinkston Creek, very small at the top (about 1 inch) but enlarging to 9 inches in the depth of a few yards. At Ruddell's Mills it has been found; and was mined on Esq. Nunn's place, to some extent, years ago.

6) "November, 28 [1872] – Specimens of silver-bearing ore found upon the farm of Mrs. Judith L. Marshall, near the Ky. River in Henry Co.

7) "March, 28 [1858] – Silver ore discovered on Willow Creek, four miles from Falmouth, in Pendleton County.

8) "August, 15 [1850] – Specimens of silver ore found near the Cumberland Falls.

9) "October, 5 [1873] – At the Louisville Exposition are exhibited some beautiful specimens of lead ore from Livingston Co., and of fluorspar from Caldwell Co.

From *History of Kentucky*, Volume Two, in the "Whitley County" chapter, the following historic account of mining silver is given.

"A Cornish miner was employed by the movers in the speculation to extract the silver from the iron ore, and he actually 'exhibited five or ten cents worth of silver from his crucibles.' But, Prof. Owen, in his report of the geological survey (vol. I, page 236), says the silver 'must have been derived either from argentiferous lead, employed in large quantities to cupel or refine the metallic ingot of iron reduced previously from the ore, or was fraudulently introduced during the process of smelting or refining – since traces of sulphuret of lead, that might be present in the ore, even if argentiferous, could not supply more that a small fraction of a grain to the ounce of ore.'"

Also found in Volume Two, from the "Henderson County" chapter. "A Lead Mine was opened, about 1857, near McElroy's gap, on the Henderson and Nashville railroad."

The following is taken from Volume Two, the "McCracken County" chapter. "*Silver and Lead.* – About 1846, considerable time and money were expended in searching for silver ore, with but very partial success; lead ore was found, but not in paying loads."

Several other accounts of lead, and silver mining are given in *History of Kentucky*, however, the following historic account, from the "Breckenridge County" chapter, is most relevant in regard to the discoveries of this investigation.

"*Minerals.* – Extensive banks of coal of fine quality are in the N.W. part of the county, near Cloverport. Lead ore has been discovered, which is said to yield lead 6 percent, more than the most noted Missouri mines."

The following excerpt was obtained through a University of Kentucky website, titled *Miscellaneous Mineral Resources in Kentucky.*
"Mining Districts"
"Kentucky was a major center for mining iron, phosphates, barite, and fluorite during the early 1900's. Mines operated for several years, until larger deposits were discovered in other parts of the United States, making Kentucky's deposits uneconomic. Some of the earliest mining in Kentucky occurred in vein deposits near Gratz in Owen County, where lead was mined for bullets during the Revolutionary War. Occasionally, some of the vein mineral deposits are mined by small operators, but currently no mines are operating in any district. However, exploration activity has been conducted by major mining companies."

It is unknown at this time if the person in charge of this lead mining operation near Gratz in Owen County, Kentucky, was Jonathan Swift's father-in-law, Gen. Daniel Roberdeau.

By this knowledge of minerals, and lead mining, one may conclude with reasonable confidence that the Jonathan Swift of this investigation was a participant or investor in lead and silver mining in the state of Kentucky.

Whether the supply of silver-bearing lead ore in Kentucky was economic or cost effective by today's mining standard is irrelevant. The fact of paramount importance pertinent to Swift Legend is that mining and smelting an undetermined amount of silver in Kentucky is possible.

Whether Swift produced large or relatively small amounts of silver bullion is immaterial. The fact that it is extremely probable he produced some silver is enough to determine that the historic and remarkable story of Jonathan Swift's silver mine is based upon actual events.

Another notation of Mr. Patten, which demonstrates the great pride and interest the Pattens took in preserving the family tradition passed down from the Swifts is found on page 124 of said Roberdeau book. As mentioned in Chapter Three of this book, Ann Roberdeau Swift was "lead out to dance by General Washington." On the margin to the side of this paragraph, Mr. Patten penciled in the following note about his great-grandmother—"I have the dress she wore on this occasion."

In speaking with a descendant of the Jonathan Swift family, it was discovered that this dress, as well as the remarkable story of it, had remained in the family until recent years.

The final points to be made in regard to Daniel Roberdeau, Jonathan Swift, and the lead mining subject, corroborate the theory presented as "Scenario #2," in this Chapter, suggesting that the Swift silver mine was under government/military control, are as follows.

1) General Daniel Roberdeau was in charge of a military/government controlled, lead mining operation

2) General Lafayette knew the Roberdeau and Swift families intimately. As previously mentioned, Jonathan and Ann Roberdeau Swift's daughter, Ann Foster Swift, was riding in General Lafayette's carriage during his triumphant visit in 1824. The following excerpts from *Genealogy of the Roberdeau Family*, further document the relationship between Lafayette, the Roberdeaus, and the Swifts.

"Lafayette, during his visit to Washington in 1825 [1824], as the nation's guest, was a frequent visitor at Colonel [Isaac, son of Daniel] Roberdeau's house, and left many treasured mementos of his visits;

some flowers that he gathered and kissed before presenting them to one of the daughters, &c. When about to return to France, the last house he was in [,] in Georgetown, was Colonel Roberdeau's, where he lingered until the mayor came and told him the procession was waiting for him..."

Also from the same chapter --
"Not only from those in their midst did expressions of sympathy come, but from afar; the aged Lafayette heard of Colonel Roberdeau's death, and sent the following beautiful expression of his feelings:

"Paris,
May 28, 1829.
"Dear Madam: It is with the deepest regret, that I have heard the heavy loss for which you are so unfortunately mourning. The opportunities I had to appreciate the Colonel's worth, my personal attachment to him, to you, dear madam, and to your amiable daughters, make me more affectionately share in your affliction. I beg you and them to accept the sympathies, regards, and best wishes, of
"Your sincere friend, Lafayette."

Swift's son, William Roberdeau, gave the following toast to Lafayette during his triumphant visit to Alexandria in 1824. "'Lafayette: one of the master workmen who assisted in fitting the keystone to the triumphal arch at Yorktown, when a victorious termination was effected, of our glorious struggle for freedom and independence.'"

Could it be that Swift purchased the Kentucky properties and had a dual objective: To be a diversion to throw people off the trail of the silver mine and to also be a mercy mission? John Filson disappeared in 1788 and in 1791 Swift purchased his first properties in Kentucky. Colonel James Harrod disappeared in 1793 and in 1794 Swift purchased the remainder of his properties, the Springfield and Greenwich indentures being the last he purchased.

The following is a very short list of those that could have been in the loop with Swift (Swift and "Co"):
1. Benjamin and William Moody
2. General Matthew Walton
3. William May –

William May, from the Coxes Station and Bardstown areas, was possibly in the loop due to his involvement with the Swift properties. He was also a very early surveyor and there is also the connection of Mr. May of Boston (as noted in Chapter Three of this book), from whom Swift learned the merchant trade. One other May connection was William and George May (brothers) who surveyed Benj. Moody's land.

4. Philip Phillips could have been in the loop due to his involvement of the Swift properties and he early on also lived in the Bardstown Coxes Station area.

5. Dr. James Craik from Alexandria, Virginia. Dr. Craik is only considered to be in the loop if the reason for cover-up scenario #2 just mentioned was true. It seems logical, considering all the evidence, that the first surgeon general could be involved in a mercy mission to prevent any further Kentucky pioneers disappearances.

There are many possible scenarios that one could create based upon the evidence of this investigation. This book is an interpretation of the facts presented. If one chooses to believe that the 20,718 ¾ acre Swift Property #1 with the Quincunx, the adjoining properties that form an excellent exit route and the many matching landmarks to be the most likely area for a silver mine, who could fault them? It should be pointed out, though, that the Bell, Barbour & Banks adjoining properties that formed the excellent exit route could have been just as useful for salting a false mine with silver ore from another mine. It is suspected that this old trick has been used in various parts of Kentucky. It is nearly the same distance from Swift's Gold Vault Property #2 to Swift's Property #1 as from Swift's Gold Vault Property #2 to Benjamin Moody's Island.

The following is the complete list of comparisons between Robert Louis Stevenson's *Treasure Island* and the Swift legend which has been formulated from the information presented in Parts One and Two of this book.

Treasure Island	Swift Legend/Investigation
1. Long John Silver	1. Jonathan Swift, who is associated with "silver" and silver mines
2. Pirate, Captain John Flint	2. Abram Flint, from Swift mining party
3. Captain Flint murders six crew members, to keep the treasure for himself.	3. Swift murders six crew members to keep the treasure for himself
4. Blind Pew, looking for treasure map at the Benbow Inn.	4. Blind Swift, looking for treasure, leaves map with Mrs. Renfro
5. Benbow Inn	5. Swift lodges at Renfor's
6. Billy Bones leaves map and journal at Benbow Inn	6. Swift leaves map and journal with Mrs. Renfro
7. *Long* John Silver's, Spy-Glass Tavern hence the name, sea-cook	7. Swift, White House Tavern on the *Long* Glades, the original sea-cook
8. Doctor Livesey	8. Doctor Craik, land speculator with Swift and George Washington's personal physician
9. Skeleton Island	9. Indian Burial Mounds near mines
10. Benjamin Gunn, "The Man of the Island"	10. Benjamin Moody, owned the *Kentucky Island*
11. The "Barsilver," left undiscovered on the island	11. Lost silver mines
12. Treasure hidden in cave	12. Treasure hidden in cave
13. Tall ships	13. Tall Ships, Swift owned a fleet
14. Pirates	14. Swift and his father-in-law called pirates
15. Widow Hawkins at the Benbow Inn	15. Widow Renfro
16 An "X marks the spot" treasure	16. An "X marks the spot" treasure site with decoy mines
17. Map and journal with directions to a treasure site	17. Map and journal with directions to a treasure site

THE THIRD NARRATIVE

PART THREE

MULTIPLE LAYERS
OF ROBERT LOUIS
STEVENSON

CHAPTER SEVEN

In Chapter One of this book, a typically known historic account of the Swift legend was presented. While there are many versions of the legend, they have mostly the same story line. Another account of the legend has been presented in the evidence and theories found in Part Two of this book.

Also in Chapter One, a case was presented to demonstrate how the stories of the Swift silver mine legend and Robert Louis Stevenson's *Treasure Island* were similar and the likelihood that Stevenson had based *Treasure Island* on the Swift stories was also presented. While the case presented in Chapter One seems to indicate a strong probability that Stevenson did use the Swift story as the genesis for *Treasure Island*, it did not prove it beyond a doubt. Part Three of this book is dedicated to prove beyond a doubt that *Treasure Island* is based upon Swift legend and that Stevenson's entire book is based solely upon Jonathan Swift, the real-life sea cook.

It is proposed that a previously unknown narrative of the Swift legend exists encoded in the pages of *Treasure Island*. It is a separate and parallel story, a hidden book within the book. It is a detailed account of Jonathan Swift's silver mining experiences and also provides Stevenson's ingenious method of pinpointing the location of the silver mine. The encoded book also provides the name of a historically unknown person who was brought to light in Part Two of this book and will be revealed later. The encoded book also reveals that a Swift journal did find its way to Stevenson through Lloyd Osbourne and that he had taken the journal from his father, Sam Osbourne.

178

Determining Probability and Verifiers

It is apparent that only those who were made aware or who suspected, due to the obvious similarities between *Treasure Island* and the Swift legend, would be able to recognize that there was an encoded message about Swift within *Treasure Island*. Only by having considerable knowledge of Jonathan Swift and the Swift legend is the code likely to be spotted.

Code: a system used for brevity or secrecy of communication, in which arbitrarily chosen words, letters or symbols are assigned definite meanings.

Code: a word, letter, number or other symbol used in a code system to represent or identify something.

Encode: to convert (a message, information etc.) into code

Cryptogram: 1) a message or writing, encode or cipher, 2) an occult symbol or representation.

By understanding that there are a wide variety of encoding techniques, and presenting little known facts pertaining to Robert Louis Stevenson, a substantial case may be presented concerning probability.

For nearly as long as humankind has been writing, we have also been writing encrypted messages. One who encodes is a cryptographer, and a cryptanalyst is one who decodes an encrypted message. The two primary requirements of encoding a message are; 1) one must actually have the ability to encrypt a concealed message into a text, and 2) one must have a message or story to be encoded.

There are numerous methods used for encoding; in fact, new ways are constantly being created. Some codes are created using a numeric system, while others use a letter or alphabet system. Codes are sometimes in one part, and others have two or more parts. Many codes such as these have been used during times of war.

While Stevenson's style of creating cryptograms has been interpreted as using both numeric and letter *verifiers*, it is proposed that his primary method of encoding was accomplished through his use of *emblems/symbolism, double entendres*, and *allegory*.

A current-day inspiration for one to become a cryptographer could be attributed to Dan Brown's book *The Da Vinci Code*. Perhaps it was Edgar Allan Poe who inspired a young Stevenson, and as previously mentioned, Stevenson's writing of *Treasure Island* was influenced by Poe's works. Present day it is not commonly known that Poe was also a famous cryptologist. It is also probable that he was influential in Sir Arthur Conan Doyle's literary work. In Conan Doyle's book, *The Dancing Men*, the great detective Sherlock Holmes solves a case of cryptic communication. In this story a strange

179

alphabetic code system using *stick men*, which resemble the ancient Scandinavian "runestave," are used by a man in the story to communicate a secret message to a woman. The stick men are openly displayed for all in the story to observe; however, only the man and woman possess the knowledge of the mysterious code alphabet.

Some codes actually refer to other worldly matters, such as the aforesaid runic alphabet. Should a Norseman wish to write a letter with an encoded message, which refers to certain elements of the twenty-four runic system called "The Elder Futhark" it could be accomplished as such – "The sun is shining brightly this morning, however, I believe it will thunder tonight." The recipient of the letter, who is also trained in the runic system, would understand that the word "sun" represents the rune called "sowilo," which is similarly shaped to a backward "Z" or a bolt of lightning. The word "thunder" would be recognized as representing the rune called "thurisaz," which resembles a hammer, and also represents the god Thor. The Celts had a similar writing code system that is called Ogham.

Another potential method of secret communication is through the art of painting, which was a primary subject matter in Dan Brown's *The Da Vinci Code*. It is very conceivable that an artist with the talent of da Vinci or Michelangelo could encrypt a hidden message into one of their masterpieces, which have been seen but unrecognized for hundreds of years. The subject matter could be something relevant to every person on earth or something trivial, which could only be identified by a specific group such as the Papacy or perhaps the powerful Medici family. In fact, many great works of art conceal esoteric truths by emblematic/symbolic means. The following description of two works of art are excellent examples of cryptic communication through the suggestive art of imagery and symbols. The first painting is of a man, writing in a darkened room with only the light from a candle being held by a simian, who represents the devil, titled "Saint Dominic and the Devil" by Pietro della Vecchia. The second is a painting in which animals are given human features, with a fox clothed in the red robe of a king, onlooking businessmen are depicted as rodents, while a rabbit protests to the fox (king), titled "His Majesty Receives" by William Holbrook Beard.

In Chapter Three of this book an excellent example of communication through the art of imagery may be found in the foreboding persona the Marquis de Lafayette symbolizes. In this imagery creation Lafayette is wearing an ancient Knights Templar apron. The black apron effectively highlights the intended instrument of communication, which is the skull and crossbones. This symbol was emblematic of a teaching which was known only to the

Templars. The apron's meaning, which is steeped in mystery, undoubtedly contained many levels of cryptic revelations.

Another example of pictures/symbols representing an esoteric teaching is the Tarot. The Tarot cards are used for divining a future outcome by some, and are tools for teaching for others. There are seventy-eight cards. Fifty-six of the cards make up four suits form the Minor Arcana, and the remaining twenty-two form the Major Arcana. Each of these cards reveals an instant story to those who possess the hidden knowledge of the Tarot.

The Church has many symbols, which are known by its members such as a cross, a crown of thorns, an empty tomb, and a risen Lord, to name only a few. The Masonic Lodge teaches its initiates through architecture and workman's tools, which are emblematic to a story or teaching that is relevant to one of the aforementioned items. A floor or mosaic tile, a column or columns, and a winding flight of stairs are a few of the teaching tools of a Mason.

The runic, art, tarot, church, and Masonic methods of telling stories through figurative, symbolic, and allegorical means are forms of cryptic communication. Only those who possess this knowledge, which was imparted to them by one of these specific forms of teaching, fully understand the lessons of the story.

This parabolic method of communication is effectively used by Stevenson to create *suggestive cryptograms* within the text of *Treasure Island*. By using this method in conjunction with other techniques, to be mentioned in the following chapters, the adventures of Jonathan Swift were encoded. Each cryptogram is suggestive in itself; when the Swift legend is regarded as the thread of meaning which binds them, they become a cumulative force.

The word *allegory* means to "speak of one subject while alluding to another." It is a figurative treatment of one subject under the guise of another, a *symbolic narrative*. It is accomplished by placing certain elements or "emblems" of a story or subject matter, which one desires to suggest or allude to, into the spoken or written words at hand. The emblematic reference or allusion to Jonathan Swift, within the text of *Treasure Island*, may partly be found in the name, John Silver. Both men share the same initials and both relate to "silver."

It has been said that when it comes to cryptology "one can use two books, and create something from nothing." The cryptographer must, therefore, leave *code verifiers* for the cryptanalyst. By these verifiers or code confirmers, a cryptanalyst may reasonability determine if the apparent cryptograms are systematic, and coincide with the story, which is considered to be the intended concealed message. For each *theory of encoded message* there must be a verifier to confirm it, and Stevenson does not disappoint in this crucial element of code breaking. By having other sources of information, evidence pertinent to the life of Robert Louis Stevenson, and of Jonathan Swift's life in Alexandria, as well as the silver mine legend, more points of similarity will be noticed while forming theories pertaining to the many cryptograms. When pieced together they create the full encoded story. These code verifiers confirm for the decoder that the suppositions, which have been formed pertaining to the cryptograms, are indeed real.

Stevenson's method of encoding was created using the story line of *Treasure Island*, characters in the story, initials of names, story objects, news and people of his time period and books he made reference to in his genesis of *Treasure Island*. These books were *At Last* by Charles Kingsley, *Tales of a Traveller* by Washington Irving and *History of Notorious Pirates* by Charles Johnson. Last and most important, it was necessary for Stevenson to have many details about Jonathan Swift and his life's adventures for him to have the story that was to be encoded.

Instead of using many different characters or objects for his encoding, he uses the same characters or objects and has multiple layers of revelations for each one. An excellent example of this can be found in Brown's book, *The Da Vinci Code*, in which one of the principle characters of his book is referred to as "the master of double-entendres" and that "he loved anything with multiple layers of meaning, codes within codes."

The Fabulist

Why Stevenson wrote *Treasure Island* with a complete story encoded into it will likely remain a mystery. Perhaps, and most likely, it was to impress fellow writers such as W. E. Henley, whom Stevenson used to bring life into Long John Silver, or for British Prime Minister Gladstone, "who read *Treasure Island* over and over" as referred to in *The Letters of Robert Louis Stevenson*.

It is not a question of whether Robert Louis Stevenson actually encrypted hidden messages or stories into his literary works, or whether he was capable of doing it. One needs only to examine his body of works to discover that he had written a number of *fables*. A fable is "a story with a moral" or "an implied story within the narrated story." The moral is the allegorical or implied message not the directly written part of the story. This art of story telling, when the unwritten or unspoken element of the story is the actual purpose of the story, is an allegory/apologue, which is a form of cryptography.

The following excerpt is from a 1901 Charles Scribner's Sons publication titled *Letters and Miscellanies of Robert Louis Stevenson*:

"The fable, as a form of literary art, had at all times a great attraction for Mr. Stevenson; and in an early review of Lord Lytton's Fables in Song he attempted to define some of its proper aims and methods. To this class of work, according to his conception of the matter, belonged essentially several of his own semi-supernatural stories, such as Will of the Mill, Markheim, and even Jekyll and Hyde; in the composition of which there was combined with the dream element, in at least an equal measure, the element of moral allegory or apologue."

Faith, Half-Faith, And No Faith At All

by

Robert Louis Stevenson

In the ancient days there went three men upon pilgrimage; one was a priest, and one was a virtuous person, and the third was an old rover with his axe.

As they went, the priest spoke about the grounds of faith.

"We find the proofs of our religion in the works of nature," said he, and beat his breast.

"That is true," said the virtuous person.

"The peacock has a scrannel voice," said the priest, "as has been laid down always in our books. How cheering!" he cried, in a voice like one that wept.

"How comforting!"

"I require no such proofs," said the virtuous person.

"Then you have no reasonable faith," said the priest.

"Great is the right, and shall prevail!" cried the virtuous person. "There is loyalty in my soul; be sure, there is loyalty in the mind of Odin."

"These are but playings upon words," returned the priest. "A sackful of such trash is nothing to the peacock."

Just then they passed a country farm where there was a peacock seated on a rail, and the bird opened its mouth and sang with the voice of a nightingale.

"Where are you now?" asked the virtuous person.

"And yet this shakes not me! Great is the truth and shall prevail!"

"The devil fly away with that peacock!" said the priest; and he was downcast for a mile or two.

But presently they came to a shrine, where a Fakeer performed miracles.

"Ah!" said the priest, "here are the true grounds of faith. The peacock

183

was but an adminicle. This is the base of our religion." And he beat upon his breast and groaned like one with colic.

"Now to me," said the virtuous person, "all this is as little to the purpose as the peacock. I believe because I see the right is great and must prevail; and this Fakeer might carry on with his conjuring tricks till doomsday, and it would not play bluff upon a man like me."

Now at this the Fakeer was so much incensed that his hand trembled; and lo! In the midst of a miracle the cards fell from up his sleeve.

"Where are you now?" asked the virtuous person. "And yet it shakes not me!"

"The devil fly away with the Fakeer!" cried the priest. "I really do not see the good of going on with this pilgrimage."

"Cheer up!" Cried the virtuous person. "Great is the right and shall prevail!"

"If you are quite sure it will prevail?" says the priest.

"I pledge my word for that," said the virtuous person.

So the other began to go on again with a better heart.

At Last one came running, and told them all was lost: that the powers of darkness had besieged the Heavenly Mansions, that Odin was to die, and evil triumph.

"I have been grossly deceived," cried the virtuous person.

"All is lost now," said the priest.

"I wonder if it is too late to make it up with the devil?" said the virtuous person.

"O, I hope not," said the priest. "And at any rate we can but try. But what are you doing with your axe?" says he to the rover.

"I am off to die with Odin," said the rover."

Another fable by Stevenson may be found in Appendix C of this book.

From *The Letters of Robert Louis Stevenson* Volume One by Booth and Mehew, there is documented proof that Stevenson had begun to think and write in code at an early age. In an 1865 letter to his Father he wrote: "My Dear Papa, I am a great deal better, but I have begun to despair of 5/-, which is a disappointment, however I can claim -/1 for being called Smout. I am going to send doctor Paul's story of Dr. Muir to the magazine (of course suppressing names). Remember the old houses please. I have no more news so good bye. R.L.B. Stevenson." Smout and Smoutty was Stevenson's nickname given to him by his father. Another note of interest in the letter is Dr. Muir. The "Dr. Muir" Stevenson wrote about was William Muir D.D. (1787-1869) who was minister of St. Stephens in Edinburgh, from 1829 to 1869. Whether Dr. James Muir and Dr. William Muir were closely related or knew each other is unknown. It is an interesting connection of the two different worlds of Stevenson and Swift by Swift's association with Dr. James Muir. Dr. James Muir was pastor of the Presbyterian Church of Alexandria and its members were largely of Scottish origin. Dr. James Muir was Swift's pastor and had died under Swift's hospitable roof.

As mentioned in Chapter Three of this book, Swift's family had come from Rotherham England prior to the year 1634 and Swift had traveled there to visit his relatives. The distance from where Swift's relatives were living in Rotherham to Stevenson's' Edinburgh is only about one half the distance across the state of Kentucky. It is likely that the people living in Edinburgh and those living in Rotherham shared many common folk tales. The Swift legend is an excellent example. This legend is known in many areas of Kentucky, Tennessee, Virginia and the Carolinas. When weighing all these facts it does not seem so improbable that the Swift legend could have been one of Stevenson's favorite childhood stories. It is likely that the Swift legend was one of the stories that Stevenson's own father had told to him. The following is an excerpt from *My First Book–"Treasure Island"* an article written by R. L. Stevenson and published in McClure's Magazine in September of 1894. In it Stevenson writes of his father—"His own stories, that every night of his life he put himself to sleep with, dealt perpetually with ships, roadside inns, robbers, old sailors, and commercial travelers before the era of steam."

Also in the "My First Book" article, there seems to be evidence and admission from Stevenson that there is a hidden story encoded in *Treasure Island*. In the article it appears that Stevenson is describing the usefulness for which a map can be for writing purposes. It also indicates there is a secret book within *Treasure Island* which is the second meaning, the double-entendre. The following is the final lines of the article, which not only sum up the possibility that Stevenson had a story to be decoded in *Treasure Island* but gives one final clue as to the content of the encoded story: "The tale has a root there; it grows in that soil; it has a spine of its own behind the words. Better if the country be real, and he has walked every foot of it and knows every milestone. But, even with imaginary places, he will do well in the beginning to provide a map. As he studies it, relations will appear that he had not thought upon. He will discover obvious though unsuspected shortcuts and footpaths for his messengers; and even when a map is not all the plot, as it was in *Treasure Island*, it will be found to be a mine of suggestion." When he wrote "a spine of its own" he hints at a hidden book within the *Treasure Island* book, and when he wrote "behind the words" he indicates that the words appearing in *Treasure Island* have encrypted meanings as well as the obvious. When he wrote—"as he studies it, relations will appear that he had not thought upon" he seems to be indicating to first study the map for clues but is also likely to be indicating that to decode it one must study it and then revelations will begin to appear. Stevenson chose his words in this article carefully and when he ended his article in the final four words with –"a mine of suggestion" he was leaving a clue to the story content of the encoded message which, of course, is a silver mine. When Stevenson wrote "He will discover obvious though unsuspected short-cuts and footpaths for his messengers," he was referring to how the characters, objects, words, initials, etc. can be used to convey a cryptic communication.

It seems that Stevenson's *My First Book–"Treasure Island"* article was designed to give hints to those who knew there was an encoded message in *Treasure Island*, and also how to decode the message. In the McClure's article he gives clues on where to find major code keys in the books, *Tales of a Traveller*, Johnson's *The General History of the Robberies and Murders of the Most Notorious Pirates*, and *At Last-A Christmas in the West Indies*, he also demonstrates how he encodes secret messages in *Treasure Island* when he mentioned such phrases as "a spine of its own behind the words," and "a mine of suggestion." To one who was aware that there is an encoded message in *Treasure Island*, these lines demonstrate some of the style of encoding Stevenson used. Stevenson could also be giving a clue to a primary encoded character when he mentions the word "mood."

There is another obvious example suggesting that Stevenson was hinting about a hidden book within *Treasure Island*, which is found in the design of the book itself. Stevenson wrote the book as if it were being narrated by two of the principle characters. Jim Hawkins, a boy of approximately eleven to fourteen years of age, which the story revolves around, is the first and primary narrator. The second narration is given by Dr. Livesey which has a much shorter account and is found exactly half way into the book, front to middle and back to middle. It is a book within the book. This book within a book alludes to Stevenson's encrypted book or— *a third narrative.*

Stevenson no doubt primarily intended the people of his lifetime to be the potential code breakers. This is evident by some of the encoding methods he used. With the clues and hints he left in his "My First Book" article and with his Dr. Livesey second narrative, which is located in the middle of *Treasure Island*, it is apparent that he wanted those who knew there was an encoded message to be able to decode it. These clues and hints helped him communicate to potential decoders that they were on the correct path by leaving these code confirmers/verifiers. Stevenson no doubt left these code verifiers to assist potential decoders and assure them that they are correct in their suppositions of his (Stevenson) encoding technique. The most evident and important of these code verifiers is found in the text at the end of *Treasure Island* and it pertains to the historically unknown man.

It is proposed that the following story titled, "The Third Narrative," is the encoded message within the pages of *Treasure Island*, the conclusions of which are based upon what is known about Jonathan Swift both the legend and the documented facts of his life. It is also based upon the suppositions and theories presented in Part Two of this book. The keys used to decode it were the documented books that Stevenson mentioned in his genesis of *Treasure Island*, Stevenson's personal letters, and the people and news of Stevenson's time period. The encoded story is a separate and parallel book with a "spine of its own" and is the "story behind the words" of Treasure Island. This short story has been formulated by the information that Stevenson has encoded into *Treasure Island*, which cannot be read as a story in its many layers of code upon code. By taking the information Stevenson provides in his method of encoding and combining it with known information about Swift's life it can be translated into a readable story. Information such as the first name of Jonathan Swift's father, Samuel, cannot be found in the encoded message, but Stevenson does provide information on Samuel Swift. Also, not all dates and ages are confirmed in the encoded message but knowing when Swift's father died from other sources of documentation one can fill in the blanks. To illustrate, on the first page of *Treasure Island*, Stevenson leaves blank the actual year the adventure takes place, "17__." It is known that Jonathan Swift was eleven years old when his father Samuel died in 1775. Samuel was placed under house arrest sometime shortly after The Boston Tea Party in 1773/74; so one may reasonably conclude that the "17__" blank year, that Stevenson omitted, is approximately 1774/75. The arrival at this conclusion will be clarified later in this book.

There are other comparisons such as this where the blanks of the code have been filled in to construct a readable story that will be clearly recognized once the decoding sections have been read.

The Third Narrative

Robert Louis Stevenson came into the possession of a Jonathan Swift journal and the entire book of *Treasure Island* is based upon Jonathan Swift of Alexandria Virginia. Stevenson chronicles the life of Jonathan Swift from the ages of eleven to fifty. Lloyd Osbourne presented the Swift journal to Stevenson and Lloyd had taken the journal from his father, Sam Osbourne. It is also likely that a map of where Swift's silver mine was located accompanied the journal or was a part of it.

The following is the information proposed to be in the Swift journal, which Sam Osbourne had owned and brought with him to California from Kentucky and Nevada, and all his other wanderings. Though most of the information now mentioned likely came from that journal, it is impossible to distinguish whether Stevenson has added information he personally knew about Swift, and it seems probable he knew a great deal.

Stevenson's Swift Silver Mine Journal

Jonathan Swift and his family, due to his father's house arrest, had a British soldier move into their house for the purpose of keeping his father, Samuel, under house surveillance. Samuel was poorly treated by the belligerent soldier and died a prisoner in his own home in 1775. Jonathan was eleven years old when his father died. When Samuel Swift was first arrested in 1773/74, his wife and children were forced into hiding. At that time they were seeking help from friends and neighbors.

It appears that Jonathan was a young man when he first became aware of the location of a Kentucky silver mine and was likely a teenager when he first visited it. A man named Flint or a man with the initials of J. F. accompanied him on one of his Kentucky visits. Another man in his party was named Benjamin Moody.

Sometime after Swift had been made aware of the silver mine and its location, it is believed that he had divulged secretive information as to where the silver mine was located. Due to this leaked information, Swift was given the job of creating a cover-up mission to cause confusion as to where the mine was located. The cover-up was a sealed orders commission. The operation was performed by Swift purchasing properties in Kentucky and by setting up pointers (a quincunx) to purposely mislead those who were seeking the silver mine. This cover-up operation was successful, and Swift found it very humorous that he had fooled the British who were looking for the real silver mine.

The journal indicates that Swift had set up at least one of these fake silver mines and possibly three. Silver ore was taken from the real silver mine to salt Swift's faked mine. The journal explains how this was done and explains that Swift was actually an American spy and was the inside man of the cover-up operation. It was Swift and a doctor who were primarily responsible for the cover-up.

The land the fake silver mine was on was a much larger property than the property of the real silver mine. The real silver mine was known by Swift and the doctor to be located on or near the property of Benjamin Moody. Moody's property is described as being located in Kentucky approximately five miles north of Springfield in Washington County. Moody's property is also mentioned as being just south of a salt lick. Benjamin Moody may have known how to produce salt. The journal also mentioned that Indian burial mounds were near Moody's property. The encoded message also states that Swift spoke with "great rapidity." After Swift's participation in the cover-up mission was completed, he returned to his normal life in Alexandria and his days of adventure in Kentucky were over.

The following are the intended objectives to be obtained in Part Three of this book:

1. To demonstrate the technique of how Stevenson encoded hidden messages in the text of *Treasure Island*.

2. To show how the encoded messages were interpreted, using what is known about the life of Jonathan Swift, considering him and the Swift silver mine legend to be the intended secret message that Stevenson had encoded.

3. To show how the many elements of the encoded messages were translated into "The Third Narrative" story and by proving that the encoded messages are referring to Jonathan Swift and his life's adventures. This demonstrates how The Third Narrative story was constructed by combining the encoded messages with what is known about Swift's life.

4. To show that there is potentially important information about the Swift silver mine legend in the encoded message.

5. To show that Robert Louis Stevenson, author of a diversity of books and fables, was likely far more complex and talented than he was already considered to be, and to prove that he was an unknown cryptologist.

Before proceeding into the cryptanalysis of Stevenson's hidden third narrative of *Treasure Island*, the subject of how quickly he wrote the book, and how that factors into the acceptance of probability in regard to his encoded story should first be addressed. As mentioned in Chapter One of this book,

"Stevenson wrote the first fifteen chapters of *Treasure Island* in fifteen days, and when he resumed writing he finished the remainder of the book in another fifteen days."

Could Stevenson have written, from square one, the entire thirty-four chapters in thirty days, and also incorporate a highly detailed encrypted story during the process? When considering this question, one must distinguish between the time needed for the writing process, and the time required for the process of creation or formulation of the story, characters, and structure of the book. The fact that he wrote Treasure Island in thirty days must in itself be proof that many months of creative preparation was needed.

It seems probable that Stevenson was familiar with the Swift silver mine legend from childhood. However, if he had first come into contact with the story through the Osbournes, he would have had several years to begin the creation process of the written story as well as the encoded one. Stevenson met Fanny Osbourne in 1876, and he had written *Treasure Island* by 1881. This five-year time period is much more time than he would have needed to formulate the emblems, symbols, and cryptograms to be planted within the written text for the encrypted story. It seems logical to state, with his vast knowledge of literature, and his past practice of writing in code, as demonstrated in the letter to his father, he would have needed only a few months to formulate the code structure before he began to write the story; although, it could have been several years. Once the complex format of the encoded story had been constructed…it was already part of the story, which was then ready to be written.

The following are the first of the many elements of Stevenson's encoded message of the Jonathan Swift silver mine story. Presentation of these elements will demonstrate how the encoded message was decoded.

Sam and Lloyd Osbourne

According to the story line of *Treasure Island*, the map and journal found its way into the hands of young Jim Hawkins believed to be eleven or twelve years old. Jim Hawkins was the primary narrator of the *Treasure Island* story. Lloyd Osbourne was in the same age bracket of Jim Hawkins when Stevenson wrote Treasure Island. Stevenson dedicated the book to Lloyd, who in a letter to W. E. Henley, states that he "owes it to."

The following excerpt is from *The Letters of Robert Louis Stevenson* edited by Bradford A. Booth and Ernest Mehew volume #3. In the portion of the letter the excerpt comes from Stevenson is speaking of being in the process of writing *Treasure Island* – "Four of them are as good as done, and the rest will come when ripe; but I am now on another lay for the moment, purely owing to Sam, this one; but I believe there's more coin in it than in any amount of crawlers: Now, see here. *The Sea Cook or Treasure Island: A Story for Boys.*"

It seems probable that Stevenson would have dedicated the book to Lloyd for obvious reasons, but when he used the words "owing to Sam" he is referring to Samuel Lloyd Osbourne, the son of Sam and Fanny Osbourne. It seems to indicate more than just loyalty to his stepson.

Jim Hawkins is a *Treasure Island* code name with multiple layers of usages; the first and primary name concealment that Stevenson provides in Jim Hawkins is Jonathan Swift. The secondary name concealment for Jim Hawkins is Lloyd Osbourne. The only reason that Stevenson included young Osbourne in the encoded story was because he had given Stevenson a Swift journal. Lloyd Osbourne had taken the Swift journal from his father, Sam. All other Jim Hawkins usages refer to Swift. The comparisons of Jim Hawkins, who found a treasure map and book and gave it to Dr. Livesey (the man who wrote the second narrative found exactly half way in the book which symbolically represents Stevenson's "third narrative"), and Lloyd Osbourne, taking his father's Swift journal and giving it to Stevenson, can be further identified by defining the code names of Sam Osbourne. The primary codename for Sam Osbourne is Israel Hands and his secondary code name, which is used as a pointer or identifier, is O'Brien.

In *Treasure Island* Israel Hands was the coxswain of the ship *Hispaniola* and also the former gunner of pirate Captain Flint. Israel Hands was a real life pirate and can be found listed in Captain Charles Johnson's *A General History of The Robberies and Murders of the Most Notorious Pirates* (Johnson's pirate book) written in 1724. In a letter to Charles Baxter in March or April 1877, Stevenson wrote—"The man with the linstock is expected in May; it makes me sick to write it." This excerpt was taken from *The Letters of Robert Louis Stevenson Volume Two* by Booth and Mehew. Stevenson was referring to Sam Osbourne who was still married to Fanny at the time. A linstock is a staff with one end forked so as to hold a lighted cloth or match and was used to fire a cannon, which was Israel Hands' job with Captain Flint.

Chapter 26 of *Treasure Island* is titled "Israel Hands," and Chapters 25 and 26 are based on the interaction of young Jim Hawkins and Israel Hands. The interaction between Hawkins and Hands represents a parting of ways. It also represents Lloyd Osbourne taking the journal from his father, Sam Osbourne. The *Treasure Island* text has Hawkins (Lloyd) defeating the coxswain (Sam). The coxswain in this case represents the one who steers the ship. The ship *Hispaniola*, in this case, represents the Swift journal. Jim Hawkins takes the *Hispaniola* away from Israel Hands and puts it into the hands of Captain

Smollett. Captain Smollett is one of two code names that represent Robert Louis Stevenson. Both aspects of the *Hispaniola* and Captain Smollett will be clarified later. One line in Chapter 25 has Hawkins telling Hands –"I'm not going back to Captain Kidd's anchorage." In other words he (Lloyd) and the journal are going to be with Stevenson/Smollett. In a line from Chapter 26, Hands says—" 'Jim', says he, 'I reckon we're fouled, you and me, and we'll have to sign articles." And in the same paragraph Hands says—" I don't have no luck, not I." When Fanny and Sam Osbourne divorced, articles would have been signed. This Stevenson clue demonstrates that he is talking about Sam and Lloyd Osbourne in this excerpt. From what has mostly been learned about Sam Osbourne, he seemed to be down on his luck in his later years; however, he was an interesting study himself and led a very fascinating and adventurous life.

When Jim Hawkins first encounters Hands on the ship in Chapter 25, Hands is engaged in a fight to the death with another pirate, an Irelander named O'Brien. After Hands kills O'Brien, Hawkins describes the corpse as having a fixed smile. Hands says to Hawkins—" He warn't no seaman anyhow." The dead man, O'Brien, was also referred to as "red cap." Although no first name is given to O'Brien, he would be called Seaman, Sailor or Smiley, giving him the initials of S.O., the same initials of Sam Osbourne making Israel Hands the primary code name for Sam Osbourne and Smiley/Seaman O'Brien confirms the identification. Jim Hawkins' (Lloyd) and Israel Hands' (Sam) initials are J. H. and I. H. "I" comes before "J" indicating that "J" (Jim) is the descendant of "I" (Israel).

Further affirmation indicating that Israel Hands is the code name of Sam Osbourne is found in Washington Irving's *Tales of a Traveller* Part 4, "The Money Diggers," under "Adventure of the Black Fisherman." In this chapter, "Sam," the black fisherman, is in a confrontation with the "red caps," which are a group of five men wearing red caps. *Tales of a Traveller* is one of the books in which Stevenson acknowledged using as the genesis of *Treasure Island*, and this demonstrates how he refers to the sources needed to decode the encoded message. This also confirms that Israel Hands who was fighting seaman O'Brien/red cap, is in fact *Sam* Osbourne and O'Brien was only a pointer, which was only one half of the encoded equation.

In the Israel Hands Chapter 26 of *Treasure Island*, where Jim Hawkins kills Israel Hands and the pistols fall from his hands, Stevenson writes— "They did not fall alone; with a choked cry, the coxswain loosed his grasp upon the shrouds, and plunged head first into the water." The encoded message Stevenson reveals in this excerpt is-- the veil of mystery surrounding the

Swift silver mine legend was unveiled when Hands let go of the shrouds of the *Hispaniola*. Shrouds in this case indicate *to veil in mystery* and the *Hispaniola* is the code name for the Swift journal. This confirms that Lloyd took the journal from Sam and gave it to Stevenson. The story of the Swift legend, which was shrouded in mystery, was now in Robert Louis Stevenson's hands. When Jim Hawkins (Lloyd Osbourne) took the *Hispaniola* (journal) from Hands (Sam Osbourne), it placed the *Hispaniola* into the control of Captain Smollett. Stevenson's two code names for himself were Captain Smollett and Dr. Livesey. Stevenson likely chose the name Smollett because of its similarity with his nickname, Smout/Smoutty. As Captain Smollett was in control of the *Hispaniola*, so was Stevenson, captain/author of *Treasure Island*. Another likely pointer that Captain Smollett is the code name for Stevenson is the English novelist Tobias George Smollett 1721-71 associating the name Smollett with novelist, Stevenson.

"The Coxswain loosed his grasp upon the shrouds and plunged head first into the water." From a 1920 Charles Scribner's Sons publication of *Treasure Island.*

Another Stevenson writing that demonstrates that Captain Smollett is the code name for Smoutty, is his fable titled, *The Persons of the Tale*. The complete short story may be found in Appendix C of this book. The story takes place between Chapters 32 and 33 of *Treasure Island*, and it is a conversational debate between Captain Smollett and Long John Silver. While part of the meaning of the story clearly can be interpreted as a struggle between good (Captain Smollett) and evil (Long John Silver), with the two men arguing the existence of God, or a creative force, represented as the Author, only the parts of the fable pertaining to this investigation will be addressed. The indicators in this story that Smollett is Smoutty are: 1) There are only two characters, John Silver and Alexander Smollett. 2) While John Silver knows that he is only a character in the *Treasure Island* story, only Captain Smollett is aware of the Author. 3) The following excerpt certainly could be interpreted as being a mirrored image of an unhappy time period in Stevenson's family life– "'I am a man that tries to do his duty, and makes a mess of it as often as not. I'm, not a very popular man at home, Silver, I'm afraid,'" and the Captain sighed." 4) In the next excerpt it appears that Stevenson is once again referring to himself, when he says, "bad as he is." Also in this excerpt Captain Smollett is aware that the Author is beginning to write again-- "'I'm glad enough to be Alexander Smollett, bad as he is; and I thank my stars upon my knees that I'm not Silver. But there's the ink-bottle opening. To quarters!'

"And indeed the Author was just then beginning to write the words: CHAPTER XXXIII"

In the article *My First Book*–"Treasure Island," published eleven years after *Treasure Island*, there is further indication that Stevenson was leaving clues for those who were aware of an encoded story within the text of *Treasure Island*. This is demonstrated in a paragraph on the next to last page of the article. In this paragraph, Stevenson is first describing how he borrowed the idea of Flint's skeleton pointer from Edgar Allan Poe and then he continues to say…"and in the same way, it was because I had made two harbors that the '*Hispaniola*' was sent on her wanderings with Israel Hands." Stevenson is referring to the wanderings of Sam Osbourne (Israel Hands) and the Swift journal (*Hispaniola*) he had in his possession during his many wanderings from Kentucky to California. Stevenson was informed of Osbourne's wanderlust, and no doubt so were many of his friends.

When one writes or speaks of ship travel, it is usually referred to as a voyage, journey, excursion or etc. Wandering is typically used to describe the actions of an individual, not to describe ship travel. There are multiple levels of cryptic communications in this excerpt. The first communication is further acknowledgement that Israel Hands is the code name for Sam Osbourne in *Treasure Island* by associating Hands with wandering. The next layer of encrypted communication is that Osbourne had kept a Swift journal (*Hispaniola*) in his possession. The final layer is that the journal (*Hispaniola*) which was in the possession of Israel Hands (Sam Osbourne) and ultimately in the possession of Dr. Livesey and Captain Smollett a.k.a.Robert Louis Stevenson.

PIECES OF EIGHT

CHAPTER EIGHT

As mentioned in the comparisons between *Treasure Island* and the Swift legend in Chapter One of this book, there are definite similarities in these two stories. One such noticeable comparison is Jon/Jonathan Swift and John Silver, Swift of course being associated with silver and both share the same initials. John Silver is not the only character in *Treasure Island* that shares a similar story line with the Swift legend. When Billy Bones leaves a treasure map and book with the widow Hawkins at the Benbow Inn, it compares with Swift leaving a map and journal with widow Renfro, who has a name similar to Benbow. When Blind Pew comes to widow Hawkins at the Benbow Inn looking for Flint's fist (treasure map), it compares to blind Swift looking for his lost silver mine and leaving his journal with Mrs. Renfro. The last of the obvious character similarities is Captain Flint who murders six of his crew so he would not have to share the treasure, compares to the very same story in Swift legend instead it was Swift's name instead of Captain Flint's.

John Silver, Billy Bones, Blind Pew and Captain Flint are the obvious characters in *Treasure Island*, and are the elements Stevenson used to demonstrate that this is a story about Swift. In total Stevenson uses seven characters of the book to introduce different elements of the Swift story, and each of these create vital components within each cryptogram. It appears that when Stevenson wrote, he chose his words at times to have more than the apparent meaning. When Stevenson used the phrase "pieces of eight," he was not

196

only referring to coins, but was also referring to the seven characters he used to encode the life of Swift. These seven characters were all developed before Stevenson reveals the name of Swift, who is eighth, and the seven characters were all pieces of eight or *pieces of Swift*.

Stevenson used the *pieces of eight* phrase several times. First, in Chapter Ten, "The Voyage," when he refers to Long John Silver's parrot named "Captain Flint." In Chapter 27 of *Treasure Island* the name of the chapter is "Pieces of Eight" and it is the last chapter in Part Five of the book. By this time, all seven of the defining characters had been introduced. The encoded name of Swift was introduced shortly after that in Chapter 29 titled "The Black Spot Again" which is in Part Six of the book titled "Captain Silver." Stevenson ended *Treasure Island* with Jim Hawkins narrating and saying "Pieces of eight! Pieces of eight!"

The following is the list of *Treasure Island* characters that Stevenson used to define Swift, and Swift completes the list as number eight:

1. Jim Hawkins
2. Billy Bones
3. Captain Flint, the pirate
4. Blind Pew
5. Mr. Blandly
6. Long John Silver
7. Captain Flint, the parrot
8. Jonathan Swift

Most of these characters have multiple usages (layers of revelation) not only to define Swift but also to help tell the encoded story. The following information demonstrates how Stevenson provided the necessary clues to establish that the seven *pieces of eight* characters are actually descriptors of Jonathan Swift's life. Other usages of the seven Swift characters will be mentioned throughout the remainder of this book.

#1 Jim Hawkins

Jim Hawkins is previously mentioned as a character with multiple usages. Stevenson demonstrated through Jim Hawkins how Lloyd Osbourne provided a Swift journal to him and that the journal came from Lloyd's father, Sam Osbourne. If an adequate case has been presented to prove the likely possibility that such a journal was given to Stevenson, then, since Jim Hawkins is the primary narrator of the *Treasure Island* story, it stands to reason that Jim Hawkins would be considered by Stevenson to be the words of the Swift journal or Swift himself. Jim Hawkins also represents a young Jonathan Swift eleven to fifteen years of age.

There are definite similarities when comparing *Treasure Island's* boy hero, Jim Hawkins, to the known boyhood life of Jonathan Swift. One such obvious comparison between the two boys, Swift and Hawkins, is that of the unwanted houseguest. In *Treasure Island*, it was the pirate, Billy Bones, who came to stay with the Hawkins at the Benbow Inn. In Swift's life, it is when Jonathan's father, Samuel, was placed under house arrest and surveillance as mentioned in Chapter Three of this book. This surveillance no doubt means that a British person/soldier was placed there to live under the same roof as the Swifts. When comparing it to the *Treasure Island* story of Billy Bones, it seems that Stevenson indicates that the surveillance person was a British solider. More will be said later about how Stevenson communicates that the pirates of the encoded story are actually the British.

In the text of *Treasure Island*, Jim Hawkins's father's life was shortened by the tyrannical Billy Bones. The following excerpt is from *Treasure Island* Chapter One. In it, Jim Hawkins (Swift) narrates his father being terrorized by Billy Bones—" I have seen him wringing his hands after such a rebuff, and I am sure the annoyance and the terror he lived in must have greatly hastened his early and unhappy death." It was shortly after Billy Bones took up lodging at the Benbow Inn that Mr. Hawkins died. This directly compares to Samuel Swift's hastened demise when he was placed under house arrest in approximately 1774 and he died from disease induced by the confinement of being a prisoner in his own home on August 31, 1775. Could Stevenson's account of this story affirm the cause of Samuel Swift's hastened death?

As mentioned in Chapter Three of this book, from *The Memoirs of Gen. Joseph Gardner Swift*, Jonathan Swift's brother, Foster, gave the following account of their father, Samuel, and British General Gage – "Among his details he said that the death of his father had occurred under the tyranny of General Gage…" In comparison, the following excerpt from Chapter I of *Treasure Island* has Stevenson describing the tyranny of Billy Bones – " My father was always saying the inn would be ruined for people would soon cease coming there to by tyrannized over and put down, and sent shivering to their beds; but I really believe his presence did us good."

Another obvious comparison between young Jim Hawkins and young Jonathan Swift is when Jim Hawkins and his mother desperately seek help in the neighboring hamlet to help secure the Benbow Inn from the pirates/British. This compares to the story of how Swift's mother, Ann Foster Swift, hid in the woods with her sons, Foster and Jonathan, whence she wrote despairing letters to influential friends begging help in freeing her husband, Samuel, from British imprisonment. The following excerpt is from Chapter Four of *Treasure Island* in which Jim Hawkins narrates and further describes the time period when he and his mother were seeking help: "We slipped along the hedges, noiseless and swift." It should be noted that in this excerpt, it is Stevenson's first use of the word "swift."

"...We slipped along the hedges, noiseless and swift..."
Illustration from a 1965 Golden Press publication of *Treasure Island*.

Stevenson directly links Jim Hawkins to three of the seven that make up the pieces of eight and they are Long John Silver, Mr. Blandly and Captain Flint, the parrot. One method that Stevenson used to link John Silver, Mr. Blandly and Jim Hawkins was by Squire Trelawney referring to each of them as "trumps." They are the only ones in the book referred to this way. One may first think that Stevenson is referring to them as a person of quality, but a trump in this case means that John Silver, Blandly and Hawkins are of the same suit or the same person at different time periods.

Stevenson further links John Silver to Jim Hawkins in the following excerpt from Chapter Seven of *Treasure Island*, in which Squire Trelawney writes in a letter, describing John Silver– "Long John Silver, he is called, and has lost a leg; but that I regarded as a recommendation, since he lost it in his country's service under the immortal Hawke." Stevenson is making two separate points in this excerpt. The first is that the time line of the encoded story is not to be confused with the constant time line of *Treasure Island*. There are two time periods he defines. The first is when Swift is young which Jim Hawkins represents. The second is when Swift is the fifty-year-old John Silver. The second point Stevenson is making is the nearly identical name of Hawke compared to Hawkins, and that Silver lost his leg while in the service of *Hawk* which alludes to his younger self, Jim *Hawkins*.

Stevenson accomplishes another method of linking Jim Hawkins to John Silver with the phrase *pieces of eight*. The only characters of the book in which Stevenson has saying the phrase *pieces of eigh*t are Long John Silver's parrot, "Captain Flint," Long John Silver and Jim Hawkins. By using this phrase, Stevenson has these three identifying themselves as one of the seven that make up the *pieces of eight* characters. As mentioned, each of these seven defines Swift, who is eventually identified after each of the seven descriptors, making Swift number eight. Stevenson further links Jim Hawkins to John Silver when he reveals the encoded name of Swift and that will be explained after links of the seven has been completed.

The following information could explain why Stevenson chose the last name *Hawkins* for *Treasure Island's* boy hero. Whether Stevenson acquired this information through a Swift journal or by other means is unknown. One of the comparisons made in this book, between *Treasure Island* and the Swift legend, has been the widow Hawkins at the Benbow Inn of *Treasure Island* to the widow Renfro of Bean Station in Tennessee. Present day Bean Station is located in Grainger County, Tennessee. Grainger County was formed in 1796 from "Hawkins" and Knox Counties. Bean Station was located in Hawkins County in 1790 and 1791, the years that Swift was reported to have been there. Bean Station is located in an area heavily known to be associated with the Swift legend and near where the Alleys settled. Robert Alley's Swift journal was in Kerr's History of Kentucky, which is also contained in Chapter One of this book, and as previously mentioned, the Alleys and the Osbournes had family connections. Bean Station is also near the city of Bristol. In *Treasure Island*, Squire Trelawney purchased the *Hispaniola* (Swift journal) at Bristol from Mr. Blandly.

Another probable Stevenson hint is in the name of Black Hills Cove where the Benbow Inn was located. It seems likely that Stevenson was referring to a famous gold mining town of his time that was in Black Hills South Dakota. Many people of Stevenson's day would likely have associated the Black Hills with the mining of precious metals. By doing this he gives more insight to the content of the encoded message, that being the mining of precious metals.

#2 Billy Bones

William (Billy) Bones is one of the principal characters in *Treasure Island* that shares a similar story line with the Swift legend. In the Swift legend, Swift brings with him on his visit to Bean Station, a journal containing a log of his silver mining activities and directions to the silver mines, and leaves the journal in the possession of widow Renfro. In *Treasure Island* Billy Bones brings with him a sea-chest with a treasure map and journal, and after he dies the map and journal are left in the possession of widow Hawkins at the Benbow Inn. This element of the story makes Billy Bones one of the descriptors of the Swift story, but the other function of the Billy Bones character, is to demonstrate that in the encoded message, (which is the viewpoint of Jonathan Swift an American) the British are considered to be the pirates or antagonists. The British are depicted as pirates, in this case, and it is likely that is what Jonathan Swift considered them to be.

The Billy Bones character and much of the story line early in *Treasure Island* was no doubt created purposely by Stevenson to bear an obvious resemblance to the "mysterious stranger" story in Chapter 4, "Wolfert Webber," of Part 4 of *Tales of a Traveller*, titled "The Money Diggers." Those who have read the works of Stevenson know that he was certainly not lacking imagination, creativity, style or any of the necessary abilities to be a great writer. Why then, did he draw so heavily and obviously from *Tales of a Traveller*? One possible answer could be, to attract attention to the similarities of the two books to aid those seeking to decode the encrypted message in *Treasure Island*. As previously mentioned, the article published in *McClure's Magazine My First Book—"Treasure Island"* seems to primarily be an aid for those attempting to decode *Treasure Island*. Stevenson wanted his encoded message to be discovered. Other ideas for *Treasure Island* that likely arose from *Tales of a Traveller* are three red crosses, great white rock, red caps, and a doctor who goes on a treasure hunt.

The name Billy Bones was likely lifted from Johnson's' pirate book. Within the chapter, "The Life of Captain Anstis," is a man named Bones, who is boatswain of the ship, *Good Fortune*. Billy Bones fits into the story line of what is known about Swift's father, Samuel. Billy Bones is interpreted to be a British soldier who moved in with the Swifts to keep surveillance on Samuel Swift. At first, all of the primary characters in *Treasure Island* seem to be of British origin, but the encoded message is based on an American viewpoint. Stevenson used several techniques throughout the encoded message to demonstrate this. In Chapter One of *Treasure Island*, Stevenson has Billy Bones showing up at the Benbow Inn and coming from the "Royale George." This is the first time in the encoded message that Stevenson refers to George III, King of England. It implies that he (Bones) was in the service of the King and a British solider. Also in Chapter One, "The Old Sea Dog at the '*Admiral Benbow*,'" he is referred to as a "'true sea-dog,' and a 'real old salt', and similar names, and saying there was the sort of man that made England terrible at sea."

There is an Alexandria, Virginia connection in Stevenson's use of "the Royal George." The following *Treasure Island* excerpt is found early in Chapter One. In it the Hawkins are inquiring about Billy Bones.

"The man who came with the barrow told us the mail had set him down the morning before at the 'Royal George'; that he had inquired what inns there were along the coast, and hearing ours well spoken of, I suppose, and described as lonely, had chosen it from the others for his place of residence. And that was all we could learn of our guest."

There are two points of comparison relevant to the book, *Treasure Island*, and to the town of Alexandria, in this excerpt. The first, is in the name "Royal George," and the second is found when Stevenson notes that it was also a place to get the "mail."

One of the most frequented taverns in Alexandria during Jonathan Swift's life was the historic "Royal George Tavern." From discussions with historians of Alexandria, history it was found that many pre-Revolutionary War discussions were said to have taken place there.

The primary point of comparison is found not only in the identical name of the two taverns, it is also in the fact that both of these Royal Georges were "mail stops." By providing not one but two points of similarity, Stevenson creates an affirmation for any potential cryptanalyst. The following excerpts are taken from *The History of Old Alexandria, Virginia*, by Mary G. Powell.

"An old newspaper advertises the mail stage arriving from the Spread Eagle at Philadelphia to the Royal George at Alexandria, leaving there every Friday for Winchester by way of Leesburg and Shepherdstown, making the return trip to Alexandria by dinner time on Wednesday. It would be of interest to know what was the most popular tavern here with the tired and hungry traveller. Probably the Royal George, as that was the booking place for the northern mail...

"In his diary of Friday, February, 1760, Washington writes that he went to a ball at Alexandria (The Royal George) 'where music and dancing was the chief Entertainment...'

"The Royal George was the booking place for mail (weekly) between Williamsburg and New York, which was carried by riders (1755), who crossed the Potomac at West's Ferry to Addison's at the mouth of Oxen Run in Maryland. This old yellow tavern was kept for a number of years by a man named Hucorne, and it is traditional that the sign bearing the effigy of George III with 'Royal George' below was changed after the Revolution to the 'George,' bearing a portrait of General Washington.

"The Royal George stood for many years an ornament to the town, and was demolished in 1857, when Harlow's grocery store was built on its site."

Billy Bones is also one of the "B" elements of *Treasure Island*. They are Billy Bones, Black Dog, the beggar Blind Pew, the black spot, Mr. Blandly, Barbecue, Ben Gunn, Benbow, "B" on the sea chest and Black Hills Cove. Three of the "B's" are of the seven *pieces of eight* descriptors of Jonathan Swift and Stevenson links them by using John Silver's nickname, "Barbecue." Stevenson further links John Silver (Jonathan Swift) to Billy Bones, Blind Pew and Mr. Blandly in the following quotation by Long John Silvers "When I was an AB master mariner I'd have come up alongside of him, hand over hand, and broached him to in a brace of old shakes, I would; but now –"

The following excerpt is from *The Letters of Robert Louis Stevenson* published by Charles Scribner's Sons, in which in a letter dated August 25, 1881 to W. E. Henley, Stevenson acknowledges and distinguishes the "B" elements of *Treasure Island*: "And now look here—this is next day—and three chapters are written and read. (Chapter I. The Old Seadog at the *Admiral Benbow*. Chapter II. Black Dog appears and disappears. Chapter III. The Black Spot.) All now heard by Lloyd, F. [Fanny], and my father and mother, with high approval. It's quite silly and horrid fun, and what I want is the best book about the Buccaneers that can be had—the latter B's above all, Blackbeard and sich, and get Nutt or Bain to send it skimming by the fastest post. And now I know you'll write to me, for 'The Sea-Cook's' sake."

Stevenson also used Billy Bones to show that the names of the characters in *Treasure Island* are not what they seem. The following excerpt is from Chapter Two of *Treasure Island* when Billy Bones is replying to Dr. Livesey who has just addressed him as Mr. Bones – "That's not my name, he interrupted."

#3 Pirate Captain John Flint

Pirate Captain John Flint is another *Treasure Island* character that shares a similar story line with the Swift legend. Anyone who knows the Swift legend, both present day and in Stevenson's time, would be familiar with the name Abram Flint. Abram Flint was one of Swift's silver mining associates, and he was known to be a violent person by the account in the Swift stories. The story describes him sword fighting with another of Swift's mining crew, a man named Fletcher. Both men were said to have been heavily drinking, and although Flint was injured, he recovered, but Fletcher died from wounds inflicted by Flint.

In *Treasure Island*, to keep the treasure for himself, Captain Flint murdered six crewmates. In Swift legend, it was Swift who murdered six crewmates for the same reason. In Swift legend, a treasure map and journal describing the whereabouts of a lost silver mine have always been at the heart of the story, and in *Treasure Island* the map is the heart of the story. In Swift legend it was Swift who was primarily known to have been the mapmaker, but in *Treasure Island*, John Flint was the cartographer and it was signed by him using only his initials – J.F. John Flint is interpreted as being a multiple layered character. Although he was used to help identify Swift by defining parts of the Swift legend, he does also represent another distinct individual of the encoded message.

#4 Blind Pew

In the story of *Treasure Island*, Blind Pew is a blind man who came to the Benbow Inn in search of Flint's treasure map. This compares with Swift legend to an older and blind Swift looking for his silver mines and his connection to widow Renfro. This similarity and Blind Pew also being one of the "B's," confirms he is one of the seven descriptors of Swift. The story components that Billy Bones, John Flint, Blind Pew and John Silver convey in *Treasure Island* are commonly known elements to the Swift story, and it makes it easy to identify these four characters as descriptors of Swift.

#5 Mr. Blandly

Squire Trelawney purchased the ship, *Hispaniola*, from Mr. Blandly. Blandly has a similarity to both the Swift legend and what is known about Jonathan Swift in that he is associated with the selling and purchasing of ships. The reasons that Mr. Blandly was created by Stevenson was to define and demonstrate: 1) that John Silver and Jim Hawkins (both Swift descriptors) are also Mr. Blandly, 2) that Swift sold ships and land (land will be clarified later), 3) the complex and dual life of Swift, that of merchant and spy, and 4) the development of the story line of the encoded message.

Both Blandly and Long John Silver were introduced in the *Treasure Island* story in Part Two of the book called "The Sea Cook" within Chapter Seven, "I Go to Bristol." "The Sea Cook" was Stevenson's original title for the book; it refers to Long John Silver. Both John Silver and Blandly are first mentioned in a letter from Squire Trelawney, written at Old Anchor Inn at Bristol, to Jim Hawkins. In the letter Squire Trelawney refers to Blandly as a "trump." This trump statement links Blandly to Jim Hawkins in Chapter Six and John Silver in Chapter Eight who were also identified as trumps by Squire Trelawney. The letter from Trelawney and the use of the word trump help to clarify what Stevenson intends to do with the letter "B." The double entendres are: 1) the "letter" from Trelawney alludes to the "letter B," and 2) "trump" means a suit of something instead of what it seems to be describing that being a desirable person. The suit is "B", in other words, Blandly, Billy Bones, Blind Pew and John Silver (Barbecue) are of the same suit.

In various places of the *Treasure Island* text, Stevenson leaves code verifiers. He does this with Blandly and John Silver in Chapter 33. The following excerpt is from the last paragraph of Chapter 33—"And there was Silver, sitting back almost out of the firelight, but eating heartily, prompt to spring forward when anything was wanted, even joining quietly in our laughter—the same bland, polite, obsequious seaman of the voyage out." By using the word "bland" to describe John Silver, Stevenson is clearly identifying Silver with the character named "Blandly." When Stevenson linked Blandly's and Silver's identities, more than one domino of the encoded message fell. This link not only served as a name verifier, but also contributes as a plot verification of the encoded message. It proves that John Silver/Blandly (both Swift descriptors) led dual lives. One personality of Swift was depicted as a pirate and the other personality was a typical merchant who sold ships. The connection of John Silver and Blandly may also indicate that the information of Swift's dual life may have come to Stevenson through a Swift journal, as this was narrated by Jim Hawkins or Swift's words.

It seems likely that Stevenson chose to use the letter "B" to serve as a pointer to a character or object that has a hidden meaning, because it is the second letter of the English alphabet. By placing a "B," representing the number two, it is an indicator that double entendres are used here. Not all of the code words are identified by a "B." The ones that are not, were all well defined by Stevenson and easily convey his cryptic communication.

#6 Long John Silver

Long John Silver and Jim Hawkins are the two primary characters in *Treasure Island*. Originally Stevenson named the book *The Sea Cook* and Long John is the sea cook. With the exception of the parrot, it has been demonstrated how Silver is linked to the seven "pieces of eight" descriptors of Swift. The following is further information pertaining to Stevenson's encrypted message, and another origin of the character development of Long John Silver. The following list demonstrates how Silver is the most similar to Jonathan Swift in description of all the *Treasure Island* characters:

1. Silver and Swift have the same initials—J.S.
2. Silver and Swift first names were the same or similar—John/Jon
3. Silver and Swift were treasure seekers
4. His last name was Silver and Swift had silver mines
5. Silver and Swift were associated with ships
6. Silver was a pirate and Swift was referred to as a pirate in some of the Swift stories
7. John Silver owned the Spyglass Tavern, and Jonathan Swift owned the White House Tavern
8. Long John Silver was associated with the pirate, Captain Flint, and Jonathan Swift was associated with Abram Flint

As mentioned in Chapter One of this book, Stevenson's acknowledged inspiration for John Silver was his friend, W.E. Henley who also had one leg. It seems likely that Stevenson once again leaves another hint at who John Silver truly was in his article in McClure's Magazine titled *My First Book–"Treasure Island."* The following excerpt is from that article and Stevenson writes-- "And then I had an idea for John Silver from which I promised myself funds of entertainment: to take an admired friend of mine (whom the reader very likely knows and admires as much as I do), to deprive him of all his finer qualities and higher graces of temperament, to leave him with nothing but his strength, his courage, his quickness and his magnificent geniality, and to try to express these in terms of the culture of a raw tarpaulin."

There are two points of interest in this excerpt. The first is when Stevenson stated he had an idea for John Silver, which was to give him some of the characteristics of Henley; it proves that the character of John Silver had already been created. The second point of interest is Stevenson's use of the word "quickness," as being one of the defining points of John Silver. In most any definition of the word *quick*, the word *swift* is used to describe it.

In regard to point number one, it is believed that Stevenson's reference to Henley, being the pattern for John Silver, was also a diversion. One may automatically accept it as obvious, that the primary reason Stevenson had chosen Henley to represent John Silver, was due to Henley's having one leg. There is no doubt that Stevenson gave John Silver some of Henley's personality by using the traits he listed; however, it is suggested that Stevenson gave John Silver one leg because of a character in one of the acknowledged code breaker books, *Tales of a Traveller*.

Once again in Part 4 of Washington Irving's *Tales of a Traveller*, in "Wolfert Webber or Golden Dreams," one of the characters of the story is a man named Peter Stuyvesant who is described in the following excerpt:

"'This will be a rough night for the money-diggers,' said mine host, as a gust of wind howled round the house, and rattled at the windows.

"'What! are they at their works again?' said an English half-pay captain, with one eye, who was a very frequent attendant at the inn.

"'Aye, are they,' said the landlord, 'and well may they be. They've had luck of late. They say a great pot of money has been dug up in the field, just behind Stuyvesant's Orchard. Folks think it must have been buried there in old times, by Peter Stuyvesant, the Dutch Governor.'

'Fudge!' said the one-eyed man of war, as he added a small portion of water to a bottom of brandy.

"'Well, you may believe it, or not, as you please,' said mine host, somewhat nettled; 'but every body knows that the old governor buried a great deal of his money at the time of the Dutch troubles, when the English red-coats seized on the province. They say, too, the old gentleman walks; aye, and in the very same dress that he wears in the picture which hangs up in the family house.'

"'Fudge!' said the half-pay officer.

"'Fudge, if you please! – But didn't Corney Van Zandt see him at midnight, stalking about the meadow with his wooden leg, and a drawn sword in his hand, that flashed like fire? And what can he be walking for, but because people have been troubling the place where he buried his money in old times?'"

The points of interest in the excerpt are as follows:

1. All of Stevenson's uses of *Tales of a Traveller* came from Part Four of the book titled "The Money Diggers."
2. It seemed that Stevenson deliberately drew attention to the similarities between *Treasure Island* and Part Four of *Tales of a Traveller.*
3. The buried treasure
4. Peter Stuyvesant is referred to as the Dutch governor
5. The great pot of money (treasure) was dug up behind Stuyvesant's Orchard
6. Peter Stuyvesant buried the treasure to hide it from the English red-coats
7. Peter Stuyvesant had a wooden leg.

The reason Stevenson chose Peter Stuyvesant to be a key for decoding his hidden message has nothing to do with the character development of John Silver, but was used entirely for the encoded story development.

As Stevenson secretly suggested in his *My First Book-"Treasure Island"* article—once one begins to study upon the encoded message, "relations will begin to appear." After it has been determined how the Stevenson method of encoding is done, not only encoded people can be decoded but encoded stories can be as well. Each key that is found, such as Peter Stuyvesant, is a portion of the encoded story and is one piece of the puzzle. The puzzle pieces must match or overlay with what is known about Swift and Stevenson's lives, which are the templates. These code keys must fit into the Swift/Stevenson pattern. In other words, if the puzzle piece fits or logically matches the pattern, it is considered a piece of the puzzle.

Long John Silver was given his wooden leg, or as it is referred to in Chapter 11 of *Treasure Island*, "timber leg" because of the encoded story Stevenson could convey by using the character of Peter Stuyvesant. The primary ingredient of the Stuyvesant story, that Stevenson intended to incorporate into his encoded message, was that Stuyvesant buried treasure to hide it from the English red-coats. The Peter Stuyvesant element is a story-line verifier, and was incorporated by Stevenson to assist in the decoding process, as well as creating the encoded story-line.

The clues that Stevenson left to assist in identifying Long John Silver with Peter Stuyvesant were: 1) Stuyvesant is a character in one of the code breaker books, *Tales of a Traveller*, which Stevenson obviously used to develop both the stories of *Treasure Island* and the encoded message, 2) Stevenson created John Silver to be a man with a wooden leg, 3) John Silver, like Stuyvesant, was connected with buried treasure, and 4) In Chapter Eight Part Two of *Treasure Island* titled, "The Sea Cook," John Silver is introduced into the story. The name of Long John Silver had previously been mentioned in Square Trelawney's letter, but in Chapter Eight is when the reader actually first meets John Silver. It is immediately in this chapter when John Silver has been introduced that Stevenson links him to Peter Stuyvesant, the "Dutch governor," by having Silver make at statement pertaining to the *Dutch*.

The following *Treasure Island* excerpt has Long John Silver talking to Jim Hawkins after they encounter Black Dog in John Silver's Spyglass Tavern—" 'See here, now, Hawkins,' said he, 'here's a blessed hard thing on a man like me, now, ain't it? There's Cap'n Trelawney – what's he to think? Here I have this confounded son of a Dutchman sitting in my own house, drinking of my own rum!'"

At this time Jim Hawkins was not aware that John Silver was the one-legged man that Billy Bones had warned him about. In the same paragraph, John Silver continues to say –

"'What could I do, with this old timber I hobble on?'"

These are the first verifiers that link Long John to Peter Stuyvesant. It has Silver identifying himself by using the word *Dutchman*, and referring to his *wooden leg* all in the same paragraph. In Chapter Eleven of *Treasure Island* titled, "What I Heard in the Apple Barrel," has John Silver once again identifying himself with Stuyvesant by referring again to his timber leg and to the Dutchmen for the second and last time. Both chapters that he refers to the Dutch, he also refers to his timber leg; therefore, making both connections each time to the one-legged Dutch Governor, Peter Stuyvesant. In Chapter Eleven of *Treasure Island*, Stevenson provides another link to the Stuyvesant story. In this chapter Jim Hawkins is, for the entire chapter, hiding inside an apple barrel for which the chapter is named. In the Stuyvesant story, the treasure was found near Stuyvesant's orchard. While an orchard cannot be provided on a ship, it can be represented symbolically by a barrel of apples. It is also in this chapter that Jim Hawkins discovers that Long John Silver is the one-legged man that he had been warned about by Billy Bones.

While researching the life of Swift's great-grandson, William H. Patten, an amazing discovery was made concerning his family lineage. This information was discovered more than a year after the cryptanalysis work of *Treasure Island* had been completed. There is a family connection pertinent to Jonathan Swift's grandson, William Swift Patten, and Wolfert Webber. Mary E. Hardman Patten, wife of William Swift Patten, descended from Wolfert Webber. From a 1939 edition of *Encyclopedia of American Biography*, a publication of The American Historical Company, Inc., New York, edited by Winfield Scott Downs, is an article about William Hardman Patten.

The following is the first two paragraphs of that article.

"PATTEN, WILLIAM, Editor, Writer, Illustrator – Through the range of his interests and the importance of his gifts, William Patten was widely recognized as one of the most versatile Americans of his generation. As an editor, he served with a number of leading publications and had to his credit such accomplishments as the creation of the celebrated series known as the 'Harvard Classics.' As a writer, his abilities were obvious to competent judges from the beginning of his career and were reflected in the many articles and monographs which came from his pen in after years. He was a talented illustrator himself, and possessed, in addition, the broadest scholarship in this field, enabling him to write with discrimination as a critic and to serve the advancement of an art with which his name will always be closely associated.

"Mr. Patten was born in New York City on November 27, 1865, a son of William Swift and Mary (Hardman) Patten. Through his father he traced his ancestry to William Patten, who came from England to Cambridge, Massachusetts, in 1635. His mother was of Dutch lineage, descended from Wolfert Webber, who lived on a well-known farm located between Chatham (Park Row) and Madison streets, and ran from Pearl to James streets, granted to him by Stuyvesant in 1650. The family has lived continuously on Manhattan Island for three hundred years. Through his father's mother, Ann Foster (Swift) Patten, the family was of French Huguenot descent. General Daniel Roberdeau was his Revolutionary ancestor."

This article establishes a Swift-Patten family connection to Wolfert Webber, which is also in the correct time-period for Stevenson, and provides documentation of a family history with Peter Stuyvesant.

A Swift family connection, relevant to one of the proposed code elements of Stevenson's encrypted story about Jonathan Swift, is certainly worth noting, however, at this time this information should be considered as coincidental. While this incredible evidence does not directly link Stevenson to the Patten family it is a "possible" affirmation, albeit one without further documentation at this time, of the Wolfert Webber code element. If documentation of a Stevenson, and Patten connection should be brought to light, it would certainly support the *Treasure Island* code theory, and could also be indicative of Stevenson's cryptogrammic use of Washington Irving's "Wolfert Webber," which he used to encode information relevant to William Swift Patten's grandfather, Jonathan Swift.

There is another very solid code-story verifier, which historically documents Peter Stuyvesant as a major part of Stevenson's encoded message about Long John Silver a.k.a. Jon Swift. The following excerpt is from Colonial New York by Michael Kammen-- "...Stuyvesant ruled for seventeen years— the longest tenure of any governor in the history of colonial New York—and he most certainly left his stamp upon the province.

"He is best remembered, perhaps, for his peg leg embroidered with silver bands, the legacy of his first military adventure."

Of the many accomplishments of Stuyvesant during these years, he is still best remembered for his "silver leg." Other various accounts of Stuyvesant were that his peg leg was made of solid silver and his nickname was "Old Silver Leg."

There should be little, if any doubt, that Stevenson primarily created the heavily encoded Long John Silver's name, and physical description, due to another man who was also called *Silver*—Old Silver Leg, Peter Stuyvesant.

211

Long John Silver
[Not Original Caption] Illustration from a 1965 publication of *Treasure Island* by the Fountain Press.

Dutch Governor Peter Stuyvesant - "Old Silver Leg"
[Not Original Caption] Illustration from the book *Peter Stuyvesant of Old New York*,
by Anna and Russel Crouse.

Another interesting similarity between John Silver and Jonathan Swift is by the initials of John Silver's wife that Stevenson provides. The following excerpt from Chapter 34 of *Treasure Island* refers to John Silver's wife—"Of Silver we have heard no more. That formidable seafaring man with one leg has *At Last* gone clean out of my life; but I daresay he met his old Negress, and perhaps still lives in comfort with her and Captain Flint." No first name is given for Silver's wife. Stevenson only told us that she was a woman of color; a "Negress," giving her the implied initials of "N.S." -- the same as Swift's wife, Nancy Swift.

John Silver represents the silver mining/treasure seeking part of Jonathan Swift's life. He also represents the part of Swift's life, which as Peter Stuyvesant determined, was spent hiding a treasure from the English red-coats. Stevenson further clarifies through John Silver that British England was actually the pirates of the encoded message. This was also found in Chapter Two, when John Silver said that he

"'...first sailed with [the pirate] England and then with Flint.'"

When Stevenson writes that John Silver a.k.a. Jon Swift "first sailed with England and then with Flint," it also further links John Silver to Jim Hawkins, as well as adding substance to the encoded story. As mentioned in Chapter Seven of this book, the encoded time period the *Treasure Island* story takes place in is 1774/75. In 1774 young Jonathan Swift a.k.a. Jim Hawkins would have been a British citizen, hence, the "first sailed with England" statement. In the normal text of *Treasure Island*, Stevenson represents John Silver (a.k.a. Swift as an adult) as a mutinous pirate, which would be the British viewpoint of him after the American Revolution.

Long John Silver was the most complex and multi-dimensional of all the *Treasure Island* characters. Stevenson presented him as a person whom others do not know whether to love or hate and even when the book ends they still do not know. His nickname was "Barbecue" which means buccaneer or pirate. He, as mentioned in Chapter Eleven of *Treasure Island*, was 50 years old.

It is likely that Stevenson had the idea to give John Silver a nickname due to a pirate mentioned in Captain Johnson's pirate book. In that book, John Walden was a one-legged pirate nicknamed "Miss Nanney." No doubt Stevenson chose to use the nickname not only to add spice to *Treasure Island*, but also for adding the needed "B" factor – Barbecue.

#7 Cap'n Flint

Cap'n Flint is Long John Silver's talking green parrot named by Silver after the famous buccaneer John Flint. The parrot's favorite saying is "pieces of eight" and by this Stevenson identifies the parrot as being one of the seven descriptors of Jonathan Swift. The parrot shares a common factor with the Swift legend in that it is named Flint. It is of course closely associated with John Silver, but the most interesting point that Stevenson has to make pertaining to the parrot is the description of its speech. The following *Treasure Island* excerpt describes the parrot's speech—"and the parrot would say, with great rapidity, 'Pieces of eight! Pieces of eight! Pieces of eight!' till you wondered that it was not out of breath, or till John threw his handkerchief over the cage."

One of the amazing things about parrots is their ability to mimic human speech. Parrot owners will describe their birds as talking high or low, fast to slow, all depending upon whom they are mimicking. Knowing this about parrots gives insight to Stevenson's intended encoded message. The primary point Stevenson is revealing with the parrot and John Silver duo is how the parrot mimics John Silver. The parrot's speech is a mirrored image of John Silver's speech, and Stevenson is saying that John Silver speaks "with great rapidity." In Chapter Three of this book when describing what is known about the appearance and characteristics of Jonathan Swift, the most notable of his characteristics was the "great rapidity of his pronunciation." Stevenson used the exact wording of an *Alexandria Gazette* article about Jonathan Swift that was written in November 1863.

Stevenson also used the parrot to demonstrate that the pirates, or antagonists, of the encoded story were the British by John Silver's statement in this *Treasure Island* excerpt – "'Now, that bird,' he would say, 'is, maybe, two hundred years old, Hawkins—they lives for ever mostly; and if anybody's seen more wickedness, it must be the devil himself. She sailed with England, the great Cap'n England, the pirate.'"

The character Black Dog is not interpreted as being one of the seven descriptors of Swift. His character does not introduce any new elements of the Swift story to the encoded message. Stevenson also refers to Black Dog as "the stranger," identifying that he is not a Swift descriptor. It seems that Black Dog was used primarily for the purpose of associating the word *dog* with the word *pirate*. Both he and Billy Bones associate "dog" with pirates. Chapter One was named for Billy Bones, "The Old Sea Dog." In fact, another clue may be found in the name *Rover* that verifies this dog/pirate word association. The name Rover, which is perhaps the most commonly recognized name pertaining to dogs, is defined in the following ways 1) A person who roves; a wanderer, 2) Archery – a mark selected at random, and 3) A pirate and/or a pirate ship. The reason for this dog/pirate word association will be presented next in the #8 Jonathan Swift section.

#8 Jonathan Swift

Jonathan Swift is revealed to be the primary person whom the encoded message is about in Part Six of *Treasure Island* titled, "Captain Silver." Jonathan Swift is the "Sea Cook" and is what *Treasure Island* is about. He is not revealed until the seven descriptors (pieces of eight) that Stevenson used to define him are developed. Stevenson represents Swift numerically by the number eight. In the text of *Treasure Island*, Stevenson seems to verify this, by using the word "swift" three times and the word "swiftly" five times; therefore, using the word *swift* a total of *eight times* throughout the book. Although the word swift is used eight times, the name Swift, does not appear at all. The Swift name actually appears in another book, which is one of the acknowledged books of genesis of *Treasure Island* that Stevenson had mentioned. As with John Silver and Peter Stuyvesant, Stevenson used the text of *Treasure Island* and *Tales of a Traveller* to set up a situation where both books corroborate a hidden message and work in partnership with each other to reveal the portion of the encoded message that he intended to tell.

The code breaking book that Stevenson used to reveal the name of Swift is *A General History Of The Robberies And Murders Of The Most Notorious Pirates* by Captain Charles Johnson. Stevenson sets up this two-book partnership in Chapter 29 of *Treasure Island*, "The Black Spot Again," and Johnson's pirate book chapter, "The Life of Captain Lowther." As previously mentioned, it seems likely that only those who were made aware by Stevenson, or those who notice the similarities between *Treasure Island* and the Swift legend, would be looking for an encoded message in *Treasure Island*. Once the possibility of a hidden story is accepted, the search for clues begins. When one is searching for clues, the logical place to begin is with Stevenson. Johnson's pirate book is one of the clues left by Stevenson; it is one of the books that he admitted using in the construction of *Treasure Island*. It is a tool that is necessary in cracking the code, which Stevenson used in partnership with his own written words in *Treasure Island*.

The following excerpt is from Captain Charles Johnson's pirate book and is found in "The Life of Captain George Lowther" chapter. In this excerpt, the pirate, George Lowther, and his crew, overtake and plunder another ship and crew—"In the spring of the year 1723, they made shift to get to sea, and steered their course for Newfoundland, and upon the banks took a schooner, called the *Swift*, John Hood master; they found a good quantity of provisions aboard her, which they very much wanted at that time, and after taking three of their hands, and plundering her of what they thought fit, they let her depart."

The following are the points of interest in this excerpt—

1. The name of the pirate captain is George Lowther.
2. The ship that was taken by George Lowther was named the *Swift*.
3. The *Swift* was a schooner.
4. The master/captain of the *Swift* was John Hood.
5. John Hood's initials are J.H.
6. The master of the *Swift's* first name is John.
7. John Hood was referred to as master of the *Swift*; a master is a person who commands a merchant vessel also referred to as Captain.

Once Stevenson found this excerpt in Johnson's pirate book and determined how he could use it, he then placed the elements of the story he intended to convey into the text of *Treasure Island*, for the purpose of creating cryptograms. The following excerpts from *Treasure Island* demonstrate how he did that. In Part Six, "Captain Silver," Chapter 29 titled, "The Black Spot Again," Stevenson has John Silver defending himself and Jim Hawkins against George Merry after he (Merry) and the other pirates have tipped Long John the Black Spot.

"'Mighty pretty,' said George. 'But how are we to get away with it, and us no ship?'

"Silver suddenly sprang up, and supporting himself with a hand against the wall: 'Now I give you warning, George,' he cried. ' One more word of your sauce, and I'll call you down and fight you. How? Why, how do I know? You had ought to tell me that you and the rest, that lost me my schooner, with interference, burn you! But not you, you can't; you hain't got the invention of a cockroach. But civil you can speak, and shall, George Merry, you may lay to that.'"

This next *Treasure Island* excerpt has John Silver tossing the Black Spot to Jim Hawkins for him to look at after he (Long John) has rebuked another pirate named Dick Johnson for cutting the Black Spot out of his (Johnson's) Bible.

"'Here, Jim—here's a cur'osity for you,' said Silver; and he tossed me the paper.

"It was a round about the size of a crown piece. One side was blank, for it had been the last leaf; the other contained a verse or two of Revelation—these words among the rest, which struck sharply home upon my mind: 'Without are dogs and murderers.'"

In these two excerpts Stevenson has acknowledged to any potential decoder that Jonathan Swift is indeed both Long John Silver and Jim Hawkins, and the following is the number of matches or hits that Stevenson set up between both *Treasure Island* and Johnson's pirate book that form the code name and theory verifiers.

1. A George is at the heart of both *Treasure Island* and Johnson's pirate book–George Merry in *Treasure Island* and George Lowther in Johnson's pirate book.

2. Both the Swift and the *Hispaniola* are schooners. This is why Stevenson made the *Hispaniola* a schooner instead of a Brig. In his *My First Book–"Treasure Island"* article Stevenson speaks of why he made the *Hispaniola* a schooner. The *Hispaniola* represents the Swift journal.

3. John Hood, master of the *Swift*, and Jim Hawkins' initials are both J. H. This is the primary reason why Stevenson gave the boy narrator a name where the initials of J. H. could be used to work in partnership with this John Hood excerpt.

4. In Johnson's pirate book, George Lowther pirated the schooner Swift and in *Treasure Island* John Silver accuses George Merry of being responsible for losing his (Silvers') schooner. When John Silver says, "lost me my schooner" he identifies himself with the ship, *Swift*, and both J.H.'s, John Hood and Jim Hawkins.

5. The pirates in Johnson's pirate book captured John Hood/J.H. and in *Treasure Island*, this excerpt is from the part of the book where the pirates have captured Jim Hawkins/J.H.–this identifies Jim Hawkins with John Hood and John Silver.

6. Captain Charles Johnson's pirate book, is one of Stevenson's acknowledged books of *Treasure Island* genesis, and is one of the code breaking books. In the second *Treasure Island* excerpt, Jim Hawkins reads the backside of the Black Spot that says, "without are dogs and murderers." The principle words in this excerpt are the two nouns, "dogs" and "murderers." As previously mentioned, Stevenson established through Billy Bones (Old Sea Dog) and Black Dog that the word *dog* represents pirates. *Dog* is a word used several times in Johnson's pirate book when referring to pirates, and the word "murders" is actually used in the title of Johnson's book, *A General History of the Robberies & Murders of the Most Notorious Pirates*.

7. The Black Spot, which had the Bible verse "without are dogs and murderers," was cut from Dick Johnson's bible. This Dick Johnson bible clearly verifies that the Captain Charles Johnson's' pirate book, the George Lowther Swift schooner, and the John Hood excerpt from

Johnson's pirate book, to be the code confirmers that Long John Silver and Jim Hawkins represent Jonathan Swift. The Black Spot from Dick *Johnson's* bible cryptically represents Captain Charles *Johnson's* book, *A General History Of The Robberies and Murders Of The Most Notorious Pirates.*

It seems likely that after Stevenson found the story about the Swift schooner in Johnson's notorious pirate book, and set up the partnership of the two books, he needed a way to further define Swift's full identity. He did this through Long John Silver. The longer version of John is Jonathan, so therefore Long John means Jonathan. Another indicator that Long John refers to the name Jonathan is in John Silver's nickname, Barbecue. When one first reads the name Long John Silver, it appears that Long John is a nickname; however, Stevenson later reveals that Barbecue is actually Silver's nickname. This seems to clarify that Stevenson was referring to the name Jonathan by his use of Long John.

There are three other similarities found in *Treasure Island* in which it seems possible Stevenson was referring to a time in Jonathan Swift's life. The first is Swift's political life. As mentioned in Chapter Three of this book, Swift was consul to seven or eight foreign nations. Stevenson could be referring to this by the title of Chapter 20, "Silver's Embassy." The second is when John Silver, also in Chapter 20, took a flag of truce to *Alexander* Smollett. This compares to the account of Swift's life when during, The War of 1812, he took a flag of truce representing his town folk in *Alexandria*. Stevenson could be referring to The War of 1812 by designing and naming Chapter 12 of *Treasure Island*, "Council of War." Stevenson reveals in Chapter 11 of *Treasure Island* that John Silver is fifty years old, which is the third similarity. When Swift, Dr. Muir, Dr. Dick and William Swann presented the flag of truce, in 1814, Swift was also fifty years old.

The Dead Man's Chest

CHAPTER NINE

Parts One and Two of this book were completed several months before the actual decoding process of *Treasure Island* had begun. At that time, only the obvious similarities between the Swift legend and *Treasure Island*, as well as the likelihood of Stevenson possessing a Swift journal (through the Osbournes) was noted. The theory of why and how Swift diverted attention from the real silver mine by setting up fake mines, presented in Part Two of this book, was not changed after the decoding process was completed. One of the objectives in the decoding process was to determine whether a number of story line verifiers could be substantiated within the text of *Treasure Island*, which could support the theories presented in Part Two.

In Part Two, the reason given that Jonathan Swift set up fake silver mines in pioneer Kentucky was to prevent the settlers and those who had heard rumors of the mine from finding the silver. In the *Treasure Island* encoded story, the reason for the cover-up was to keep British England from finding the mine. The methods Swift used to pull off the diversion or cover-up presented in Part Two of this book, and the encoded method of cover-up in *Treasure Island*, are almost identically described which will be presented as it was interpreted.

In the *Treasure Island* encoded message, Stevenson not only defines Swift as keeping the location of the silver mine from England, but also as being a spy working against England. Stevenson represented England in the most interesting of ways, as being pirates. Before the reason for cover-up, methods used, and spy factor parts of the encoded message are presented, two important encoded story line development elements will be presented.

#1 The Hispaniola: The *Treasure Island* ship, *Hispaniola*, is another of Stevenson's code words with multiple layers of revelations. The first cryptic communication the code word, *Hispaniola*, defined was that it represents Swift's journal. Stevenson's second use of the *Hispaniola*, is to represent land. *Hispaniola* is an island in the West Indies and is mentioned prominently in two of the code breaking books: *At Last—a Christmas in the West Indies*, and Captain Johnson's pirates book. It is an island that was regularly visited by pirates. It seems likely that Stevenson chose to name the ship, *Hispaniola*, for that reason, and because it was mentioned twice in the life of Captain Lowther chapter in Johnson's pirate book. Another reason for Stevenson's naming the ship *Hispaniola*, will be presented later.

As mentioned, the *Hispaniola's* second purpose is to represent land, specifically bounded property, which is represented by an island. This is communicated by Stevenson by the map of the *Treasure Island* and is described at the beginning of Chapter Twelve. The three primary hills of the *Treasure Island* are named for sails of a ship, and are described by John Silver as being located on the island running north to south. The north hill is called the Foremast Hill; the middle and largest hill is called Main, or Mainmast, and is also referred to as Spyglass Hill, and the southern most hill is called Mizzenmast Hill.

In the encoded story, the *Hispaniola* represents the bounded property, which Squire Trelawney had purchased from Jonathan Swift, whom Stevenson represented as Mr. Blandly. Two vessels are identified by Stevenson in the *Treasure Island* text that is found upon the island on dry ground. The first is the "coracle," which was made by Ben Gunn, and the second is the *Walrus* that was Captain Flint's old pirate ship in which each represent bounded property. The coracle represents the smaller of the two properties, and the *Walrus* represents the larger tract of land. More will be said of the properties represented by these vessels and how the *Hispaniola* and *Walrus* are actually the same ship.

#2 Code Name "Redruth": Why would Stevenson need to represent two different tracts of property in his encoded message? What is the Swift legend about? The answer to both questions is—a silver mine. Stevenson's cryptic communication of a silver mine is defined by the *Treasure Island* character Tom Redruth. The Redruth code name comes from one of the code breaking books, mentioned as sources of genesis by Stevenson, titled *At Last—a Christmas in the West Indies* by Charles Kingsley. Once again Stevenson communicates his intended encoded message, by partnering another book with his *Treasure Island* text. The following excerpt shows how he identifies Tom

Redruth, of *Treasure Island,* with a silver mine. The excerpt is found in the very early pages of Chapter One in *At Last:*

"But almost the most interesting group of all was one of the Cornish miners, from the well-known old Redruth and Camborne County, and the old sacred hill of Carn-brea, who were going to seek their fortunes awhile in silver mines among the Andes, …"

On the first page of Chapter Seven in *Treasure Island,* Stevenson verifies that Tom Redruth represents a silver mine. Stevenson does this by referring to him as "old Redruth," just as it was worded in *At Last.* Tom Redruth was the oldest of Jim Hawkins's party, and was the first of the party to be killed by pirates on the island.

The Swift Quincunx
a.k.a.
Silver's Jolly Roger

Once it was determined that Stevenson had brought the story elements of bounded property, and a silver mine, into the message of the encoded story, it seemed to make sense that he could have encoded the actual whereabouts of the silver mine. Stevenson not only provides the location of the country and state, that the legendary Swift silver mine is in, but he also identifies the county, and indicates a specific area of that county in his cryptic communication.

In this book there have been two "X marks the spot" documentations, presented that pertain to the Swift silver mine legend. The first document presented was the 1788 land entry of John Filson presented in Chapter One and Four of this book. In this document it says that Swift had described to Filson, how the mine was identified by the "X marks the spot" method, and was described as being in the center of the four cardinal points. The second documentation is based upon piecing together old land surveys to approximate the location of Swift Property #1, the 20,718 ¾ tract. While the second documentation has not been verified, it seems probable that some part of Swift Property #1 was in the cross hairs of the four "view towns" as mentioned in Chapter Four.

The quincunx or "X" element of the Swift legend was a huge factor pertaining not only to the Swift legend but also in the suppositions presented in Part Two of this book. Stevenson likely also considered the "X" factor to be very important, due to his efforts in defining it in the encoded message.

One of the methods Stevenson used to create a quincunx, that marks a silver mine, was using the British Union Jack flag. As mentioned, old Tom Redruth was the first of the party to be killed by pirates on the *Treasure Island.*

Of all the many characters that were killed on the island, Stevenson only buried Tom Redruth. When Stevenson buried Redruth, he was placed in the earth covered with the Union Jack flag, which can be found in Chapter 18 and 19 of *Treasure Island*. Old Tom Redruth represents a silver mine in the earth and Stevenson creates the "X" with the Union Jack which is made up of three crosses or "X's."

The British Union Jack Flag

The following excerpt is from the *Encyclopaedia Britannica*, 1949 edition—"The national flag of the British empire is the Union Jack in which are combined in union the crosses of St. George, St. Andrew and St. Patrick. St. George had long been a patron saint of England, and his banner of silver with a cross gules its national ensign. St. Andrew in the same way was the patron saint of Scotland, and his banner of azure with a saltire silver the national ensign of Scotland." This account of the history of the Union Jack goes on to say that it was in 1801 that "a cross styled like that of St. Patrick, a saltire gules, in a field silver, was incorporated in the union flag."

The idea of the three red crosses, on the John Flint map of the *Treasure Island*, may have come to Stevenson through *Tales of a Traveller*, in Part Four under, "Sam the Black Fisherman." However, the three red crosses of the map represent the three crosses of the Union Jack, which covers or marks the spot of old Tom Redruth, who represents a silver mine. From the *Encyclopaedia's* description of the Union Jack, Stevenson could have also been hinting about silver mines. One cross mentions "a banner of silver" (St. George), another cross mentions a "saltire silver" (St. Andrew), and the third cross mentions "in a field silver" (St. Patrick).

Stevenson defines two separate bounded tracts of property on *Treasure Island*, by using the *Walrus/Hispaniola* to represent the larger tract of land, and Ben Gunn's *coracle* represents the smaller tract of land. The larger tract (*Walrus*) in the encoded message represents a fake silver mine set up by Swift. Old Tom Redruth represents this fake mine, and Stevenson refers to it as "The Dead Man's Chest." "The Dead Man's Chest" is an island named by pirates, and is mentioned early in Chapter One of Charles Kingsley's *At Last*, which is one of the code breaking books. "The Dead Man's Chest" island, represents the bounded tract of land that the fake mine is on, and is referred to by this name only by the pirates in *Treasure Island*.

Stevenson goes into considerable detail in describing the fake mine, "The Dead Man's Chest." He defines the time in which the initial set up of "The Dead Man's Chest" was done, and he also defines the scam of selling it (the *Hispaniola*, a.k.a. *Walrus*) to Squire Trelawney.

The first account of Jonathan Swift, represented by Jim Hawkins and John Silver, which initially set up the fake mine, is found in Chapter 14 of *Treasure Island*, "The First Blow." In this chapter Jim Hawkins has just landed for the first time upon *Treasure Island*. Only he, John Silver, and the pirates are on the island at this time. Stevenson's encoded message does not follow a normal time line. Different times are represented by different symbols, the *Hispaniola* represents a current time line and *Walrus* represents the *Hispaniola* (fake silver mine property) at an earlier time period. This account where Jim Hawkins is first on the island with only the pirates represents the time when Jonathan Swift first came to Kentucky to scout out and set up a fake silver mine.

Stevenson defines the act of doing this by four characters: a man named Tom, a man named Alan, John Silver and Jim Hawkins. In this chapter, the man named Alan is first killed by the pirates, who accompanied Silver and Hawkins to the island, then the next man killed is Tom. Jim Hawkins (the narrator or the words of Swift) describes in detail how the man named Tom, is brutally murdered by John Silver. Stevenson also uses the story line of *Treasure Island*, in conjunction with the encoded message, to convey the full message. This is done when the pirates look for the treasure, and find the "X marks the spot" only to find that it had been rifled.

Much of Stevenson's encoded message is delivered in two, three, or more different stages and each must be identified to determine the full message. The man named Tom, is Tom Redruth, and at this time in Chapter 14, the significance of a dead man named Tom has not been fully defined. It is later in Chapters 18 and 19, when Stevenson establishes the importance of a dead man named Tom, through Tom Redruth, who represents a silver mine with the Union Jack representing "X marks the spot," which indicates where the treasure is buried. Therefore, the cryptic message being said when John Silver kills Tom is: John Silver is setting up the dead Tom (fake silver mine), which the pirates refer to as "The Dead Man's Chest."

The significance of the man named Alan, and the cryptic communication that he defines, is not fully understood until Chapter 31 of "The Treasure Hunt—Flint's Pointer," and Chapter 33, "The Fall of a Chieftain." It is in these chapters that Stevenson clearly reveals the "X marks the spot factor," in both *Treasure Island*, and Swift legend, is an elaborately set up fake silver mine. "Alan" represents the "X." He is mentioned by Silver just before he kills Tom and by Tom after the pirates murdered Alan. This interaction in Chapter 14 links Silver, Tom and Alan, and through Tom Redruth other upcoming encoded information is identified. The upcoming old Tom Redruth information marks the trio as significant encoded story line code keys. Stevenson uses only the first names of a character, in which he later identifies and defines, three different times. These characters are "Tom" a.k.a. Tom Redruth, "Alan," and "Ben," who will be mentioned later.

The following *Treasure Island* excerpt is from Chapter 14, "The First Blow." In it John Silver is responding to Tom (with no last name) after he has just heard Alan's death cry, "'That?' returned Silver, smiling away, but warier than ever, his eye a mere pin-point in his face, but gleaming like a crumb of glass. 'That? Oh, I reckon that'll be Alan.'"

The two primary encoded subject matters presented by Stevenson in this paragraph, are the identification of Alan, and the description of John Silver's eye. The two important words pertaining to the encoded message are *Alan* and *pin-point*. Stevenson's double entendres are that Alan is the pin-pointer. To one having an enjoyable time reading *Treasure Island*, the term pin-point means the size of the point of a pin. To the encoded message it means that Alan is the means of identifying the location of Flint's treasure. Alan is Allardyce, the skeleton, mentioned in Chapter 31, "The Treasure Hunt—Flint's Pointer," and is also Flint's Pointer or "X marks the spot." Another likely reference made by Stevenson pertaining to Silver's eye, may be found near the end of his Fable, *The Persons of the Tale*, which is found in Appendix C of this book. In this reference Captain Smollett is addressing Long John Silver and says— "'But he's on the right side; and you mind your eye!'" This story takes place between Chapters 32 and 33 of *Treasure Island*, which is when the fake or rifled treasure site has been identified.

This next *Treasure Island* excerpt comes from Chapter 31, "The Treasure

Hunt--Flint's Pointer" and has John Silver speaking to one of the pirates, Tom Morgan, after finding the skeleton and discovering that it is a pointer to the treasure--

> "'I thought so,' cried the cook; 'this here is a p'inter. Right up there is our line for the Pole Star and the jolly dollars. But, by thunder! if it don't make me cold inside to think of Flint. This is one of his jokes, and no mistake. Him and these six was alone here; he killed 'em, every man; and this one he hauled here and laid down by compass, shiver my timbers! They're long bones, and the hair's been yellow. Ay that would be Allardyce. You mind Allardyce, Tom Morgan?'"

The points of interest in this paragraph are—
1. It is John Silver who identifies the skeleton as a pointer.
2. The use of the term "jolly dollars," means the treasure is marked by the four cardinal points, meaning the pointer is a quincunx represented by Stevenson as a *Jolly Roger*.
3. The skeleton/Allardyce is identified as Flint's pointer to the treasure.
4. Silver describes the bones as long bones, which are the bones that make up the "X" in a Jolly Roger called cross-bones.
5. John Silver speaks to Tom Morgan in this paragraph. This identifies the skeleton pointer Allardyce/Alan with a Tom, which represents a silver mine.

This next *Treasure Island* excerpt is from Chapter 33, "The Fall of a Chieftain." In this excerpt Stevenson establishes, in his encoded message, that the silver mine (Tom Redruth), marked by the quincunx (a.k.a. Union Jack a.k.a. Jolly Roger a.k.a. Flint's Fist a.k.a. "X,") is a fake and it was John Silver (Jonathan Swift) who was responsible for setting up the diversion. The following action takes place after the pirates discover the truth, that there is no treasure at the treasure site–

> "He was raising his arm and his voice, and plainly meant to lead a charge. But just then—Crack! Crack! Crack! —three musket-shots flashed out of the thicket. Merry tumbled head foremost into the excavation; the man with the bandage spun round like a teetotum, and fell all his length upon his side, where he lay dead, but still twitching; and the other three turned and ran for it with all their might.
> "Before you could wink, Long John had fired two barrels of a pistol into the struggling Merry; and so the man rolled up his eyes at him in the last agony, 'George,' said he, 'I reckon I settled you.'"

"'There ain't a thing left here,' said Merry, still feeling around amoung the bones."
From a 1920 Charles Scribner's Sons publication of *Treasure Island*.

The points of interest and cryptic communications in these excerpts are:

1. George Merry tumbled head first into the treasure site. When Stevenson specified head, foremost he is identifying the skull of the Jolly Roger.

2. The man with the bandage who was killed and lay dead. When Stevenson described that he spun like a teetotum, and fell all his length upon his side, where he lay dead he is identifying the crossbones of the Jolly Roger. A teetotum is a type of die having four sides, each marked with a different initial letter, spun with the fingers in an old game of chance. The four sides of the teetotum represent the four cardinal points north, south, east and west forming the "X" or pointer to the treasure.

3. When Long John says to George Merry "'George I reckon I settled you.'" George Merry represents England. His name not only implies King George, but also *merry* old England. In the fable, *The Persons of the Tale*, Stevenson clearly indicates that George Merry represents the King of England. In the following two excerpts John Silver, who represents the encoded words of Stevenson's Swift journal, is speaking disparagingly about King George III not once but twice to the face of the faithful British Captain, Alexander Smollett a.k.a Smoutty: A) "'Such a thing as a Author?' returned John, derisively. 'And who better'n me? And the p'int is, if the Author made you, he made Long John, and he made Hands, and Pew, and George Merry—not that George is up to much, for he's little more'n a name...'" B) " 'It's a fact he seemed to be against George Merry,' Silver admitted musingly. 'But George is little more'n a name at the best of it,' he added brightening..." In these excerpts Stevenson demonstrates the viewpoint of Swift, as well as most Americans of the late 1700's, pertaining to the throne of England, by implying that King George III was a figurehead and that Parliament is the primary power of the British government. In this usage Stevenson also uses George Merry to further identify the quincunx. As mentioned, one representation of the quincunx is the flag of England (the Union Jack) which marked Tom Redruth (who represents a fake silver mine) and one of the crosses or "X's" in the Union Jack represents St. George—a patron saint of England—therefore; Tom Redruth also represents, by way of the Union Jack, England. When Long John (Swift) said, "'I settled you'" it represents that he was responsible for setting up "The Dead Man's Chest."

4. In this *teetotum* excerpt Stevenson provides a brazenly obvious affirmation for a cryptanalyst. It verifies that he intends to communicate that

228

the teetotum/dice reference, which takes place at the rifled treasure site, does indeed represent a skull and crossbones. The simple method of decoding this cryptogram is attained through knowing the slang or cryptic word for dice, which is "bones."

By identifying that this rifled treasure site is associated with a "skull and crossbones" Stevenson cryptically links it with the Jolly Roger pointer called, "Allardyce."

"..the man with the bandage spun round like a teetotum, and fell all his length upon his side..." [Not Original Caption] From a 1920 Charles Scribner's Sons publication of *Treasure Island*.

Further, Stevenson story line verification, of the encoded story structure, is found in the name "Allardyce." As mentioned, Alan and Allardyce represent the crossbones of Stevenson's Jolly Roger/quincunx. Stevenson further defines this, by using both *Alan* (AL) and *dyce* (teetotum) in the name "Allardyce." The following breakdown of the name Allardyce demonstrates how he cryptically communicates that *Alan* and *Allardyce* is the Jolly Roger. "All" or "Al" represent "Alan," "ar" represents the word "are," and "dyce" represents the four-sided "teetotum."

It seems possible that Stevenson intended to include the ship's mate, Mr. Arrow, into this Flint's pointer puzzle. Like Alan, who was the first killed by pirates on the island, Mr. Arrow was the very first casualty of the expedition. The name "Arrow" could certainly be used to indicate a pointer. Stevenson could also have had Mr. Arrow in mind in the name Allardyce—"All" or "Al" represent Alan, "ar" represents Arrow, "dyce" represents teetotum.

For this skeleton pointer (Jolly Roger) Stevenson left yet another clue to be found in his *My First Book– "Treasure Island"* article. In the article, Stevenson acknowledged that he borrowed the idea of the skeleton from Edgar Allan Poe. It seems certain that Stevenson named the skeleton-pointer, Allardyce and Alan, due to Poe's middle name—"Allan." This Stevenson clue (Allan) about Flint's pointer is both a theory of code name and code story verifier.

The significance of a vessel (ship or boat) found upon dry land is partly defined by Stevenson during this treasure hunt. This *Treasure Island* excerpt from Chapter 32, "The Treasure Hunt – The Voice Among the Trees," describes the treasure site–

> "Before us was a great excavation, not very recent, for the sides had fallen in and grass had sprouted on the bottom. In this were the shaft of a pick broken in two and the boards of several packing-cases strewn around. On one of these boards I saw, branded with a hot iron, the name *Walrus*—the name of Flint's old ship.
> "All was clear to probation. The *cache* had been found and rifled; the seven hundred thousand pounds were gone!"

As previously mentioned the *Hispaniola* and *Walrus* are actually the very same ship. Stevenson defines this when two different flags are flown over the ship. When Stevenson has the Union Jack flown over the *Hispaniola*, it represents Squire Trelawney's property or land. When the Jolly Roger is flown over it in Chapter 19, "The Garrison In the Stockade," it represents Flint's old ship, *Walrus*, or property that Flint had previously owned. Both Flint and Mr. Blandly are descriptors of Swift. When Stevenson has Mr. Blandly, who is Swift, selling Squire Trelawney the *Hispaniola* (property), it means that Swift (Blandly) is selling the *Walrus*, which is Flint's (Swift's) previously owned property.

This property (land) the *Hispaniola* and the *Walrus* represent, is the rifled treasure site and is defined by Stevenson by the *board* with the word *Walrus* branded into it. It is property that Swift/Flint had previously owned and had set up as a fake silver mine. He confirms this by describing the contents of the excavation, when he described the "shaft" of a pick. Stevenson describes it as only the shaft of the pick not the pick itself. His use of the word shaft instead of the more commonly used word *handle*, is an indicator or verifier that an encoded message is contained in this sentence. The encoded message he intends to communicate is something that every silver mine must have, which is a *shaft* or mineshaft.

The cumulated information of this mineshaft cryptogram, and points number 2 and 4, in regard to the teetotum, dice/bones, and Allardyce revelation, very efficiently define that Stevenson is indeed alluding to a silver mine, which is identified by Allardyce, which is an "X marks the spot pointer" to the treasure.

According to the findings of this investigation, amazingly, there are two different properties connected to the Swift legend, which are marked by the four cardinal points or *pointers*. The first is the 1,000 acre property that Swift had told John Filson about, and the second is Swift Property #1, the 20,718 ¾ acre tract. It is possible that both of these properties are referenced by Stevenson in his "X marks the spot," "rifled treasure" *Walrus* property. The one most likely referred to, is the 20,718¾ acres that Swift purchased in 1791 from Mordecai Barbour. Swift sold the property to James Kerr in 1792 and Kerr sold Swift's old ship (property), the *Walrus*, (the 20,718 ¾ acres) to Robert Walsh in 1795. In Stevenson's, *My First Book–"Treasure Island"* article in McClure's magazine Stevenson acknowledged that it was his father who named Flint's old ship *Walrus*. Could the name *Walrus* be the code name for Walsh?

In *Treasure Island*'s Chapter Seven, "I Go To Bristol," Squire Trelawney writes that Mr. Blandly (Swift) got the *Hispaniola* for the "merest trifle." When Jonathan Swift conveyed the 20,718 ¾ acre tract to James Kerr, he also sold it for the merest trifle of five shillings. Whether or not James Kerr was mentioned in Stevenson's Swift silver mine journal is unknown. It is also unknown if Stevenson's code name for Kerr is Squire Trelawney. Squire Trelawney was the one Mr. Blandly (Swift) sold the *Hispaniola* (fake silver mine) to, and, from Swift's point of view (the encoded message) was considered to be British represented as a pirate, dog, or cur; Kerr, and cur being pronounced the same.

Some affirmation of this may be found in the following excerpt, found in Chapter 28, "In the enemy's camp," by Stevenson mentioning both of the characters referred to as dogs, Billy Bones the sea-dog, and Black Dog, while also referring to the faked chart which alludes to the fake silver mine property Kerr purchased from Swift.

"'I'll put one to that,' cried the old mahogany-faced seaman—Morgan by name—whom I had seen in Long John's public house upon the quays of Bristol. 'It was him that knowed Black Dog.'
"'Well, and see here,' added the sea cook. 'I'll put another again to that, by thunder! for it was this same boy that faked the chart from Billy Bones. First and last, we've split upon Jim Hawkins!'"

Stevenson's use of the words dog, and pirate is not done to deprecate dogs or pirates. These words are used for their emblematic value. In fact he seemed to have a favorable regard for *rovers* as seen in his fable *Faith, Half-Faith, And No Faith At All*, which is included in Chapter Seven of this book. In this story the rover's name indicates that he may have failed the judgment of mankind's standard of acceptance; however, he is the only one to pass the test of his God.

The primary reason the 20,718 ¾ acres are considered to be the *Hispaniola* (a.k.a *Walrus* a.k.a, "The Dead Man's Chest") is because of its size. The *Hispaniola* represents a much larger property than the "coracle" property. Swift Property #1, is believed to be the *Walrus* property, but for the sake of consideration, the John Filson property should also be considered. Neither Swift nor Filson ever owned this property; Filson had only made a land entry. He is, however, the only documented person known to be associated with Swift and a silver mine. Since John Filson is not only connected with Swift, and the silver mine, but also with a property that has the "X" factor, could John Flint actually be the code name for John Filson in both *Treasure Island* and Swift legend?

As unlikely as it may initially seem, the following ten points compare Filson and Flint:

1. Flint is a good substitute name for Filson, FLI/FIL, just as Munday is an excellent substitute name for Moody.
2. Filson and Flint share common first names, John.
3. Both have the same initials - J.F.
4. John Filson is known to be associated with the Swift legend.

5. John Filson was known for being Kentucky's first historian and first cartographer.
6. The famous *Treasure Island* map was made by John Flint and he signed it only by his initials-- J.F.
7. John Filson's 1,000 acre land entry mentioned Swift, a silver mine and "X marks the spot."
8. John Flint's treasure site was marked with Flint's pointer or "X marks the spot."
9. By the 1788 land entry we know that John Filson and Jon Swift a.k.a. John Silver knew each other from their treasure hunting escapades.
10. From the story of *Treasure Island* we know that John Flint and John Silver a.k.a Jon Swift knew each other from their treasure hunting escapades.

It seems unlikely at first, but when all things are considered, it is not impossible to believe that John Flint is the code name for John Filson.

Stevenson's first clues to the "X marks the spot" story line were presented very early in the book. The first was in the name of Billy *Bones* (representing the Jolly Roger/Quincunx creation of Swift), and the second clue was in *Mrs. Crossley's bag*. In Chapter Four of *Treasure Island*, "The Sea Chest," when Jim Hawkins and his mother were seeking help from the neighboring folk, Mrs. Hawkins took a bag from Mrs. Crossley to put money in, which was from Billy Bones' sea chest. Mrs. Hawkins only took the money owed to her by Billy Bones, leaving the rest of his money in the old sea chest. Mrs. Crossley represents the cross bones, or "X," of the fake Jolly Roger silver mine. Stevenson defines that the fake silver mine as being salted with money from the real silver mine. This is represented by the small amount of money that Mrs. Hawkins took from Billy Bones' sea chest. Billy Bones' sea chest represents the real silver mine. More will be explained about this later.

This "X mark the spot" over a fake silver mine element of the story, is what Stevenson was referring to and had left a hint about, when he finished his *My First Book–"Treasure Island"* article with the final four words, "a mine of suggestion."

The Spy-Glass Embassy

In Part Two of this book, theories were presented to suggest that Jonathan Swift's Kentucky land purchases, were actually part of a complex cover-up operation. The purpose of the cover-up operation was to confuse, overwhelm, and divert attention away from the real silver mine, and to attract interest to the fake silver mine on Swift's properties. Further theories presented in Part Two of this book, were that the reason for this diversion was because the silver mine had been used as a bargaining chip during the Revolutionary War, with either France, Spain, Holland or all three. It was also suggested in Part Two, that if this scenario should happen to be correct, then the cover-up operation was likely conceived at the very highest level of government. The possibility of Dr. James Craik's involvement in the cover-up was also presented. It was suggested in these theories that Jonathan Swift's participation during this cover-up, could indicate he was, for a time period, active military in merchant guise.

In Stevenson's encoded message, Swift's (John Silver's) covert operation earned him the title of spy. Once Stevenson's method of encoding was broken, and the identity of all the Swift descriptors had been determined, it became apparent that Stevenson clearly identified Long John Silver as a spy. The following is a partial list confirming that Stevenson provided information into the encoded message, which refers to Long John Silver (Swift) as a spy working against England:

1. The most obvious spy confirmation is in the name of Long John Silver's tavern, or public house, "The Spy-Glass."

2. From Chapter 33, "The Fall of a Chieftain," the following excerpt describes both the pirates, and John Silver's reactions, after learning the treasure had been rifled. The pirates' reaction was that of surprise and anger. John Silver's reaction was that of a man who already knew the treasure was not there. "There never was such an overturn in this world. Each of these six men was as though he had been struck. But with Silver the blow passed almost instantly. Every thought of his soul had been set full-stretch, like a racer, on that money; well, he was brought up in a single second, dead; and he kept his head, found his temper, and changed his plan before the others had had time to realize the disappointment." Jim Hawkins, who is another Swift descriptor, narrates this paragraph; he also represents Swift's own words, or the words of Stevenson's Swift journal, therefore; this is Swift describing his own actions and reactions. Long John Silver was informed by Dr. Livesey, in a hint, previous to the treasure hunt, that there would be no treasure there, which indicates that Dr. Livesey was also part of the cover-up. More will be said later pertaining to Dr. Livesey's involvement.

3. The following excerpt, found shortly after the previous excerpt in Chapter 33, further describes the action of the pirates (George Merry) and John Silver at the rifled treasure site, and is a solid encoded story line verifier, proving that Long John Silver is playing a duel role or

double-agent. " 'Dig away, boys,' said Silver, with the coolest insolence; 'you'll find some pig-nuts and I shouldn't wonder.' 'Pig-nuts!' repeated Merry, in a scream. 'Mates, do you hear that? I tell you, now, that man there knew it all along. Look in the face of him, and you'll see it wrote there.' " This excerpt also further defines that Stevenson's encoded message, considers England as the pirates. The offended party in this excerpt is the pirates represented by George Merry whom Stevenson uses to represent King George III, St. George in the Union Jack, and Merry Old England.

4. Another description where Long John shows no reaction, due to previous knowledge, is represented by Jim Hawkins and occurred when Captain Smollett presented him (Silver) with an accurate copy of Flint's map without the red "X's" and is found early in Chapter 12, "Council of War." Captain Smollett represents England in this case. Since Jim Hawkins, who is one of the Swift descriptors, was fully familiar with Flint's map, and the location of the "X's," he represents Long John's memory or past. Another Stevenson symbol indicating that Jim Hawkins also represents John Silver's past, can be found in Chapter 31, "The Treasure Hunt—Flint's Pointer," when Jim Hawkins and John Silver are connected by a rope, and Hawkins describes that he "followed obediently after the sea cook." The encoded message is that Jim Hawkins is John Silver's past.

5. This next excerpt, found in Chapter 28, "In the Enemy's Camp," has John Silver admitting, by way of Jim Hawkins whom represents Silver's past, that he faked the chart from Billy Bones, and by it Stevenson could be implying that Swift provided fake treasure maps. "'Well, and see here,' added the sea cook. 'I'll put another again to that, by thunder! for it was this same boy that faked the chart from Billy Bones. First and last we've split upon Jim Hawkins!'"

6. Stevenson writes that Long John Silver "was accused of playing double" in Chapter 30—"On Parole."

7. Stevenson refers to Long John as, "already doubly a traitor," in Chapter 31, "Flint's Pointer."

8. It is Long John who identifies the fake treasure site, and the pointer, Allardyce, in Chapter 31, "Flint's Pointer." This indicates that John Silver was familiar with that treasure site.

9. Since Mr. Blandly is also another descriptor of Swift, he and Silver also represent the dual life of Swift. Mr. Blandly is the Dr. Jekyll to John Silver's Mr. Hyde, or in this case Mr. Hide. John Silver represents the

"Past and Present"
Illustration from an Atheneum Book's for Young Readers publication of *Treasure Island*. [Not Original Caption] Illustrations copyright 1911 Simon & Schuster Inc. Copyright renewed.

Swift of the cover-up mission (spy) and Mr. Blandly represents the merchant, politician, and normal life of Jonathan Swift.

10. When George Merry had tumbled head first into the rifled treasure site, and John Silver had fired both barrels of his pistol into "the struggling Merry" Silver said, "'George,' said he, 'I reckon I settled you.'" This is likely an indication that Swift was the one responsible for setting up the fake silver mines. Verification comes from knowing Long John was responsible for the demise of the ship's mate, Mr. Arrow. *Arrow*, could certainly be compared to the *skeleton pointer*, All"ar"dyce. Symbolically, and cryptically Mr. Arrow is also the "*dead man* pointer.*"

11. In Chapter Nine, "Powder and Arms," Stevenson sets up an interaction between Captain Smollett, Squire Trelawney, and Dr. Livesey. In their conversations Captain Smollett is complaining that word of the treasure site has been leaked out. In Part Two of this book, a theory was presented as to why a silver mine cover-up was needed. The theory was that Jonathan Swift had leaked the information about the Kentucky silver mine by either word of mouth, caught at sea, or at his wharf with silver ore or bars. The following *Treasure Island* excerpt from Chapter Nine, "Powder and Arms," seems to support these theories–

" 'I'll tell you what I've heard myself,' continued Captain Smollett: 'that you have a map of an island; that there's crosses on the map to show where treasure is; and that the island lies—' And then he named the latitude and longitude exactly.
'I never told that,' cried the squire, 'to a soul.'
'The hands know it, sir,' returned the captain.
'Livesey, that must have been you or Hawkins,' cried the squire."

Being that Jim Hawkins is John Silver and Jonathan Swift, this *Treasure Island* excerpt seems to support the theory that Jonathan Swift had possibly leaked information of the silver mine. This would also support the theory presented of why a silver mine cover-up was needed.

12. As mentioned under "Long John Silver" in Chapter Eight of this book, the essential component of Peter Stuyvesant, from *Tales of a Traveller*, which Stevenson needed to convey, was the story of Stuyvesant hiding his treasure from the British redcoats. This story component is a primary story line verifier for the encoded message and again demonstrates that Stevenson is saying that Swift was working against England.

13. Another Stevenson hint, and indicator, that Long John Silver was involved in a fake silver mine transaction is found in Chapter 33, "The Fall of a Chieftain." In this excerpt Squire Trelawney is delivering a tongue lashing to John Silver—"'John Silver,' he said, 'you're a prodigious villain and imposter—a monstrous imposter, sir. I am told I am not to prosecute you. Well, then I will not. But the dead men, sir, hang about your neck like millstones.'" The points of interest in this excerpt are: (a) it is Squire Trelawney who is calling John Silver an imposter, (b) Trelawney used the word imposter, instead of other words, that may seem to be more appropriate-- such as--traitor, mutineer, murderer, crook, pirate etc, (c) Squire Trelawney owned the *Hispaniola*, which represents the fake silver mine, and this conversation takes place shortly after it had been determined that there was no treasure at the site. In other words, Squire Trelawney had just found out he had purchased "The Dead Man's Chest," instead of the real *Hispaniola*.

14. The Flint treasure map ends up in the possession of John Silver and it was Dr. Livesey who gave it to him. In Chapter 30, "On Parole," the Doctor is giving Silver advice by telling him, "look out for squalls when you find it." The Doctor is referring to the fake treasure site. The following passage found at the end of Chapter 30, has the Doctor giving advice to Silver, and offering to help him and Jim Hawkins. "'My second is a piece of advice: Keep the boy close beside you, and when you need help, halloo. I'm off to seek it for you, and that itself will show you if I speak at random. Goodbye, Jim.'" On the first page of the next chapter, "Flint's Pointer," Stevenson leaves a clue, which not only implies Silver/Swift was a double-agent, but he may have received his orders from the Doctor. Silver says "'And now, Jim, we're to go in for this here treasure hunting, with sealed orders, too, and I don't like it; and you and me must stick close, back to back like, and we'll save our necks in spite of fate and fortune.'" When John Silver says that he is operating "with sealed orders," in following the story of *Treasure Island*, it is merely another cute Stevenson description of John Silver's speech. But when what is known of the encoded story is considered, it becomes a story line verifier for Stevenson's encrypted communication, that John Silver is a spy. Comparing this with the facts and theories presented in Parts One and Two of this book, one cannot help but remember the meeting of Swift, Dr. Craik, Colonels Hooe, and Henley who dined with George Washington at Mount Vernon and wonder if the sealed orders John Silver (Swift) spoke of were dated

November 26, 1786. As it was with Dr. James Muir (Swift's pastor) and Dr. William Muir (pastor of Edinburgh Presbyterian Church), it is unknown if the Colonel Henley who dined at Mount Vernon with Jonathan Swift (the real Long John Silver), and Dr. James Craik was related to Ernest Henley's family. As previously mentioned, Ernest Henley was acknowledged by Stevenson, to be the pattern of John Silver's character traits, and was a close friend of Stevenson's. This Swift/Henley connection once again demonstrates as the Stevenson/ Sam Osborne/Robert Alley connection did that it was not improbable for Stevenson to have access to Swift's silver mine stories.

15. The following excerpt from Chapter 30, "On Parole, " finds Dr. Livesey talking to Jim Hawkins, after he has just found out that Hawkins did not betray his party, but instead was actually responsible for the success of the mission. "'There is a kind of fate in this,' he observed, when I had done. 'Every step, it's you that saves our lives; and do you suppose by any chance that we are going to let you lose yours? That would be a poor return, my boy. You found out the plot; you found Ben Gunn—the best deed that ever you did, or will do, though you live to ninety.'" In this excerpt Dr. Livesey acknowledges Jim Hawkins' importance in the treasure hunt. In this case Dr. Livesey is speaking to a young John Silver represented by Jim Hawkins. Jim Hawkins, or the younger John Silver, had learned that it was Ben Gunn who actually had the treasure. Through Jim Hawkins, Dr. Livesey also knew that Ben Gunn had the real treasure and that Flint's map and that treasure site was worthless.

16. The last Stevenson indicator or clue presented here, that John Silver was a spy is found in Chapter 34, "And Last." In this quotation one of the three remaining marooned pirates shot at Long John as he and the remaining party leave *Treasure Island.* Jim Hawkins narrates, *"At Last,* seeing the ship still bore on her course, and was now swiftly drawing out of earshot, one of them – I know not which it was – leapt to his feet with a hoarse cry, whipped his musket to his shoulder, and sent a shot whistling over Silver's head and though the mainsail."

In this paragraph Stevenson uses the word *swift* (swiftly) for the eighth and final time. When the pirate shoots at Silver, and the bullet goes through the ships *mainsail,* Stevenson is defining that the pirates (England) found out about Swift's double-agent/spy dealings. The hill called the mainsail on the island, is also called the Spy-Glass, which is also the name of Long John Silver's public-house, and by this action Stevenson defines that John Silver was a spy. The importance of this paragraph and all the code elements that it verifies cannot be over stated. The following code elements should be considered story-line theory, and character theory validations when measuring the sum of their revelations:

A. Stevenson identifies Long John Silver as a spy when he names Silver's tavern/public house "Spy-Glass."

B. Chapter Eight of *Treasure Island* is titled, "At The Sign of the 'Spy-Glass.'"

C. Jonathan Swift is represented by Stevenson numerically by the number *eight*. Stevenson defines him in the encoded story by using the seven descriptors. The seven descriptors make up the "pieces of eight."

D. Stevenson uses the word swift (swiftly) for the eighth and final time in this paragraph.

E. Stevenson is alluding to the "Spy-Glass" Tavern when the pirate's bullet passes by John Silver's head and goes into the *mainsail*. The mainsail hill on *Treasure Island* is also called Spy-Glass. This pirate's bullet further confirms that John Silver is a spy. This Spy-Glass reference also refers to the number eight by means of Chapter Eight, "At the Sign of the Spy-Glass."

F. Stevenson confirms in this paragraph that the number *eight* represents both *Swift*, and the word *spy* numerically. This is done by the eighth, and final use of the word, swift and by naming Chapter Eight, "At the Sign of the Spy-Glass."

G. By using the word swift for the eighth and final time, coupled with Swift being the eighth of the pieces of eight, it solidifies the connection between Swift and Silver who was the owner of The Spy-Glass Tavern, which is represented by Chapter Eight.

H. In this one paragraph, Stevenson uses the word swift for the eighth time, and also refers to Long John Silver. By this, Stevenson links Jonathan Swift, the number eight, and John Silver together. By these code elements one may conclude with certainty Stevenson is cryptically communicating that the secret and actual identity of Long John Silver is indeed, Jonathan Swift.

Knowing this about Jonathan Swift (a.k.a. Long John Silver) one final deduction may be made, which is, the daily special at the White House Tavern (a.k.a. Spy-Glass Tavern) was *always* red herring.

Robert Louis Stevenson
Picture of Stevenson from a 1901 Charles Scribner's Sons publication titled *The Letters of Robert Louis Stevenson Vol. 1.*

Washington Irving
Author of *Tales of a Traveller*

Peter Stuyvesant
Dutch Governor of New York

D.L. Moody
Famous Evangelist of the Nineteenth Century

Ira Sanky
Great singer and song leader of the Moody Revivals

Free Assembly Hall
Stevenson's mother attended the Moody Revivals in Edinburgh.

Moody Preaching

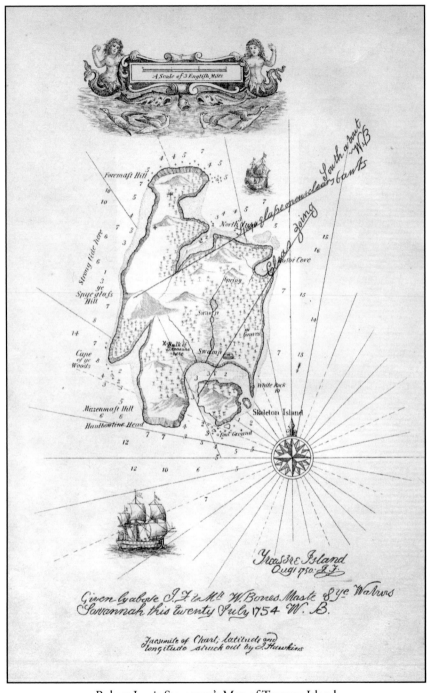

Robert Louis Stevenson's Map of Treasure Island
From a 1901 Charles Scribner's Sons publication of *Treasure Island* from *The Novels and Tales of Robert Louis Stevenson.*

A Notable Singer, Preacher, Coracle and Half-Idiot Maroon

CHAPTER 10

In Part Two of this book, comparisons were made between the *Treasure Island* character Ben Gunn and Benjamin Moody, who owned property in Washington County, Kentucky. At that time the only point to be made was the similarity of their names, and the possibility that both had common connections to the Swift legend. In the theories presented, it was suggested that Benjamin Moody was actually the man known in Swift legend as Munday. It is now suggested that Benjamin Moody is also represented as the *Treasure Island* character Benjamin Gunn.

The significance of finding a historically unknown man's name encoded within the text of *Treasure Island,* and the support it lends to the theories presented in Part Two of this book, is huge. In *Treasure Island,* it is Captain Flint's treasure that John Silver is in search of, which was worthless, because it was discovered that Ben Gunn actually had the treasure. In the theories presented in Part Two of this book, it was proposed that Jonathan Swift was leading people on a wild goose chase by setting up fake silver mines. The reason Swift did this was to divert attention from the real silver mine which has been proposed to be in Washington County, Kentucky. One of the four considered locations in that county was Benjamin Moody's land. Stevenson's cryptic communication of Benjamin Moody is perhaps the closest to conclusive proof that the theories presented in Part Two of this book may have a degree of merit.

Having the name of Moody to go on from the initial Swift investigation proved to be very useful in the decoding process. From the book *Selected Letters of Robert Louis Stevenson*, edited by Ernest Mehew, a Stevenson and Moody connection was found. The following excerpt is from that book, and has Stevenson corresponding with Frances Sitwell, Thursday the fifteenth of January 1874–"I have some journals sent me about the Edinburgh revival and I have made myself nearly sick over them. It is disheartening beyond expression. I wish I had been there that I might have seen the movement near at hand; but I am afraid I should have taken up a testimony and made everybody at home very much out of it." In this excerpt Stevenson is referring to the great American evangelists, Dwight L. Moody and Ira D. Sankey. The journals he refers to were most likely sent to him by his mother who attended the revival.

This next excerpt is from *The Letters of Robert Louis Stevenson, Volume One* edited by Bradford A. Booth and Ernest Mehew, and it reveals even more of Stevenson's feelings toward the Moody and Sankey revivals. This letter was sent to Charles Baxter from Stevenson on the same day as the previous letter, January 15, 1874–"You are a good fellow to send me all these things; a beastly good fellow. The Lord bless you. Have you been revivalled yet? They sent me magazines about it; the obscenest rubbish I was ever acquainted with." The paragraph this was taken from has Stevenson further expressing his dislike for the revival, which is not mentioned in this book.

Also in Volume One of Booth and Mehew's book, is a letter from Stevenson to his parents dated Monday 22, December, 1873 in which Stevenson refers to Ira Sankey in a less than flattering way–"It was as well you sent me a paper or I should never have known who 'Hanky' was; he is not happily named; these syllables have been already made familiar to the B'r'ish Public in a manner quite the reverse of serious…"

These letters prove that D.L. Moody and Ira Sankey had made an enormous impression on Stevenson even though, to be sure, it was the opposite result that both evangelists would have hoped for. In these letters it is known that Stevenson came into possession of several journals/magazines describing D.L. Moody, Ira Sankey and their revival. It seems probable that D.L. Moody may have never known for certain that a doctrine of his, no doubt mentioned in these magazines, would end up in Stevenson's most famous book, *Treasure Island,* as a creed of the world's most famous pirate—Long John Silver.

The Moody and Sankey revivals held in England, Ireland, and Scotland, were enormously successful and influenced thousands upon thousands of people. It has been said that D.L. Moody may have been the greatest of evangelists. This next excerpt is from the book *Moody: His Words, Work, And Workers* edited by Reverend W. H. Daniels, A.M. and it describes how Stevenson's Edinburgh was influenced by the revivals:

"In thousands of Christian households the deepest interest was felt by parents for their children, and by masters and mistresses for their servants; and so universal was this, that Dr. Horatius Bonar declares his belief 'that there was scarcely a Christian household in all Edinburgh in which there were not one or more persons converted during this revival.'"

Dwight Moody was the evangelist and Ira Sankey was the great singer and song leader. Many of the creeds and doctrines of D.L. Moody would have been common knowledge to nearly all in Edinburgh, especially those who attended the revivals or had received his magazines.

The following excerpt is from *The Life and Work of Dwight L. Moody* by Reverend J. Wilbur Chapman, D.D. and is one of Moody's creeds titled--

"Don't Cut Anything Out of the Bible"

"Then there are other people who say, 'I believe in the Bible, but not in the supernatural side of it.' They go on reading the Bible with a pen-knife, cutting out this and that and the other thing. Now, if I have a right to cut out a certain portion of the Bible, I think my friend has the same right, and you would have a queer book, if everybody cut out what he wanted to. Every liar would cut out everything about lying. Every drunkard would cut out what he did not like. It is a most absurd statement for a man to say he will have nothing to do with the supernatural. If you are going to throw off the supernatural, you might as well burn your Bibles at once. For if you take the supernatural out of the book, you take Jesus Christ out of it."

This knowledge about Moody and Sankey is the first of many layers of cryptograms that Stevenson would need to fully define Benjamin Moody. There are three points of interest in this Moody creed, the first being the name of Moody. The second is the title of this creed, "Don't Cut Anything Out of the Bible." The third is the reference to cutting out of the Bible with a pen-knife.

This next *Treasure Island* passage is taken from the third paragraph of

Chapter 29, "The Black Spot Again." In this quotation Jim Hawkins narrates how the pirates are preparing the black spot for John Silver. "…I could just make out that he had a book as well as a knife in his hand; and was still wondering how anything so incongruous had come in their possession, when the kneeling figure rose once more to his feet, and the whole party began to move together towards the house."

The points of interest in this Chapter 29 excerpt are as follows: Jim Hawkins identifies that the pirates have a book; the word incongruous is used to describe how extremely unlikely it is that any of these pirates should have a book; the encrypted meaning is that Stevenson put the book here for a reason. At this point that book has not yet been identified as a Bible. A piece of one of the pages of the book (Bible) was cut out by the pirate with a knife.

This next *Treasure Island* excerpt shortly follows the previous quotation and it is Long John Silver's response to being given the black spot. " 'The black spot! I thought so,' he observed. 'Where might you have got the paper? Why, hillo! look here, now: this ain't lucky! You've gone and cut this out of a Bible. What fool's cut a Bible?' "

It was Stevenson's intention to use this Bible cutting line to attract the attention of anyone working on decoding his secret story in *Treasure Island*. This seems to indicate that he primarily intended to communicate his encrypted message to friends of his own time period. His reason for using this famous D. L. Moody creed was to introduce the name "Moody" into the structure of the encoded message.

Stevenson's referral in this excerpt to Moody's "Don't Cut Anything Out of the Bible" creed is alluded to more than once, in fact, the entirety of Chapter 29 is constructed around it. To stress the cryptic importance of the pirates cutting out of a Bible, he sets up a hilarious interaction between Long John Silver and the pirate named Dick. In these excerpts, Stevenson's brilliant use of Long John Silver's distinctive pirate dialect could arguably be interpreted as the most comical dialogue to be found within the pages of *Treasure Island*, and it effectively creates a very memorable moment. The following is the continuation of that conversation, which has the pirate named Morgan responding to John Silver's question, "What fool's cut a Bible?"

" 'Ah, there!' said Morgan – 'there! Wot did I say? No good'll come o' that, I said.'

" 'Well, you've about fixed it now, among you,' continued Silver. 'You'll all swing now, I reckon. What soft-hearted lubber had a Bible?'

" 'It was Dick,' said one.

" 'Dick, was it? Then Dick can get to prayers,' said Silver. 'He's seen his slice of luck, has Dick, and you may lay to that.' "

The following excerpt is found further into the text of Chapter 29, after Long John has talked his way out of the "black spot" –

" 'Silver!' they cried. 'Barbecue for ever! Barbecue for cap'n!'

" 'So that's the toon, is it?' cried the cook.

" 'George, I reckon you'll have to wait another turn, friend; and lucky for you I'm not a vengeful man. But that was never my way. And now, shipmates, this black spot? 'Tain't much good now, is it? Dick's crossed his luck and spoiled his Bible, and that's about all.'

" 'It'll do to kiss the book on still, won't it?' growled Dick, who was evidently uneasy at the curse he had brought upon himself.

" 'A Bible with a bit cut out!' returned Silver derisively. 'Not it. It don't bind no more'n a ballad-book.' "

The next step for Stevenson was to attach the Moody name to the *Treasure Island* character, Ben Gunn. Ben Gunn, as was Israel Hands, was a name found by Stevenson in Captain Charles Johnson's pirate book, which is one of the code breaking books. In Johnson's pirate book Ben Gunn is spelled with one "N" and is found in "The Life of Captain Roberts" chapter. Stevenson attaches the Moody name to *Treasure Island's* Ben Gunn, by using the black spot *again*. He does this in Chapter 29 titled, "The Black Spot Again." The reason Stevenson named Chapter 29 "The Black Spot Again," is because he used it for two separate revelations. The first use of this Chapter 29 black spot was to define Swift, as mentioned in Chapter Eight of this book within #8 Jonathan Swift.

As previously mentioned on the back of the black spot, which had been cut out of a Bible, were the words—"without are dogs and murderers." The nouns of this Bible verse are dogs and murderers and the first letters of these nouns are – "D" and "M." This is Stevenson's second use of this black spot done for the purpose of adding another layer of cryptic communication, this time pertaining to Dwight Moody, or "D.M."

By keeping the initials D.M. in mind Stevenson completes, for a decoder, the attachment of the Moody name to Ben Gunn as shown in this next *Treasure Island* excerpt from Chapter 32, "The Treasure Hunt—The Voice Among the Trees." In this paragraph Ben Gunn is pretending to be Captain Flint to frighten the pirates by saying what the pirates knew to be the last words ever spoken by Captain Flint– "'Darby M'Graw,' it wailed—for that is the word that best describes the sound—'Darby M'Graw! Darby M'Graw!' Again and again and again; and then rising a little higher, and with an oath that I leave out, 'Fetch aft the rum, Darby!'" By Ben Gunn saying Darby M'Graw, Stevenson has made the Dwight Moody/Ben Gunn connection by Darby M'Graw's initials, "D.M."

There is one other Moody reference to be found in *Treasure Island,* taken from a paragraph in Johnson's pirate book, from "The Life of Captain Roberts" chapter– "…That he bullied well among them who dared not make any reply, but was very easy with his friends, who knew him; for Moody, on this occasion, took a large glass from him, and threatened to blow his brains out (a favorite phrase with these pirates), if he muttered at it."

This Stevenson reference and verifier for Moody can be found in *Treasure Island,* Chapter 26 titled "Israel Hands," in which Jim Hawkins says– "'One more step, Mr. Hands,' said I, 'and I'll blow your brains out…'"

Christopher Moody is the pirate referred to in Johnson's *Notorious Pirates,* who is mentioned several times in the Captain Roberts chapter. By using this second Moody reference, Stevenson defines that it is the name of Moody he intends to identify, not Dwight or Christopher. One may reasonably conclude that Stevenson, as with John Silver, and Jonathan Swift (J. S.'s), is using the first name of Ben or Benjamin Gunn, to convey the actual name to be decoded, Ben Moody.

The code name theory verifier revealed by Stevenson to confirm the name of Moody within *Treasure Island,* is the best and most obvious of the code verifiers, of the entire encoded message structure. This undeniably was necessary for him to do in order to describe a historically unknown man who died a hundred years before *Treasure Island* was published. This Moody name verifier can be found at the end of *Treasure Island* in Chapter 34 and Jim Hawkins is describing how the surviving party lived after the *Treasure Island* expedition. In this excerpt the narrator, Jim Hawkins, gives an account of Ben Gunn:

> "…As for Ben Gunn, he got a thousand pounds, which he spent or lost in three weeks, or, to be exact, in nineteen days, for he was back begging on the twentieth. Then he was given a lodge to keep, exactly as he had feared upon the island; and he still lives, a great favorite, though something of a butt, with the country boys, and a notable singer in church on Sundays and saints' days."

The "notable singer" mentioned in this excerpt is Stevenson cryptically referring to Ira Sankey the notable singer of the Moody revivals. By doing this Stevenson is acknowledging that the Dwight Moody clues he provided are indeed to be identified with Ben Gunn. By connecting Ben Gunn, a church, and a notable singer, all in one sentence, Stevenson does not leave a decoder in doubt as to whether the name of Moody is the intended cryptic communication. By this Stevenson has clearly defined the name of a historically unknown person. To rank all the code verifiers by clarity and importance, this and point number sixteen of Swift as a spy, should be considered the mainsail of code verifiers. If only one encoded message was decoded from the text of *Treasure Island* and this being the name of "Benjamin Moody" it would be the one thing that would best support the theories presented in Part Two of this book.

By recognizing Dwight L. Moody's don't cut anything out of the Bible creed, and by following the path of decoding, which has just been demonstrated, one may confidently conclude that Stevenson has encoded the name Moody. Stevenson did however leave other clues and hints for guiding a decoder in determining the Moody name. The following quotation is taken from a paragraph in Chapter 33, "The Fall of a Chieftain." In it Jim Hawkins narrates and Stevenson leaves a clue– "...It was a story that profoundly interested Silver; and Ben Gunn, the half-idiot maroon, was the hero from beginning to end."

When Stevenson refers to Ben Gunn as half-idiot, he is referring to the word "moody" or one who exhibits sharply varying moods. A person who is happy half the time and sad half the time is a moody person. Stevenson further assists in defining Moody by referring to Ben Gunn as the maroon and Ben Gunn refers to himself as marooned in Chapter 15, "The Man of the Island." The word marooned has similar letters to the word moody.

It is probable that Stevenson was leaving clues pertaining to Moody in his 1894 article in McClure's Magazine *My First Book-"Treasure Island."* The following excerpt is from this article and in it Stevenson is describing his writing style of *Treasure Island*:

"'...Compare it with the almost contemporary 'Merry Men;' one may prefer the one style, one the other— 'tis an affair of character, perhaps of mood; but no expert can fail to see that the one is much more difficult, and the other much easier, to maintain.'"

By using the word "mood," it seems likely Stevenson intended it to be yet another clue left by him in this article. There is one more hint, left by Stevenson, about the name Ben Moody. It was Ben Gunn who rifled the cache from Flint's treasure site and moved it to his cave. This *Treasure Island* excerpt is found in Chapter 33, "The Fall of a Chieftain" and it describes the location of the cave:

"Ben, in his long, lonely wanderings about the island, had found the skeleton—it was he that had rifled it; he had found the treasure; he had dug it up (it was the shaft of his pickaxe that lay broken in the excavation); he had carried it on his back, in many weary journeys, from the foot of the tall pine to a cave he had on the two-pointed hill at the north-east angle of the island, and there it had lain stored in safety since two months before the arrival of the *Hispaniola*."

The points of interest in this excerpt are: it is Ben Gunn who does have the treasure; Stevenson clarifies that it was only the shaft of the pickaxe remaining in the fake treasure site, and Ben Gunn's cave is on the two-pointed hill. Stevenson's idea for the two-pointed hill may have come from one of the cover pages of *At Last* by Charles Kingsley, which is a logo for the MacMillan Publishing Company. It is an "M" within an "M" and the inner "M" resembles a two-pointed hill. Stevenson uses this image of a large capital "M" to represent Ben Gunn's (Moody's) property giving him the initials of B.M.

1889 Logo for The MacMillan
Publishing Company

In Stevenson's encoded message, Ben Gunn/Moody, Dr. Livesey and John Silver/Swift were all part of the cover-up. Stevenson first conveys this when Ben Gunn assists John Silver in escaping, mentioned in the final chapter of *Treasure Island*. As previously mentioned, Ben is one of the names used by Stevenson at a time when no last name was given, and the full identity was revealed later. In Chapter Eight, "At the Sign Of the 'Spy-Glass,'" Stevenson cryptically introduced Ben Gunn seven chapters before he is officially introduced in Chapter Fifteen. In Chapter Eight, Ben is in the Spy-Glass Tavern and seems to be at John Silver's command, which is indicated when Silver tells him to run and catch Black Dog. John Silver later tells Jim Hawkins that, "Ben's a good runner; few seamen run better than Ben."

The next reference made to Ben Gunn being fleet of foot is found in Chapter 15 where he is officially introduced as Ben Gunn and Jim Hawkins describes first seeing him; "...From trunk to trunk the creature flitted like a deer, running manlike on two legs, but unlike any man that I had ever seen, stooping almost double as it ran. Yet a man it was, I could no longer be in doubt about that." Another running reference is made in Chapter 33, "The Fall of a Chieftain," by Jim Hawkins when he describes– "Ben Gunn, being fleet of foot."

Each of these fleet of foot references make it clear that Ben Gunn is also the Ben at the Spy-Glass Tavern in Chapter Eight. The Ben who at John Silver's command ran after Black Dog is also Ben Gunn the man who set Silver free. As mentioned in Part Two of this book, Jonathan Swift (John Silver) went to church with the Moody (Gunn) family.

Ben's, "fleet of foot" ability is referred to three times by Stevenson.
[Not Original Caption] Illustration from a 1954 Nelson Doubleday
publication of *Treasure Island.*

This identification of Ben Gunn at the Spy-Glass Tavern (White House Tavern in Alexandria), demonstrates how the time line of the encoded message is not the same as the story of *Treasure Island*. When Ben Gunn is fully identified in Chapter 15, he tells Jim Hawkins that he had been "marooned three years agone." This may have been done by Stevenson to cryptically reveal that it had been three years from the time Jonathan Swift (Jim Hawkins) met Ben Moody (Ben Gunn) in Alexandria to the time of Swift's first visit to Kentucky and the silver mine. If this is what Stevenson was revealing, it could indicate the age of Swift during his first Kentucky visit. The year 1784 is the year to base it upon. As mentioned in Chapter Three of this book, 1784 is the first year where documentation can be found which establishes Swift's home as in Alexandria, Virginia. It was also in 1783 or 1784 that Benjamin Moody died. Taking three years from this date gives an approximate date of 1780. It seems logical to add at least two years to the three making an approximate year of 1778.

Jonathan Swift was born in 1764; this would mean that Swift was approximately 14 to 17 years old when he first came to Kentucky. Coming at it from another angle, Jim Hawkins has always been considered to be from 11 to 14 years of age. Adding the three years to this would mean that Swift was again approximately between 14 and 17 years of age upon his first Kentucky visit. This is, of course, based upon the supposition that Stevenson was conveying in his encryption, the three-year message. There is one other shred of evidence that could lend support to this estimated age of Swift, on his first Kentucky visit, and it is based upon knowing that Swift learned the merchant trade under Mr. May of Boston. It is also based upon the silver mine diversion theories presented in Part Two of this book.

By the theories presented in Part Two of this book, pertaining to Swift diverting attention from the theoretical silver mine in Washington County Kentucky, a supposition can be formed pertaining to Mr. May. It seems that Swift owned his own business in 1784, at 20 years of age. Much of the property Swift purchased in Kentucky was through William May of Bardstown, Kentucky. If Swift was in Kentucky, in 1778 or 1779, he would have been a 14 or 15-year-old apprentice, and in the company of Colonel Joseph May. If Swift divulged information pertaining to the silver mine's whereabouts, then he likely also mentioned his superior, Mr. May. Purchasing property through William May would further confuse those seeking the mine, by diverting attention from Mr. May of Boston to William May of Bardstown. This could also explain the lengthy time period during which Swift had not seen the silver mines, as mentioned in the Swift legend. If Jonathan Swift were in

Kentucky in 1778, then, when he first purchased land in 1791 and in 1794, it would be a 13 to 16 year time gap. Whether Stevenson, did or did not intend to communicate a specific time period for when Swift was first in Kentucky, he did portray a-very-much alive Ben Moody, represented by Ben Gunn and a time period of three years.

The following excerpt from *The Virginia Magazine of History and Biography Volume VI* could indicate the reason why Benjamin Moody became the owner of the Washington County Kentucky properties, especially if his family had been familiar with any land interests of the Moody pirates.

"...The extremely interesting chapter on Piracy is taken largely, though with due acknowledgment, from Hughson and other investigators; but General McCrady has clearly shown the injustice of the term 'Carolina Pirates,' and has drawn for us a very just distinction between pirates like Worley, 'Blackbeard,' and Steele Bonnet, and the men who hled [held] legal commissions as privateers under William and Mary or the 'good Queen Anne.' No one, probably, better understood the difference than the miscreants who were hung in chains at White Point. Governors Blake, Archdale, Quarry and others were accused, perhaps unjustly, of trafficking with these 'gentlemen adventurers;' but the pirates themselves were no more Carolinians than were the Spaniards who harassed and threatened the Province.

"It was not until 1718-19 that Governor Robert Johnson and Vice-Admiral William Rhett exterminated the nefarious hordes of Bonnet, Moody and Worley, while Governor Spotswood of Virginia did similar service by the infamous crew of Blackbeard..."

Finding Ben Gunn's Coracle

Ben Gunn's two-pointed hill is not marked with an "X" on Flint's map. Stevenson does, however, define, with amazing accuracy, the location of Ben Gunn's (Moody's) treasure. As previously mentioned, the coracle, which belonged to Ben Gunn, represents bounded property. The property it could represent is Benjamin Moody's land in Washington County Kentucky. In Chapter 15 Ben Gunn tells Jim Hawkins, "I keep her under the white rock," referring to his boat the "coracle." While the coracle represents Ben Moody's land, the white rock represents salt. When Stevenson describes the coracle as being under the white rock, the encrypted meaning is that Ben Moody's (Gunn's) property is south of a salt rock or salt lick. As mentioned in Part Two of this book, Benjamin Moody's property is located just south of Matthew Walton's famous Salt Lick. (Refer to Map #4 in Chapter 5 and document A-3 in Chapter 6 of this book).

Stevenson makes two references that link Ben Gunn to salt, one directly and the other implied. In Chapter 33, "The Fall of a Chieftain," Stevenson writes-- "...Ben Gunn's cave was well supplied with goat's meat salted by himself..." If Ben Gunn (Moody) lived on an island in the ocean, which he did not, he could have manufactured salt from it. Part of Ben Moody's (Gunn's) property was an inland island where a salt lick would be needed to produce salt-- Walton's lick was just across the creek.

In addition to the white rock (salt) reference, Stevenson's implied (or encoded) method of linking Ben Gunn to salt is done by using the coracle and cheese. A coracle was a small rounded boat made of wickerwork and covered with skins of animals; in this case it was goat. These little boats were used in Wales, Ireland and part of Western England.

The one thing that Ben Gunn wanted more than anything was cheese—he craved it. These references to cheese and the coracle, which both relate directly only to Ben Gunn, is another Stevenson clue. The fact that Ben Gunn can manufacture salt, and that he loves cheese, but does not know how to make it, indicates that Stevenson is referring to Cheshire, England. Cheshire has always been known for two things: cheese and salt. Cheshire is also located in Western England, linking it to the coracle, and it also borders Flint County. Stevenson is not saying that Ben Gunn (Moody) came from Cheshire, England; the sole point he is concerned with making is to associate Ben Gunn (Moody) with salt. Ben Gunn had access to plenty of goats on *Treasure Island*, but he did not know how to make cheese, yet he could produce salt. Whether or not this encoded message tells us anything about Benjamin Moody's participation in the silver mine operation is unknown.

Since the *Hispaniola* and *Walrus* represent Swift's old property of 20,718 ¾ acres, Stevenson used a much smaller boat, a coracle, to represent Ben Moody's 4,800 acres according to the original surveys. Ben Gunn's cave is in the two-pointed hill, located at the Northeast angle of the island, and represents Benjamin Moody's land marked with a capital "M." By using the scale of the island provided on Flint's map, Gunn's cave is located approximately four, to five miles north of the stockade with the kettle *spring*, of *Treasure Island*. This is the same distance from *Springfield*, in Washington County, to Moody's 4,800 acres, which is directly north of Springfield. More information pertaining to the location of Benjamin Moody's property will be provided later.

Ben, Ben Gunn, Benbow and the "B" Sea Chest

Stevenson left several encoded clues to demonstrate that Billy Bones' sea chest cryptically represents the real treasure (silver mine) in which Ben Gunn

(Moody) possessed. The first clue is in the name Benbow. "Ben" and "bow" represent Ben Gunn's (Moody's) "X." The bow also represents a gift, or a more appropriate word in this story, a prize. *Prize* is a code word used by pirates to identify the word "treasure," and pirates marked their treasure with an "X" or Jolly Roger. A bow can symbolically represent an "X." With the three "X's" of Flint's map, the Union Jack, and the encoded Jolly Roger, which all represent treasure markers, one cannot doubt that Stevenson's encrypted communication of Benbow is "Ben's treasure."

"Billy Bones "B" sea chest at the Benbow Inn, which Black Dog, Blind Pew the beggar, and Barbeque all seek." [Not Original Caption]
Illustration from a 1955 Whitman Publishing Company publication
of *Treasure Island.*

Another Stevenson clue is found in the name of Billy Bones. As mentioned, it is probable that Stevenson lifted the name of Bones from Captain Johnson's pirate book. Captain Johnson's man named Bones, was the boatswain of the ship, *Good Fortune*. This ship, named *Good Fortune,* indicates that Billy Bones, and more specifically his sea chest, represent the real treasure. The sea chest is marked with a "B" burnt into it, and is found in Chapter Four of *Treasure Island.* This "B" is a marker from Stevenson to identify that the sea chest has more than one meaning or a double entendre.

Stevenson leaves another clue that the sea chest represents Ben Gunn's treasure, in the description of the chest's contents. Jim Hawkins describes, in Chapter Four, the money found in the chest as being from "…all countries and sizes - doubloons, and louis-d'ors, and guineas, and pieces of eight, and I know not what besides, all shaken together at random." In Chapter 34, "And Last," Stevenson cryptically compares the contents of the sea chest to Ben Gunn's treasure. Jim Hawkins narrates —"It was a strange collection, like Billy Bones's hoard for the diversity of coinage, but so much larger and so much more varied that I think I never had more pleasure than in sorting them. English, French, Spanish, Portuguese, Georges, and Louises, doubloons and double guineas and moidores and sequins…" One type of money not mentioned in Ben Gunn's treasure, which was in Billy Bones' sea chest, was pieces of eight. No doubt Stevenson did this to show that Ben Gunn is an encoded character with a separate identity, and is not one of the Swift descriptors or pieces of eight.

As previously mentioned, Mrs. Crossley's bag represents the fake silver mine. Stevenson further defines this when Mrs. Hawkins takes a small amount of money from Billy Bones' sea chest and puts it into Mrs. Crossley's bag. Mrs. Crossley's bag represents the fake silver mine marked by the "X," and the money in it represents a salted treasure site.

It appears that Stevenson is leaving an encrypted communication as to what Ben Gunn's (Moody's) treasure actually is in Chapter 30, "On Parole." The following excerpt, taken from this chapter, has Dr. Livesey describing Ben Gunn to Jim Hawkins-- "'Oh, by Jupiter, and talking of Ben Gunn! why, this is the mischief in person. Silver!' he cried, 'Silver! —I'll give you a piece of advice,' he continued as the cook drew near again; 'don't you be in any great hurry after that treasure.'" If one is only following the story line of *Treasure Island,* it seems that Dr. Livesey is merely calling out to John Silver. However, when one realizes that *Treasure Island* is actually a story about the Swift silver mine legend, the Dr. Livesey quote takes on a different meaning. When Livesey is describing Ben Gunn, and says Silver all in the same breath, it is Stevenson revealing that the actual treasure is—a silver mine. There is also the black hills cove clue, where the Benbow Inn is located, referring to mining and also the mining shaft (broken pickaxe shaft) reference at the rifled treasure site. Put all these clues together, and one will have a silver mine as the encoded treasure.

Locating Treasure Island

Once it has been determined that Robert Louis Stevenson's book, *Treasure Island* was based upon the Swift silver mine legend, the general location for *Treasure Island* is immediately known. The Swift silver mine is known to have been in or near Kentucky in the United States of America. Stevenson did, however, leave other clues that the *Treasure Island* was in North America. The first and most obvious is in John Flint's map of the island. The island can easily be compared to a crude early drawing of North America.

The *Treasure Island* maps considered in this investigation are 1) A photocopy of a map sent via internet from Beinecke Library at Yale University taken from an 1885 edition of *Treasure Island*. 2) An exact duplicate of the 1885 map, just described, from a 1901 *Treasure Island* edition by Charles Scribner's Sons (see picture). 3) Another *Treasure Island* publication, whose map is very near, or the same is a popular 1911 edition illustrated by N.C. Wyeth, which can be found in bookstores today. 4) A *Treasure Island* publication, which the map is nearly identical, is from Puffin Books. This edition has Long John Silver on the cover wearing a cocked-hat, with a red, instead of green, parrot sitting on his shoulder with the moon in the background. These maps are not the one that Lloyd Osbourne and Stevenson created together. That original map was lost, and is mentioned by Stevenson in his *My First Book—"Treasure Island"* article. Stevenson recreated the map mentioned in the 1883 first edition.

In Chapter 33, "The Fall of a Chieftain," Stevenson left another North America clue at the rifled treasure site, when John Silver tells the pirates, "'Dig away, boys,' said Silver, with the coolest insolence; 'you'll find some pig-nuts and I shouldn't wonder.'" A pig-nut is the nut from a type of hickory tree native to North America. Stevenson also mentions rattlesnakes in Chapter 14, which are found in North and Spanish (South) America. In Chapter 34, "And Last," Jim Hawkins narrates as the party is leaving the island; "…We laid her head for the nearest port in Spanish America…" When Stevenson says that the *Hispaniola* was headed for the nearest Spanish America port, it indicates they were not in Spanish America to begin with.

Kentucky

In Part Two of this book, the inland island of Benjamin Moody was compared to Stevenson's *Treasure Island*, showing yet another similarity between the two stories. It seems likely that a property nearly surrounded by water, where a silver mine is possibly located, could have been in a Stevenson/ Sam Osbourne Swift journal or perhaps it was known to Stevenson by other means, which influenced the naming of *Treasure Island*. However, for purposes of being able to tell the story of a real and fake silver mine, which was located a considerable distance apart, Stevenson was referring to the state of Kentucky when naming *Treasure Island*. The state of *Kentucky* is Stevenson's encoded "*Treasure Island*."

In the encoded message, Ben Gunn, or Ben Moody, is the important figure in Kentucky because of a silver mine he may have had there. Stevenson refers to Ben Gunn as "The Man of the Island," which is the title of Chapter "Fifteen." The chapter title, and number, is Stevenson's first Kentucky clue. Kentucky was the *fifteenth* state admitted into the United States, and Ben Moody's property was located there. On the *Treasure Island* map, graves are marked in an area, which would be near Kentucky. The gravesite is north of the stockade. In Chapter 15, "The Man of the Island," Ben Gunn refers to the graves as the "cetemery" (cemetery) and "mounds" where he would go to pray. He considered the mounds/gravesite his place of worship, which is yet another Stevenson reference that Ben Gunn is the evangelist, Dwight L. Moody. As mentioned in Part Two of this book, Indian burial mounds are likely to be found in Washington County, Kentucky.

Upon closer examination of Robert Louis Stevenson's (Flint's) *Treasure Island* map, one will observe the letter "M" above the letter "G" in Graves. As mentioned in this chapter, Stevenson designates the "two-pointed hill" as being where Ben Gunn's (Moody's) treasure cave is located. Also mentioned, was the fact that the image of a two-pointed hill creates a capital "M" which stands for "Moody." The location of the "M" on Stevenson's crude *Treasure Island* map of North America is very near where Benjamin Moody's island property was located in Washington County, Kentucky. This "M" on the map is a major code clue left by Stevenson, but one must have the previously mentioned elements of the code puzzle to understand it. The "M" also represents "Mine."

Another Stevenson clue that the *Treasure Island* is Kentucky is found in Chapter 31, "And Last," when Jim Hawkins refers to the party's– "dark and bloody sojourn on the island." As previously mentioned in Part One of this book, The Native Americans referred to Kentucky as the "dark and bloody ground."

Identifying Kentucky as the *Treasure Island*, completes Stevenson's meaning of the most famous line from *Treasure Island*–

"Fifteen men on the dead man's chest—
Yo-ho-ho, and a bottle of rum!"

Fifteen refers to Kentucky, dead man's chest refers to Jonathan Swift's fake silver mine property and yo-ho-ho means that either Swift or Stevenson (or both) considered misleading the British with the fake Kentucky silver mine, very humorous. The property (*Hispaniola*/the dead man's chest,) Squire Trelawney purchased from Jonathan Swift (Mr. Blandly) would most likely have been the 20,718 ¾ acres Swift purchased in 1791, though Stevenson could have been referring to any of the Jonathan Swift properties.

Loopholes, Stockade, Kettle Spring, Job Anderson and Washington County Kentucky

The information of Ben Moody's (Ben Gunn's) property (the coracle) being south (under) of Walton's Salt Lick (white rock) is another interestingly similar comparison between the Swift legends according to the findings and theories presented in Part Two of this book and Stevenson's *Treasure Island*. It is nearly worthless, however, unless an encoded message identifying Washington County can be logically substantiated.

Stevenson identifies Washington County, Kentucky in Part Four of *Treasure Island* titled, "The Stockade." The Stockade is where Stevenson identified the name Moody by using the line, "don't cut anything out of the Bible" and the initials, D. M., on the back of the Black Spot. Another similarity between *Treasure Island*, and the Swift legend, is the kettle in the spring, also found in Part Four, "The Stockade." This next excerpt from Chapter 19, "The Garrison in the Stockade," has Jim Hawkins describing the spring and kettle– "…There was a porch at the door, and under this porch the little spring welled up into an artificial basin of a rather odd kind—no other than a great ship's kettle of iron, with the bottom knocked out, and sunk 'to her bearings', as the captain said, among the sand." This compares with the story of Matthew Walton's old salt kettle, left at Moody's land, across from Walton's lick, mentioned in Part Two of this book.

Stevenson uses the stockade, and the pirate Job Anderson, as directional/locational indicators to reveal that the stockade of *Treasure Island* is located in Washington County Kentucky. With the clues left by Stevenson, identifying Kentucky as the *Treasure Island*, along with it being common knowledge that Swift's silver mine was in Kentucky, Stevenson was able to identify Washington County cryptically and ingeniously with little effort. The first Job Anderson directional clue is found in Chapter 18, "End of the First Day's Fighting," and is narrated by Dr. Livesey– "…We struck the enclosure [stockade] about the middle of the south side, and, almost at the same time, seven mutineers—Job Anderson, the boatswain, at their head—appeared in full cry at the southwestern corner." The point of interest is that Job Anderson is associated with a directional indicator, that being the "south-western corner."

Stevenson's next use of the locational indicator named Job Anderson is found in Chapter 21, "The Attack," and is narrated by Jim Hawkins – "The head of Job Anderson, the boatswain, appeared at the middle loophole." The directional and locational indicators represented here are middle and north. The side of the stockade that has the five loopholes is on the north side. All other sides have two loopholes each, and this is clarified in Chapter 21, therefore, the only side of the stockade with a middle loophole is the north side.

The next Job Anderson clue, is found in Chapter 21, shortly after the previously stated excerpt, and is narrated by Jim Hawkins – "Mechanically I obeyed, turned eastwards, and with my cutlass raised, ran round the corner of the house. Next moment I was face to face with Anderson."

The points of interest are:

1. Jim Hawkins ran eastwards when he exited the stockade. The door of the stockade is located on the south side (porch side). When Jim Hawkins ran around the southeast corner of the stockade, he would then be headed in a North/Northeast direction.
2. When Jim Hawkins is running North to Northeast, he is soon face to face with Job Anderson, which Stevenson refers to only as Anderson.
3. In this clue, Job Anderson's location is North/Northeast.

Stevenson, of course, did not mention Washington County, Kentucky in the text of *Treasure Island*. His method of encoding Washington County was in defining a bordering Kentucky county, and describing the proximity of the stockade, where Ben Moody was identified, in relation to that county. The name of the Kentucky county mentioned in the text of *Treasure Island*, is "Anderson."

A "southwest corner," was the first Job Anderson directional clue, and the southwest corner of Anderson County is approximately in the middle of north Washington County. The second Job Anderson clue, was "north" and "middle," and as just mentioned, the southwest corner of Anderson County line is located in the north and middle of Washington County. The third clue has Anderson being located somewhere in the "north or northeast" from the stockade; this indicates that the stockade would be located to the south or southwest of Job Anderson/Anderson County. This would place the stockade in the north/northwest area of Washington County. Since it is unlikely that Jim Hawkins made a perfect ninety-degree turn when he went around the corner of the stockade, it seems probable that Stevenson meant to identify this Job Anderson directional clue as northeast instead of north. This would place the stockade to the southwest of Anderson County's southwest corner, and mean that Stevenson's encoded stockade was located in northwest Washington County, using the Anderson County line as the east-west divider.

Benjamin Moody's (Ben Gunn's) island property (coracle), and Matthew Walton's salt lick and kettle (white rock and stockade with kettle spring), were located in the northwest of Washington County. All of the Job Anderson (Anderson County) clues were left by Stevenson in Part Four of *Treasure Island* titled, "The Stockade." By using Anderson County, Stevenson is clearly indicating that the treasure is located in northern Washington County. Had the treasure/silver mine been located in south Washington County, he would have made Job Anderson's last name either Marion or Boyle. Had the silver mine been in the east or west, Stevenson would have named Job Anderson either Mercer or Nelson. Marion, Boyle, Mercer and Nelson are the county names that border Washington County on the south, east and west.

Another cryptogram of encoded communication to be mentioned in this book is the likelihood that Stevenson was referring to yet another quincunx/ Jolly Roger. It is another layer of encoded communication, where Stevenson uses the loopholes again. When Job Anderson's head appeared in the middle of the five loopholes, it seems to represent another quincunx. Jim Hawkins narrates in "The Attack," Chapter 21 – "…In a moment, the four pirates had swarmed up the mound and were upon us. The head of Job Anderson, the boatswain, appeared at the middle loophole." The four pirates mentioned in this excerpt represent the four cardinal points that make up the crossbones and Job Anderson's head in the middle loophole represent the skull of the Jolly Roger. Another significant Stevenson clue in this excerpt is the mention of the mound. This identifies the graves/mounds of Ben Gunn with the stockade.

The difference between this quincunx/Jolly Roger, and the Jolly Roger of the Dead Man's Chest (fake silver mine), is that these pirates are alive. The Dead Man's Chest property was represented by the dead Tom Redruth, and the Tom (also Redruth) that John Silver had killed. Also, it was marked with dead pirates killed by John Flint, that Stevenson represented by the treasure pointer, Allardyce. Tom Morgan is one of the three pirates that were left marooned upon the island at the conclusion of *Treasure Island*. This Tom represents a live Tom or a real silver mine, and "The bar silver" that remained upon the island mentioned at the end of the book.

These live pirates at the loopholes also represent the real treasure/silver mine. The quincunx, represented by the five loopholes and Job Anderson, also represents the man named Bones in Captain Johnson's pirate book. There are two boatswains referred to by Stevenson, one in the story of *Treasure Island*, and the other is encoded. The first is Job Anderson, boatswain of the *Hispaniola*, and the second is the man named Bones, who was boatswain of the ship named *Good Fortune*.

The real treasure/silver mine is also the real *Hispaniola*. The ship (property) named *Hispaniola* by Mr. Blandly (John Silver and Jonathan Swift) was not the real *Hispaniola*; it was a fake. When Stevenson used the name *Hispaniola*, a name which implies—Spanish land, he is identifying a property/ land that was once Spanish occupied with a silver mine. This is what Squire Trelawney thought he was purchasing when he bought the *Hispaniola* from Mr. Blandly. As mentioned in Part Two of this book, D.P. Casteel found a Spanish marker in the year 1915, and it was located in north Washington County, Kentucky. It is probable, if there is a silver mine in north Washington County, the Spaniards marked it by the four cardinal points using rocks piled up at each point. The silver mine would have been marked in a way that the Spaniards would easily recognize it, but not so obvious that everyone would be able to identify it, as Swift did with the Dead Man's Chest.

Ben Gunn and Ben Moody had another similarity. Ben Gunn was referred to as the maroon or marooned. In the late 1770s and early 1780s, north Washington County, as well as, most of Kentucky, was unpopulated. Being in north Washington County during this time period could be compared to being marooned.

WHATEVER REMAINS

" W hen you have eliminated all which is impossible, then whatever remains, however improbable, must be the truth." ~ *Sherlock Holmes*
From, The Adventure of the Blanched Soldier, a short story by Sir Arthur Conan Doyle, about a soldier believed to be a leper.

To research and investigate Jonathan Swift and Robert Louis Stevenson has been a great honor and a thrilling adventure of discovery. The findings and theories presented in this book should only be considered the steam off the tip of an iceberg. It is hoped, however, that this steam will aid in finding the tip. There is no doubt that what was presented in this book raises more questions than it has answered. One such question could be: Why did Stevenson identify Swift numerically with the number eight? In an attempt to answer that question one more will be asked: What is the primary theory presented in this book that Swift was responsible for? The answer is: Setting up pointers for a fake silver mine. In this book the pointers have been referred to as quincunx, Union Jack, Alan, Allardyce, Jolly Roger, Flint's Fist, Mrs. Crossley's bag, "X" or three red crosses, and dead man named Tom a.k.a. the Dead Man's Chest. Each of these pointers represents an "X" with the treasure being located at its intersecting point. It seems likely that Stevenson chose the number eight for the purpose of further defining/verifying his encoded story of Swift. Since it is theorized that Swift was responsible for making an "X," it is probable that Stevenson chose the only number which itself makes an "X," and that is "*8*." By combining the revelations of "*8*" makes an "X," and "*8*" represents "Swift," he further confirms the encoded story-line theory that, Jonathan Swift set up an "X marks the spot" quincunx on a counterfeit silver mine.

Another question to be asked would be does the "B" factor of Stevenson's encoded message also refer to the adjoining property owners of Swift Property #1? The names of those property owners were, Bell, Barbour and Banks, and as mentioned in Part Two of this book, Swift Property #1 was originally owned by Mordecai Barbour (refer to Appendix A of this book, sections A4 thru A9).

Whether there was a lost or hidden silver mine somewhere in Washington County, or anywhere in Kentucky, after 220 years still remains unknown. There is only one thing to be certain of at this time, which is that the story of the Swift silver mine legend is real. It has been proposed that this very real story was Stevenson's true inspiration for one of the world's most beloved books—*Treasure Island*.

Although most geologists indicate the chance of a silver mine in Kentucky is unlikely, there was at one time something that gave birth to the silver mine stories. There are three likely possibilities, the first being that a great store of Spanish silver was brought to and hidden in Kentucky with the intention of retrieving it later. If such a cache of silver was found, it could have been the source of the silver mine stories. The second is that the government, to expedite the settlement of the Kentucky wilderness, used the Swift silver mine stories. Also along these lines, it is a known fact that the silver mine stories was used by wealthy land speculators to increase their land's value. The third possibility is that an undetermined amount of silver was extracted from a vein of silver-bearing galena somewhere in Kentucky. The Washington County area is both a logical and possible location for Kentucky's lost silver mine a.k.a "*Treasure Island*." If after all that has been revealed in this book, one re-reads The Swift Journal from Kerr's *History of Kentucky*, and purposefully intend to see it as a diversion, the story of the man named Munday will read very differently than it did when it was first read.

As mentioned at the end of this chapter, Tom Morgan, who was alive at the end of the *Treasure Island* story, represents the *real* silver mine. The dead Tom Redruth represents the faked silver mine. Stevenson verifies this Tom Morgan encoded story theory in this excerpt from the end of Chapter 33, "The Fall of the Chieftain"—"…Yet there were still three upon that island—Silver, and old Morgan, and Ben Gunn—who had each taken his share of these crimes, as each had hoped in vain to share in the reward."

The encoded message points of interest are 1) Stevenson refers to John Silver, Tom Morgan, and Ben Gunn as "three" who were still upon the *Treasure Island*. 2) John Silver and Ben Gunn were not two of the three pirates left marooned on the *Treasure Island* at the end of the story. 3) Tom Morgan was one of the three remaining pirates left marooned on *Treasure Island*. 4) Stevenson alludes to the three remaining pirates by this Silver, old Morgan, and Ben Gunn reference. 5) Tom Morgan is referred to in this excerpt as *old* Morgan and in doing this; Stevenson alludes to old Tom Redruth. 6) When Stevenson alludes that old Morgan is to be compared to old Redruth (both Toms) he creates a new silver mine connection to old Tom Morgan. 7) Tom Morgan represents the real silver mine, or the genuine Hispaniola, and Stevenson confirms this when he (Morgan) is mentioned along with Silver (silver) and Ben Gunn, the man who was actually known to be in possession of the treasure. 8) Stevenson encodes, that Silver is silver bars or silver ore, old Morgan is the silver mine and Ben Gunn is Ben Moody who is the primary subject pertaining to the *Treasure Island*.

As mentioned in Chapter Nine of this book, Stevenson named the *Treasure Island* character, Tom Redruth, because of the reference of Redruth and silver mines in Charles Kingsley's book, *At Last*; but why did he refer to the faked and genuine silver mines as a "Tom?" Once again, the three Toms of *Treasure Island* are 1) Old Tom Morgan; who cryptically represents the genuine silver mine. 2) The man referred to only as Tom, who was killed by Long John Silver in which this action represented setting up a faked silver mine (Dead Man's Chest). 3) Old Tom Redruth, represents the rifled (fake) treasure site, and is also the completed identity of the man named only Tom.

One reason that Stevenson used a common first name was to purposefully link the three Toms for the cause of defining his encoded story. Stevenson used the name "Tom" and the word "old" to accomplish this, when he refers to both Tom Redruth and Tom Morgan as "old." As he chose to use the number eight, which makes an "X," it seems probable that he used the name "Tom," to confirm an encoded story theory rather than picking a name at random.

The code elements of the *Treasure Island* character, Tom Morgan are 1) He is referred to as "Old" and "Tom" which links him to the character "Old Tom Redruth" and the man named Tom who is also Redruth. 2) His name is Tom Morgan and his initials are T.M. 3) He was left marooned on the island (Kentucky) at the end of the story. 4) Old Tom Morgan was mentioned in the same sentence and sequence with (John) Silver and Ben Gunn which cryptically links the metal silver, Ben Moody, and Tom Morgan.

As mentioned in Chapter Six of this book, Ben Moody's island property was divided among his children after his death. When it was divided, and the re-survey was performed in 1797, the 5,226 (4,800 original survey) acres were separated into six tracts or lots. Lot #1 of Benjamin Moody's land went to his son, Thomas. "Tom" Moody's Lot #1 property was an 805 acre tract and was also the property which was directly across from Walton's Salt Lick. This tract of land can be viewed in Chapter Six of this book, identified as A-3. Tom Moody's land is in the *northwest* section of the 1797 re-survey. Note: Benjamin Moody Sr. is referred to as Captain in genealogical files found in the Washington County Clerk's Office.

The code connections which can be made between the *Treasure Island* character Tom Morgan and Tom Moody are: 1) They both share Tom as a first name. 2) Both of their initials are T.M. 3) Stevenson linked Silver, Tom Morgan and Ben Gunn/Ben Moody in the Chapter 33 excerpt. 4) Tom Moody and Benjamin Moody are linked as father and son. 5) Tom Morgan and Tom Moody were left on the island. As mentioned in Chapter Six of this book, Tom Moody married Mary Berry, who was the daughter of Richard Berry, and lived adjacent to the Moody land in Washington County, Kentucky which establishes that Thomas's residence was there.

Another layer of revelation one may deduce from the two Toms is, the fake Tom indicates a deliberate pattern of duplication. By creating the two Toms, Stevenson is able to perfectly convey within his encoded story, Jonathan Swift's silver mine twist, which was presented in Part Two of this book. In real life, and in *Treasure Island*, Jonathan Swift's and Long John Silver's "Tom" was Tom Redruth (a.k.a. the fake silver mine,) the dead man named only Tom (also Redruth), and the counterfeit Hispaniola (a.k.a. the Dead Man's Chest). Ben Gunn's (Ben Moody's) "Tom" was Tom Morgan (a.k.a. the real silver mine a.k.a. the genuine Hispaniola.) By using the name Tom in both cases, Stevenson demonstrates that Swift's/Silver's counterfeit silver mine, had notable similarities to Ben Moody's/Ben Gunn's genuine silver mine.

These two Toms of *Treasure Island*, seem to support the theory and scenario presented in Part Two of this book. The theory was that Jonathan Swift's intention and objective, was to purchase properties in Kentucky with similar landmarks, people and etc. to the island property in Washington County, Kentucky, which was owned by Benjamin Moody. In fact hard evidence exists which seem to substantiate that Swift was also duplicating his own Kentucky land purchases to further confuse all known information pertaining to the silver mine subject.

From the Dr. James Craik communiqué, (see original document identified as A-1 in Chapter Two or transcribed document in Appendix A identified as A-1 in this book) one finds that *the Doctor* is interested in two properties, one with 20,720 acres and the other with 20,718 ¾ acres. The 20,718 ¾ acre tract is the Swift Property #1 tract with the quincunx in Breckinridge

County, Kentucky and the 20,720 acres mentioned compose Swift Properties #4 thru #8. The 1791 Swift Property #1 had 20,718¾ acres all in one tract. Swift Properties #4 thru #8 totaling 20,720 acres is the five-parcel package that Swift sold to Dr. Craik in 1794 which is only one and one quarter acres more than Swift Property #1. In other words, Swift and Co. put together the five-parcel land package to duplicate Swift Property #1.

Why Stevenson used Tom Moody's first name for old Redruth and old Morgan, instead of his brothers', William or Benjamin Jr., or his sisters', Sarah, Ann or Frances is suspect but unknown. Could it be that Thomas' (Tom's) Lot #1 tract of 805 acres is significant to this story and investigation?

When Stevenson refers to the "bar silver" which remains on the island, he is alluding to a silver mine. Tom Morgan who remained marooned on the island represents that silver mine. The connection Stevenson makes in this "Silver, old Morgan and Ben Gunn" excerpt seems to determine that Ben Gunn (a.k.a Ben Moody) owned a silver mine. In other words, Tom Morgan (code name for Tom Moody) represents the silver mine which is on the inland island property of the man that Stevenson's encoded message referred to as "The man of the island," Benjamin Moody.

It is proposed that the location (or locations) of the legendary Swift silver mine has been identified and revealed in this investigative study. The primary location presented is the Quincunx property, also identified as Swift Property #1, and "The Dead Man's Chest," which is located in Breckinridge and Hardin Counties in Kentucky. The secondary locations are Swift Properties #4 thru #8, which is the five-parcel land package the Doctor purchased, and Swift's "Greenwich" property is also considered a site. Swift's "Gold Vault Property" should also be considered significant.

It is believed that the "rifled treasure site" of *Treasure Island*, referred to by Stevenson, was Swift Property #1. Flint's pointer, "Allardyce," identified its location. It seems probable at one time, this property contained a mineshaft, and silver ore was brought in from another source, to "salt" this counterfeit silver mine. It is unlikely; however, there is any recorded evidence to support this theory. These Swift properties have been referred to as, "faked silver mines," nevertheless; not one of them should be completely ruled out as a possible site.

As it is with Stevenson's portrayal of Long John Silver, a man the reader knows not whether to love or hate, or to fear or respect, the same paradox exists with Jonathan Swift. Some of the traditional stories, such as "Tale #2" in Chapter One of this book, portray him in a dark and negative manner, and, as mentioned in "Scenario #1" of Chapter Six of this book, there is evidence which could be interpreted, if one chooses, to support the stories of a murderous Swift. However, if one chooses to believe that things are not always as they appear, an alternate conclusion must be accepted. Considering the possibility of a high-level cover-up operation, in which he was only a participant, and the solid evidence presented in Chapter Three of this book of his good character, it is proposed, that the man responsible for these faked Kentucky silver mines could, just as logically be considered, a silent and unsung "American hero." There was no personal financial gain for his work in Kentucky, and it is believed that the cover-up operation was done in service of his country. Like his father, Samuel, and their forebears, he was instrumental in the founding of the United States of America, and it is sincerely hoped that this book has brought a positive light to the extraordinary life of Jonathan Swift.

If there was an actual silver mine in Kentucky, it is probable that it was owned by someone else, such as, Benjamin Moody, not Swift. Although Swift's silver mine was only a diversion, it is as historically significant as a genuine silver mine, because it was *designed* to be, as Robert Louis Stevenson described it… "a mine of suggestion."

Appendices

Appendix A

A-1

DEED BOOK PAGE #843

By virtue of a power of attorney from Doctor James Craik Senior of Alexandria dated this third day of September 1793. I have received of Jonathan Swift for said Craik his heirs Executors Administrators or assigns peaceable and quiet possession of twenty thousand seven hundred and twenty acres of land situated on the waters of Green River in the County of Hardin and State of Kentucky with his general warranty Deed of them to the said Craik and all the papers of the same and will deliver them to the said Craik or his aforesaid by the Records both of Hardin and Nelson County they appear to be perfectly free and clear from all encumbrances and are superior in quality, and situation to the twenty thousand seven hundred and eighteen acres and three quarter of an acre of land on Rough Creek which I could not receive in consequence of their being encumbered. Witness my hand at Bairds Town Kentucky this fourth day of March 1794   John Taylor attorney in fact for James Craik Senior

A-2

DEED BOOK PAGE #844

Received of John Taylor a letter directed to Doctor James Craik Senior of Alexandria containing a conveyance of general warranty dated the 19th day of February 1794 from me to the said Craik for twenty thousand seven hundred and twenty acres of Land in the County of Hardin and state of Kentucky and Recorded in said County with all the papers of the same that the said Taylor received of me which I promise bind and oblige myself to deliver to the said Craik or his heirs Executors Administrators or assigns Witness my hand at Bairds Town Kentucky this fourth day of March 1794 "Jonathan Swift"

Transcribed Survey of Mordecai Barbour
20,718 ¾ Acres

"Surveyed for Mordecai Barbour 20,718 ¾ of land by virtue of two treasury warrant numbers 188000, [18800] 18817 in Nelson County on the waters of Rough Creek beginning at two small white oaks where Bells line of his 75,000 [acre] survey now belonging to Blair Elliott and Company intersects a line of Barbour and Banks 60,000 acre survey thence along Barbour and Banks line North 72 degrees West

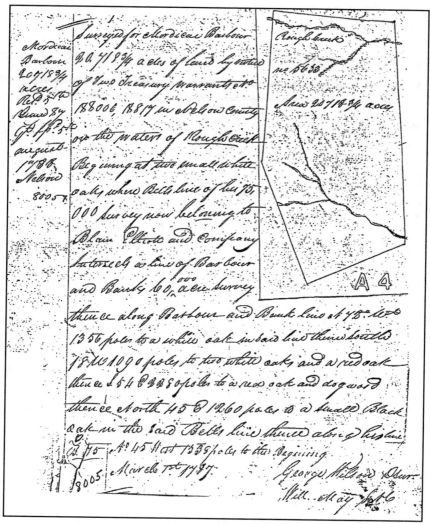

A-4

277

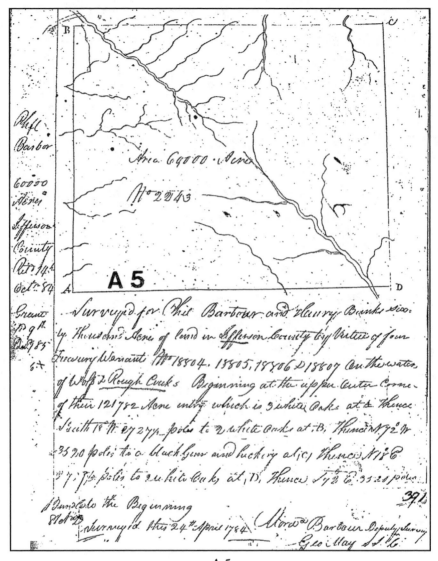

A-5

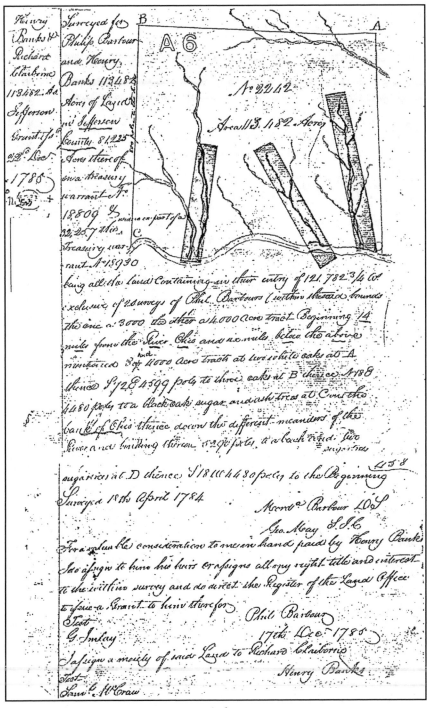

A-6

141 poles crossing Otter creek & passing said Mays corner & continuing the same course with a line of May, Bannister & Company's 2000 acre survey 20 poles further to a maple on the bank of Ohio thence up the same binding therewith to the Beginning.

July 29th 1788

Richd Woolfolk aſst

Will May SWC

Surveyed for William Bell aſsee 75,000 acres of Land on 14 Treasury Warrants No 7982, 17986, 17981, 17990, 17979, 17980, 17984, 17974, 17978, 17987, 17976, 17989, 17985 16298, in Nelson County on Rough creek adjoining Barbour & Banks second 50,000 acre survey on the South west

Beginning at two hickories and Oak the most Southwardly corner of the said Barbour & Banks two surveys of 50,000 Acres each, which lies upon the waters of Otter & the creeks, also 80 poles Southwest from McWilliam's Beginning of his 98,000 acre survey thence North 45 W 4000 poles with the lines of the above mentioned Surveys to their lower corner three white Oaks near a large Spring, thence S 45 W 3000 poles to a spanish Oak & two small white Oaks, thence S 45 E 4000 poles to three black Oaks white Oak & Dogwood, thence N 45 E 3000 poles to the Beginning.

George Wilson SS

March 1st 1787

Will May SWC

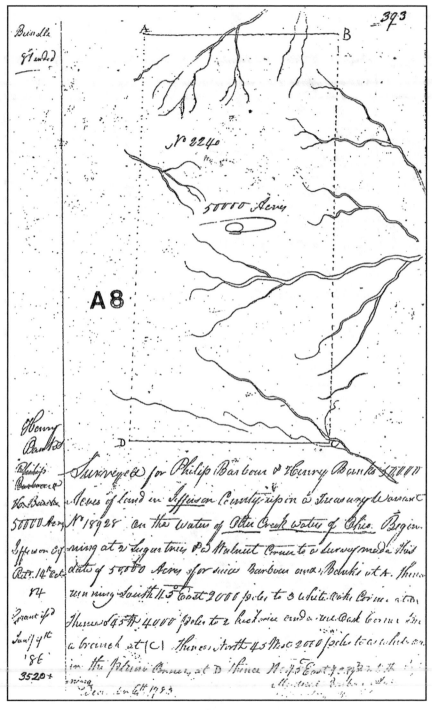

A-8

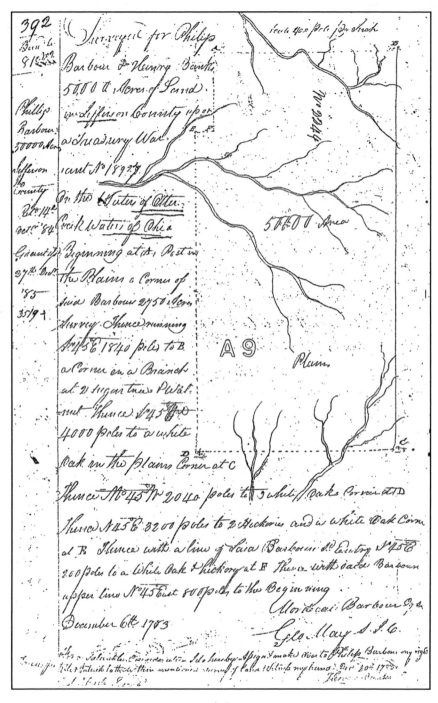

A-9

1,356 poles to a white oak in said line thence South 18 degrees West 1,090 poles to two white oaks and a red oak thence South 54 degrees East 2,280 poles to a red oak and dogwood thence North 45 degrees East 1,260 poles to a small black oak in the said Bells line, thence along his line North 45 degrees West 1,538 poles to the beginning."

Surveyed March 1st 1787

George Wilson, Deputy Surveyor
Will May, Surveyor Nelson County

(See Appendix A, Map # 2 identified as #1 and Swift Property #1, and 20,718 ¾ acres showing the placement of this property. To view the original survey, see Appendix A, identified as A4.)

Transcribed Survey of Phil Barbour and Henry Banks
60,000 Acres

"Surveyed for Phil Barbour and Henry Banks sixty thousand acres of land in Jefferson County by virtue of four treasury warrant numbers 18804, 18805, 18806, and 18807 on the waters of Wolf and Rough Creeks   Beginning at the upper outer corner of their 121,782 acre entry which is three white oaks at A Thence South 18 degrees West 2,727 1/2 poles to two white oaks at, B, Thence North 72 degrees West 3,520 poles to a black gum and hickory at, C, Thence North 18 degrees East 2,727 1/2 poles to two white oaks at, D, Thence South 72 degrees East 3,520 poles to the beginning."

Surveyed this 24th April 1784

Mordecai Barbour, Deputy Surveyor
George May, Surveyor Jefferson County

(See Appendix A, Map # 2 identified as #3 and 60,000 acres showing the placement of this property. To view the original survey, see Appendix A, identified as A5.)

Transcribed Survey of Philip Barbour and Henry Banks
113,482 Acres

"Surveyed for Philip Barbour and Henry Banks 113,482 acres of land in Jefferson County, 81,225 acres thereof in a treasury warrant number 18809 and 32,257 [acres] being part of a Treasury warrant number 18930 being all the land containing in their entry of 121,782 ¾ acres exclusive of 2 surveys of Phil Barbours (within the said bounds the one a 3,000 the other a 4,000 acre tract.)   Beginning 14 miles from the river Ohio and six miles below the above mentioned 3 and 4000 acre tracts at two white oaks at A thence South 72 degrees East 4,599 poles to three oaks at B thence North 18 degrees East 4,480 poles to a black oak sugar and ash trees at C on the bank of the Ohio thence down the different meanders of the river and binding thereon 5,290 poles to a beech and two sugar trees at D thence South 18 degrees West 4,480 poles to the beginning."

Surveyed 18th April 1784

Mordecai Barbour, Deputy Surveyor
George May, Surveyor Jefferson County

(See Appendix A, Map # 2 identified as #3 and 113,482 acres showing the placement of this property. To view the original survey, see Appendix A, identified as A6.)

Transcribed Survey of William Bell
75,000 Acres

"Surveyed for William Bell assignee 75,000 acres of land on 14 Treasury Warrants number 17982, 17986, 17981, 17990, 17979, 17980, 17984, 17974, 17978, 17987, 17976, 17989, 17985, 16298 in Nelson County on Rough Creek adjoining Barbour and Banks second 50,000 acre survey on the Southwest   Beginning at two hickories and red oak the most Southwardly corner of the said Barbour and Banks two surveys of 50,000 acres each, which lies upon the waters of Otter and Mill Creeks also 80 poles Southwest from W. Mc William's beginning of his 98,000 acre survey thence North 45 degrees West 4,000 poles with the lines of the above mentioned, Surveys to their lower corner three white oaks near a large spring, thence South 45 degrees West 3,000 poles to a Spanish oak and two small white oaks, thence South 45 degrees East 4,000 poles to three black oaks white oak and dogwood, thence North 45 degrees East 3,000 poles to the beginning." March 1st 1787   George   Wilson, Deputy Surveyor

Will May, Surveyor Nelson County

(See Appendix A, Map # 2 identified as #3 and 75,000 acres showing the placement of this property. To view the original survey, see Appendix A, identified as A7.)

Transcribed Survey of Philip Barbour and Henry Banks
50,000 Acres

"Surveyed for Philip Barbour and Henry Banks 50,000 acres of land in Jefferson County upon a Treasury Warrant number 18928 on the waters of Otter Creek [being the] waters of Ohio. Beginning at 2 sugar trees and a walnut corner to a Survey made this date of 50,000 acres for said Barbour and Banks at A thence running South 45 degrees East 2,000 poles to 3 white oaks corner at B thence South 45 degrees West 4,000 poles to 2 hickories and a red oak corner on a branch at C thence North 45 degrees West 2,000 poles to a white oak in the plains corner at D thence North 45 degrees East 4,000 poles to the beginning." December 6th 1783

Mordecai Barbour, Deputy Surveyor

George May, Surveyor Jefferson County

(See Appendix A, Map # 2 identified as #3 and the "lower" 50,000 acres showing the placement of this property. To view the original survey, see Appendix A, identified as A8.)

Transcribed Survey of Philip Barbour and Henry Banks
50,000 Acres

"Surveyed for Philip Barbour and Henry Banks 50,000 acres of land in Jefferson County upon a Treasury Warrant number 18927. On the waters of Otter Creek [being the] waters of Ohio Beginning at, A, Post in the plains a corner of said Barbours 2,750 acre survey Thence running South 45 degrees East 1,840 poles to B a corner on a branch at 2 sugar trees and walnut Thence South 45 degrees West 4,000 poles to a white oak in the plains corner at C Thence North 45 degrees West 2,040 poles to 3 white oaks corner at D Thence North 45 degrees East 3,200 poles to 2 hickories and a white oak corner at E Thence with a line of said Barbours said Entry South 45 degrees East 200 poles to a white oak and hickory at F Thence with said Barbours upper line North 45 degrees East 800 poles to the Beginning."

December 6th 1783   Mordecai Barbour, Deputy Surveyor
                                     George May, Surveyor Jefferson County

(See Appendix A, Map # 2 identified as #3 and the "upper" 50,000 acres showing the placement of this property. To view the original survey, see Appendix A, identified as A9.)

APPENDIX B

B-1

This Indenture made this twenty third Day of March in The year of our Lord Seventeen hundred and ninety five between James Kerr and Julia his Wife of the town of Alexandria in the County of Fairfax and Commonwealth of Virginia of the one part and Robert Walsh of Baltimore town in Baltimore County in the state of Maryland Merchant of the other part WITNESSETH that the said James Kerr and Julia his Wife for and in consideration of the sum of Ten thousand Dollars current money of the United States of America to the said James Kerr in hand paid by the said Robert Walsh at or before Sealing and Delivery of these presents the receipt Whereof he Doth hereby acknowledge and thereof Doth for ever acquit and Discharge the said Robert Welsh his heirs executors and Administrators they the said James Kerr and his said Wife Julia have given, granted, Bargained, sold, aliened, released and confirmed and by these presents do give grant Bargain sell alien release and confirm unto the said Robert Walsh his heirs and assigns forever a certain tract or parcel of land Containing TWENTY THOUSAND SEVEN HUNDRED AND EIGHTEEN ACRES AND THREE QUARTERS of an ACRE of land as by survey made and returned unto the land office of Virginia situate and being in the County of Nelson in the District of Kentucky for which twenty thousand seven hundred and eighteen acres and three quarters of an acre of land a patent was granted by the Commonwealth of Virginia unto Mordecai Barbour Esquire bearing date the fifth day of August in the year of our Lord one thousand seven hundred and eighty eight under the hand of Edmund Randolph then Governor of Virginia and under the seal of said Commonwealth and which lands with the patent was conveyed by the said Mordecai Barbour Esquire to a certain Jonathan Swift by Indenture bearing date the fifteenth day of September in the year of Our Lord One Thousand Seven Hundred and Ninety One and by the said Jonathan Swift Conveyed to the said James Kerr by Deed bearing date the eight day of May in the year of Our Lord One thousand Seven hundred and Ninety two and is bounded as follows Viz., BEGINNING at two small white oaks where Bells line of his Seventy thousand acre survey now belonging to Blair Elliott and Company intersects a line of Barbour and Banks Sixty thousand acre survey thence along Barbour and Banks line North seventy two Degrees West thirteen hundred and fifty six poles to a white oak in said line thence south eighteen Degrees West One thousand and ninety poles to two white oaks and a red oak thence South fifty four Degrees East two thousand two hundred and eighty poles to a red oak and Dogwood thence North forty five Degrees East twelve hundred and sixty poles to a small black oak in the said Bells line thence along his line North forty five Degrees West fifteen hundred and thirty eight poles to the BEGINNING reference being had to the said patent will more fully appear Together with all houses woods, underwoods, waters, water courses ways commodities hereditaments privileges Advantages advantages and appurtenances Whatsoever to the said tract of land belonging or in any wise appertaining and the Reversion and Reversions Remainder and remainders Rents Issues and profits thereof and of every part and parcel thereof AND also all [?] right title Interest property Claim and Demand Whatsoever of them the said James Kerr and Julia his Wife of unto and out of the said tract of Land above Mentioned and Described and of on and to every part and parcel thereof TO HAVE AND TO HOLD the said tract of Land Hereditaments and all and singular the premises hereby granted with their and every of their appurtenances unto the said Robert Walsh his heirs and assigns to the only proper use and behoof of of him the said Robert Walsh his heirs and assigns for ever and to or for no other use intent or purpose Whatsoever and the said James Kerr for himself his heirs executors administrators doth hereby Covenant Grant and agree to and with the said Robert Walsh his heirs and assigns that he the said James Kerr and his heirs the tract or parcel of land above Mentioned and hereby granted against him the said James Kerr and his heirs and against all and every other person and persons Whatsoever lawfully claiming [a to?] claim unto the said Robert Walsh his heirs and assigns shall and will warrant and forever Defend by these Presents.

In Witness whereof the said James Kerr and Julia his wife have hereunto set their hands and affixed their seals to the Day and year just above written and also doth hereby Warrant and Defend the said lands to be clear of all taxes or other encumbrances to the Day of the Date hereof signed sealed and delivered in presence of

James Terrell   James Kerr
John Ambrose   Julia Kerr
P___ K_____?

Received of Robert Walsh the sum of Ten thousand Dollars current money of the United States of America being the full consideration money mentioned in the within Deed Witness my hand and this Twenty third Day of March in the year One Thousand Seven Hundred and Ninety five   James Kerr   P____ K_____?

James Kerr This day appeared before us the subscribers two Justices of the peace in and for the County of Fairfax and acknowledged the foregoing Deed and relinquished all his Right and property to the Lands Mentioned therein given under our hands This 16th Day of April 1795

George Gilpin
Wm Herbert

FAIRFAX COUNTY

The Commonwealth of Virginia to Richard Conway George Gilpin and William Herbert Gentlemen of Fairfax County Greeting Whereas James Kerr and Julia his wife By Their Certain Indenture of Bargain and sale bearing Date this 23rd Day of March 1795 have sold and conveyed unto Robert Walsh the fee simple estate of a Certain tract or parcel of land Containing twenty Thousand Seven hundred and eighteen Acres and three quarters of an acre lying and being in the county of Nelson and District of Kentucky with the appurtenances and Whereas the said Julia cannot Conveniently Travel to the County Court of Nelson to make acknowledgement of the said Conveyance Therefore we do give unto you or any two or more of you power to receive the Acknowledgement which the said Julia shall be willing to make before you of the conveyance aforesaid contained in the said Indenture which is hereto annexed and we do further desire you or any two or more of you personally to go to the said Julia and receive her acknowledgement of the same and examine her privily and apart from The said James her husband whether she doth the same freely and voluntarily without his persuasion or threats and Whether she be willing that the same should be recorded in the co. court of Nelson and when you have received her acknowledgement and examined her as aforesaid that you Distinctly and openly certify the said court of Nelson, under your hands and seals sending then I here the [said] Indenture and this writ witness Peter Wagoner clerk of the Court of Fairfax This 24th day of March 1795 P Wagener clerk Fairfax, In obedience to the within commission to us directed we did personally go to the said Julia Kerr wife of said James Kerr and examine her privily and Apart from the said James her husband Touching her Relinquishment of Dower of in and to the within mentioned Lands and premises who acknowledged that she same freely and voluntarily without the threats of persuasion of her husband and that she was willing that the same together with this writ should be recorded in the county Court of Nelson and District of Kentucky given under our hands and seals this 15th Day of April 1795.

Richard Conway   Carried to Julia 25 and recorded
Wm Herbert

B-2

This Indenture made this first day of March in the year of our Lord ONE THOUSAND SEVEN HUNDRED AND NINETY TWO between Jonathan Swift and Ann his wife of the town of Alexandria in the County of Fairfax and State of Virginia of the one part and Stephen Cook of the said town of Alexandria in the County of Fairfax and State of Virginia of the other, Witnesseth that the said Jonathan Swift and Ann his wife as will for and in consideration of an unliquidated Georgia Certificate dated the 29th July 1777 for three hundred and Eighty Six pounds fifteen shillings and signed Obryan and [Wade?] and three rights of land situated and being, in the Township of Otisfield in the County of Cumberland in the State of Massachusetts conveyed to the said Jonathan Swift by the said Stephen Cook in an Instrument bearing equal and even date with these presents as for and in consideration of the sum of five shillings current money of Virginia to him in hand paid by the said Stephen Cook at or before the ensealing and delivery of these presents the receipt whereof he doth hereby acknowledge and thereof doth acquit and discharge the said Stephen Cook his heirs Executors and administrators they the said Jonathan Swift and Ann his wife have given granted bargained and sold aliened released and confirmed and by these presents do give grant bargain sell alien release convey and confirm unto the said Stephen Cook and heirs and assigns forever a certain tract or parcel of land containing FIVE THOUSAND ACRES as by survey bearing date Twentieth of May ONE THOUSAND SEVEN HUNDRED AND EIGHTY NINE situated and being in the county of Nelson in the District of Kentucky and for which a patent was granted to Robert Brook Voss Esquire of the County of Culpepper and State aforesaid bearing the third day of March in the year of Our Lord ONE THOUSAND SEVEN HUNDRED AND NINTY ONE under the hand of Beverly Randolph Esquire Governor of Virginia and under the seal of the said State, and the said lands was afterwards conveyed by the said Robert Brook Voss and Janett his wife to the said Jonathan Swift by a special warranty deed bearing date the [blank] day of November in the year of our Lord ONE THOUSAND SEVEN HUNDRED AND NINETY ONE the said tract of land being bounded as follows viz, beginning at a white oak and sugar tree the north east corner of Myers preemption that includes Hynes lick running thence with a line thereof S 10 E 230 poles to a white oak and black oak thence with Hynes line N 85 east 110 poles to a large white oak corner to Camps preemption thence with a line thereof S 85 east 260 poles to his corner two box white oaks thence S 5 W 94 poles to a stake corner to Hynes survey thence with a line of the same S 45 E 360 poles to a black oak and gum on Nash's line thence with his line N 45 E 40 poles to a white oak thence S 45 E 180 poles to two white oaks thence S 45 W 80 poles to a white oak dogwood and black oak thence south 260 poles to two white oaks S 45 W 54 poles to a stake in a line of William Mays 1600 acre survey thence with the said line S 65 E 195 poles to his corner a white oak and Spanish oak on a drain of Cedar Creek thence N 73 E 682 POLES CROSSING Cedar Creek to a white oak thence N 35 West 1434 poles crossing the last mentioned creek to a stake thence S 73 W 788 poles to the BEGINNING Reference being had to the survey and patent aforesaid will fully and clearly appear and all houses, trees, woods, underwoods, waters, water courses, profits, commodities, hereditaments and appurtenances whatsoever to the said tract of land belonging or in any wise appurtaining and the reversion and reversions remainder and remainders rents issues and profits thereof and of every part and parcel thereof – To have and to hold the said tract of land, hereditaments and all and singular the premises hereby granted with their and every of their appurtenances unto him the said Stephen Cook his heirs and assigns to the only proper use and behoof of him the said Stephen Cook his heirs and assigns forever and the said Jonathan Swift for himself and his heirs Executors and administrators doth covenant grant and agree to and with the said Stephen Cook his heirs and assigns that the said Jonathan Swift and his heirs the said tract of land hereditiments and all and singular the premises hereby granted with their and every of their appurtenances unto him the said Stephen Cook his heirs and assigns against the claim and demand of him the said Jonathan Swift and his heirs and all and every other person or persons whatsoever claiming by from or under him shall and will warrant and forever defend by these presents In witness whereof the parties hereunto set their hands and affixed their seals the day and year before mentioned and Ann the wife of the said Jonathan Swift in token of her free will and consent to this bargain and sale and full relinquishment and quit claim of all her right of dower and thirds off and in the within granted premises hath also set her hand and affixed her seal the day and year above mentioned.

Signed sealed and delivered   Jonathan Swift
In presence of   Ann Swift
Philip Wanton, George Washington Dent,
John Liggert, Andrew Ramsay

At a court held for the County of Fairfax 21st May 1792 Jonathan Swift acknowledged this deed to be his act and deed which together with the commission and return of or the privy examination of Ann Swift wife of the said Jonathan and ordered to be recorded

Test. P. Waggoner clerk

Nelson
Personally appeared before us two of the Justices of the Peace in and for the County of Nelson Jonathan Swift acknowledged this Indenture by him subscribed to be his act and deed given under our hands this 22nd day of February 1794.

Gabriel Cox
Andrew Hynes

Endorsed as follows
Fairfax County
The Commonwealth of Virginia to George Gilpin William Herbert and R. Conway Esqrs of the County of Fairfax Gentlemen greeting, Whereas Jonathan Swift and Ann his wife by their certain Indenture of bargain and sale bearing date the first day of March 1792 have sold and conveyed unto Stephen Cook the fee simple estate of Five Thousand Acres of land with the appurtenances lying and being in the county of Nelson in the District of Kentucky and whereas the said Ann cannot conveniently travel to our said court to make acknowledgement of said conveyance therefore we do give unto you or any two or more of you power to receive the acknowledgment which the said Ann shall be willing to make before you of the conveyance aforesaid contained in the said Indenture which is hereto annexed and we do therefore desire you or any two or more of you personally to go to the said Ann and receive her acknowledgment of the same and examine her privily and apart from the said Jonathan her husband whether she doth the same freely and voluntarily without his persuasion or threats and whether she be willing to the same should be recorded in our said County Court of Fairfax and when you have received her acknowledgment and examined her as aforesaid that you distinctly and openly certify her thereof in our said Court under our seals sending then there this said Indenture and this writ Witness Peter Waggoner clerk of the said Court this nineteenth day of May One Thousand Seven Hundred and Ninety Two.

Peter Waggoner C.C.

Fairfax County To Wit,
Pursuant to the within commission to us directed we the subscribers did this day privily and apart from her husband did examine the within Ann Swift whether she was willing to the within mentioned sale, To which she answered in the affirmative and signed and acknowledged the deed hereunto annexed in our presence declaring it to be her free and voluntary act without any threats or persuasions of her said husband Given under our hands and seals the 10th day of May 1792—

George Gilpin
Will Herbert

I the clerk of the Hardin Circuit Court in the State of Kentucky do certify that at a court of quarter session began and held for Hardin County at the Court House in Elizabeth Town on Tuesday the 25th day of February 1795 the following entry was made To Wit, "A Deed from Jonathan Swift and Ann his wife to Stephen Cook having been acknowledged before George Gilpin and William Herbert two of the Magistrates of Fairfax County is here again acknowledged by the said Swift and ordered to be recorded" Which in pursuance of an act of the General Assembly of Kentucky approved Nov.2nd 1820 directing the clerk of the Hardin Circuit Court to perform certain duties I have certified upon the record the original not being in the office Given Under my hand this 5th day of October 1821

Sam Haycraft clerk

B-3

This Indenture made the twenty sixth day of February One Thousand Seven Hundred and Ninety Four between Jadia L. Ashcraft of the County of Hardin which was formerly a part of Nelson and also a part of Jefferson and State of Kentucky of the one part and Jonathan Swift of the town of Alexandria in the county of Fairfax and State of Virginia of the other Witnesseth that the said Jadia L. Ashcraft for and in consideration of the sum of five shillings current money of Virginia to him in hand paid by the said Jonathan Swift at and before the ensealing and delivery of these Presents the Receipt whereof he doth hereby acknowledge and thereof doth acquit and discharge the said Jonathan Swift his heirs Executors and Administrators, he the said Jadiah Ashcraft has granted bargained and sold made over and transferred conveyed and confirmed and by these presents doth grant bargain and sell make over transfer convey and confirm unto the said Jonathan Swift his heirs and assigns forever a certain tract or parcel of land on the waters of Green River in the aforesaid County of Hardin BEGINNING at a beech and hickory twenty poles below the mouth of the second large west branch of Bear Creek about fifteen miles meander measure above the mouth of said creek being also a corner to Willis Greens Seven hundred and fifty acre survey running with a line of the same North 15 degrees east two hundred and twenty poles to two gums on a ridge then north 40 degrees west three hundred and fifty poles to a white oak corner to James Craiks land then with the division line north 83[53?] degrees east four hundred poles to a post then south one hundred and ten poles to a haw bush corner to Helms land then south 9d 30m west one hundred and ninety five poles to an ash on the side of the knobs then south 45 degrees east forty two poles to a beech on the west bank of Bear Creek and in said Helms lower line marked H thence down with the meanders of the creek binding thereon to the BEGINNING containing FIVE HUNDRED AND SIXTY EIGHT ACRES being part of a patent of twelve hundred and seventy six acres granted to the said Jadiah Ashcraft bearing date the 23rd day of May One Thousand Seven Hundred and Eighty Six and all houses, gardens, orchards, meadows, woods, underwoods, waters and water courses profits commodities hereditiments appurtenances whatsoever to the said estate belonging or in any wise appurtaining and also all the right title and interest of the said Jadiah Ashcraft of in and to the same to have and to hold the said estate with all and singular the premises and appurtenances unto the said Jonathan

Swift his heirs and assigns forever and the said Jadiah Ashcraft for himself his heirs Executors and Administrators covenant and agrees with the said Jonathan Swift his heirs and assigns that the said premises hereby granted now are and so forever hereafter shall remain and be free and clear from all former and other gifts grants bargains sales dower Rights and title of dower judgements Executions titles troubles claims and incumberances whatsoever made done committed and offered by the said Jadiah Ashcraft and lastly the said Jadiah Ashcraft the said estate hereby grant with all and singular the premises and appurtenances thereunto belonging unto the said Jonathan Swift his heirs and assigns shall and will warrant and forever defend against the claim or demands of all persons whatsoever, in Witness whereof the said Jadiah Ashcraft hath hereunto set his hand and seal the day and year first above written

    Jadiah Ashcraft
    By his attorney
    Daniel Ashcraft
    Signed sealed and delivered in presence of
    Isaac Morrison   Phillip Phillips   John Taylor
    Received of Jonathan Swift the consideration within mentioned Witness my hand this 26th day of February 1794   Jadiah Ashcraft
                             By his attorney
                             Daniel Ashcraft

    Witness
    Isaac Morrison
    Phillip Phillips
    John Taylor

    Hardin County
    Personally appeared before me Phillip Phillips Esquire one of the Judges of the Court of quarter session for said County Daniel Ashcraft and acknowledged this Indenture by him Subscribed to be his act and deed Given under my hand this 28th day of February 1794   Phillip Phillips

B-4

    THIS INDENTURE made the first day of August in the year of our Lord one thousand seven hundred and ninety five between Jonathan Swift of the Town of Alexandria in the county of Fairfax and Commonwealth of Virginia Merchant of the one part and James Craik of the said town county and Commonwealth physician of the other part Witnesseth that the said Jonathan Swift for and in consideration of the sum of [word crossed out] five shillings current money of Virginia to him in hand paid by the said James Craik at and before the ensealing and delivery of these presents the receipt whereof he doth hereby acknowledge and thereof doth acquit and discharge the said James Craik his heirs Executors and Administrators He the said Jonathan Swift has granted bargained and sold aliened released made over transferred conveyed and confirmed and by these presents doth grant bargain and sell alien release and make over transfer convey and confirm unto the said James Craik his heirs and assigns forever a certain tract or parcel of land situate lying and being on the waters of Green River in the county of Hardin and State of Kentucky BEGINNING at a beech and hickory 20 poles below the mouth of the second large west branch of Bear Creek about 15 miles meander measure above the mouth of the said creek being also a corner to Willis Green's 750 acre survey running with a line of the same north 15 degrees east 270 poles to two gums on a ridge then north 40 degrees west 350 poles to a white oak corner to James Craik's lands then with the Division Line north 53 degrees east 400 poles to a post then south 110 poles to a Haw bush corner to Helm's Lands then south 9D 30m west 195 poles to a beech on the West bank of Bear Creek and in the said Helms lower line marked TH thence Down with the meanders of the creek binding thereon to the BEGINNING containing 568 acres being part of a parcel of 1276 acres granted to Jadiah Ashcraft Esquire bearing date the 23rd day of May 1786 and was by the said Jadiah Ashcraft conveyed to said Jonathan Swift by deed recorded in the county of Hardin bearing date the 26th Day of February 1794 reference being had to the same and patent and survey will more fully and clearly appear. And all houses buildings, gardens, orchards, meadows, woods, underwoods, huntings, fisherys, quarries, coals, licks, Mines, Metals, Oars of Minerals of any kind above upon or under the ground and all the waters and water courses, profits, commodities, heraditaments and appurtenances whatsoever to the said Estate belonging or in any wise appurtaining and the reversion and reversions, remainder and remainders, rents, issues and profits thereof and of every part and parcel thereof and also all the right title interest and estate of him the said Jonathan Swift of in and to the same. To have and to hold the said lands together with all and singular the privileges and appurtenances unto the said James Craik his heirs and assigns forever to the only proper use benefit and behoof of him the said James Craik his heirs and assigns forever. And the said Jonathan Swift for himself his heirs Executors and Administrators doth covenant promise and grant to and with the said James Craik his heirs Executors Administrators and assigns that the said James Craik his heirs and assigns shall and may forever hereafter peaceably and quietly have hold use own possess and enjoy the aforesaid estate with all and singular the premises hereby granted with their and every of their appurtenances_____?_____

Interruption or denial of him the said Jonathan Swift his heirs or assigns and that the said premises hereby granted now are and so forever hereafter shall remain and be free and clear of and from all former and other grants bargains sales Dower right and title of Dower judgments executions titles troubles charges claims and encumbrances whatsoever made done committed or suffered by the said Jonathan Swift. Lastly the aforesaid lands with all and singular the premises and appurtenances thereunto belonging unto the said James Craik his heirs and assigns shall and will warrant and forever defend against the claims or demands of all persons whatsoever. In Witness whereof the said Jonathan Swift has hereunto set his hand and affixed his seal the day and year first above written.

JONATHAN SWIFT
Signed sealed and delivered in the presence of
Joseph Riddle
Scudamore Nickolls
Lemuel Bent

And Ann wife of the said Jonathan in token of her free will and consent to this indenture of bargain and sale of her full relinquishment of her right of Dower and thirds of in and to the said within premises hath set her hand and affixed her seal the day and year first above written,

Ann Swift

Witnesses
Scudamore Nickolls
Joseph Riddle
Lemuel Bent
Received of Doctor James Craik the consideration within mentioned   Witness
my hand this 1st day of August one thousand seven hundred ninety five
Witnesses
Scudamore Nickolls
Joseph Riddle   }   Jonathan Swift
Lemuel Bent

B-5

This Indenture made this nineteenth day of February in the year of our Lord one thousand seven hundred and ninety four between Phillip Phillips Esquire and Susanna his wife of the County of Hardin and State of Kentucky of the one part and Jonathan Swift of the town of Alexandria in the County of Fairfax and State of Virginia Merchant of the other part Witnesseth that the said Phillip Phillips and Susanna his wife for and in consideration of the sum of five shillings current money of Kentucky to them in hand paid by the said Jonathan Swift at and before the ensealing and delivery of these presents the receipt whereof they do hereby acknowledge and thereof doth acquit and discharge the said Jonathan Swift his heirs executors and administrators they the said Phillip Phillips and Susanna his wife have given, granted, bargained and sold, aliened, released, made over, transferred and confirmed and by these presents doth grant bargain and sell, alien, release, make over, transfer, convey and confirm unto the said Jonathan Swift and his heirs and assigns forever a certain tract or parcel of land situate lying and being on the waters of Green River in the County of Hardin formerly a part of Nelson and State of Kentucky BEGINNING A at two white oaks and ash south west corner to William Fryes nine hundred and seventy acre survey thence running south twelve degrees west five hundred and twenty poles to a black gum white ash and sugar tree north west corner to Phillip Phillips four hundred acre survey thence with his line south twenty five degrees west two hundred and fifty three poles to a white oak thence south twenty two degrees east one hundred and forty poles to a dogwood, black oak and white oak corner to Jane Grants five hundred acre survey thence with a line of the same south forty degrees west two hundred and two poles to three white oaks thence south fifty degrees east two hundred poles to a large ash corner to Jadiah Ashcraft lands thence with a line thereof south fifty three west four hundred and eighty poles to a gum and hickory corner to Willis Greens seven hundred and fifty acre survey on the second large branch of Bear Creek then with said Greens line north twenty five west five hundred poles to a large white oak thence with the said Greens upper line south sixty five west two hundred and forty poles to a white oak and beech corner to William Mays six thousand acre survey   B   thence with a line of the same south sixty eight west one thousand and sixty five poles to a sassafras and white oak on the waters of Big Reedy thence with a line of John Cockey Owings land north thirty west four hundred and six poles to two chestnuts near the head of Raymers fork of Caney north fifty one east eleven hundred and twenty poles crossing several branches of Caney to a poplar and white oak corner to said Owings land   C   and James and Robert Nourses part of this same patent thence with the Nourses line south sixty degrees east six hundred and thirty four poles thence north thirty degrees east four hundred and sixty eight poles thence north sixty west three hundred and sixty seven poles then north 30 degrees east five hundred and seventy poles to a white oak then north 86 degrees east two hundred and sixty six poles to a white oak corner to Elizabeth Ashcrafts four hundred acre survey on the first west branch of Bear Creek below the clay lick back then south 39 degrees east three hundred and seventy poles to the BEGINNING containing EIGHT THOUSAND NINE HUNDRED AND TWELVE ACRES contained in a patent of Eleven thousand Eight hundred and Seventy acres granted to the said Phillip Phillips Esquire bearing date the twenty fifth day of May one thousand seven hundred and ninety also one other tract or parcel of land situate lying and being on the waters of Green River in the said County of Hardin and State aforesaid BEGIN-NING   B   at a white oak and beech on the second large west branch of Bear Creek a branch of Green River corner to Willis Greens seven hundred and fifty acre survey and running thence south 68 degrees west one thousand and sixty poles with a line of Phillip Phillips eleven thousand eight hundred and seventy acre survey to a sassafras and white oak on the head of one of the main branches of Big Reedy then south 30 degrees east four hundred and sixty three poles to a post then with Mays division line north 68 degrees east one thousand and twenty poles to a small white oak in the aforesaid Greens line then with the said line north 25 degrees west four hundred and eighty three poles to the BEGINNING containing THREE THOUSAND ACRES part of a Six Thousand Acre grant obtained by William May Esquire by virtue of a part of two treasury warrants #15114, #17446 and was by the said William May Esquire and Mary his wife conveyed to the said Phillip Phillips Esquire by their deed bearing date the nineteenth day of February one thousand seven hundred and ninety four also one other tract or parcel of land adjoining the aforesaid Eleven thousand Eight hundred and Seventy acre survey of the said Phillip Phillips BEGINNING at a large ash corner to the said survey and running with a line of the same south 53 degrees west four hundred and eighty poles to a gum and hickory corner to Willis Greens seven hundred and fifty acre survey then with a line of the same south 40 degrees east fifty poles to a white oak then with the division line north fifty three degrees east four hundred poles to a post then south one hundred and ten poles to a haw bush corner to Helms land then with his line east one hundred and ninety two poles to a black oak then north forty six degrees west seventy poles to a white oak then north twenty degrees east one hundred poles with Keiths line to a sycamore and buck eye then north forty six degrees west with Kerkendalls line one hundred and thirty poles to a black oak and poplar corner to Jane Grants land then with the same north fifty degrees west two hundred poles to the BEGINNING containing SEVEN

HUNDRED AND EIGHT ACRES part of a patent of Twelve Hundred and Seventy Six acres granted to Jadiah Ashcraft Esquire bearing date the twenty third day of May one thousand seven hundred and eight six and was by the said Jadiah Ashcraft Esquire conveyed to the said Phillip Phillips Esquire by his deed bearing date the nineteenth day of February one thousand seven hundred and ninety four also one other tract or parcel of land on the waters of Green River in the County of Hardin and State aforesaid BEGINNING at the north west corner of Joseph Barnetts two thousand five hundred acre survey being a beech and ash standing one pole south of a large run branch of the middle fork of Indian Camp Creek thence with a line thereof south one degree west seven hundred poles to a white oak corner to James Taylors land then with Madisons Line west two hundred and twenty poles to a red oak and dogwood corner to John Thomases land thence north three hundred and twenty poles to a poplar and swamp oak thence with said Thomas, Phillips and Hines [Helms?] lines west twelve hundred and eighty two poles to a black oak and poplar in Walker Daniels line thence with the same north three hundred and nineteen poles to a white oak corner to Abraham Deals land thence with his line east one hundred and ninety seven poles to a black oak north two hundred and twenty nine poles to a black oak in Lewises line thence with the same south eighty one and a half degrees east thirteen hundred and twenty poles to the BEGINNING containing FOUR THOUSAND SEVEN HUNDRED ACRES a grant for which with name of said Phillip Phillips was obtained by virtue of part of a treasury warrant #14790 – Also one other tract or parcel of land adjoining the above at the north east corner BEGINNING at a beech and ash about one pole from the bank of a large run one of the main branches of the Indian Camp Creek and on the south side of the same being also a corner to Joseph Barnetts land running thence north one degree east five hundred and forty poles to a dogwood and gum by the head of one of the main branches of said creek and in the line of John Mays seven hundred and eighty acre survey thence with the same south eighty five and a half degrees east one hundred poles to a hickory on the east side of a drain of said creek then north four degrees and a half east two hundred and five poles to two white oaks on the north side of a ridge and near the head of the first run and emptying in on the south side of Caney below the Brushy Pond fork then south eighty five and a half degrees east six hundred and ninety poles to a stake then south 42 degrees west six hundred and fifty poles to a stake in May Bannister and Company line then north 88 degrees west two hundred and ten poles to two cherry trees and dogwood by the head of a drain being also a corner to said Barnetts land then west five hundred and thirty poles to the BEGINNING containing THREE THOUSAND FOUR HUNDRED ACRES being half of the land contained in a patent of six thousand eight hundred acres granted to William May Esquire bearing date the tenth day of July one thousand seven hundred and eighty six and was by the said William May Esquire and Mary his wife conveyed to the said Phillip Phillips Esquire by their deed bearing date the nineteenth day of February one thousand seven hundred and ninety four and all houses, buildings, gardens, orchards, meadows. Woods, underwoods, quarries, coals, licks, Mines, Metals or Minerals or Ore of and kind above upon or under the ground and all waters and water courses, profits, commodities, hereditaments, and appurtenances whatsoever to the said estates or tracts of land belonging or in any wise appurtaining and the reversion and reversions, remainder and remainders, rents, issues and profits thereof and every part and parcel thereof and also all the estate right titles and interest of the said Phillip Phillips Esquire and Susanna his wife of and to the same to have and to hold the said estates or parcels of land with all and singular the privileges or appurtences thereunto belonging unto the said Jonathan Swift his heirs and assigns forever to the only proper use benefit and behoof of the said Jonathan Swift his heirs and assigns forever and the said Phillip Phillips Esquire for himself his heirs, executors and administrators doth covenant and promise and grant to and with the said Jonathan Swift his heirs executors, administrators and assigns that the said Jonathan Swift his heirs and assigns shall and may forever hereafter peaceably and quietly have, hold, use, occupy, possess and enjoy the aforesaid estate with all and singular the premises hereby granted with their and every of their appurtences thereunto belonging without the let suit trouble interruption or denial of him the said Phillip Phillips Esquire his heirs and assigns and that the said premises hereby granted now are and so forever hereafter shall remain and be free and clear from all former and other gifts grants bargains sales, dower judgments, executions, titles troubles, charges, claims and encumbrances whatsoever made done committed or suffered by the said Phillip Phillips and lastly the said Phillip Phillips and his heirs the said estates tracts or parcels of land hereby granted with all and singular the premises and appurtences thereunto belonging unto the said Jonathan Swift his heirs and assigns shall and will warrant and forever defend against the claim and demand of all persons whatsoever In Witness whereof the said Phillip Phillips and Susanne his wife have hereunto set their hands and affixed their seals the day and year first above written.

Phillip Phillips
Susannah Phillips

Signed sealed and delivered
In presence of
William May
Benjamin Frye
Robert C. Foster
Gabriel Cox
Witnesses to Susannah
Phillips Signing---
Joseph Barnett
John Taylor

Received of Jonathan Swift the consideration within mentioned witness my hand this 19th day of February one thousand seven hundred and ninety four.

P. Phillips

Witness
William May
Benjamin Frye
Robert C. Foster
Gabriel Cox

Nelson County

Personally appeared before us two of the Justices of the Peace in and for the County of Nelson Phillip Phillips Esquire acknowledged this Indenture by the subscribed to be his free act and deed given under our hand this 19th day of February 1794.   Benj. Frye

Gabriel Cox

B-6

This Indenture made this nineteenth day of February in the year of Our Lord One Thousand Seven Hundred and Ninety Four between William May and Mary his wife of the county of Nelson and State of Kentucky of the one part and Phillip Phillips of the county of Hardin and State aforesaid of the other Witness that the said William May and Mary his wife for and in consideration of the sum of five shillings current money of Kentucky to him in hand paid by the said Phillip Phillips the receipt whereof they do hereby acknowledge and thereof do acquit and discharge the said Phillip Phillips his heirs executors and administrators they the said William May and Mary his wife have bargained and sold and by these presents doth grant bargain and sell unto the said Phillip Phillips his heirs and assigns a certain tract or parcel of land lying and being in the water of Green River in the County of Hardin formerly part of Nelson and State of Kentucky being part of Mays six thousand acre survey on the west side of Bear Creek a branch of Green River and bounded as followeth, BEGINNING at a white oak and beech on the second large fork of Bear Creek corner to Willis Greens seven hundred and fifty acre survey and running thence south sixty nine degrees west one thousand and sixty poles with a line of Phillip Phillips eleven thousand eight hundred and seventy acre survey to a sassafras and white oak on the head of one of the main branches of Big Reedy Creek, then south thirty degrees east four hundred and sixty three poles to a post, thence with said Mays division line north sixty nine degrees east one thousand and seventy poles to a small white oak in the aforesaid Greens line thence with his said line north twenty five degrees west four hundred and sixty three poles to the BEGINNING containing THREE THOUSAND ACRES being one half a six thousand acre patent granted to the said William May by virtue of treasury warrants No. 15114, 17446 also all the right title interest and estate of the said William May and Mary his wife of in and to the same, to have and to hold the said tract or parcel of land with all its appurtenances and privileges thereunto belonging or any wise appurtaining also one other tract or parcel of land lying and being in the said County of Hardin and State aforesaid on the dividing ridge between the southern branches of Big Caney and the waters of Welches Creek and Indian Camp Creek waters of Green River BEGINNING at a beech and ash about one pole from the bank of a large run being one of the main branches of Indian Camp Creek and on the south side of the same being at a corner to Joseph Barnetts land running thence north one degree east five hundred and forty poles to a dogwood and gum by the head of one of the main branches of said creek and in the line of John Mays seven hundred and fifty acre survey then with the same south eighty five and a half degrees east one hundred poles to a hickory on the east side of a drain of said creek then north four and a half degrees east two hundred and five poles to two white oaks on the north side of a ridge and near the head of the first run emptying on the south side of Caney below the Brushy Pond fork thence south eighty five and a half degrees east six hundred and ninety poles to a stake thence south four and a half degrees west six hundred and fifty poles to a stake in John Mays line thence north eighty eight west two hundred and ten poles to two cherry trees and a dogwood by the side of a drain being also a corner to said Barnetts land then west five hundred and thirty poles to the BEGINNING , containing THREE THOUSAND FOUR HUNDRED ACRES being one half the land contained in a patent of six thousand eight hundred acres granted to the said William May bearing date the tenth day of July one thousand seven hundred and eighty six also all the right title interest and estate of the said William May and Mary his wife of in and to the same to have and to hold the said tract or parcel of land with all its privileges and appurtenances thereunto belonging or in any wise appurtaining to the said Phillip Phillips and to his heirs and assigns forever and the said William May and Mary his wife for themselves and their heirs do covenant and agree with the said Phillip Phillips and his heirs and assigns to warrant and forever defend the aforesaid two tracts or parcels of land with their appurtenances to the said Phillip Phillips and his heirs and assigns [against?] themselves and their heirs and all persons claiming by from or under them in Witness whereof the said William May and Mary his wife have hereunto Set their hands and seals the day and year first above written.

William May

Mary May

Signed sealed and delivered
In presence of
Benjamin Frye, Gabriel Cox
Robert C. Foster
Received of Phillip Phillips Esquire the consideration within mentioned Witness my hand this 19th day of February one thousand seven hundred and ninety four

William May

Mary May

Witness
Robert C. Foster
Benjamin Frye
Gabriel Cox

Nelson County
Personally appeared before us two of the Justices of the Peace in and for said County William May Esquire and Mary his wife and acknowledged this Indenture by them subscribed to be their free act and deed given under our hand, this 19th day of February 1794.

Benjamin Frye

State of Kentucky}

Nelson County
I Benjamin Grayson clerk of the County Court and Court of quarter sessions for said County do hereby certify that Benjamin Frye and Gabriel Cox Gentlemen

before whom the above acknowledgement was made and who have subscribed their names thereto were at the day of the date thereof and State are Justices of the peace in and for the County aforesaid and due faith and credit is to be given to any act done by them when acting in their official character. In testimony whereof I have hereunto set my hand and annexed the seal of my office this twenty second day of February in the year of Our Lord one thousand seven hundred and ninety four.

Benjamin Grayson

I the clerk of the Hardin Circuit Court in the State of Kentucky do certify that at a Court of quarter session begun and held for Hardin County at the Courthouse in Elizabeth Town on Tuesday the 25th day of February 1794 the following entry was made To Wit, Deed from William May and Mary his wife to Phillip Phillips being duly acknowledged before Benjamin Frye and Gabriel Cox two of the Justices of the Peace for Nelson County and certificate from the clerk of said County that they are such [was] presented and ordered to be recorded which in pursuance of an act of the General Assembly of Kentucky appeared Nov. 2nd 1820 directing the clerk of the Hardin Circuit Court to perform certain duties I have certified upon the record the original not being in the office .Given under my hand this 5th day of October 1821.

Sam Haycraft clerk

B-7

This Indenture made this nineteenth day of February in the year of our Lord one thousand seven hundred and ninety four between Jadiah Ashcraft Esquire of the County of Hardin formerly a part of Nelson which was formerly a part of Jefferson County and State of Kentucky of the one part and Phillip Phillips Esquire of the said County of Hardin and State of Kentucky of the other Witnesseth that the said Jadiah Ashcraft for and in consideration of the sum of five shillings current money of Kentucky to him in hand paid by the said Phillip Phillips at and before the ensealing and delivery of these presents the receipt whereof they do hereby acknowledge and therefore doth acquit and discharge the said Phillip Phillips his heirs executors and administrators. The said Jadiah Ashcraft has bargained and sold aliened released made over transferred and confirmed and by these presents doth give grant bargain sell alien release make over transfer convey and confirm, unto the said Phillip Phillips his heirs and assigns forever a certain tract or parcel of land lying and being on the waters of Green River in the said County of Hardin and State of Kentucky BEGINNING at a large ash corner to Phillip Phillips eleven thousand eight hundred and seventy acre survey and running with a line of the same south 53 degrees west four hundred and eighty poles to a gum and hickory corner to Willis Greens seven hundred and fifty acre survey then with a line of the same south 40 degrees east fifty poles to a white oak then with the division line north fifty three degrees east four hundred poles to a stake then south one hundred and ten poles to a haw bush corner to Helms land then with his line east one hundred and ninety two poles to a black oak then north 46 degrees west seventy poles to a white oak then north 20 degrees east one hundred poles with Keith's line to a sycamore and buck eye then north 33 degrees west with Kerkendales line one hundred and thirty poles to a black oak and poplar corner to Jane Grants

land then with the same north 50 degrees west two hundred poles to the BEGIN-
NING containing [left blank but is known to be "seven"] hundred and eight acres
part of a twelve hundred and seventy six acres granted to the said Jadiah Ashcraft
bearing date the twenty third day of May one thousand seven hundred and eighty
six and all houses, buildings, gardens, orchards, meadows, woods, underwoods, quarries, coals, licks, Mines, Metals, Ores, or Minerals of any kind above upon or under
the ground and all waters and water courses profits, commodities, hereditaments
and appurtenances whatsoever to the said estate of tract of land belonging or in any
wise appurtaining and the reversion and reversions, remainder and remainders, rent,
issues, and profits thereof and of every part or parcel thereof and also all the right
title interest and estate of the said Jadiah Ashcraft of in and to the same to have and
to hold the said estate or tract of land with all and singular the premises thereunto
belonging and will all and every appurtenance and appurtenances to the said Phillip
Phillips his heirs and assigns forever to the only proper use benefit and behoof of him
the said Phillips his heirs and assigns forever and the said Jadiah Ashcraft for himself
his heirs executors and administrators doth covenant and grant to and with the said
Phillip Phillips his heirs executors administrators and assigns shall and may forever
hereafter peaceably and quietly have hold, use, occupy and enjoy the aforesaid estate
with all and singular the premises hereby granted with these and every of their appurtenances thereunto belonging without let suit trouble interruption or denial of him
the said Jadiah Ashcraft his heirs or assigns and that the said premises hereby granted
now are and so forever hereafter shall remain and be free and clear from all former
and other gifts, grants, bargains, sales, dower right and title of dower judgments executions titles troubles claims and encumbrances whatsoever made done committed
or suffered by the said Jadiah Ashcraft and lastly the said Jadiah Ashcraft and his heirs
the said estate or tract of land hereby granted with all and singular the premises and
appurtenances thereunto belonging unto the said Phillip Phillips his heirs and assigns
shall and will warrant and forever defend against the claim or demand of all persons
whatsoever In Testimony whereof the said Jadiah Ashcraft hereunto set his hand and
affixed his seal the day and year first above written

> Jadiah Ashcraft
> By his attorney
> Daniel Ashcraft

Signed sealed and delivered
in presence of at and before
the ensealing and delivery of
these presents between the tenth
and eleventh line first underlined
before signed.
Received of Phillip Phillips Esquire the consideration of within mentioned Witness my hand this 19th day of February one thousand seven hundred and ninety
four

> Daniel Ashcraft for
> Jadiah Ashcraft

Witness
John Taylor

Jonathan Swift

Joseph Barnett

I the clerk of the Hardin Circuit Court in the State of Kentucky do certify that at a court of quarter session began and held for the County of Hardin at the Courthouse in Elizabeth Town on Tuesday the 25th day of February 1794 the following entry was made, to wit, "A deed from Jadiah Ashcraft by Daniel Ashcraft his attorney in fact to Phillip Phillips was acknowledged and ordered to be recorded which in pursuance of an act of the General Assembly of Kentucky approved November 2nd 1820 directing the clerk of the Hardin Circuit Court to perform certain duties I have certified upon the record the original deed not being in the office Given under my hand this 6th day of October 1821.

Sam Haycraft clerk

B-8

This Indenture made the twentieth day of February in the year of our Lord one thousand seven hundred and ninety four between Jonathan Swift and Ann his wife in the town of Alexandria in the county of Fairfax and Commonwealth of Virginia Merchant of the one part and James Craik Esquire Senior of the same Town County and Commonwealth Physician of the other part Witnesseth that the said Jonathan Swift and Ann his wife for and in consideration of the sum of five shillings current money of Virginia to him in hand paid by the said James Craik at and before the ensealing and delivery of these presents the receipt whereof they do hereby acknowledge and thereof doth acquit and discharge the said James Craik his heirs executors and administrators, they the said Jonathan Swift and Ann his wife have given, granted, bargained, sold and aliened, released, made over, conveyed, transferred and confirmed and by these presents doth grant, bargain and sell, alien, release, make over, transfer, convey and confirm unto the said James Craik and his heirs and assigns forever, A certain tract or parcel of land situate lying, and being on the waters of Green River in the County of Hardin formerly a part of Nelson and State of Kentucky BEGINNING at two white oaks and ash south west corner to William Mays nine hundred and seventy acre survey then running south twelve degrees west five hundred and twenty poles to a black gum white oak and sugartree north west corner to Phillip Phillips four hundred acre survey then with his line south 25 west two hundred and fifty three poles to a black oak then south 22 east one hundred and forty poles to two dogwoods, black oak and white oak corner to Jane Grants four hundred acre survey then with a line of the same south 40 west two hundred and two poles to three white oaks thence south 50 degrees east two hundred poles to a large ash corner to Jediah Ashcraft land thence with a line thereof south 53 west four hundred and eighty poles to a gum and hickory corner to Willis Greens seven hundred and fifty acre survey on the second large branch of Bear Creek thence with said Greens line north 25 west five hundred poles to a white oak then with said Greens upper line south 65 west two hundred and forty poles to a white oak and beech corner to William Mays six thousand acre survey thence with a line of the same south 68 west one thousand and sixty five poles to a sassafras and white oak on the waters of Big Ready thence with a line of John Cockey Owings north 30 degrees west four

302

hundred and six poles to two chestnuts near the head of Raymers fork of Caney north 51 degrees east eleven hundred and twenty poles crossing several branches of Caney to a poplar and white oak corner to said Owings land and James and Robert Nourses land part of this same patent thence with Nourses line south 60 degrees east six hundred and thirty four poles then north 30 degrees east four hundred and sixty eight poles then north 60 degrees west three hundred and eighty seven poles then north 30 degrees east five hundred and seventy poles to a white oak then north 86 degrees east two hundred and sixty six poles to a white oak corner to Elizabeth Ashcrafts four hundred acre survey on the first west branch of Bear Creek below the clay lick fork then south 39 degrees east three hundred and seventy poles to the BEGINNING containing EIGHT THOUSAND NINE HUNDRED AND TWELVE ACRES contained in a patent of Eleven Thousand Eight Hundred and Seventy acres granted to Phillip Phillips Esquire bearing date the 23rd day of May one thousand seven hundred and ninety and was by the said Phillip Phillips Esquire and Susanna his wife conveyed to the said Jonathan Swift by this deed bearing date the nineteenth day of February one thousand seven hundred and ninety four ALSO one other tract or parcel of land situated lying and being on the waters of Green River in the said County of Hardin and State aforesaid BEGINNING B at a white oak and beech on the second large west branch of Bear Creek a branch of Green River corner to Willis Greens seven hundred and fifty acre survey and running thence south 69 degrees west one thousand and sixty poles with a line of Phillip Phillips eleven thousand eight hundred and seventy acre survey to a sassafras and white oak on the head of one of the main branches of Big Reedy Creek then south 30 degrees east four hundred and sixty three poles to a post then with Mays division line north 68 degrees east one thousand and seventy poles to a small white oak in the aforesaid Greens line then with his said line north 25 degrees west four hundred and sixty three poles to the BEGINNING containing THREE THOUSAND ACRES part of a six thousand acre grant obtained by William May Esquire by virtue of a part of two treasury warrants #15114, #17446 and was by the said William May Esquire and Mary his wife conveyed to Phillip Phillips Esquire by their deed bearing, date the nineteenth day of February one thousand seven hundred and ninety four and was by the said Phillip Phillips Esquire and Susanna his wife conveyed to the said Jonathan Swift by their deed bearing, date the nineteenth day of February one thousand seven hundred and ninety four ALSO one other tract or parcel of land adjoining the aforesaid eleven thousand eight hundred and twenty acre survey of the said Phillip Phillips BEGINNING at a large ash corner to the said survey and running with a line of the same south 53 degrees west four hundred and eighty poles to a gum and hickory corner to Willis Greens seven hundred and fifty acre survey then with a line of the same south 40 degrees east fifty poles to a white oak then with the division line north 53 degrees east four hundred poles to a post then south one hundred and ten poles to a haw bush corner to Helms land then with his line east 192 poles to a black oak then north 46 degrees west 70 poles to a white oak then north 20 degrees east 100 poles with Keiths line to a sycamore and buckeye then north 33 degrees west with Kirkendales line 130 poles to a black oak and poplar corner to Jane Grants land then with the same north 50 degrees west two hundred poles to the BEGINNING containing SEVEN HUNDRED AND EIGHT ACRES part of a patent of twelve hundred and seventy six acres granted Jadiah Ashcraft Esquire 23rd day of May 1786 and was by the said Jadiah Ashcraft Esquire conveyed to Phillip Phillips Esquire by his deed bearing date the nineteenth day of February one thousand seven hundred and ninety four and was by the same Phillip Phillips Esquire and Susanna his wife conveyed to the said Jonathan Swift by their deed bearing date the nineteenth day of February one thousand seven hundred and ninety four ALSO one other tract or parcel of land on the waters of Green River in the County of Hardin and State aforesaid BEGINNING at the north west corner of Joseph Barnetts two thousand five hundred acre survey being a beech and ash standing one pole south of a large run branch of the middle fork of Indian Camp Creek thence with a line thereof south 1 degree west seven hundred poles to a white oak corner to James Taylors land thence with Madisons line two hundred and twenty poles to a red oak and dogwood corner to John Thomases land thence north three hundred and twenty poles to a poplar and swamp oak thence with said Thomas, Phillips and Hines [Helms?] lines west twelve hundred and eighty two poles to a black oak and poplar in Walker Daniels line thence with the same north three hundred and nineteen poles to a white oak corner to Abraham Deals land then with his line east one hundred and ninety seven poles to a black oak north two hundred and twenty nine poles to a black oak in Lewises line thence with the same south 81 and one half degrees east thirteen hundred and twenty poles to the BEGINNING containing FOUR THOUSAND SEVEN HUNDRED ACRES a grant for which in the name of Phillip Phillips Esquire was obtained by virtue of part of a treasury warrant #14790 and was by the said Phillip Phillips Esquire and Susannah his wife conveyed to the said Jonathan Swift by their deed bearing date the nineteenth day of February one thousand seven hundred and ninety four. ALSO one other tract or parcel of land adjoining the above at the north east corner BEGINNING at a beech and ash about one pole from the bank of a large run one of the main branches of Indian Camp Creek and on the south side of the same being also a corner to Joseph Barnetts land running thence north one degree east five hundred and forty poles to a dogwood and gum by the head of one of the main branches of said creek and in the line of John Mays seven hundred and eighty acre survey then with the same south 85 and one half degrees east one hundred poles to a hickory on the east side of a drain of said creek then north 4 and one half degrees east two hundred and five poles to two white oaks on the north side of a ridge and near the head of the first run and emptying in on the south side of Caney below the Brushy Pond fork thence south 85 and one half east six hundred and ninety poles to a stake then south 4 and one half degrees west six hundred and fifty poles to a stake in May Bannister and Co. line then north 88 degrees west two hundred and ten poles to two cherry trees and dogwood by the head of a drain being also a corner to said Barnetts land then west five hundred and thirty poles to the BEGINNING containing THREE THOUSAND FOUR HUNDRED ACRES being half the land contained in a patent of six thousand eight hundred acres granted to William May Esquire bearing date the tenth day of July one thousand seven hundred and eighty six and was by the said William May Esquire and Mary his wife conveyed to the said Phillip Phillips Esquire by their deed bearing date the nineteenth day of February one thousand seven hundred and ninety four and by the said Phillip Phillips and Susannah his wife conveyed to the said Jonathan Swift by their deed bearing date the nineteenth day of February one thousand seven hundred and ninety four reference being had to the same or to the records of Hardin County in the aforesaid State of Kentucky will more fully and clearly appear-- And all houses, buildings, gardens, orchards, meadows, woods and underwoods, quarries, coals, licks, Mines, Metals, Minerals or ores of any kind above upon or under the ground and all waters and water courses, profits, commodities, hereditaments and appurtenances whatsoever to the said estates or tracts of land belonging or in any wise appurtaining and the reversion and reversions, remainder and remainders, rents issues and profits thereof and every part and parcel thereof and also all the estate right title and interest of the said Jonathan Swift of in and to the same to have and to hold the said estates or parcels of land with all and singular the privileges and appurtenances thereunto belonging unto the said James Craik Esquire his heirs and assigns forever to the only proper use, benefit and behoof of him the said James Craik his heirs and assigns forever and the said Jonathan Swift for himself his heirs executors and administrators doth covenant and promise and grant to and with the said James Craik his heirs, executors and administrators and assigns that the said James Craik his heirs and assigns shall and may forever hereafter peaceably and quietly have, hold, use, occupy, possess and enjoy the aforesaid estates with all and singular the premises hereby granted with their and every of their appurtenances thereunto belonging, without the let suit trouble interruptions or denial of him the said Jonathan Swift his heirs or assigns and that the said premises hereby granted now are and so forever hereafter shall remain and be free and clear from all former and other gifts, grants, bargains, sales, dower right and title of dower judgments executions titles troubles charges claims and encumberances whatsoever made done committed or suffered by the said Jonathan Swift and lastly the said Jonathan Swift and his heirs the said estates tracts or parcels of land with all and singular the premises and appurtenances thereunto belonging unto the said James Craik Esquire his heirs and assigns shall and will warrant and forever defend against the claims or demands of all persons whatsoever.

In testimony whereof the said Jonathan Swift and Ann his wife have hereunto set their hands and affixed their seals the day and year first above written

Jonathan Swift

Signed sealed and delivered
In presence of
John Taylor   Robert Ward
Robert C. Foster   David Phillips
Received of James Craik Senior Esquire the consideration within mentioned Witness my hand this twentieth day of February one thousand seven hundred and ninety four

Jonathan Swift

Witness
John Taylor   Robert Ward
Robert C. Foster   David Phillips

Kentucky Nelson Co.
Personally appeared before us two Justices of the Peace in and for the County of Nelson Jonathan Swift acknowledged this Indenture by him subscribed to be his free act and deed Given under our hands this 20th day of February 1794.

Gabriel Cox

Andrew Hynes

State of Kentucky Nelson County

I Benjamin Grayson clerk of the County Circuit and Court of quarter session for said County do hereby certify that Benjamin Frye, Gabriel Cox and Andrew Hynes Gentlemen before whom the annexed deed were acknowledged and who have subscribed their names thereto were at the time of doing the same and still are Justices of the Peace in and for the County aforesaid and that due faith and credit is to be given to any act done by them when acting in their official character in testimony whereof I have hereunto set my hand and affixed the seal of my office this twenty second day of February in the year of our Lord seventeen hundred and ninety four

Benj. Grayson

I the clerk of the Hardin Circuit Court in the State of Kentucky do certify that at a court of quarter sessions began and held for Hardin Co. on Tuesday the 25th day of February 1794, the following order was made, to wit, "A deed from Jonathan Swift and Ann his wife to James Craik Esquire was acknowledged by said Jonathan and ordered to record" which fact in pursuance of an act of the general assembly of Kentucky entitled "An act .directing the clerk of the Hardin Circuit Court to perform certain duties" approved November 2nd 1820. I have certified upon the record, the original deed not being in the office given under my hand this 7th day of August 1834.

Sam Haycraft clerk

B-9

This Indenture made the fourth day of August in the year of our Lord one thousand seven hundred and ninety four between Daniel Ferry Esquire of the County of Nelson and State of Kentucky of the one part and Jonathan Swift of the town of Alexandria in the County of Fairfax and State of Virginia Merchant of the other part Witnesseth that the said Daniel Ferry for and in consideration of the sum of five shillings current money of Virginia to him in hand paid by the said Jonathan Swift at and before the ensealing and delivery of these presents the receipt whereof he doth hereby acknowledge and thereof doth acquit and discharge the said Jonathan Swift his heirs executors and administrators the said Daniel Ferry has granted, bargained and sold, aliened, released, made over, transferred, conveyed and confirmed and by these presents doth grant, bargain and sell, alien, release, make over, transfer, convey and confirm unto the said Jonathan Swift his heirs and assigns forever a certain tract or parcel of land called GREENWICH situate, lying and being in the County of Hardin formerly a part of Nelson and State of Kentucky on the north side of Green River and bounded as followeth, To Wit, BEGINNING at two black oaks a white oak and hickory the south east corner of Joseph Lewises nine thousand seven hundred and seventy eight acre survey and standing in the line of Isaac Morrisons four thousand seven hundred acre survey thence due north seven hundred and seventy poles to two blacks, a white oak, poplar, and hickory thence east six hundred and twelve poles and a half to a white oak thence south seven hundred and seventy poles to a post thence west six hundred and twelve poles and a half to the BEGINNING

306

containing THREE THOUSAND AND NINE HUNDRED ACRES being part of a patent of five thousand acres granted to William May Esquire surveyor of the county of Nelson by the Commonwealth of Virginia bearing date the first day of June in the year of our Lord one thousand seven hundred and eighty six and was by the said William May Esquire and Mary his wife conveyed to the said Daniel Ferry by their deed bearing date the fifteenth day of July [actually April] in the year of our Lord one thousand seven hundred and ninety four and all houses, buildings, out houses, gardens, orchards, meadows, woods, underwoods, hunting, fisheries, quarries, coals, licks, Mines, Metals, Ores or Minerals of any kind above upon or under the ground and all waters and water courses, profits, commodities, hereditiments and appurtenances whatsoever to said estate belonging or in any wise appurtaining and the reversion and reversions remainder and remainders, rents issues and profits thereof and of every part and parcel thereof and also all the right title interest and estate of the said Daniel Ferry of in and to the same to have and to hold the said estate with all and singular the privileges and appurtenances unto the said Jonathan Swift his heirs and assigns forever and the said Daniel Ferry for himself his heirs executors and administrators doth covenant promise and grant to and with the said Jonathan Swift his heirs executors administrators and assigns that the said Jonathan Swift his heirs and assigns shall and may forever hereafter peaceably and quietly have hold use occupy possess and enjoy the aforesaid estate with all and singular the premises hereby granted with their and every of their appurtenances without the let suit trouble interruption or denial of him the said Daniel Ferry his heirs or assigns and that the said premises hereby granted now are and to forever hereafter shall remain and be free clear and from all former and other gifts grants bargains sales dowers rights and titles of dower judgments executions titles troubles charges and encumbrances whatsoever made done committed or suffered by the said Daniel Ferry and lastly the aforesaid estate with all and singular the premises and appurtenances thereunto belonging unto the said Jonathan Swift his heirs and assigns shall and will warrant and forever defend against the claim demands persons whatever In Witness whereof the said Daniel Ferry has hereunto set his hand and affixed his seal the day and year first above written.

Daniel Ferry

Signed sealed and delivered in presence of
Thomas Lewis, Amos Allison, Charles Bennett

Received of Jonathan Swift the consideration within mentioned Witness my hand this fourth day of August one thousand seven hundred and ninety four.

Daniel Ferry

Witness
Thomas Lewis, Amos Allison, Charles Bennett

Virginia Fairfax
Personally appeared before us two of the Justices of the Peace in and for the County of Fairfax Daniel Ferry Esquire and acknowledged this Indenture by him subscribed to be his free act and deed given under our hands and seals at Alexandria the fourth day of August In the year of our Lord one thousand seven hundred and ninety four.

R. Hooe
William Herbert

Virginia Fairfax County

I Peter Waggoner clerk of Fairfax County Court do hereby certify that Robert Hooe and William Herbert Gentlemen before whom the annexed deeds appear to have been acknowledged was at the time of doing the same and now are two Justices of the Peace in and from the County aforesaid duly commissioned and sworn and that to all certificates by them in their official capacity so given due faith and credit as and ought to be given thereto as well in Justice Court as thereof in testimony whereof I have hereunto set my hand and affixed the seal of the said County this 6th day of August 1794 and in the 19th year of American Independence.

Peter Waggoner

At a Court of quarter session held for Hardin County the 23rd day of June 1795 this Indenture of bargain and sale together with the certificate endorsed was exhibited in Court and ordered to be recorded

Test.   D. May   Clerk Hardin County Quarter session

B-10

THIS INDENTURE made this fourth day of August in the year of our Lord One Thousand Seven Hundred and Ninety Four Between Daniel Ferry Esquire of the County of Nelson and State of Kentucky of the one part and Jonathan Swift of the town of Alexandria in the County of Fairfax and State of Virginia Merchant of the other part witnesseth that the said Daniel Ferry for and in consideration of the sum of five shillings current money of Virginia to him in hand paid by the said Jonathan Swift at and before the ensealing and delivering of these Same presents the Receipt whereof he doth hereby acknowledge and thereof doth acquit and discharge the said Jonathan Swift his heirs Executors and Administrators the said Daniel Ferry has granted bargained and sold aliened Released made over transferred Conveyed and confirmed and by these presents doth grant bargain and sell alien Release make over transfer convey and confirm unto the said Jonathan Swift and his heirs and assigns forever a certain tract or parcel of land [____?] called SPRINGFIELD situate laying and being in the County of Hardin formerly a part of Nelson County and State of Kentucky on the waters of Green River between Little Reedy and Welches Creek and bounded as followeth To wit, BEGINNING at a white oak and ash South West corner to William Mays land on said Reedy and on the West side of said creek about two miles from Green River by the head of a drain Running thence Sixty seven degrees West Fifteen hundred and Sixty eight poles to two white oaks and Gum in John May John Bannisters line Thence with the Same North forty five degrees East Fourteen hundred and Ninety Three poles to two Maples and a White Oak corner to Lewises Six thousand acre Survey thence with the line thereof South Eighty eight degrees East three hundred and eighty poles to a white oak in the line of William Mays land on little Reedy thence with the same South two degrees West Sixteen hundred and seventy poles to the BEGINNING Containing NINE THOUSAND TWO HUNDRED ACRES for which a Patent was granted to William May

Esquire Surveyor of the County of Nelson by the Commonwealth of Virginia bearing date the tenth day of July in the year of Our Lord One Thousand Seven Hundred and eighty Six and was by the said William May and Mary his wife conveyed to the said Daniel Ferry by deed bearing date the fifteenth day of July in the year of Our Lord One Thousand Seven Hundred and Ninety Four and all houses buildings out houses gardens orchards meadows woods trees underwoods huntings fisheries quarries coals licks Mines Metals Ores or Minerals of any kind above upon or under the ground and all waters and water courses profits commodities hereditiments and appurtenances whatsoever to the said belonging or in any wise appurtaining and the revision and revisions Remainder and Remainders Rents issues and profits thereof and of every part and parcel thereof and also all the right Title Interest and Estate of the said Daniel Ferry of in and to the same to have and to hold the said Estate with all and Singular the privileges and appurtenances to the said Jonathan Swift his heirs and assigns forever the only proper use benefit and behoof of the said Jonathan Swift and the said Daniel Ferry for himself his heirs Executors and Administrators doth covenant promise and grant to and with the said Jonathan Swift his heirs Executors Administrators and assigns that the said Jonathan Swift his heirs and assigns Shall and may forever hereafter Peacefully and quietly have hold use occupy possess and enjoy the aforesaid Estate with all and Singular the premises hereby granted with their and every of their appurtenances without the let suit trouble Interruption or denial of him the said Daniel Ferry his heirs or assigns and that the said premises hereby granted now are and so forever hereafter Shall remain and be free and clear from all former and other grants Bargains Sales dower right and title of dower Judgments Executions Titles Troubles charges and encumbrances Whatsoever made done and committed and suffered by the said Daniel Ferry and lastly the aforesaid Estate tract or parcel of land with all and Singular the premises and appurtenances thereunto belonging unto the said Jonathan Swift his heirs and assigns Shall and will Warrant and forever defend against the claim or demands of all persons whatsoever In witness whereof the said Daniel Ferry has hereunto set his hand affixed his Seal the day and year first above written.

Daniel Ferry

Signed Sealed and delivered in presence of
Thomas Lewis
Amos Allison
Charles Bennett
Received of Jonathan Swift the consideration mentioned with my hand this-
fourth day August One Thousand Seven Hundred and Ninety Four

Daniel Ferry

Witness
Thomas Lewis, Amos Allison, Charles Bennett

Virginia Fairfax
Personally appeared before us two of the Justices of the Peace in and for the County of Fairfax Daniel Ferry Esquire acknowledges this Indenture by him subscribed to be his free act and deed Given unto our hands and Seals at Alexandria this fourth day of August One Thousand Seven Hundred and Ninety Four

Robert Townsend Hooe
William Herbert
At a court of quarter sessions held for the County of Hardin the 23rd day of June 1795 this Indenture together with the Certificate thereof was presented in court and ordered to be Recorded   Test.   D. May   Clerk Hardin County   Quarter session

B-11

This Indenture made this fifteenth day of April in the year of our Lord one thousand seven hundred and ninety five between William May Esquire and Mary his wife of the County of Nelson and State of Kentucky of the one part and Daniel Ferry Esquire of the said County and State of the other part Witnesseth that the said William May and Mary his wife for and in consideration of five shillings current money of Kentucky to them in hand paid by the said Daniel Ferry at and before the ensealing and delivering of these presents the receipt whereof they do hereby acknowledge and thereof doth acquit and discharge the said Daniel Ferry his heirs executors and administrators they the said William May and Mary his wife have granted bargained and sold aliened, released and conveyed and by these presents doth grant, bargain and sell alien, release and convey to the said Daniel Ferry his heirs and assigns forever a certain tract or parcel of land situate lying and being in the County of Hardin formerly a part of Nelson and State of Kentucky on the north side of Green River and bounded as followeth, To Wit, BEGINNING at two black oaks a white oak and hickory the south east corner of Joseph Lewises nine thousand seven hundred and twenty eight acre survey and standing in the north line of Isaac Morrisons four thousand seven hundred acre survey thence due north seven hundred and seventy poles to two black oaks a white oak and poplar and hickory thence east one thousand and nineteen poles to an ash, poplar, hickory and black oak thence due south seven hundred and seventy poles to three white oaks and a hickory thence due west one thousand and nineteen poles to the BEGINNING containing FIVE THOUSAND ACRES a patent for which was granted by the Commonwealth of Virginia to the said William May bearing date the first day of June in the year of our Lord one thousand seven hundred and eighty six reference being had to the same will more fully and clearly appear and all houses, buildings, yards, orchards, meadows, woods, underwoods, quarry, coals, licks, Mines, Metals, Ores or Minerals of any kind and all waters and water courses, profits, commodities and appurtenances to the said tract of land belonging or in any wise appertaining and also all the right title interest and estate of the said William May and Mary his wife of in and to the same to have and to hold the said tract of land with all its privileges and appurtenances to the said Daniel Ferry and his heirs and assigns forever and the said William May and Mary his wife for themselves their heirs, executors, administrators doth covenant and agree with the said Daniel Ferry and his heirs and assigns to warrant and forever defend the aforesaid tract of land with the appurtenances to the said Daniel Ferry his heirs or assigns against them and their heirs and all persons claiming by from or under them. In Witness whereof the said William May and Mary his wife has hereunto set their hands and seals the day and year first above written.

William May

Mary May

Signed sealed and delivered in presence of
William McClung, John Rowan
Bladen Ashley, Isaac Larue

Received of Daniel Ferry the consideration within mentioned this 15th day of
April 1795 Witness my hand this 15th day of July one thousand seven hundred and
ninety four

Will May

Witness
Ro[bert]Breckinridge
Will McClung

Nelson County
Personally appeared before us two of the Justices of the Peace in and for said
County in the State of Kentucky William May Esquire and Mary his wife and acknowledged this Indenture by them subscribed to be their free act and deed given
under our hands this--

At a Court of quarter session held for the county of Hardin the 23rd day of
June 1795 This Indenture together with the receipt endorsed thereon was proved by
the oaths William McClung, John Rowan and Bladen Ashley Witnesses thereto and
ordered to be recorded.

Test. D. May clerk Hardin County quarter sessions

B-12

This Indenture made this fifteenth day of April in the year of our Lord One
Thousand Seven Hundred and Ninety Five between William May Esquire and Mary
his wife of the County of Nelson and State of Kentucky of the one part and Daniel Ferry Esquire of the said County and State of the other part Witnesseth that
the said William May and Mary his wife for and in consideration of five Shillings
current money of Kentucky to them in hand paid by the said Daniel Ferry at and
before the sealing and delivering of these presents the receipt whereof they do hereby
acknowledge and they doth acquit and discharge the said Daniel Ferry his heirs Executors Administrators they the said William May and Mary his wife have granted
bargained and sold and by these presents doth grant bargain and sell alien and release
and make over to the said Daniel Ferry his heirs and assigns forever a certain tract
or parcel of land lying and being in the county of Hardin formerly a part of Nelson
and State aforesaid on the waters of Green River Between Little Reedy and Welshes
creek and bounded as followeth To wit, BEGINNING at a white oak and a south
west corner to William Mays land in said Reedy on the west side of said creek about
two miles from Green River by the head of a drain running thence north sixty seven
degrees west fifteen hundred and sixty eight poles to two white oaks and a gum in
John Mays John Bannisters line thence with the same North forty five degrees east
fourteen hundred and ninety three poles to two maples and white oak corner to Lew-

311

ises six thousand acre survey thence with the line thereof south eighty eight degrees east three hundred and eighty poles to a white oak in the line of William Mays land on Little Reedy thence with the same south two degrees west sixteen hundred and seventy poles to the BEGINNING containing NINE THOUSAND TWO HUNDRED ACRES for which a patent was granted by the Commonwealth of Virginia to the said William May bearing date the 10th day of July in the year of our Lord One Thousand Seven Hundred and Eighty Six Reference being had to the same will more fully and clearly appear and all houses buildings gardens orchards meadows woods and underwoods quarries coals licks Mines or Metals Ores or Minerals of any kind and all waters and water courses profits commodities and appurtenances to the said tract of land belonging or in any wise appertaining and also all the Right Title Interests and Estate of the said William May and Mary his wife of and in and to the same to have and to hold the said tract of land with all its privileges and appurtenances to thesaidDanielFerryandtohis heirs and assigns forever and the said William May and Mary his wife for themselves their heirs do covenant and agree with the said Daniel Ferry and his heirs and assigns to warrant and forever defend the aforesaid tract of land with the appurtenances to the said Daniel Ferry and his heirs and assigns against themselves and their heirs and all persons claiming by from or under them in witness whereof the said William May and Mary his wife have hereunto by their hands and seals the day and year first above written

William May
Mary May

Signed sealed and delivered in presence of
William McClung
John Rowan
Bladen Ashley
Isaac Larue
Received of Daniel Ferry the considerations within mentioned witness My hand this fifteenth day of April One Thousand Seven Hundred and Ninety Five

William May

WITNESS   R. Breckinridge

Nelson [County]
Personally appeared before us two Justices of the Peace in and for the County of Nelson in the State of Kentucky William May Esquire and Mary his wife acknowledged this Indenture by Subscribed to be their free act and deed given under our hand this—

At a court of quarter Session held for Hardin County this 23rd day of June 1795 This Indenture was proved by the oaths of William McClung, John Rowan, Bladen Ashley together with a certificate thereon and ordered to be recorded

Test. D. May   Clerk Hardin County Quarter session

19 Nelson County S[superscript t]

This day came Stephen May before us Two of the Justices of the peace for said County and acknowledged the Within Deed &c The said Martha Being examined apart from her husband relinquished her right of Dower given under Our hands this 15[superscript th] Day of Dec[superscript r] 1795

Nelson County S[superscript t]

William Kenzy
Gabriel Cox

I Certify that a true Copy of the Within Deed is recorded in the record Book B page 101 in My office Given under m[y] hand as Clerk of said County Court February 2[superscript nd] 1796

Ben Grayson

at a Court of Quarter Sessions held for the County of Hardin the 27 Day of April 1796 this Indenture of Bargain and Sale was presented in Court together with the relinquishment of the right of Dower and a Certificate also on the back thereof and ordered to record Teste

James May C D C H C

B 1

This *Indenture* made this twenty third Day of March in The year of Our Lord ~~seventeen~~ hundred and ninety five between James Keer and Julia his Wife of the Town of Alexandria in the County of Fairf[ax] and Commonwealth of Virginia of the One part and Robert Walsh of Baltimore town in Baltimore County in the State of Maryland Martha of the Other part WitNesseth that the said James Keer and Julia his Wife for and in Consideration of the Sum of Ten thousan Dollars Current Money of the United States of America to The said James Keer in hand paid by the said Robert Walsh at or before Sealing and Delivery of these presents the receipt Whereof he Doth hereby Acknowledge and thereof Doth for ever acquit and Dis charge the said Robert Walsh his heirs Executors and

[margin left:]
Rec[superscript d]
&c
&c
Given to
A. Hubbard
Keer
to
Walsh

Laws 3718

20 and Administrators they the said James Keer & his said Wife Julia have given, granted, Bargained, sold, Aliened released and Confirmed and by these presents do give grant Bargain Sell alien release and confirm Unto the said Robert Walsh his heirs and assigns for ever a certain tract or parcel of Land Containing *twenty Thous* = *and seven hundred and eighteen* acres and three quar = ters of an Acre of Land as by Survey Made and returned into the Land Office of Virginia situate and being in the County of Nelson in the District of Kentucky. For Which Twenty thousand Seven hundred and eighteen Acres and three Quarters of an acre of Land a patent was granted by the Commonwealth of Virginia Unto Mordecai Bar = bour Esquire bearing date the fifth day of August in the year of Our Seven

[left margin:] and one Thousand hundred and eighty eight Under the hand of Edmund Randolph Then Governor of Virginia and Under the Seal of Said Com

[left margin:] be and Seven / therein the / rording Silla

monwealth and which Lands with the patent was conveyed by the said Mordecai Barbour Esquire to a certain Jonathan Swift by Indenture bearing date the fifteenth day of September in the year of Our Lord One Thousand Seven hundred and Ninety One and by the said Jonathan Swift conveyed to the said James Keer by Deed bearing date the eighth day of May in the year of Our Lord One thousand Seven hundred and Ninety Two and is bounded as follows *Viz: BEGINING* at two Small White Oaks where Bells line of this Twenty thousand acre Survey now belonging to Blair Elliott and Company intersects a line of Barbour and Banks Sixty thousand acre Survey Thence along Barbour and Banks line North Seventy two Degrees West Thirteen hundred and fifty Six poles to a White Oak in said line thence South eighteen Degrees West One thousand and Ninety poles to two White Oaks and

This Indenture made this first day of March in the Year of our Lord One thousand Seven hundred and Ninety two between Jonathan Swift and Ann his Wife of the Town of Alexandria in the County of Fairfax and State of Virginia of the one part and Stephen Cook of the said Town of Alexandria in the County of Fairfax and State of Virginia of the other Part Whereas that the said Jonathan Swift and Ann his Wife is Seller for and in Consideration of an Unliquidated Georgia Certificate dated this 29th July 1777 for three hundred and Eighty six pounds fifteen Shillings and Signed O Bryan and Evans and three eighths of land Situated and being in the the Township of Oldfield in the County of Cumberland in the State of Massachusetts Conveyed to the said Jonathan Swift by the said Stephen Cook in an Instrument bearing equal and even date with these presents as for and in Consideration of the Sum of five Shillings Current Money of Virginia to him in hand paid by the said Stephen Cook at or before the ensealing and delivery of these presents the receipt whereof he doth hereby acknowledge and thereof doth acquit and discharge the said Stephen Cook his heirs Executors and administrators they the said Jonathan Swift and Ann his Wife have given granted bargained and sold aliened Released and Confirmed and by these Presents do give grant bargain sell alien Release convey and confirm Unto the said Stephen Cook his heirs and assigns forever a Certain tract or parcel of land Containing five thousand acres as by Survey bearing date Twentieth of May One thousand Seven hundred and Eighty nine Situated and being in the County of Nelson in the District of Kentucky and for which a patent was granted to Robert Brook Abr Esquire of the County of Culpepper and State aforesaid bearing the third day of March in the Year of Our Lord One thousand Seven hundred and Ninety one under the hand of Beverly Randolph Esquire Governor of Virginia and under the

B-2

315

an act of the General Assembly of Kentucky Entitled an act directing the Clerk of the Hardin Circuit Court to perform certain duties &c. November 2nd 1825 I have Certified upon the Record the original true Not being in the office Given Under my hand this 6th day of October 1821

Saml Haycraft Jr CHC

B 3

This Indenture made the Twenty sixth day of February One thousand Seven hundred and Ninety four between Jediah Ashcraft of the County of Hardin which was formerly a part of Nelson and also a part of Jefferson and State of Kentucky of the one part and Jonathan Swift of the Town of Alexandria in the County of Fairfax and State of Virginia of the other Witnesseth that the said Jediah Ashcraft for and in Consideration of the Sum of five Shillings Current money of Virginia to him in hand paid by the said Jonathan Swift at and before the ensealing and delivery of these Presents the Receipt whereof he doth hereby acknowledge doth acquit and discharge the said Jonathan Swift his Executors and Administrators, He the said Jediah Ashcraft has granted bargained and Sold made over and transfered Conveyed and Confirmed and by these presents doth grant bargain and sell make over transfer Convey and Confirm Unto the said Jonathan Swift his heirs and afsigns forever a Certain tract or Parcel of land on the waters of Trim River in the aforesaid County of Hardin Beginning at a Beech and Hickory twenty poles below the mouth of the Second large West branch of Bear Creek about fifteen Miles meander measure above the mouth of said creek being also a Corner to Miller Grams Seven hundred and fifty acres thence running with a line of the Same North 15° East Two hundred and Twenty Poles to two Gums on a Ridge then North 40 West Three hundred and fifty poles to a White Oak Corner to James Crocks land then with this Same line North 23 East four hundred poles to a post then South one hundred and ten poles to a Hawbush Corner to Helms land then South 9° 30 West One hundred and Ninety five poles to an ash in the side of the Knobbs then South 45 East forty two poles to a Beech on the West bank of Bear Creek and on Said Helms lower line Marked H then down with the meanders of the Creek binding thereon to the Beginning Containing five hundred and Sixty Eight acres being part of a Patent of Twelve hundred and Seventy Six acres granted to the Said Jediah Ashcraft bearing date the 25° day of May One thousand Seven hundred and Eighty Six and all houses gardens Orchards Meadows Woods

Underwood

This Indenture made the first day of August in the year of our Lord one thousand seven hundred and Twenty five between Jonathan Swift of the Town of Alexandria in the County of Fairfax and Commonwealth of Virginia Merchant of the one part and James Craik of the said Town County Commonwealth physician of the other part Witnesseth that the said Jonathan Swift for and in consideration of the sum of five shillings Current Money of Virginia to him in hand paid by the said James Craik at and before the ensealing and delivery of these presents the receipt whereof he doth hereby Acknowledge and thereof doth Remise and discharge the said James Craik his heirs Executors and administrators He the said Jonathan Swift has granted bargained and sold aliened released and over transferred conveyed and confirmed And by these presents doth grant bargain and sell alien release and make over transfer convey and Confirm unto the said James Craik and his heirs and assigns forever a certain tract or parcel of Land situate lying and being on the waters of Green river in the County of Hardin and State of Kentucky. Beginning at a beech & hickory 2 poles below the mouth of the second large west branch of bear neck about 15 miles meander measure above the mouth of said Creek being also a corner to Willis Green's 450 acre survey running with a line of the same North 15° East 240 poles to two Gums on a ridge then North 40 degrees West 350 poles to a white Oak corner to James Craik's Lands then with the Division Line North 53 degrees East 400 poles to a post then south 110 poles to a Haw bush Corner to Helms Land then south 9° 30′ West 195 poles to an

Interruption or denial of him the said Jonathan Swift his heirs or assigns and that the said premises hereby granted now are and so forever hereafter shall now and and before and clear of from all former & other grants bargains sales Dower right and title of Dower Judgments Executions titles troubles charges claims and Incumbrances whatsoever made done Committed or suffered by the said Jonathan Swift. Lastly the aforesaid lands with all and Singular the premises and appurtenances thereunto belonging unto the said James Craik his heirs and assigns shall and will warrant and forever defend against the claims or Demands of all persons whatsoever. In Witness whereof the said Jonathan Swift has hereunto set his hand and affixed his seal the day and year first above Written

Jonathan Swift (LS)

Signed Sealed &
delivered in presence of
Joseph Riddle
Feudamore Nicholls
Lem'l Bent

And Ann Wife of the said Jonathan in token of her free will & consent to this Indenture & bargain & Sale of her full relinquishment of her right of Dower and thirds of in and to the said within Premises hath caused her hand and affixed her seal the day & year first above Written

Ann Swift (LS)

Witness
Feudamore Nicholls
Joseph Riddle
Lemuel Bent

Received of Doct'r James Craik the Consideration with in mentioned Witness my hand this 1'st day of august one thousand seven hundred Ninety five

Witness
Feudamore Nicholls
Joseph Riddle
Lem'l Bent

Jonathan Swift

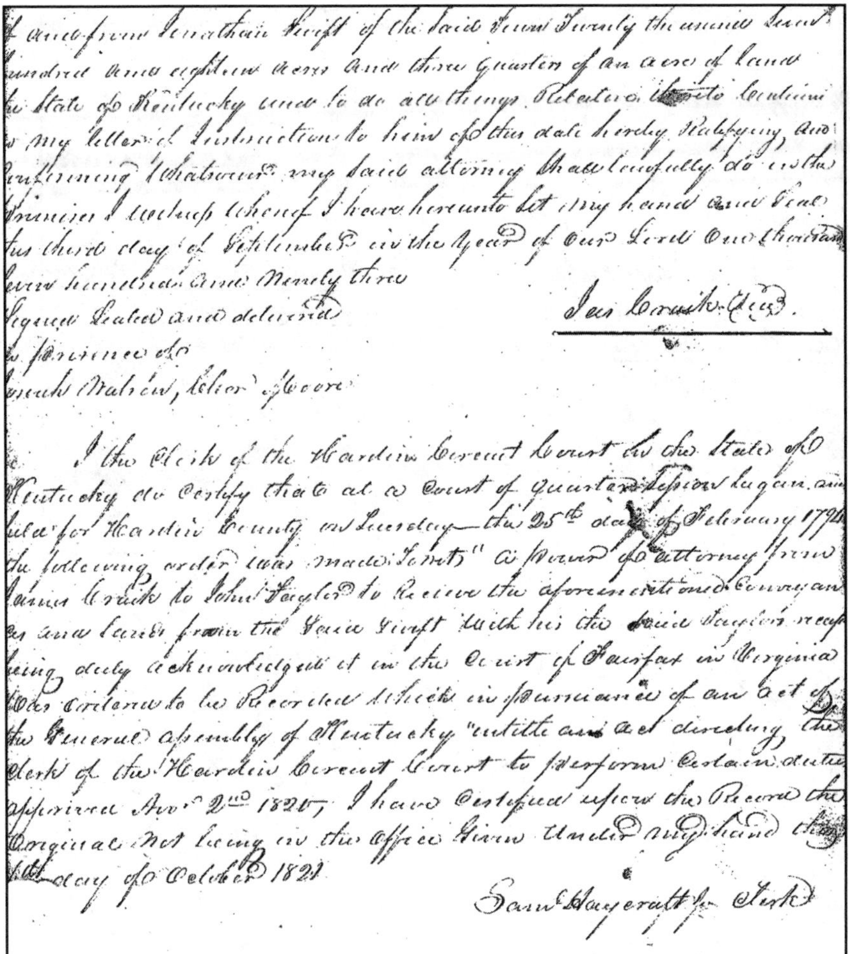

[L]and from Jonathan Swift of the said Town Twenty thousand [sev]en hundred and eighteen acres and three quarters of an acre of land [in t]he State of Kentucky and to do all things relative thereto contain[ed i]n my letter of instruction to him of this date hereby ratifying and confirming whatever my said attorney shall lawfully do in the premises. In witness whereof I have hereunto set my hand and seal this third day of September in the year of our Lord one thousand seven hundred and ninety three

Signed sealed and delivered in presence of
Joseph Walker, Elias Moore

Jas Craik (Seal)

I the Clerk of the Hardin Circuit Court in the State of Kentucky do certify that at a Court of Quarter Session begun and held for Hardin County on Tuesday the 25th day of February 1794 the following order was made towit " a Power of attorney from James Craik to John Taylor to receive the aforementioned conveyances and lands from the said Swift with his the said Taylor's receipt being duly acknowledged in the Court of Fairfax in Virginia was ordered to be recorded which in pursuance of an act of the General Assembly of Kentucky "entitled an act directing the Clerk of the Hardin Circuit Court to perform certain duties approved Nov 2nd 1820, I have certified upon the Record the original not being in the office Given under my hand this 4th day of October 1821

Saml Haycraft Jr Clerk

B-5

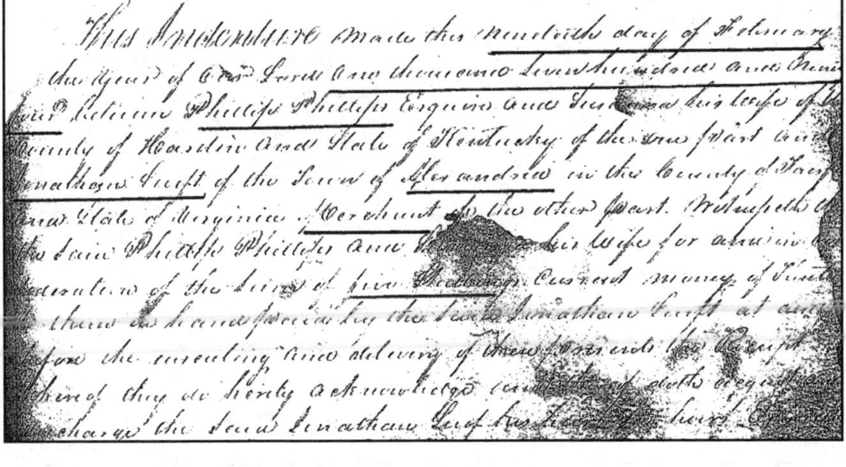

This Indenture made this nineteenth day of February [in] the year of our Lord one thousand seven hundred and ninety four between Phillips Phillips Esquire and Susanna his wife of the County of Hardin and State of Kentucky of the one part and Jonathan Swift of the Town of Alexandria in the County of Fairfax and State of Virginia Merchant of the other part. Witnesseth that the said Phillips Phillips and [illegible] his wife for and in consideration of the sum of five shillings current money of Virginia to them in hand paid by the said Jonathan Swift at and before the ensealing and delivery of these presents the receipt whereof they do hereby acknowledge [illegible] discharge the said Jonathan Swift his heirs [illegible]

directing the Clerk of the Hardin Circuit Court to perform certain
duties I have Certified upon the Record the Original not being in
the office Given Under my hand this 8th day of October 1821

E. W. Haycraft Clerk

This Indenture made this ninedaenth day of February
in the Year of Our Lord One thousand seven hundred and ??
four between William May and Mary his Wife of the County of
Nelson and State of Kentucky of the one part and Phillip
Phillips of the County of Hardin and State aforesaid of the
Nelson that the said William May and Mary his Wife for and in
Consideration of the sum of five Shillings Current money of Kentucky
to him in hand paid by the said Phillip Phillips the Receipt where
they do hereby acknowledge and thereof do acquit and discharge
said Phillip Phillips his heirs Executors and administrators they the said
William May and Mary his Wife have bargained and sold and
by these presents doth grant bargain and sell unto the said P.
Phillips his heirs and assigns a Certain tract or parcel of land ly
and being in the waters of Green River in the County of Hardin
formerly part of Nelson and State of Kentucky being part of a tract
six thousand acres survey on the West side of Bear Creek a
of Green River and bounded as follows, Beginning B at a W
Oak and Beech on the second large fork of Bear Creek Corner
to Willis Green seven hundred and fifty acre survey and running
thence South sixty Nine degrees West One thousand and sixty f
with a line of Phillip Phillips Eleven thousand eight hundred an
seventy acre survey to a Sassafras and White Oak on the head of on
of the main branches of Big Rudy Creek, then South thirty degrees
four hundred and sixty three poles to a Post, thence with said
decanus line North sixty Nine degrees East one thousand and sev
poles to a Small White Oak in the aforesaid Greens line th
with his said line North twenty five degrees West four hund
and sixty three poles to the Beginning Containing three thousand
acres being one half a six thousand acre Patent granted to
said William May by virtue of a Treasury Warrants No. 18
17446 also all the Right Title Interest and Estate of the said
William May and Mary his Wife of in and to the same
have and to hold the said tract or parcel of land with all
Appurtenances and Privileges thereunto belonging or any wis

B-6

Phillips being duly acknowledged before Benjamin Frye
and Gabriel ___ two of the Justices of the Peace for Nelson
County and Certificate from the Clerk of said County that
they are such Was presented and ordered to be Recorded
Which in pursuance of an act of the General Assembly of
Kentucky approved Nov. 2nd 1820 directing the Clerk of
the Hardin Circuit Court to perform certain duties I have
Certified upon the Record the original not being in the office
Given Under my hand this 5th day of October 1821.
Saml. Haycraft Jr. Clk.

This INDENTURE made this Nineteenth day of
February in the Year of our Lord One thousand Seven
hundred and Ninety four Between Jacob Ashcraft Esqr.
of the County of Hardin formerly a part of Nelson which
was formerly a part of Jefferson County and State of Kentucky
of the One part and Phillip Phillips Esqr. of the said County
of Hardin and State of Kentucky of the Other Witnesseth that
the said Jacob Ashcraft for and in Consideration of the Sum
of five Shillings Current money of Kentucky to him in hand
paid by the said Phillip Phillips at and before the ensealing
and delivery of these presents the Receipt whereof they do
hereby acknowledge and therefore doth acquit and discharge
the said Phillip Phillips his heirs Executors and administrators
the said Jacob Ashcraft has bargained bargained and ___
aliened released made over transferred and Confirmed and
by these presents doth give grant bargain sell alien Release
Make over transfer Convey and Confirm, Unto the said
Phillip Phillips his heirs and assigns forever a Certain tract
or parcel of land lying and being on the Waters of Green
River in the said Vicinity of Hardin and State of Kentucky
Beginning at a large Ash B. Corner to Phillip Phillips
Eleven thousand Eight hundred and Seventy acre Survey
and Running With a line of the same South 5 B West
four hundred and Eighty poles to a Gum and Hickory
Corner to Willis Green's Seven hundred and fifty acre Survey
then With a line of the same South 50 East fifty poles

This Indenture made the Seventeenth day of February in the year of our Lord one thousand Seven hundred and twenty five between Jonathan Swift and Ann his Wife of the Town of Alexandria in the County of Fairfax and Commonwealth of Virginia Merchant of the one part and James Craik Esqr Surgeon of the Town County and Commonwealth Physician of the other part Witnesseth that the said Jonathan Swift and Ann his Wife for and in Consideration of the Sum of five Shillings Current money of Virginia to them in hand paid by the said James Craik at and before the ensealing and delivery of these presents the Receipt whereof they do hereby acknowledge and thereof doth acquit and discharge the said James Craik his heirs Executors and Administrators they the said Jonathan Swift and Ann his Wife have given granted bargained and aliened released made over conveyed transferred and Confirmed and by these presents doth grant bargain and sell alien Release make over transfer Convey and Confirm unto the said James Craik and his heirs and assigns forever, A certain tract or parcel of land Situate lying and being on the waters of Green River in the County of Hartford formerly a part of Bell and State of Kentucky Beginning at two White Oaks and Ash South West Corner to William Knapp Nine hundred and twenty acre Survey then running South Sixteen degrees West five hundred and Twenty poles to two Black Gum White Oaks and Sugartree North East corner to Phillips Phillips Four hundred acre twenty three with his line South 25 West Two hundred and fifty three poles to a Black Oak then South 22 East One hundred and forty poles to two Dogwoods Black Oak and White Oak corner to James Grant four hundred acre Survey then North of the same fifty 40 West Two hundred and twenty to three White Oaks then South 50 East Two hundred poles to Ash Corner to Ashcraft Land thence with a line South 50 West four hundred and Eighty poles to a Gum and Hickory Corner to William Greens Seven hundred and fifty acre Survey on the Second Long branch of bear Creek thence North twenty West five

B-8

322

Received of Jonathan Swift the consideration mentioned with
my hand this fourth day August One thousand seven hundred and
ninety four

Witness   Daniel Ferry {Seal}
Thomas Lewis, Amos Allison,
Charles Bennett

        Virginia Fairfax Sc.
                Personally appeared before us two of the Justices of the
Peace in and for the County of Fairfax Daniel Ferry Esquire ack___
this Indenture by him subscribed to be his free act and deed Given ___
Our hands and seals at Alexandria this fourth day of August One
thousand seven hundred and Ninety four
                                        Robert R T Hood {Seal}
                                        William Hubert {Seal}

        At a Court of quarter Session held for the County of Hardin
23d day of June 1795 this Indenture together with the Certificate the___
was Presented in Court and Ordered to be Recorded
                                        Test D. May C. H.

B 9

This Indenture made the fourth day of August in the ___
of Our Lord One thousand Seven hundred and Ninety four Bet___
Daniel Ferry Esquire of the County of Nelson and State of Kentucky
of the One Part and Jonathan Swift of the Town of Alexandria in ___
County of Fairfax and State of Virginia Merchant of the other par___
Witnesseth that the said Daniel Ferry for and in consideration of
sum of five Shillings current money of Virginia to him in hand ___
by the said Jonathan Swift at and before the sealing and deliv___
of these presents the Receipt whereof he doth hereby acknowledge and ___
doth acquit and discharge the said Jonathan Swift his heirs Exec___
admin___ the said Daniel Ferry has granted bargained and sold a___
Released made over transferred Conveyed and confirmed and by ___
Presents doth grant bargain and sell alien Release Make Over Tran___
Convey and Confirm unto the said Jonathan Swift his heirs and assigns
forever a certain tract or Parcel of land called Greenwich Situate
lying and being in the County of Hardin formerly a Part of N___
and State of Kentucky on the North Side of Green River and bounded
as followeth To Wit, Beginning at two Black Oaks a White Oak
Hickory the South East Corner of ___ ___ ___ thousand ___
                                                    ___

Nelson §—

Personally appeared before us two Justices of the Peace in and for the County of Nelson in the State of Kentucky M May Esquire and Mary his Wife, acknowledged this Indenture by subscribed to be their free act and deed Given under our hand this —

At a court of quarter Session held for Hardin County 23rd day of June 1795 This Indenture was proved by the Oaths of William McClung John Renan Bladen Ashby together with a Cert thereon and Ordered to be recorded ⹀ Test Q. May 6, 76, 6, 2;

This Indenture made this fourth day of August in the of our Lord One thousand seven hundred and Ninety four Betw Daniel Perry Esquire of the County of Nelson and State of Kentuc of the One Part and Jonathan Swift of the Town of Alexandria in the of Fairfax and State of Virginia Merchant of the other Part Witnesseth the said Daniel Perry for and in Consideration of the Sum of five Current Money of Virginia to him in hand paid by the said Jona Swift at and before the ensealing and delivering of these presents Receipt whereof he doth hereby acknowledge and thereof doth acquit and discharge the said Jonathan Swift his heirs Exors and admors said Daniel Perry has granted bargained and sold aliened Rele made over transfered Conveyed and Confirmed and by these pre doth grant bargain and sell alien Release make over transfer Convey and Confirm unto the said Jonathan Swift and his heirs and assigns forever a certain tract or parcel of land entituled Called Springfield scituate lying and being in the County of H formerly a Part of Nelson County and State of Kentucky on the West of Green River between little Rudy and Welches Creek and bounde as followeth To wit; Beginning at a White Oak and ash South West Co to William May's land on said Rudy and on the West side of said about two miles from Green River by the head of a drain Running thence Sixty two degrees West Fifteen hundred and Sixty eight po to two White Oaks and Gum in John May's John Bannister's Yea thence with his land North forty five degrees East Fourteen hundred and Ninety three poles to two Maples and a White Oak Corner to A. Hammond's survey thence with the line thereof South Eighty together with the Certificates and other therein was produced in Court and admitted to Record.

Test Wm May Cl, HC, C, 2,

This Indenture made this fifteenth day of April in the Year of Our Lord One thousand seven hundred and Ninety five Between William May Esquire and Mary his Wife of the County of Nelson and State of Kentucky of the One Part and Daniel Terry Esquire of the said County and State of the other part Witnesseth that the said William May and Mary his Wife for and in Consideration of five Shillings Current Money of Kentucky to them in hand paid by the said Daniel Terry at and before the ensealing and delivering of these presents the Receipt whereof they do hereby acknowledge and thereof doth acquit and discharge the said Daniel Terry his heirs Exors and Admors they the said William May and Mary his Wife have granted bargained and Sold aliened released and Conveyed and by these presents doth grant bargain and sell alien Release and Convey to the said Daniel Terry his heirs and assigns forever a Certain tract or parcel of Land situate lying and being in the County of Hardin formerly a part of Nelson and State of Kentucky on the North side of Nolin Lick run and described as followeth to Wit, Beginning at Two White Oaks a White Oak and Hickory the South East Corner of Joseph Lewis survey ... and twenty eight acre survey and standing in the ... ... James Ray's four thousand seven hundred acre survey thence due North three hundred and twenty poles to two Black Oaks a White Oak and Poplar and Hickory thence East One thousand and Nineteen poles to an ash Poplar Hickory and Black Oak thence due South three hundred and twenty poles to three White Oaks and a Hickory thence due West One thousand and Nineteen poles to the Beginning Containing two thousand acres a Patent for which was granted by the Commonwealth of Virginia to the said William May bearing date the first day of June in the Year of Our Lord One thousand seven hundred and Eighty six reference being had to the same, will More fully and clearly appear and all houses buildings gards Orchards, Meadows, Woods, Underwoods, Quarrys, Coals, Licks, Mines, Metals, Ores or Minerals of any kind and all Waters and Water Courses Profits Commodities and appurtenances to the said tract of land Belonging or in any wise appertaining and also all the right Title Interest and Estate of the said William May and Mary his Wife of in and to the same To have and to hold the said Tract of land with all its priveledges and appurtenances to the said Daniel Terry and his heirs and assigns

covenant and agree with the with the said Daniel Terry and his h
and assigns to warrant and forever defend the aforesaid tract of land with i
appurtenances to the said Daniel Terry his heirs or assigns against th
and their heirs and all persons claiming by from or under them i
Witness whereof the said William May and Mary his wife ha
hereunto set their hands and seals the day and year first above wr
Signed sealed and delivered in presence of
William McClung, John Rowan — William May (Seal)
Bladen Ashby, Isaac Larue — Mary May (Seal)

Received of Daniel Terry the Consideration within mention
this 13th day of April 1795 Witness my hand this 13th day of July
thousand seven hundred and ninety four
Witness — Will May
Ro Breckinridge, Will McClung

Nelson Sct
Personally appeared before us two of the Justices
the Peace in and for said County in the State of Kentucky William
May Esquire and Mary his wife and acknowledged this Indenture
by them subscribed to be their free act and deed Given under ou
hands this —
At a Court of Quarter Session held for the County of Hard
the 23rd day of June 1795 This Indenture together with the Receipt en
thereon was proved by the oaths William McClung John Rowan a
Bladen Ashby Witnesses thereto and ordered to be recorded
Test D May C,H,C,Q,

This Indenture made this fifteenth day of April in
year of Our Lord One thousand seven hundred and Ninety five b
William May Esquire and Mary his wife of the County of Nels
and State of Kentucky of the one part and Daniel Terry Esquire
the said County and State of the other Part Witnesseth that the
said William May and Mary his wife for and in consideration
of five Shillings Current Money of Kentucky to them in hand paid
the said Daniel Terry at and before the sealing and delivering and
these presents the Receipt whereof they do hereby acknowledge and th
[illegible] acquit and discharge the said Daniel Terry his heirs Exec
[illegible] the said William May and Mary his wife

B-12

shall and will warrant and forever defend against the
claims or demands of All persons whatsoever. In Testimony
whereof the said Jediah Ashcraft hereunto set his hand and
affixed his seal the day and year first above written

Signed Sealed and delivered   Jediah Ashcraft {Seal}
in Presence of us and before   by his Attorney
the ensealing and delivery of   Daniel Ashcraft
these presents between the sixth
and eleventh line first interlined
before signed

Received of Phillip Phillips Esqr. the Consideration
within mentioned — Witness my hand this 19th day of February
One thousand Seven hundred and ninety four
Witness   Daniel Ashcraft for
John Taylor   Jedeah Ashcraft
Jonathan Swift
Joseph Barnes

I the Clerk of the Hardin Circuit Court in the
State of Kentucky do certify that at a Court of Quarter Session
begun and held for the County of Hardin at the Courthouse in
Elizabeth Town on Tuesday the 25th day of February 1794 the following
entry was made to wit, A Deed from Jedah Ashcraft by Daniel
Ashcraft his attorney in fact to Phillip Phillips was acknowledged
Ordered to be Recorded, which in Pursuance of an act of the
assembly of Kentucky Approved Novr 2nd 1820 directing the Clerk
said Court to perform certain duties I have
     Done & the Original Deed not being in the office Given
to the Recorder this 6th day of October 1821

               David Hayeraft J Clerk

B-13

To all persons to Whom these presents Shall Come I
James Kisack of the Town of Alexandria County of Fairfax
Commonwealth of Virginia Send Greeting Know Ye that for
Causes and Considerations me thereunto moving I have
ordained Constituted and appointed and by these presents
make Ordain Constitute and appoint John Taylor of the said

327

B-13

B-13

APPENDIX C

THE PERSONS OF THE TALE

AFTER the 32nd chapter of *Treasure Island*, two of the puppets strolled out to have a pipe before business should begin again, and met in an open place not far from the story.

"Good-morning, Cap'n," said the first, with a man-o'-war salute, and a beaming countenance.

"Ah, Silver!" grunted the other. "You're in a bad way, Silver."

"Now, Cap'n Smollett," remonstrated Silver, "dooty is dooty, as I knows, and none better; but we're off dooty now; and I can't see no call to keep up the morality business."

"You're a damned rogue, my man," said the Captain.

"Come, come, Cap'n, be just," returned the other. "There's no call to be angry with me in earnest. I'm on'y a chara'ter in a sea story. I don't really exist."

"Well, I don't really exist either," says the Captain, "which seems to meet that."

"I wouldn't set no limits to what a virtuous chara'ter might consider argument," responded Silver. "But I'm the villain of this tale, I am; and speaking as one sea-faring man to another, what I want to know is, what's the odds?"

"Were you never taught your catechism?" said the Captain. "Don't you know there's such a thing as an Author?"

"Such a thing as a Author?" returned John, derisively. "And who better'n me? And the p'int is, if the Author made you, he made Long John, and he made Hands, and Pew, and George Merry - not that George is up to much, for he's little more'n a name; and he made Flint, what there is of him; and he made this here mutiny, you keep such a work about; and he had Tom Redruth shot; and - well, if that's a Author, give me Pew!"

329

"Don't you believe in a future state?" said Smollett. "Do you think there's nothing but the present story-paper?"

"I don't rightly know for that," said Silver; "and I don't see what it's got to do with it, anyway. What I know is this: if there is sich a thing as a Author, I'm his favourite chara'ter. He does me fathoms better'n he does you - fathoms, he does. And he likes doing me. He keeps me on deck mostly all the time, crutch and all; and he leaves you measling in the hold, where nobody can't see you, nor wants to, and you may lay to that! If there is a Author, by thunder, but he's on my side, and you may lay to it!"

"I see he's giving you a long rope," said the Captain. "But that can't change a man's convictions. I know the Author respects me; I feel it in my bones; when you and I had that talk at the blockhouse door, who do you think he was for, my man?"

"And don't he respect me?" cried Silver. "Ah, you should 'a' heard me putting down my mutiny, George Merry and Morgan and that lot, no longer ago'n last chapter; you'd heard something then! You'd 'a' seen what the Author thinks o' me! But come now, do you consider yourself a virtuous chara'ter clean through?"

"God forbid!" said Captain Smollett, solemnly. "I am a man that tries to do his duty, and makes a mess of it as often as not. I'm not a very popular man at home, Silver, I'm afraid!" and the Captain sighed.

"Ah," says Silver. "Then how about this sequel of yours? Are you to be Cap'n Smollett just the same as ever, and not very popular at home, says you? And if so, why, it's *Treasure Island* over again, by thunder; and I'll be Long John, and Pew'll be Pew, and we'll have another mutiny, as like as not. Or are you to be somebody else? And if so, why, what the better are you? and what the worse am I?"

"Why, look here, my man," returned the Captain, "I can't understand how this story comes about at all, can I? I can't see how you and I, who don't exist, should get to speaking here, and smoke our pipes for all the world like reality? Very well, then, who am I to pipe up with my opinions? I know the Author's on the side of good; he tells me so, it runs out of his pen as he writes. Well, that's all I need to know; I'll take my chance upon the rest."

"It's a fact he seemed to be against George Merry," Silver admitted, musingly. "But George is little more'n a name at the best of it," he added, brightening.

And to get into soundings for once. What is this good? I made a mutiny, and I been a gentleman o' fortune; well, but by all stories, you ain't no such saint. I'm a man that keeps company very easy; even by your own account,

330

you ain't, and to my certain knowledge you're a devil to haze. Which is which? Which is good, and which bad? Ah, you tell me that! Here we are in stays, and you may lay to it!"

"We're none of us perfect," replied the Captain. "That's a fact of religion, my man. All I can say is, I try to do my duty; and if you try to do yours, I can't compliment you on your success."

"And so you was the judge, was you?" said Silver, derisively.

"I would be both judge and hangman for you, my man, and never turn a hair," returned the Captain. "But I get beyond that: it mayn't be sound theology, but it's common sense, that what is good is useful too - or there and thereabout, for I don't set up to be a thinker. Now, where would a story go to if there were no virtuous characters?"

"If you go to that," replied Silver, "where would a story begin, if there wasn't no villains?"

"Well, that's pretty much my thought," said Captain Smollett. "The Author has to get a story; that's what he wants; and to get a story, and to have a man like the doctor (say) given a proper chance, he has to put in men like you and Hands. But he's on the right side; and you mind your eye ! You're not through this story yet; there's trouble coming for you."

"What'll you bet?" asked John.

"Much I care if there ain't," returned the Captain. "I'm glad enough to be Alexander Smollett, bad as he is; and I thank my stars upon my knees that I'm not Silver. But there's the ink-bottle opening. To quarters!"

And indeed the Author was just then beginning to write the words:
CHAPTER XXXIII.

BIBLIOGRAPHY

1.   Booth, Bradford A. and Ernest Mehew. *The Letters of Robert Louis Stevenson Volume One, 1854-April 1874*. *The Letters of Robert Louis Stevenson Volume Two, April 1874-July 1879*. *The Letters of Robert Louis Stevenson Volume Three, August 1879-September 1882*. *The Letters of Robert Louis Stevenson Volume Four, October 1882-June 1884*. *The Letters of Robert Louis Stevenson Volume Five, July 1884-August 1887*. *The Letters of Robert Louis Stevenson Volume Six, August 1887-September 1890*. *The Letters of Robert Louis Stevenson Volume Seven, September 1890-December 1892*. *The Letters of Robert Louis Stevenson Volume Eight,* January 1893-December 1894. New Haven and London: Yale University Press, 1994 & 1995.

2.   Brockett, F. L. *Lodge of Washington, A History of the Alexandria Washington Lodge #22, A.F. & A.M. of Alexandria, Virginia 1783-1876*. Virginia, Alexandria: G. H. Ramey & Son, 1899.

3.   Brookes-Smith, Joan E., compiler. *Master Index Virginia Surveys and Grants 1774-1791*. Kentucky, Frankfort: Kentucky Historical Society.

4.   Brookes-Smith, Joan E., editor. *Index for Old Kentucky Surveys and Grants*. Kentucky, Frankfort: microfilmed by Kentucky Historical Society, 1973-1974.

5.   Brown, Dan. *The Da Vinci Code*. New York, New York: Doubleday, 2003.

6.   Buchanan, Roberdeau. *Genealogy of the Roberdeau Family.* Washington D.C.: Joseph L. Pearson, 1876.

7.   Callow, Philip. *Louis: A Life of Robert Louis Stevenson*. Illinois, Chicago: Ivan R. Dee, Publisher, 2001.

8.   Cappon, Lester J and Stella F. Duff. *Virginia Gazette Index 1736-1780, Vol. II*. Virginia, Williamsburg: The Institute of Early American History and Culture, 1950.

9.   Chapman, Rev. John Wilbur. *The Life and Work of Dwight L. Moody*. Pennsylvania, Philadelphia: Clark & Co., 1900.

10.   Chinn, George Morgan. *Kentucky Settlement and Statehood 1750-1800*. Kentucky, Frankfort: The Kentucky Historical Society, 1975.

11.   Cook, Michael C.G. Kentucky *Record Series, Mercer County Kentucky Records Volume I*. Indiana, Evansville: Cook Publications, 1987.

12.   Cook, Michael and Bettie Anne Cook, editors and indexers. *Pioneer History of Washington County, Kentucky.* Kentucky, Owensboro: Cook and McDowell Publications, 1980.

13.   Daniels, Rev. W. H., editor. *Moody: His Words, Work, and Workers*. Nelson & Phillips, 1877.

14.   Durrett, Reuben T. *John Filson, The First Historian of Kentucky. His Life*

and Writings. Kentucky, Louisville: John P. Morton and Company, 1884.

15. Elliot, Jean. *Kindly But Alien Hands.* Virginia, Alexandria: From the files of the Alexandria Virginia Library, Kate Waller Barrett Branch, Colross file.n.p.: n. pub.

16. Elliot, Jean. *"Kindly But Alien Hands." The Princeton Recollector, A Monthly Journal of Local History Vol. VI, No. 10.* Virginia, Alexandria: From the files of the Alexandria Virginia Library, Kate Waller Barrett Branch, Colross file: Princeton History Project, 1981.

17. Gjernes, Marylou. *"Presbyterians and Alexandria 1770-1830."* Virginia, Alexandria: From the Alexandria Virginia Library, Kate Waller Barrett Branch. n.p.: n. pub. April 20, 1977.

18. Hawthorne, Bess L. *Hannah Boone and Her Descendants.* Vermont, Burlington: Chedwato Service, 1960.

19. Hennessy, James Pope. *Robert Louis Stevenson.* New York, New York: Simon and Schuster, 1974.

20. Henson, Michael Paul. *John Swift's Lost Silver Mines, Journal-Maps-Research* Kentucky, Louisville: United Christian Printing Service, 1975.

21. Henson, Michael Paul. *Lost Silver Mines and Buried Treasures of Kentucky.* Kentucky, Louisville: United Christian Printing Service, 1972.

22. Hiatt, Marty and Craig Roberts Scott. *Implied Marriages of Fairfax County Virginia.* Georgia, Athens: Iberian Publishing Company, 1994.

23. Hollan, Catherine B. cataloguer and exhibitor. *Three Centuries of Alexandria Silver.* Virginia, Alexandria: The Lyceum, October 28, 1994 – January 31, 1995.

24. Hurst, David, consultant. *Washington County, Kentucky Bicentennial History 1792-1992.* Kentucky, Paducah: Turner Publishing Company, 1991.

25. Irving, Washington. *The Works of Washington Irving Volume IX: The Sketch Book and Tales of a Traveller.* New York, New York: G. P. Putnam's Sons, 1881.

26. Jackson, Donald and Dorothy Twohig, editors. *The Diaries of George Washington Volumes 4 & 5 July 1786-December 1789 and 1784-June 1786.* Virginia, Charlottesville: University Press of Virginia, 1976-1979.

27. Jillson, Willard Rouse, Sc.D. *Old Kentucky Entries and Deeds.* Maryland, Baltimore: Genealogical Publishing Co., Inc., 1987.

28. Johnson, Captain Charles. *A General History Of The Robberies And Murders Of The Most Notorious Pirates.* Connecticut, Guilford: The Lyons Press, 1998, 2002, originally published 1724.

29. Kammen, Michael. *Colonial New York: A History.* New York: Charles Scriber's Sons, 1975, Second Printing 1987.

30. Kerr, Judge Charles, editor. *History of Kentucky Volume I.* New York and Chicago: The American Historical Society, 1922.

31. King, J. Estelle Stewart, compiler, 133 N. Wetherly Drive, Beverly Hills, California. *Abstract of Wills and Inventories Fairfax, County, Virginia. 1742-1801.* n.p.: n.pub. 1936.

32. Kingsley, Charles. *At Last: A Christmas in the West Indies.* London and New York: MacMillan and Co., 1889.

33. Kleber, John E. *The Kentucky Encyclopedia.* Kentucky, Lexington: University Press of Kentucky, June 1992.

34. Kurlansky, Mark. *Salt A World History.* New York, New York: Penguin Books LTD., 2002.

35. Mackay, Margaret. *The Violent Friend: The Story of Robert Louis Stevenson.* New York, Garden City: Doubleday & Company, Inc., 1968.

36. McMurtry, R. Gerald. *The Kentucky Lincolns on Mill Creek.* Elizabethtown, Kentucky: From the Brown-Pusey House Elizabethtown, Kentucky.

37. Mehew, Ernest. *Selected Letters of Robert Louis Stevenson.* New Haven and London: Yale University Press, 1997.

38. Miller, T. Michael. *Portrait of a Town Alexandria District of Columbia (Virginia) 1820-1830.* Maryland, Bowie: Heritage Books, Inc., 1995.

39. Miller, T. Michael. *Artisans and Merchants of Alexandria, Virginia 1784-1820 Volume 1, Artisans and Merchants of Alexandria, Virginia 1780-1820 Volume 2.* Maryland, Bowie: Heritage Books, Inc., 1990 & 1992.

40. Munson, James D. *Alexandria, Virginia, Alexandria Hustings Court Deeds 1797-1801 Volume 2.* Maryland, Bowie: Heritage Books, Inc., 1991.

41. Munson, James D. *Alexandria, Virginia, Alexandria Hustings Court Deeds 1783-1797.* Maryland, Bowie: Heritage Books, Inc.

42. Netherton, Nan, Donald Sweig, Janice Artemel, Partrica Hickin, Patrick Reed. *Fairfax County, Virginia A History.* Virginia, Fairfax: Fairfax County Board of Supervisors, 1978.

43. Pippenger, Wesley E. and James D. Munson. *The Virginia Journal and Alexandria Advertiser Volumes I-V.* Maryland, Westminster: Willow Bend Books, 2000-2002.

44. Powell, Mary G. and indexed by Wesley E. Pippenger. *The History of Old Alexandria, Virginia from July 13, 1749 to May 24, 1861.* Maryland, Westminster: Willow Bend Books, 2000.

45. Prothro, Kimberly and Dennis A. Knepper. *Historical and Archaeological Investigation of Roberdeau's Wharf at Harborside.* Washington, D.C.: Engineering-Science, Inc., July 1989.

46. Scribner's Sons, Charles. *The Letters of Robert Louis Stevenson: Volume One. The Novels and Tales of Robert Louis Stevenson.* New York: Charles Scribner's Sons, 1901.

47. Smith, Sarah B. *Legends of Nelson County.* Bardstown, Kentucky: From the Nelson Co. Public Library in Bardstown Kentucky (library reference number R976.9495 Smit).

48. Smith, William Francis and T. Michael Miller. *A Seaport Saga Portrait of Old Alexandria, Virginia.* Missouri, Marceline: Walsworth Publishing Co., 1981.

49. Smoot, Betty Carter. *Days In An Old Town.* Virginia, Alexandria: From the files of the Alexandria Virginia Library, Kate Waller Barrett Branch, 1934.

50. Sparacio, Ruth and Sam. *Fairfax County, Virginia Deed Book 1797-1798.* Virginia, McLean: The Antient Press.

51. Sparacio, Ruth and Sam. *Virginia County Court Records Deed Abstracts of Fairfax County, Virginia 1791-1792,* Virginia, McClean: The Antient Press. 1994.

52. Steely, Michael S. *Swift's Silver Mines and Related Appalachian Treasures.* Tennessee, Johnson City: The Overmountain Press, 1995.

53. Stevenson, Robert Louis. *The Silverado Squatters.* Utah, Sandy: Quiet Vision Publishing, 1999-2000.

54. Stevenson, Robert Louis. *Treasure Island.* New York, New York: Penguin Books Ltd., 1994, originally published 1883.

55. Stevenson, Robert Louis. *My First Book–"Treasure Island."* Illinois, Chicago: McClure's Magazine, September 1894.

56. Sutton, Rita (Kennedy). *Part One: Early Osbornes on Clinch River.* Virginia, Wise: Historical Society of Southwest Virginia, 1973.

57. Swift, General Joseph Gardner. *The Memoirs of Gen. Joseph Gardner Swift, LL. D., U.S.A., First Graduate of the United States Military Academy, West Point.* Massachusetts, Worcester: F.S. Blanchard & Co., 1890 by Harrison Ellery.

58. Taylor, Barbara E. *The Silver and the Silversmiths of Alexandria, Virginia.* Virginia, Alexandria: From the Alexandria Virginia Library, Kate Waller Barrett Branch. n.p.: n.pub. April 20, 1976.

59. Teele, A.K., editor. *The History of Milton, Mass. 1640 to 1887.* Kentucky, Louisville: From the National Society Sons of the American Revolution Library Louisville, Kentucky, publisher unknown, 1887.

60. Terry, Thomas P. *United States Treasure Atlas Volume 4.* Wisconsin, La Crosse: Specialty Publishing Company, February 1985.

61. The Grayson County Historical Society. *Historical Sketches and Family Histories, Grayson County, Kentucky.* Kentucky, Elizabethtown: From the records of the Brown-Pusey House, Inc., 2002.

62. The Virginia Historical Society. *The Virginia Magazine of History and Biography Volume VI.* Virginia, Richmond: House of the Society, June 1899.

63. Tyler, Lyon G. M.A., LL. D. *Tyler's Quarterly Historical and Genealogical Magazine Volume IX.* Virginia, Richmond: Richmond Press, Inc., Printers, 1928.

64. Unknown compiler. *Register of Baptisms, Marriages and Funerals During the Ministry of the Rev. Dr., James Muir in the Presbyterian Church of Alexandria, D.C.* Virginia, Alexandria: From the Alexandria Virginia Library, Kate Waller Barrett Branch. n.p.: n.pub.

65. Vedeler, Dr. Harold. *Old Presbyterian Meeting House.* Virginia, Alexandria: second printing, January 1997, revised May 19, 1999.

66. Wardell, Patrick G. *Alexandria City and County Virginia Wills, Administrations and Guardian Bonds 1800-1870.* Maryland, Bowie: Heritage Books, Inc., 1986.

67. Wilson, Robert H. *The Story of Old Town & "Gentry Row" in Alexandria, Virginia.* Pennsylvania, Kennett Square: Robert H. Wilson Crosslands, 1983.

68. Wright, F. Edward and Wesley E. Pippenger. *Early Church Records of Alexandria City and Fairfax County, Virginia.* Maryland, Bowie: Heritage Books, Inc., 1996 and 1997.

Art and Resources

Map #1 and Map #4 — *Kentucky Atlas and Gazetteer.* Maine, Yarmouth: Delorme, 2001, www.delorme.com.

Map #2 and Map #3 — *Streams of Kentucky,* by U.S. Geological Survey, 1958.

Map #2a and Map #2b — *Kentucky County Maps,* Wisconsin, Lyndon Station: Thomas Publications LTD.

Portrait of "George Washington at Princeton" provided by The Indianapolis Museum of Art, accession number 53.64 – Charles Willson Peale and Charles Peale Polk, oil on canvas.

Portrait of "General Joseph Gardner Swift" provided by the U.S. Army Corps of Engineers.

Pictures of "Belaire/Colross" provided by the local History/Special Collections Department of the Alexandria Public Library.

Pictures of "Colross" archeological excavation provided by Rita Holtz of the Alexandria Public Library.

Picture of "Colross at Princeton" provided by the Princeton Day School, New Jersey.

Portrait of "Ann Roberdeau Swift" (Mrs. Jonathan Swift) provided from the Collection of The New-York Historical Society, accession number #1953.93.

Portraits of "Dr. James Craik" and "The Marquis de LaFayette" provided by The Alexandria-Washington Lodge #22. "Copyright Alexandria-Washington Lodge #22 A.F. & A.M. all rights reserved. Photography by Arthur W. Pierson, Falls Church, Virginia."

Portrait of "John Filson" provided by The Filson Historical Society, Louisville Kentucky.

Portrait of "Peter Stuyvesant" obtained from the book, *Historic New York—Being the Second Series of the Half Moon Papers.* Edited by Maud Wilder Goodwin, Alice Carrington Royce, Ruth Putnam and Eva Palmer Brownell and published by G. P. Putnam's Sons, New York, 1899.

Portraits of "D. L. Moody" and "Ira D. Sankey" obtained from the book, *Moody: His Words, Work and Workers.* Edited by Rev. W. H. Daniels, A.M. and published by Nelson & Phillips, New York and Hitchcock and Walden, Cincinnati, Chicago and St. Louis, 1877.

Pictures of "Free Assembly Hall, Edinburgh. Awakening the Time of Mr. Moody's Meetings" and "Mr. Moody Preaching in the Great Opera House, Haymarket, London" obtained from the book, *The Life and Work of Dwight L. Moody.* Written by Rev. J. Wilber Chapman, D.D. and published by Clark & Co., Philadelphia, PA, 1900.

Portrait of "Washington Irving" obtained from the book, *The Life and Letters of*

Washington Irving Volume I. Written by Pierre E. Irving and published by George Bell and Sons, London, 1908.

Pictures of "Sand Knob" courtesy of Mr. Dennis Watson.

Portraits of "Foster Swift, M. D." and "Mrs. Foster Swift" obtained from the book, *The Memoirs of Gen. Joseph Gardner Swift, LL. D., U.S.A., First Graduate of the United States Military Academy, West Point.* Published by Blanchard & Co., Massachusetts, Worcester: F.S 1890 by Harrison Ellery.

Picture of "Robert Louis Stevenson" obtained from the book, *The Letters of Robert Louis Stevenson Volume I.* Selected and edited by Sidney Colvin and published by Charles Scribner's Sons, New York, 1901.

Picture of "Robert Louis Stevenson's Map of Treasure Island" obtained from Charles Scribner's Sons, Robert Louis Stevenson collection, titled *Robert Louis Stevenson Volume II—Treasure Island,* published 1901.

ABOUT THE AUTHOR

Robert A. Prather and his wife Karen live outside the small town of Garrett, near Fort Knox Kentucky, and for the past twenty-five years have owned and operated a small business there. He is an ongoing student of history and pre-history, and is a member of the Falls of the Ohio Archaeological Society. Mr. Prather is a 32nd degree Mason and past D.D.G.M. He is an amateur investigator and research scientist. This is Mr. Prather's first book.

INDEX

341

For more great titles visit us at www.acclaimpress.com